THE GREAT UNKNOWN

Mountain journeys in the Southern Alps

For Kirsty + James,

To the many adventures into the great unknown of life!

Best,
Jane — on behalf of Geoff

Dedicated to John Rundle, John Nankervis, and all who draw inspiration from journeys in the mountains.

The name 'The Great Unknown' was given by A.P. Thomson, John Pascoe, Gavin Malcolmson and Duncan Hall to a peak at the western end of the Garden of Eden ice plateau in December 1934. To them, the peak was a metaphor for all the remote unexplored country in the vicinity; and their attempt to climb it from Adverse Creek had failed.

The mountain was also written about by Paul Powell, after the first ascent of it in 1939: 'The Great Unknown was the mystery that we felt on this cornerpost of wild and rugged country.'

The Great Unknown can also be a metaphor for our own journeys to remote mountains and our personal discovery of these places. For me the unknown has always been a spark that has driven trips. It carries with it the excitement of simply being alive, that every day can bring new experiences, new learnings, new understandings of who and what we are. Few places deliver that experience of discovery as meaningfully as the mountains.

THE GREAT UNKNOWN

Mountain journeys in the Southern Alps

GEOFF SPEARPOINT

We must closely guard the welfare of our National Parks and Reserves. These should not be regarded as the property of our minister or the government. They belong to the people of today and tomorrow. We must fight for their protection if necessary.

Fred Vosseler

First published in 2019 by Potton & Burton

Potton & Burton
319 Hardy Street, PO Box 221, Nelson, New Zealand
pottonandburton.co.nz

© Geoff Spearpoint

Maps by Roger Smith, Geographx

ISBN 978 1 98 855002 2

Printed in China by Midas Printing International Ltd

This book is copyright. Apart from any fair dealing for the purposes of private study, research, criticism or review, as permitted under the Copyright Act, no part may be reproduced by any process without the permission of the publishers.

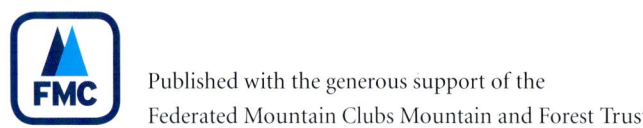

Published with the generous support of the Federated Mountain Clubs Mountain and Forest Trust

CONTENTS

- **7** INTRODUCTION

- **15** KAHURANGI
  - 16 The Dragons Teeth
  - 19 Garibaldi Ridge
  - 21 Mt Kendall
  - 24 Mt Owen to the Matiri Range & The Haystack

- **29** SPENSER MOUNTAINS
  - 30 To see the Faerie Queene
  - 34 Thompson Pass & Mt Una
  - 36 There and back
  - 38 Kehu Peak

- **41** KAIKOURA RANGES
  - 42 Seaward: the frost report on Mt Manakau
  - 46 Inland: Tapuae-o-Uenuku classic

- **51** THE WAIMAKARIRI TO THE HOKITIKA
  - 52 Christmas at Sir Robert Hut
  - 56 Along the Main Divide
  - 58 Mathias to the Waimakariri
  - 62 Clarkes Pass: What could possibly go wrong?
  - 64 Main Divide traverse above the Whitcombe Valley

- **69** THE BRACKEN SNOWFIELD
  - 70 The County face of Mt Evans
  - 75 Stormed out
  - 76 Bracken to the Gardens
  - 79 Off to Ivory Lake
  - 82 Winter snows on the Bracken

- **85** THE GARDEN OF EDEN ICE PLATEAU
  - 86 Storm on Adams Col
  - 90 The North Ridge of Mt Kensington
  - 94 Big day out
  - 96 To The Great Unknown

- **101** RANGITATA, THE MOUNTAINS OF EREWHON
  - 102 The Warrior
  - 106 Amazon Peak
  - 108 Mt Arrowsmith
  - 111 Mt D'Archiac

- **115** ELIE DE BEAUMONT TO AORAKI MT COOK
  - 116 The West Peak of Elie De Beaumont
  - 120 Wilczek Peak, the Callery and Price Range
  - 123 Aoraki Mt Cook grand traverse
  - 126 Murchison–Tasman glaciers traverse

- **131** THE BALFOUR, NAVIGATOR & SIERRA RANGES
  - 132 Across the Balfour Range
  - 137 The Navigator
  - 140 Mt Sefton
  - 144 The Sierra Range & Douglas Neve

- **149** THE HOOKER WILDERNESS
  - 150 Scissor slabs to the Makawhio Valley
  - 154 Karangarua–Fettes Peak–Mahitahi
  - 158 Otoko–Marks Flat–Moeraki
  - 162 The Solution to Mt Hooker

- **167** FROM THE OKURU TO THE WILKIN
  - 168 Selborne Range traverse
  - 172 The dark side of the Divide
  - 176 Moirs mission
  - 178 Winter wilderness

- **183** THE HAAST RANGE, VOLTA GLACIER & MT ASPIRING
  - 184 Haast Range traverse
  - 188 Not rock solid: an Eros encounter
  - 194 Viva la Volta

- **199** THE OLIVINES & RED MOUNTAIN
  - 200 Olivine–Volta traverse
  - 204 Desperation Pass, the Olivine Ice Plateau & Red Mountain
  - 210 A land of beyond
  - 214 In Barrington country

- **221** FIORDLAND & THE DARRANS
  - 222 Harrison–Tutoko
  - 226 The Light and the Dark
  - 230 Transit–Sinbad
  - 234 Windward River tops–Coronation Peak–Precipice Cove

- **239** AFTERWORD: BACK OF BEYOND
- **241** ACKNOWLEDGEMENTS
- **242** BIBLIOGRAPHY, NOTES, REFERENCES & GUIDEBOOKS

INTRODUCTION

So strange it is we wish to go,
Or so they say who may not know,
Not know the breath of mountain air,
Nor feel the feeling of no care;
Not know what nomads ever knew
Or do the things that they would do,
Or watch the cloudmist fade and go
Lester Masters, 'Some There Are'

THE EXPERIENCE

The mountains speak. They draw us in, take us on missions into unseen corners, cast spells and sometimes let us on their summits. They throw us into gorges, stun us with their peaks, drag us into heroic struggles, forge fantastic friendships, and change our lives forever. To those with their eyes open, mountains can lead to a new reality.

They steer us to the back of beyond then chase us home again, drunk on adventure, scratched, torn and grinning, back to lectures and work, where few know or understand where we've been. How can the excitement of outrageous days in the mountains be explained?

But there is an exhilaration in living with nature on nature's terms, sleeping out under a universe of stars, finding ways into hidden valleys and camping on remote ice plateaus where the mountains rise sharp as frosted greywacke. Being in the mountains is about the joy of being alive, and that's what the journeys in this book are about.

Sometimes the tops offer wonderful days in the sun, swanning around in unexpected tarns, lazing in warm, stony hollows on the crest of peaks, and afternoon glissades in sugar-snow back to camp. On others, they can lead into a morass of wind, rain, hail and snow, where effort becomes impotent and the world crashes into the space of a cage, lashing us to the hillside. That is the thing about the mountains. They offer everything but promise nothing. The experiences we have in them depend on what we choose to pursue.

This book is about the experience of being there, of living in the land and hearing it breathe, feeling it roar, listening to its pulse. Feeling the shock when an icefall cracks away overhead, seeing puffs of rock dust as a boulder pulverises down a gully nearby. Not just watching the rivers rise and fall but being part of and controlled by them. Every good trip has a level of uncertain outcome. It keeps the mind focused.

It is also about focusing on what is around you. Seeing seiches in alpine lakes from strong winds, or cooking dinner on a rock outcrop where the steam sifts while the sun sets, and the mountains bare their teeth until darkness swallows them. It is listening to a bush robin defending its territory in sharp strident notes that are reminiscent of a stone skipping over flat water.

It is lying tucked under a bivvy rock in some isolated valley with a fire scented by *Olearia* and *Phyllocladus* heating the billy for a brew, while drizzle and rain alternate with the mist rolling in and out among the scrubby bluffs. In an Otago University Tramping Club magazine, *ANTICS* 2003, Kelvin Lloyd wrote, 'It's a timeless experience to sit out the weather under a dry rock overhang in the middle of the wilderness. Try it some time.'

THE JOURNEYS

Strictly speaking, the Southern Alps/Kā Tiritiri o te Moana (from here on, written as Southern Alps) begin at The Divide on the Milford road and finish at Nelson Lakes. In this book Kahurangi, the Kaikoura ranges, and Fiordland are included as well.

Throughout the Southern Alps, many remote ice plateaus and wild mountain ranges have gained a reputation amongst backcountry trampers and climbers for their beauty, isolation and challenge. This book celebrates those places. A few well-known peaks are also here, including Aoraki Mt Cook, but mostly it is about those lesser known, less-frequented wilderness mountains.

In each chapter I have singled out three or four trips and written about them briefly, based on my diaries. These mountain trips are part of a personal journey of 50 years of tramping and climbing in the more remote mountains of the Southern Alps.

The photos were taken on a variety of trips, not always the trips described, to reflect each region. Similarly, lines marked on the maps are there to make sense of the stories, rather than for any other purpose. They are certainly not recommended routes and are sometimes particularly unhealthy places to end up in. The aim of the book is to inspire, not be a guide.

In most cases I have brought an eclectic mix of historical adventures into these accounts as well. Over the decades, thousands of kiwis have tramped to, climbed in, and explored for themselves these magical, wild, and little-known places, and many more have dreamed and schemed of doing so. Part of the uniqueness of these places is their very isolation and the shared experience of this among friends and generations of like-minded people.

HERITAGE

New Zealanders have been pursuing transalpine tramping and mountaineering trips in the Southern Alps for over 120 years. For instance, W.G. Grave and his companions returned year after year to explore northern Fiordland in the 1890s. And over the years there have been many other people similarly inspired.

Roland Rodda, George Moir, Tom Fyfe, Jack Ede, Howard Boddy, S.A. Wiren, Gordon Speden, Jim Dennistoun, Dora de Beer, John Pascoe, Marie Byles, Stan Conway, Ray Chapman, Merle Sweney, Alan Willis, Scott Gilkison, Paul Powell, J.T. Holloway, Ian Whitehead, Arnold Heine, Bill Beaven, Norm Hardie, the Brough brothers, Peter Bain, John Nankervis, Kelvin Lloyd, and many more have been involved in such trips. The journeys in this book celebrate our transalpine exploring tradition.

Sometimes their explorations were re-explorations, as earlier waves of people explored these mountains first, beginning with Māori and continuing through to gold prospectors, surveyors, geologists and others.

A.P. Harper, Charlie Douglas and A. Woodham experienced the challenge of their surroundings back in 1894, when camped near Lemmer Peak and the Franz Josef Glacier.

Towards midnight the gale increased, and the wind howled around us in furious gusts, trying to dislodge the fly which was flapping about in an alarming manner. Douglas had just said, 'It is deuced lucky that we tied her down so well,' when a squall struck us again, and after a brief struggle with the canvas it broke a rope, and in half a second the whole arrangement had gone away in the darkness . . . The wind seemed literally to leap on us, driving the hail with almost irresistible force, and making it very difficult to rig up any kind of shelter.

It was the tramping and mountaineering club scene from the 1920s that really fostered transalpine trips. *Moir's Guide*, which covers routes between Aoraki Mt Cook and Fiordland, was first printed almost a century ago. Pascoe's guide, *The Southern Alps, from the Kaikouras to the Rangitata*, came out almost 70 years ago. In a skilled amateur world where connections reached into survey departments, local communities, and included capable bushmen,

PREVIOUS PAGE The Volta side of Mt Aspiring (right), with the Coxcomb Ridge on the left.
OPPOSITE Approaching Seal Col on the Barrier Range above the Dart River, with Desperation Pass to the left.

mountaineers and hunters, club parties enthusiastically sought out both the known and the unknown to explore. A small number employed local guides on these journeys, but most did not.

Keen parties often committed all their Christmas holidays to these climbing and tramping trips in the Southern Alps on adventures of often up to 20 days. They were passionate about the journeys, and they made friendships and memories that lasted a lifetime.

There was something romantic and exciting about unravelling new places and truths in a landscape where government surveys were still inaccurate or vague, then producing updated maps in mountaineering and tramping club journals. Although this drove a number of exploratory alpine journeys, for the most part, people sought clarity in these places out of their own curiosity.

'The most joyous days in my mountain memory are those spent in pioneering new routes, in the exploration of unvisited valleys, in the working out and placing of unmapped physical features. It is in the unravelling of the unknown that the prettiest problems and the most generous rewards are to be found,' wrote W. Scott Gilkison, in *Peaks, Packs and Mountain Tracks*, in 1940.

CHANGING GEAR

In days before plastic, clothes and food were carried in waterproof, light Japara (waxed cotton) bags, made for the purpose. This changed to the more familiar nylon and plastic bags in the 1950s and 1960s. Tents, too, were of dry Japara, and parkas, of oiled Japara. Hobnails and Tricouni on leather-soled boots changed to rubber Vibram soles in New Zealand during the 1950s (after Italian Vitale Bramani began producing them in 1937. Six of his friends had been killed in a mountaineering accident, which he blamed on poor footwear).

Swanndri bush shirts and jackets are a New Zealand invention, and became popular with those in the outdoors all over the country. Many trampers and climbers used them from 1914 onwards, until lighter, synthetic polypro and fleece fabrics began to take over in the 1970s. Sleeping bags, originally just square blankets, have been filled with various materials (my first one, handed down from my parents, was filled with kapok), but New Zealand

OPPOSITE A view of the Ramsay Glacier and lake with Mt Whitcombe behind and Lauper Peak to the right, from a camp on Butler Saddle above the upper Rakaia.
RIGHT New Zealand's mountain parrot, the kea, at work on a pack.

companies such as Fairydown have been making feather-down bags since the 1920s, and it supplied the 1953 Everest Expedition with them.

Packs have been through many transitions. Initially, sacks with shoulder straps gave way during the 1930s and 1940s to steel A-frame packs such as the Bergen. From the end of WWII, H-framed packs such as the classic Mountain Mule dominated, until Macpac frameless (then internal frame) packs were created in the 1970s. These began a new evolution towards the simple, lighter packs of today.

Another item carried on many trips until the 1970s was a half axe, giving those with fire skills the ability to produce a cooking fire in virtually any weather. Primus stoves were also a feature of transalpine trips, running on kerosene, then switching to a petroleum distillate (white spirits, Fuelite) in the 1960s. Today, Jetboil gas stoves are increasing in popularity.

Before the 1970s, entering remote alpine areas required parties to back themselves. No contoured maps, little route information, little accurate weather prediction, no locator beacons, no GPS and little chance of aerial rescue meant being as self-sufficient for all eventualities as possible.

Even what food to take in has improved. Before WWII, many foods were sundried: beans, raisins, soup, fruit, dried meat and bacon, rice, flour, bread and butter. Then, new ranges of freeze-dried foods appeared. Vegetables, meat, macaroni, milk and egg powder all helped to reduce pack weights. Today, the choice seems almost endless.

All these advances have helped enable new approaches to transalpine journeys, offering the ability to pick weather, carry light gear and food, and cover much more ground. New opportunities are there for the exploring, and remote places have never been so accessible on foot.

PERSONAL PERSPECTIVE

In many ways, a transalpine approach is a return to our earlier mountaineering roots and soaks up the full richness the mountains offer. The mountains, the gorges, the forest, the scrub, the tussock, the rock and the ice are all seamlessly connected. The experience of that completeness, in which both tramping and climbing skills are required, is what sparks and attracts me.

Each place in the mountains is different. There is only one Olivine Range, one Volta Glacier, one Bracken Snowfield. Though these are all in Wilderness Areas, they each offer very unique experiences. Wilderness Areas are designed to protect the cultural experience of wilderness that many outdoor New Zealanders have sought in the mountains for more than a century.

One of the consequences for me of wilderness journeys is the realisation that nature, not ourselves, will be in charge on this planet in the longer term. Currently we have taken on the task of gardening our wild lands and we should do this because nature left to its own devices would consign many species to extinction. But that leaves a conflict between human selection and natural selection. Humans assume the right to live all over the planet. Currently other species are also claiming that right, abetted by natural selection.

Despite that, I have an acute awareness of the need to look out for the mountains, for both future generations and the land itself. I feel passionate that we have a duty of care to see our wild and remote places, plants and animals looked after.

To me, we don't so much own the mountains as belong to them. I like the Te Urewera concept that these places, and likewise the mountains, are their own persons, not owned by anyone, and that we are all guardians of their make no mistake. There is an unspoken connection many in outdoors circles share that you won't find in 'park plans' or 'management documents', but which is at the heart of our relationship with our wild lands.

Which brings us back to the journeys and the experience. There are still some untravelled places; the Bare Rocky Range between the Karangarua River and the Makawhio, culminating in Fettes Peak has never been traversed, to my knowledge. But really, chasing down smaller and smaller corners to tick off has a fanciful quality about it. Who knows where humans have been in the last millennium in the mountains, and really, does it matter? The joy is to discover these places for ourselves. A place doesn't need the validity of 'first' to have meaning. These trips are our unknowns, and we give the places new meaning by our own trips. And if they are great trips, they stand on their own.

Empower your own journeys, choose your own lines. Part of venturing into the unknown is accepting that sometimes you'll get it wrong and there will be a need to back off. That's part of the journey. If you want a real challenge, leave the map and GPS at home. I once went to the Olivine Plateau with just a page from an AA motoring map (due to forgetting the contoured map). This gives wilderness a chance. Each trip, like every surfing wave, is unique. Embrace the adventure. Some fantastic trips are waiting to be discovered.

mana. Likewise, the mountains aren't just an environment for challenge. They are an environment shared with a multitude of plants and animals.

The mountains help to support and define us. An intense emotional connection develops for many trampers and mountaineers with places in the wilds. This isn't about views or scenery or just observing. It is a spiritual connection that has long since replaced formal religion for many. For me, it is where I go for solace, to reflect and meditate on the world, for friendship in the company of fellow outdoor folk, as well as for adventure.

As a society, New Zealanders may not express such feelings much, but

OPPOSITE The upper Tuke Gorge in the Mikonui Catchment.
ABOVE The endangered rock wren, or tuke, lives entirely above the bushline, from Kahurangi to Fiordland.

N
Collingwood
Golden Bay
60
Aorere River >
THE DRAGONS TEETH
Brown Cow Ridge
Lead Hills
Boulder Lake
Anatoki River >
Adelaide Tarn
Trident
Dragons Teeth
Anatoki Peak
DOUGLAS RANGE
Drunken Sailors
Lonely Lake
< Burgoo Strm
DEVIL RANGE
Lake Stanley
Mt Snowdon
Island Lake
Fenella Hut
Waingaro River >
LOCKETT RANGE
Cobb River >
Iron Hill
PEEL RANGE
Cobb Reservoir
0
5
10 km

N
0
5
10 km
< Leslie River
GARIBALDI RIDGE
Pyramid
Karamea Bend
Silvermine Creek >
< Karamea River
ARTHUR RANGE
HERBERT RANGE
< Crow River
< Kakapo River
Karamea River >
< Little Wanganui River
Mt Kendall
Moonstone Lake
MT KENDALL
Mt Gomorrah
GARIBALDI RIDGE
Mt Luna
Biggs Tops
Gibbs Track
Mt Patriarch
Johnson River >
Whangapeka River >
Whangapeka River >
Rolling River
MATIRI RANGE
Hurricane Hut
< Mokihinui River (Nth)
Fyffe River >
The Needle
The Haystack
Mt Owen
MT OWEN TO THE
MATIRI RANGE AND HAYSTACK
Thousand Acre Plateau
< Matiri River
< Owen River
Lake Matiri
Matiri River (West) >
6
< Buller River

CHAPTER 1
KAHURANGI

Kahurangi is an ancient land of diverse landscapes, ranging from the friendly Cobb Valley to the remote Karamea catchment, the seldom travelled valleys of the North Mokihinui Valley and the upper Matiri Valley. Although never really alpine, Kahurangi has some wild and remote corners, full of challenge, and the following four trips have been chosen to reflect this.

The bedrock varies throughout, and this, along with rainfall gradients, has helped create a vibrant and diverse flora. The Dragons Teeth are just plain rugged, and so is Mt Kendall. The Garibaldi tops and especially the Thousand Acres Plateau on the Matiri Range are more like the setting for Sir Arthur Conan Doyle's *The Lost World*, high tussock plateaus above rings of bluffs in places few parties ever visit.

Some areas of Kahurangi saw an early interest by farmers for grazing and much of the region was scoured for minerals by keen prospectors. In 1929, then again in 1968, major earthquakes devastated whole catchments, particularly to the south, and much of the damage still affects significant areas. Despite this, the whole region is a tramping mecca full of outstanding adventures of all grades.

The high route over the Dragons Teeth is a standout trip, but equally great journeys can be put together traversing Garibaldi Ridge or ascending Mt Kendall. All of them will need a head for heights, good navigational skills, good weather, and luck. Garibaldi is probably the least accessible, while offering challenging and exposed scrambling. Here are four good journeys for those who want a challenge.

THE DRAGONS TEETH

BROWN COW RIDGE–BOULDER LAKE–ADELAIDE TARN– DRAGONS TEETH–LONELY LAKE–LOCKETT RANGE–IRON HILL

6 DAYS: 28 DECEMBER 2008–2 JANUARY 2009

GS WITH PHIL & VICKY NOVIS, LINDA LILBURNE AND CHRYS HORN

To traverse the teeth of a dragon – what an excellent concept for a trip. First, we consulted the Dragon's oracle, Warwick Briggs, who has been over the Dragons Teeth about 60 times. Despite listening intently, we went away thinking the riddles of the route might be too clever for us. We would just have to talk nicely to the dragon itself and keep our eyes peeled.

Credit for the first traverse of the high route over the Dragons Teeth in the late 1960s belongs to Keith Marshall. Keith explored the route on many forays while based at Adelaide Tarn Hut, and he was also responsible for putting the wire cable up through a gnarly bluff section. When this was removed in the 1990s, once it had become too badly rusted and unsafe, the section became known as the Wireless.

The delightful names of this area, the Dragons Teeth, Yuletide Peak, the Drunken Sailors, Lonely Lake, were all dreamed up by Frank and Berna Soper and Keith Marshall when exploring the area in the 1960s. What a legacy. They formed the Golden Bay Alpine and Tramping Club and drove the building process for Boulder Lake Hut (1961), Adelaide Tarn Hut (1964) and in 1973, Lonely Lake Hut.

From Bainham, our homage to the dragon began up Brown Cow Ridge to Boulder Lake and then continued to a campsite on the tops near Green Saddle. Phil cut the eight dinner carrots into 28 pieces, and then Vicky pointed out this made it a 28-carat meal. We were in for some good food on this trip.

By lunchtime next day we were already camped above Adelaide Tarn, so we spent the afternoon investigating the start of the high route. Sidling above the bush under Mt Douglas, we found the odd cairn and 'Marshall marker': round painted lids put in to mark the route by Keith Marshall. But in many places there wasn't much to indicate anything. It was a tricky little route, sneaking over the Nose. Keith must have had a lot of fun sorting that line out.

ABOVE At the top of the wireless bluff on the Dragons Teeth high route.
OPPOSITE Approaching the Dragons Teeth (left). Mt Douglas and Mt Trident (L–R), above Adelaide Tarn.

Bluffs, slabs, scrubby beech, and some serious drops below kept us focused. At the bottom of the Wireless we turned around and headed back to camp.

While three of the party headed for the low route past the Teeth next morning, two of us headed for the high route, and after three and a half hours we had scrambled up the Wireless wall and sat in tussock on the spur above. The day was perfect, so we set out to pick the Teeth. Steep, exhilarating scrambles took us to the top of both peaks. On top of the highest peak I found a heart-shaped rock. It isn't every day you get to tear out the heart of a dragon and sneak away with it.

Time beckoned and we still had a way to go. Swinging towards the bluffs of Anatoki Peak we picked up a light trail with the odd Marshall marker, but often the route was more tenuous. Scree and scaly vegetation led up into the bluffs and we popped out on what you might call the right leg of the dragon, the Anatoki Peak spur. We wandered up to the peak, then slept out lower down, waking to drizzle and mist.

Anatoki Peak is still a long way from the Drunken Sailors, and the country between isn't straightforward. The range here forms the dragon's backbone. As Linda and I started to feel our way along in the mist next morning, Phil arrived. He had come along here the night before, and soon we were reunited with the rest of the party, dropping down to Lonely Lake, with its cute little hut. This hut had a makeover in 2016, thanks to Golden Bay volunteers Gaylene Wilkinson and Peter Fullerton.

The trip continued along the Douglas and Lockett Range tops, but the essence of the Dragons Teeth journey was over. Now it just remained for us to head out over Iron Hill and down into the Cobb Valley.

Dracophyllum forest high above the Karamea River.

GARIBALDI RIDGE

WANGAPEKA TRACK–KAKAPO RIVER–HERBERT RANGE–GARIBALDI RIDGE–LUNA TOPS–GIBBS TRACK

8 DAYS: 28 DECEMBER 1994–4 JANUARY 1995
GS WITH SVEN BRABYN, BARBARA BROWN, GAYLENE WILKINSON AND DAVID GLENNY

Garibaldi Ridge stands out like a bulwark, rising to rocky summits from the bushed ranges surrounding it: a genuine battleship of bluffs. Our aim was to reach this wild and isolated range, find a way up on to the tops through the big sandstone bluffs flanking it, then traverse east and find a way off, down to the Karamea River.

Who was Garibaldi? In stature, Garibaldi the man matches Garibaldi the Ridge. Born in 1807, Guiseppe Garibaldi was a gifted guerrilla leader who led many military campaigns to free Italy of foreign rule, achieving mythic status in the process. His support for those less well-off was admired internationally.

We began Garibaldi the Ridge in drizzle, three days after Christmas 1994, when five of us headed up the Wangapeka Track with eight days' food. The weather around Christmas is always a lottery. Heavier rain fell all the next day, too, and most of this travel was off track. Working our way through the scrub we crossed Kakapo Saddle, then descended the valley beyond, soaked and cold, to reach Kakapo Hut, with the light fading.

There was a sweetness to arriving at the dry hut. The fire soon crackled, the first brew boiled, and we changed into dry clothes. And there was an even greater sweetness to be curled up warm and dry on a foam mattress, drifting in and out of sleep, embers still glowing in the fire and listening to the rain drum heavily on the tin roof. It was better than the Hilton.

Like a castle surrounded by a moat, the Herbert Range snakes from Kendall Ridge to Garibaldi Ridge, surrounded by the Karamea River and its gorges. We climbed a steep spur through kāmahi to reach the range at Twenty Four Tarn Basin, but thick mist hid the tarns and it was raining again.

At the head of Jupiter Creek the range crest dips into the bush, but mostly the forest is open, with Dr Seuss-like *Dracophyllum* trees. Underfoot, their long amber leaves were very slippery. Dave managed to fold one over the bridge of his nose, giving the effect of a long beak, confusing the local weka.

Few people come this way, so we were surprised – then concerned – when we caught sight of a partly hidden, musty tent. Inside were personal family letters, biblical texts, and photos. Wherever the owner was, this was no ordinary camp, and it left us wondering. Afterwards, enquiries indicated it belonged to one Gerald Cover, who believed the Lord was coming and the end of the world was near, so he had retreated to the mountains in anticipation of this apocalypse.

We celebrated New Year's Eve camped at the bushline overlooking Silvermine Creek, with the bluffs of Garibaldi Ridge spread before us. West of Pyramid, access is fairly straightforward on to the range, but on the first day of 1995, we climbed a spur to 1418 metres midway along, wending through stunted beech and dodging bluffs. Although we had chosen a line of weakness, we still had to poke around to get up. The bluffs towards Pyramid bulged like Popeye's muscles, big walls with curved edges, protecting mostly easier country above. Parts of Garibaldi Ridge are easy to traverse, but places where the ridge narrows, such as west of the 1418-metre spur, travel options become very difficult. Garibaldi Ridge certainly has some challenges to it.

The quartz sandstones of Pyramid give way to limestone in the sandstone further east, and as we crossed karst country on the ridge plateau, sinkholes appeared. We trod carefully. This place, on the edge of the Tasman Wilderness, is like a lost world, and looking over the edge into the abyss we could see the lower Karamea only about 2 kilometres away, but over 1000 metres lower.

With morning, our route lay along the range, over 1430 metres, and out to Sandy Peak to pick up a leading ridge down to the Karamea/Silvermine forks. It wasn't a good route. Blades of rock, boulders in the bush and scrappy vegetation on a hot day wore us down, but we reached the river for a swim about four in the afternoon. Partway down we stumbled across a big timber beam and a small waterhole. There is more history in these places than one might suppose.

MT KENDALL

WANGAPEKA RIVER–MT PATRIARCH–LUNA RIDGE–MOONSTONE LAKE–MT KENDALL–KARAMEA RIVER–BIGGS TOPS–WANGAPEKA VALLEY

8 DAYS: 25 FEBRUARY 2017–4 MARCH 2017
GS WITH ROBIN MCNEILL AND GARRY NIXON

Mt Kendall is a bit off the radar. Sleeping out on top of Mt Owen 20 years ago, I remember my attention was drawn to the peak's craggy granite summit dominating the horizon high above the upper Karamea Valley and it went on my to-do list.

Compared with other journeys Garry and Robin have dragged me through, this one was pretty mellow, with eight days up our sleeves and actual tracks most of the way. We crossed the Wangapeka River and climbed up to John Reid Hut on a hot summer's afternoon, to find two other local parties there.

Meeting others in the hills is always interesting, hearing where they have come from and are going to, sharing experiences and discovering mutual friends. We slept out under the trees, with stars twinkling beyond, curled up on a bed of *Dicranaloma* moss. In the dark hours, a shadowy morepork swooped close to check me out, wings flustering the air, leaving me wide awake.

After a side trip up Mt Patriarch, we descended to Kiwi Saddle Hut. No people, but lots of birds. A weka skulked around looking for gaiters to loot, robins puffed up and declared the place theirs, tomtits tweedled and fantails swooped after sandflies. They were busy here. Somewhere out across the Taylor, a kaka called. Birds often seem to congregate like this. You see none for hours, then come across a place where the branches are alive with movement and song. With the birds' friendliness, some cloud and fine drizzle, a comfy hut and an open fire, we were seduced to stay, before heading over Mt Luna next day.

This turned out well too. After a warm lunchtime sunbathe on the summit with Robin's primus chuttering away, we curled up for a quick snooze. I like to take these opportunities.

Down in the Karamea by Moonstone Lake, sandflies and mosquitoes had taken complete charge of the few abysmal campsites. Maybe that is what distracted Garry when, having made a brew, he went to settle the leaves in the age-old tradition of swinging the billy. Braced with legs apart, arm extended, he swung a full circle, swung again, at which point the billy and brew sailed off into the scrub, leaving Garry holding the wire handle. I think next time he will pay more attention to how he fixes the handle on.

Mt Kendall proved to be a big day out. In the dusty light of daybreak, we headed up the spur on the true right of Mars Creek, and this provided open travel through much of the forest, if a bit bluffy at the bushline. Swinging into the basin south of the ridge, we picked our way up through tussock, granite bedrock and old screes, although water up here was very scarce.

The peak seemed in the bag until we reached the summit block, and then it didn't. Gendarmes on the south ridge made that route look unlikely, so we scrambled up to a col on the north-east ridge instead. Close up, this looked

LEFT Looking across Silvermine Creek to Pyramid (right) on Garibaldi Ridge.
BELOW Garry swinging the billy to settle tea leaves.

worse, but we got out our rope and gave it a nudge. It nudged back. Steep, loose rock, hard earth, and plenty of exposure, particularly to the north, made us stand back for another look. It didn't look flash but, scrambling up onto a tiny shelf at the base of the bluffs, carrying the rope, I picked my way up the first tricky section. Then I wasn't keen to go back. The steepness continued but, fortunately, little chimneys and an occasional tussock helped. On top, my first concern was to see if the south ridge was better. The gendarmes all had easier routes around the back, but even so, slabs still proved to be a bit of a scramble, with big bluffs below creating exposure. Robin and Garry came up that way, pleased as punch, and we were all chuffed to see a pair of rock wrens bobbing and fussing around on top.

Mt Kendall is 1762 metres, but there is a higher peak 500 metres to the south-west at 1771 metres. While the other two headed back towards the bushline, I headed over to that peak, enjoying glorious views in the late afternoon light from the summit. A simple but unexpected metal plaque on a boulder nearby was dedicated to Frances Broad. I gave her a silent hug for the vigil she keeps in such a stunning setting.

There is a third high peak to Mt Kendall. Out towards the north-west, 1.5 kilometres along the ridge, is a 1746-metre peak. Someone who has been along the Dragons Teeth and is looking for a challenge might have an interesting time traversing Kendall Ridge and climbing all of this.

By the time I rejoined the others at the bushline, it was 7 p.m. I was largely resigned to a night out, but Garry took off at a sprint, and some fine, fast navigating saw us fly down the ridge. By nightfall we were almost there, stumbling the last few hundred metres with our torches. We'd been away for over 12 hours, but for me it felt like 24.

Our route out of the Karamea led us over the Biggs Tops, Stone Creek, and through a bit of strife, but ended with long kilometres tramping down the Wangapeka Track. Parts of the Wangapeka are very scenic, with cramped gorges full of rapids and rock outcrops, and emerald pools. Huts like Kings Creek are a reminder of earlier mining, and why the excellent benched track is here at all.

Hochstetter's geological survey of the area in 1859 led to prospectors finding gold in the Wangapeka Valley, and the subsequent rushes began. As a consequence, the surveyor John Rochfort and his assistants, financed by Nelson Provincial Council, cut a rough track up the Wangapeka and down to Karamea Bend.

Gold was also found on the Mt Arthur Tablelands in 1865. Miners prospected everywhere and, almost as quickly, farmers began pushing their stock up tracks to the tops to graze, particularly on the Tablelands and in the Cobb Valley, which was grazed continuously from 1875 until the Cobb dam was built in the 1940s.

Who would have thought at the time – certainly not the miners, graziers, Lands and Survey department or provincial authorities who poured money and effort into these pack tracks – that they would create such a perfect network for tramping in the region.

ABOVE The summit of Mt Kendall. A slightly higher summit exists out to the left.
OPPOSITE Along Kendall Ridge from near the summit. The Garibaldi tops are visible in the distance.

MT OWEN TO THE MATIRI RANGE & THE HAYSTACK

ROLLING RIVER–MT OWEN–FYFE RIVER–MATIRI HEADWATERS–HAYSTACK RANGE–THOUSAND ACRES PLATEAU–MATIRI VALLEY

7 DAYS: 10 DECEMBER–16 DECEMBER 1977
GS WITH VICKY FROUDE AND CHRIS MANSELL

I've always been drawn to wild, isolated places. They have a sense of mystery, of challenge, of the unknown. The only information I had about the Matiri was a map, but sometimes maps can lead you astray. Our inch-to-mile map showed inviting flats and lakes in a tributary of the Matiri River draining from the east. I envisaged easy travel in a quiet corner that few visited. Instead, we found a land frozen in chaos, the result of the 1929 and 1968 earthquakes. I'll know next time.

Three of us set out up the Rolling River near Tapawera to traverse over Mt Owen, cross the Fyfe Valley and navigate over into the Matiri. From there, we would approach the Haystack Range, cross Thousand Acres Plateau and descend to the road in the Matiri Valley near Murchison.

It all sounded simple enough, but the challenges began early on. By the time we were finding our way over Mt Owen, 300 millimetres of fresh snow covered the karst landscape, and we were in a whiteout. If this wasn't enough, static electricity in the air started to hum – a distinctly unpleasant experience. We descended from 1732 metres into the Fyfe and camped that night in the head of Sandstone Creek, near a little lake.

Next day, with the rain getting heavier, we stood in a branch of the Matiri wondering what had hit us. Much of the valley was covered in landslide debris with log jams and boulders buried under cutty grass, lawyer and dense scrub, making travel slow, hard work. We worked together as a team, supporting each other, taking turns to lead rather than frittering away the energy by all pursuing separate routes.

After a huge day, which ended with some tricky bush-navigation avoiding a lake at the forks where blind valleys led to sump holes, we stumbled in wet twilight down towards the Matiri River and found a large, dry overhang, about 30 metres above the river. Dry dead wood for a fire lay everywhere. It was a perfect campsite. Sometimes you deserve to get lucky.

From Hurricane Hut up-valley we headed west onto the Matiri Range, Haystack and The Needle. Dramatic scarps at all angles swept along the sides of the range. Spiky Spaniard grass, *Dracophyllum* and tough flax flourished where it was less steep, while higher up were bold rock outcrops. Once on the crest, though, the land dipped gently to the west, and the scented tussock gave good travel.

Larrikin Creek drained away from Haystack into the colossal Mokihinui catchment, but it was the flat, tussocky Hundred Acre Plateau under Mt Misery, and the Thousand Acres Plateau, which caught our eye, perched up on pedestals. On them a million sundews raised their sticky fingers, mānuka and mountain beech fringed the drier land and red tussock waved for kilometre after kilometre. It was a stunning place. We thankfully picked up a Forest Service track at Larrikin Hut and headed towards the lower Matiri Valley.

We were all but out, and Vicky had exams to sit at university. However, stormy weather the night before had brought the rivers up, and the West Branch just before the roadend was in high flood, with logs bobbing past. Boulders rumbled below, and we were forced to return to an old slab hut where some hunters had a good fire going. We had no choice but to wait.

OPPOSITE The view north from Mt Owen. Mt Kendall on the left horizon, Mt Patriarch, centre right.
OVERLEAF (LEFT) Looking out at The Haystack from The Needle on the Matiri Range. Thousand Acres Plateau extends out to the right in the distance, above Larrikin Creek.
OVERLEAF (RIGHT) Hundred Acre Plateau, or Devils Dining Table, on the Matiri Range. The slight rise on the plateau is called Mt Misery.

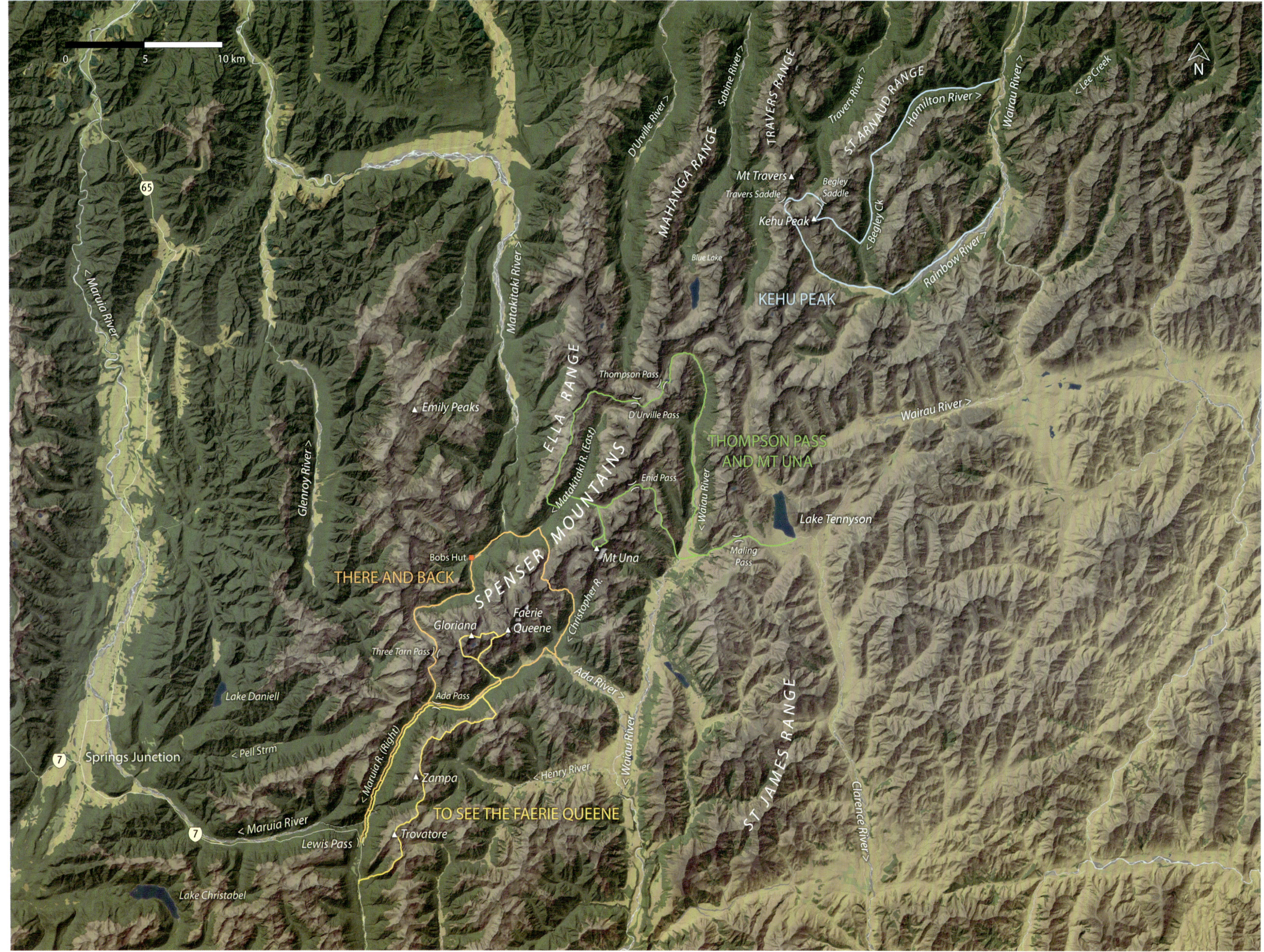

CHAPTER 2
SPENSER MOUNTAINS

Every landscape in the hills has its own aura. Some places are wild and confronting. Others, like the Spenser Mountains, have an ambience that is welcoming, attractive and accommodating. Here is a land of snowy summits, strings of grassy river flats, gorgeous clear rivers and often clean bushlines where beech forest flows into tussock and tarns. These are mellow mountains, with numerous peaks over 2000 metres to climb or traverse in all seasons. Lying on the Main Divide between the Matakitaki River, D'Urville, and Sabine on one side and the Waiau Valley, Lake Tennyson and Wairau tributaries on the other, the Spensers have a few slithers of semi-permanent ice tucked under Mt Una, but the name Glacier Gully is a bit optimistic.

Generations of trampers and climbers have enjoyed the Spensers. Tony Nolan of the Tararua Tramping Club party based in the Ada Valley during Christmas 1958 wrote:

From our camp on the grassy meadows, some battled their way up to the snowline, retreating pell-mell when they came face to face with a herd of hogsbacks; others burnt up the calories chasing Canadian geese around Lake Pagget with photographic or malicious intent. A sports meeting was held on the lawn in the evening, and a brightly decorated Christmas tree appeared. Christmas Eve ended with a singsong around a suitable bonfire. We rather feared that some over-zealous culler had skittled the old boy's reindeer for Father Christmas failed to call that night.

The following routes, 'To see the Faerie Queene' and 'Thompson Pass and Mt Una', were both great trips, but for more challenge, try a tops traverse from Mt Una to Three Tarn Pass incorporating Faerie Queene and Gloriana Peak.

TO SEE THE FAERIE QUEENE

MARUIA RIVER–ADA PASS–ADA RIVER–FAERIE QUEENE– GLORIANA–ADA VALLEY–ZAMPA TOPS–TROVATORE

4 DAYS: 6 –9 APRIL 2007
GS WITH MURRAY PRESLAND, TONY JAEGERS, BRENDAN QUIRKE, ALWYN COURTENAY, TONY LAVO, TONY BIRTWISTLE AND CHRIS KEEN

It was Easter. I arrived from Christchurch, Murray's vanload came from the Hutt Valley, Wellington, and we joined up at Lewis Pass, full of banter and anticipation. The track we began on up the Maruia River Right Branch is part of the St James Walkway, and offers fast travel through forests of beech, lush liverworts and mosses.

Ada Pass must be one of the easiest crossings of the Southern Alps. We rolled gently over it down towards Camera Gully in the Ada Valley, to camp at the edge of the bush. It was an idyllic setting, and we cranked up a fire and lay back with our steaming mugs. Off in the night forest, stags stalked with their hormones racing, roaring belligerently like upset bar patrons.

Travers and Maling came into this area in March 1860 and named the Spenser Mountains after the English poet Edmund Spenser. Spenser's epic poem 'The Faerie Queene', written in 1590, is composed of several books, each of which tells the story of a medieval knight with a particular virtue. Gloriana is the Faerie Queene who ruled over Faerieland, and while the poem is partly rooted in English and Irish history, there is a natural fit between this beautiful landscape and those evocative names. Other characters in the poem include Una and Duessa, also frozen in this local landscape as mountains.

With morning we set out to conquer the Faerie Queene ourselves, but virtue and honour never came into it. Battling through pole beech up Camera Gully (we didn't pick a good line) we reached the tussock to find we'd lost a knight already. However, he turned up shortly afterwards. Up past a waterfall, we followed the basin to the north-east onto the range and headed east along it. Scrambling along the greywacke rock ridge we ran into the Faerie Queene's defences. Dry mists drew down around us but we kept steadfast along the crest, climbing easy buttresses until we sat on the summit to munch lunch. Seventy-four years earlier, R.S. Odell had been here on the first ascent, in 1933.

The day was mild and only half done so, returning the way we had come, we set our sights on Gloriana. She was draped in mist, too, but this time wet mist, where the rocks were greasy and treacherous. We moved steadily up, though, and by 4.30 p.m. the top was ours. (In 1938 a party of 10 is reported to have made the first ascent.) We headed home in a whiteout, and with daylight fading, plunged down, reaching the bush at dark. We had now moved from a whiteout to a blackout, but our route choices were better than in the morning, and torches saw us back feasting before the fire at nine o'clock.

We had come in up the river valleys. To go out, we chose the tops between the Ada and Henry that lead past Philosophers Knob and Zampa – idyllic tops with *Chionochloa australis*, short, shiny carpet grass, to walk on. This can get slippery, but in such mellow country over a couple of fine days it was simply easy travelling. Mixed with it were yellow *Racomitrium* moss species, pale green-grey mats of sticky *Celmisia* and bare rocky outcrops. The day felt like a royal tour of the Spenser Mountains, with Gloriana and Faerie Queene clear in the autumn sun, rising above the flats and forests of the Ada. It was a privilege to be there.

The tarn under Zampa offered a perfect campsite, and I slid into my sleeping bag under a three-quarter moon and a sky littered with diamonds. What a country and planet to live on. You can keep Mars; I'm staying here.

On our last perfect day we dropped into Henry Saddle, climbed out steeply and finished our traverse of Faerieland over Trovatore, Travers Peak and the track down through the bush to the Lewis Pass Road.

OPPOSITE Morning light on Faerie Queene, from a tarn above the Ada-Christopher forks.
OVERLEAF (LEFT) The western Spenser Mountains, Ada Valley and Pass, from near Philosophers Knob.
OVERLEAF (RIGHT) Zampa tarns with the rabbit ears of Gloriana Peak (centre) and Faerie Queene to the right.

THOMPSON PASS & MT UNA

MALING PASS–WAIAU RIVER–THOMPSON PASS–
D'URVILLE PASS–DAVID SADDLE–ELLA RANGE–MATAKITAKI
RIVER EAST BRANCH–MT UNA–ENID PASS–WAIAU RIVER–
MALING PASS

6 DAYS: 1–6 APRIL 1999
GS WITH BARBARA BROWN, SVEN BRABYN, LYNETTE HARTLEY, JEFF HALL,
LARS BRABYN, MARK PICKERING AND ADRIAN GRIERSON

There isn't much shelter from the wind at Lake Tennyson, so we slept in the back of the car. Station wagons are handy like that, but we had to leave it behind in the morning. Too heavy. Following the bulldozed track, we crossed Maling Pass to drop into the Waiau. The upper Waiau, tucked under the Spenser Divide, embodies many of the best aspects of the Spensers, and is now part of the Te Araroa Trail, linking Nelson Lakes with Lewis Pass. In 2018, a farmer-philanthropist paid for the new six-bunk Waiau Hut near here; a very generous act of giving back to the outdoor community.

Back in Easter 1999, the place was secluded, Caroline Creek Biv was in good condition, and the welcome from the sandflies very enthusiastic. We camped in the last patch of bush up-valley.

Higher up the Waiau in a landscape full of gorgeous places lay Lake Thompson, sparkling like a jewel. Enchanted, we wandered around finding ever-better campsites, tarns within tarns, and water like crystal. But it was too early for camping, and after two hours lingering we headed over Thompson Pass.

Sidling across the head of the D'Urville River to D'Urville Pass we were initially forced up around a rocky gut, but the rest of the way was easy. From there, we kept our height, over boulders and bedrock overlooking the East Matakitaki, past a small tarn, across benches under David Saddle to find a high campsite at about 1800 metres. A full, frosty moon hung in the sky as evening cloud cleared.

Tops on this southern extension to the Ella Range above the East Matakitaki roll gently down for kilometres, watered by tarns, with views of all the central Spenser Mountains. It was about as cruisy and scenic as tops-tramping gets. To the south stood Mt Una, first climbed in November 1938 by Tom Newth and Ray Husband, and which we were to attempt later in the trip. They walked from Hanmer, taking a horse to carry their packs, and Husband noted: 'I might mention here that a packhorse should be included in a climber's equipment, and Tom is busy designing a horse-shoe crampon for travel on the glaciers further south.'

Open red and silver beech led us down off the range about 10 minutes below the tidy East Matakitaki Hut. Across the valley an old track through mountain beech led us back towards the Spenser tops again. From here Mt Una (2300 metres) could be climbed, and morning found us picking our way south up a staircase of boulders and scree, corkscrewing up a nifty little gully tucked in west of the peak. Scrambling up broken but wonderfully patterned greywacke rock, we reached a chimney just before the ridge. A boulder jammed in it made climbing awkward, so the rope was used for security. Then we were on top, on the most brilliant of autumn days.

OPPOSITE On Mt Una, Easter 1999. Adrian, Barb (sitting), Lynette, Jeff and Lars. The Spenser Mountains stretch away to the right towards Faerie Queene.

RIGHT Dawn light on the Glacier Burn face of Mt Una (right) and Duessa Peak (centre). Seen from the St James Range.

Directly below us, remnants of ice clung to the base of bluffs in Glacier Gully. To the south, Duessa Peak was dwarfed, but rugged for all that. A friend, Graham McCallum, was on the first ascent of Duessa in 1947, along with B. Hildreth, J. Rogers and L. Verry. The ridge to the north-east from Mt Una proved a better descent route than the way we had come, and by 3 p.m. we were back at our campsite and packing furiously so as to cross the range that night. Over Enid Pass we kept our height and sidled south into another tarn basin for the night. All that remained was to return to the Waiau Valley and Lake Tennyson.

At this stage, St James Station hadn't been sold to the government and we didn't have permission to cross it. Descending from Maling Pass, we turned a corner and there, not far away, the owner was trundling up towards us on a bulldozer. There was no chance to avoid a discussion – however, on our side, we were only tramping and had no rifles or dogs. And we were leaving.

We met up. The inevitable question of 'who gave you permission to be here?' occurred. Quick as a flash, one of our party said, 'You did.' Confusion set in. 'Did I?' The audacity was breathtaking, but it worked. In no time we were merrily chatting to him about the weather, where we had been and what he was up to. Never let it be said that trampers don't do their bit to foster friendships.

THERE AND BACK

MARUIA–THREE TARN PASS–MATAKITAKI VALLEY–
CHRISTOPHER RIVER–ADA VALLEY–MARUIA

8 DAYS: 14–21 AUGUST 1977
GS WITH SHONA MAXWELL

The Spenser Mountains might be idyllic in summer, but winter is a different story. Shona and I had hitched to Lewis Pass during the August holidays, then tramped up to Ada Pass. Heavy snow lay on the mountains. Our plan was to cross over them into the isolated flats and forest of the Matakitaki headwaters then, in a different part of the range, cross back to the east.

Our route crossed the range at 1986 metres and is today called Three Tarn Pass. It was not named on the map then. As we drew closer, the tarns weren't visible; they were asleep in a mountain world under thick white blankets. Snow flurried around, turning to rain as we descended, and icy crusts of snow cut our bare legs. That night we reached the bushline and lit a good fire, turning cold misery into comfort. Down by the stream a blue duck (also known as whio) whistled to us at twilight.

All night it rained. We woke early at four, ravenous after the previous day's snow-plugging, and we made up some instant pudding. I love such random actions; it is liberating just responding to hunger in a tent in the middle of the night. Full, we went back to sleep.

Later in the morning we continued to Bobs Hut. Bobs had a good coat of orange paint on it then and looked very inviting with the steady rain falling. I like the big open fireplaces in the old Forest Service huts. When coming in cold and wet, with dry wood in the porch, the fire can be roaring within minutes, and a billy swinging from a bit of number-8 wire. It is part of a culture that stretches back for over a century; the fire is far and away more communal and friendlier and doesn't require the support of the oil industry to boil a brew and keep warm.

Because we were concerned about getting back over the range, we set the alarm for 5.30 a.m. A blazed track took us to a slightly hairy two-wire crossing of the West Branch where balance was imperative, then we were away up the Matakitaki East Branch to the first grass flat and heading back towards the Spenser Divide. A fine morning had turned heavily overcast, and in deep snow with a windslab crust, we reached the divide at 4 p.m. Now to find a way off. We sidled across dodgy slopes to plug down to the bushline in a branch of the Christopher Valley, which flows into the Ada. It began snowing in the night.

Coming down next morning through gorgeous open mountain beech forest with a floor of Dicranaloma moss, we came across unmistakable stock puddles, some of it fresh. We were back on the fringes of St James Station, with loose herds of bulls and cattle. Until 2008 much of the Spenser Mountains was part of St James Station, managed by the Stevenson family, and was famous for its semi-wild horses, which have been there since the 1920s.

We spent the night in the little Christopher Cullers Hut, curled up by the fire. The rising sun melted a veil of low cloud away down-valley, and Faerie Queene glittered in a gown of white, serene above olive forests and frosted grass flats. All day we pottered around the reflective shores of Lake Paget, watching paradise ducks and Canada geese. We continued on in the still winter air. Friendly riflemen, tomtits, grey warblers, South Island robins, kea, goldfinches and bellbirds with their fluid calls seemed as tranquil as the waters.

Evening found us tucked under a high canopy of mature forest looking out on the last flat up the Ada, with frost forming on the grass. I always choose campsites tucked under a bush fringe whenever I can. There are many advantages. Trees are like a roof. On a fine night they keep most of the dew off my sleeping bag or the tent. They also keep the cold at a distance. Most flats become frost hollows in winter and getting up to breakfast in wet or frozen grass isn't much fun when a drier alternative is so easy.

The moon was down to a quarter, and only the flickering bonfire lit up nearby tree trunks. As we lay by the dying fire well after midnight we were both shocked bolt upright by a bloodcurdling, loud series of unearthly shrieks coming from directly above us in the canopy. The shrieks stopped as quickly as they'd started and we strained to listen in the silence. With no warning they began again, weird and frightening. This happened a few times. We used what battery we had left in our torches, but saw nothing, and nothing moved.

What on earth was it? A possum? I've heard a lot of possums at night, and I've slept out many hundreds of nights before and since and never heard

Ada Cullers Hut. In 1977, it had an open fire, which was very welcome in August.

anything vaguely like this. Possums can be pretty screechy and raucous but this was on a whole other level, beginning with full intensity and finishing as abruptly. I wrote in my diary at the time 'One bird at night . . . screeched like hell – an ominous, threatening sound, almost like a raucous dog growling. Don't know what it was.'

I've always been keen on my native birds, but running through them in my head, I dismissed everything I knew. Then, when I read through my bird books back home, the call of the Laughing Owl, which has been described as 'unearthly yells', maniacal and 'dreadfully doleful shrieks of sudden high intensity' fitted very well. The trouble was, they were probably extinct. The last specimen was found in 1914 in South Canterbury. Still, reports from isolated places east of the Southern Alps persisted until the 1960s. Who knows?

KEHU PEAK

HAMILTON RIVER–BEGLEY CREEK–KEHU PEAK–BEGLEY SADDLE–TRAVERS SADDLE–RAINBOW PASS–RAINBOW RIVER

3 DAYS: 20–23 OCTOBER 1978

GS WITH JOHN NANKERVIS, JOHN COCKS AND MARTIN POTTER

The Spenser Mountains are full of adventures for long weekends, in both mellow and rough country. Some of the peaks such as Kehu are a little isolated and don't see many climbs, making them interesting, but we had another reason to be in the area at this time: not only was ours a transalpine climbing trip but also we were paying homage to our friend Pat Begley.

Pat was chief guide of the Tararua Tramping Club when he tragically drowned during Easter 1978 in the Murchison River in Mount Cook National Park. Begley Creek, Begley Hut and Begley Saddle were well established on the maps long before Pat arrived in New Zealand in 1963, but they were touchstones for us to remember this friend along our way.

Nank's VW Beetle skittled along the Wairau–Hanmer Springs Hydro Road with a throaty roar and scraping the undercarriage on marginal fords was all part of the excitement. I was glad it wasn't my car, and I hoped it would get us back.

Heading up through the beech forest of the Hamilton Valley, we then tramped through drizzle until we were in the snow before the bushline. Higher, we crossed over into Begley Creek and scurried downstream to the hedonistic pleasures of a Forest Service hut: a mattress, fire and shelter.

On a sparkling fine Sunday morning, we swung down one branch through the bush and back up another to leave our packs below Begley Saddle. Approaching Kehu Peak from the east out of Begley Creek, we sorted climbing gear, then cramponed up snowy basins that steepened considerably towards the top.

Kehu Peak (2220 metres), is a little gem off most people's radar, lying between the northern Spenser Mountains and the southern St Arnaud Range. It was named in 1947 by the first ascent party of L.J. Dumbleton, J. Stanton, J. Taylor and R. Lamberton, who wrote: 'We are suggesting the name Kehu for this peak, after the Maori whose invaluable services to Brunner and to other explorers do not seem to have been adequately recognised.'

Range after snow-layered range peeled away in front of us as we sat in a warm sun identifying what we could see and munching snacks. Later, we crossed Begley Saddle, dropped into the upper Travers, climbed up to Travers Saddle, then camped higher still on snow near Rainbow Pass.

Winter is officially over by Labour weekend, but no one told Jack Frost. The night was very cold. On steep snow the next day we descended into the Rainbow, and once the slope eased, sat on our bums and slid. Unsettled skies cuffed us down the valley, on a long slog back to the road and car.

ABOVE Travers Saddle, below the southern faces of Mt Travers, with Mt Cupola in the distance, seen from the route up to Rainbow Pass.
OPPOSITE Deep snow high on Kehu Peak. Martin is following John (Cocks), with the upper Begley Valley behind.

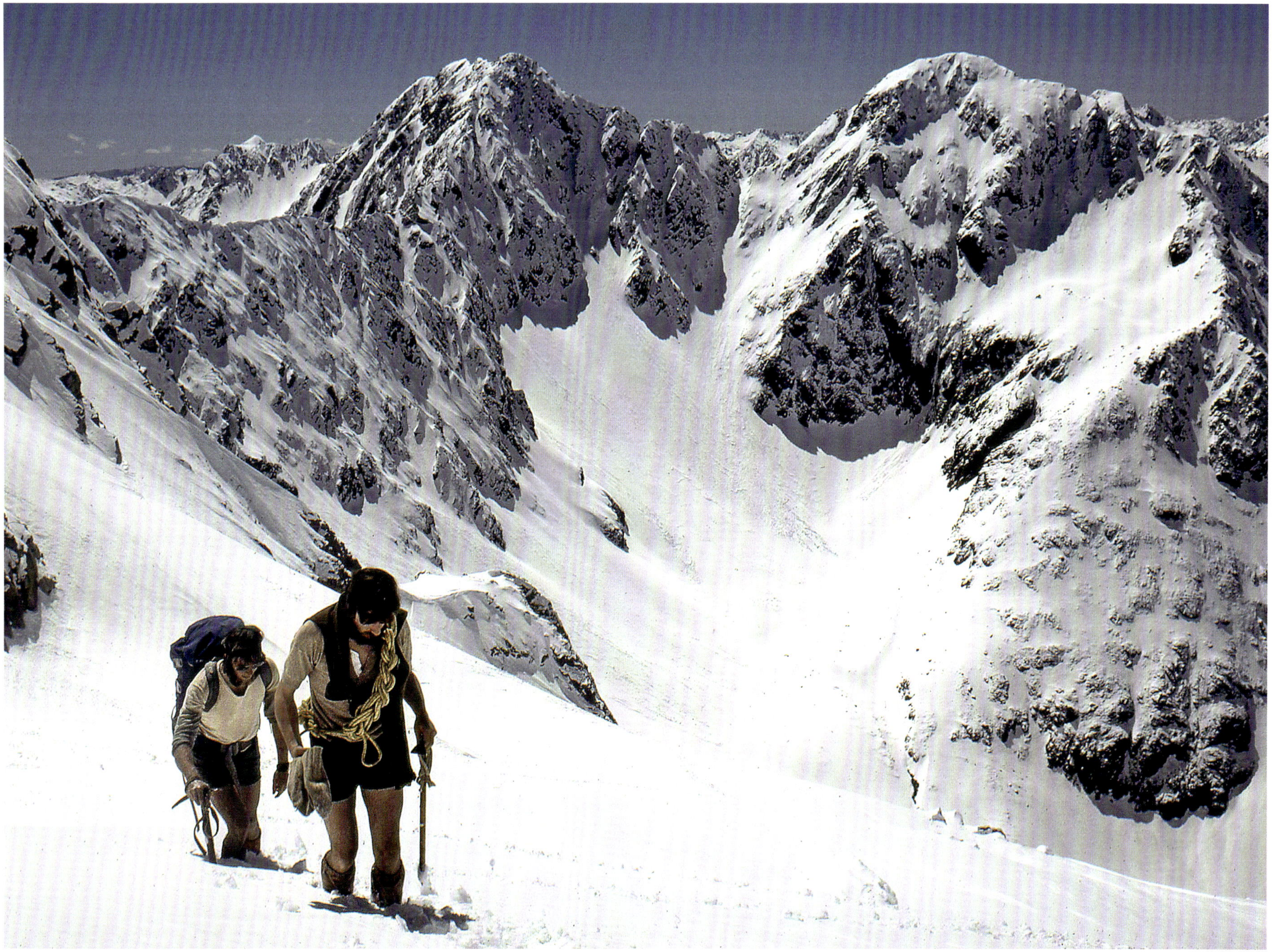

THE FROST REPORT ON MT MANAKAU

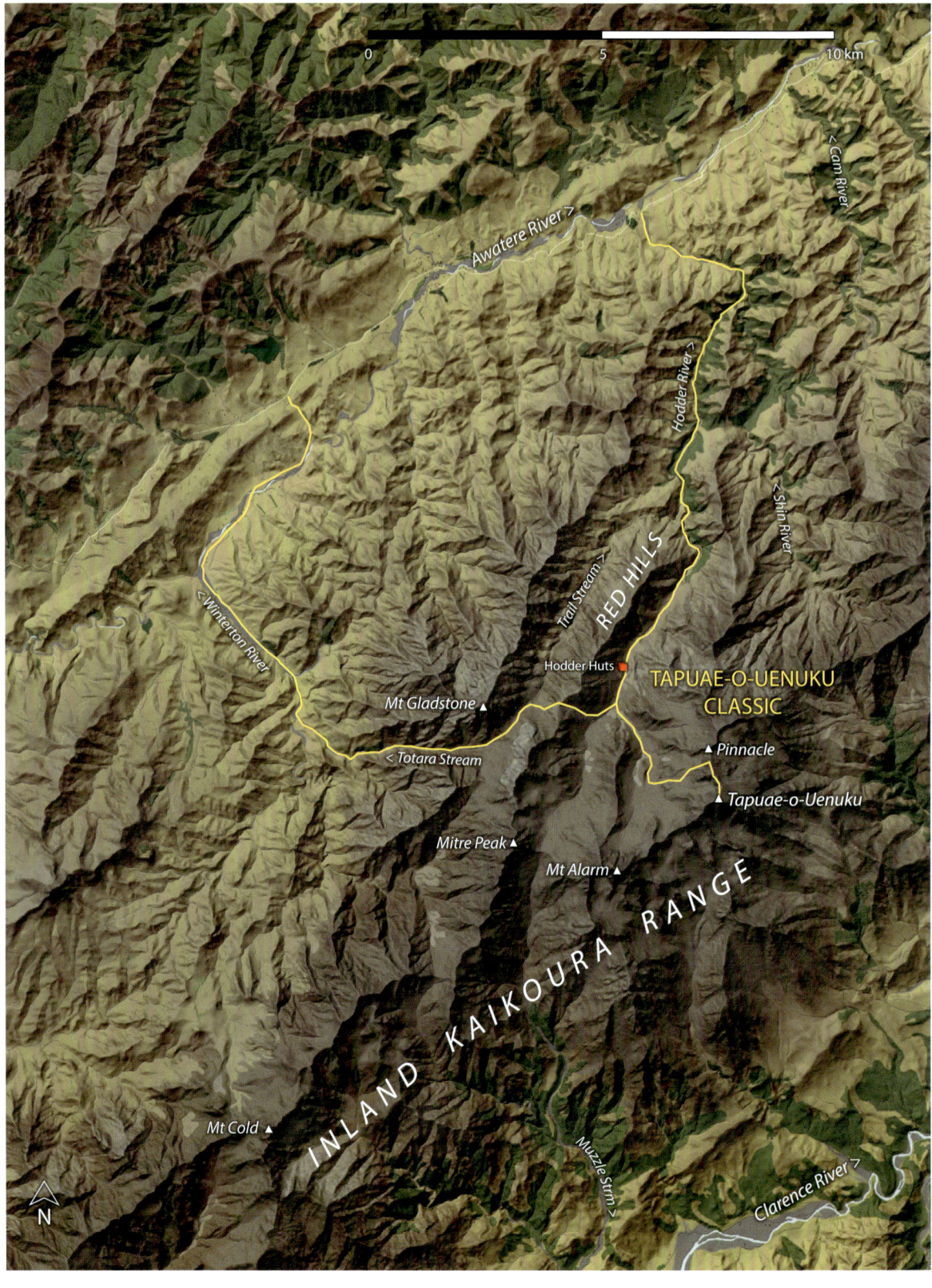

Clarence River
Fidget Strm
Dubious Strm
SEAWARD KAIKOURA RANGE
Te ao Whekere
▲ *Manakau*
▲ *Uwerau*
▲ *Mt Saunders*
< Sice Ck
Hapuku Hut
▲ *Snowflake*
Kowhai Saddle
< Kowhai River
Hapuku River >
▲ *Mt Fyffe*
①

0 5 10 km
N

TAPUAE-O-UENUKU CLASSIC

Cam River
Awatere River >
Hodder River >
Shin River
< Winterton River
Trail Stream >
RED HILLS
Hodder Huts
▲ *Mt Gladstone*
< Totara Stream
▲ *Pinnacle*
▲ *Tapuae-o-Uenuku*
▲ *Mitre Peak*
▲ *Mt Alarm*
INLAND KAIKOURA RANGE
▲ *Mt Cold*
Muzzle Strm >
Clarence River >

0 5 10 km
N

CHAPTER 3
KAIKOURA RANGES

There are two Kaikoura ranges, the Inland and the Seaward, divided by the Clarence River. Everywhere the shattered greywacke rock of which both ranges are comprised shows through – in the gravel riverbeds, the gorges, and on the high peaks.

Barren and scrubby, it is a harsh and uncompromising landscape interlocked with the wind and the cold. The place has a fierce character of its own, and I love that extremity.

Despite this, in good conditions the mountains are not particularly difficult to climb by their standard routes and there are other well-established, but usually unmarked, trails throughout this landscape as well. It is thought the first ascent of Mt Manakau in the Seaward Range, for instance, was in the 1870s by local James Ingram.

Nehemiah McRae was probably the first recorded climber of the Inland Range's highest peak, Mt Tapuae-o-Uenuku, in 1864. He reportedly left a £5 note in a bottle up there. Other ascents followed, the note disappeared, and later a cheque was left for $1,000,000 . . . but it wasn't signed. Morgan Carkeek placed a trig on the summit in 1895. A winter ascent didn't follow until August 1941 when Bert Esquilant and Steven Brockett reached the summit. The following day they attempted Mt Alarm, but frostbitten feet forced a retreat. Since then, many others have felt the blow of the frostbite hammer in the Kaikoura ranges.

The classic journey here is a trip up the Hodder River with all its 80 or so crossings to the Hodder Huts and an ascent of Mt Tapuae-o-Uenuku, followed by a return via Trail Stream to the Hodder or, alternatively, Totara Stream and the Winterton Valley.

SEAWARD: THE FROST REPORT ON MT MANAKAU

HAPUKU RIVER–MT MANAKAU–MT UWERAU–HAPUKU RIVER

3 DAYS: 8–10 MAY 1971

GS WITH LAUCHIE DUFF

It was May, and from Wellington the Kaikoura ranges looked inviting under a dusting of snow. Definitely time to take the iceaxe for a walk.

We had our sights set on Mt Manakau; at 2608 metres it is the highest peak in the Seaward Range. Our trip wasn't anything new or fancy, but this one became memorable for the cold and a lack of water. You can prepare for them both and we didn't prepare for either.

In the 1930s, a Mr E. (Ted) Brown reportedly climbed Mt Manakau from Fidget Stream and traversed over Uwerau and Mt Fyffe en route to Kaikōura in one day. Others were not so lucky. In July 1964, during an ascent of Mt Manakau, a Christchurch mountaineer was blown into a gut on the Kowhai slopes of Mt Uwerau and killed.

Our trip from the coastal highway up the Hapuku River led through a rugged little gorge under stately tōtara, matai and miro trees. Later we sat around a fire in the blackness. The memory of that fire would taunt us the next night.

Leaving packs and most of our gear behind in the morning, we headed up Surveyor Spur. Fresh powdery snow covered the mountain down to 2000 metres. With short daylight hours it was nearly three o'clock before we were on the summit of Mt Manakau, where Lauchie managed a handstand to celebrate. We'd intended to simply come back the same way, but that seemed a bit boring. Instead, we looked across at Mt Uwerau, and thought, why not traverse it? We knew nothing about Mt Uwerau, but surely it couldn't be that hard.

Catching our boot tops in the bright afternoon snow we bombed off Manakau along the ridge, taking our time on the steep bits. Many places had a thin veneer of frost-shattered shingle over bedrock that was nasty to move around on. A few minor pinnacles slowed us further. So, by the time the sun had bulged its way down behind the snowy Spensers, and Messrs Orange, Vermillion, Amber, Crimson, Indigo, and Violet were fading into black, we were still at about 2100 metres, scrambling in bluffs. It was time to stop.

'What's the time, Lauchie?' I enquired, as we carved out a channel in a short section of shingle to lie in.

'Half-past six.'

We ripped open the end of a large plastic bag, and by top and tailing we could get most of our bodies in. I wore everything I had, of course. Shorts, overtrousers, singlet, a small holey jersey and my light Japara parka. Underneath us we laid the rope, but it was damp. Jack Frost chilled his way in everywhere, preventing sleep.

'What's the time, Lauchie?'

'Half-past seven.'

From our kea roost we looked out over the head of the Kowhai River.

It wasn't until 1965 that Geoff Harrow, a Canterbury mountaineer who was holidaying in Kaikōura, went on a search for Hutton's shearwaters after hearing stories from local hunters. Until then it had been unknown where they bred. His investigations turned up several sites, including one in the head of the adjacent Kowhai.

'What's the time?'

'Nine o'clock.'

An incredible moonrise over a glittering sea was followed by another bout of shivering and a deepening of the trench. A tube of condensed milk went down well between us. It wasn't much for dinner, but it was all we had.

Go on, sky, damn you, turn pink. We shuffled arms and legs to ease pins and needles. We shuffled to retain heat, but with every move we lost more. The cold came from everywhere. Silently, the full moon coasted over the snows of Manakau. We huddled together, trying to conserve that priceless stuff called heat and warmth.

'What's the time . . .'

Deep cold is an insidious, debilitating tyrant. We weren't the first to suffer at the hands of a malignant frost high in the Kaikoura ranges, and others have paid much higher prices, but we still shivered uncontrollably, hour after hour. Beside us, hoar ice crystals grew three or four centimetres long from out of the gravel.

It is true that the darkest hour is just before dawn, and for us, it was also the coldest.

The bright amber moon slowly spiked itself to extinction way over on the Spensers, the same way the sun had, an eternity before. Yet, away out to sea, an oval of mushroom pink was forming to replace the disappearing moon's brightness. The peaks and valleys to the north-east began to glow until finally, finally, the sun appeared.

Suddenly we were laughing and thawing. Stiff joints came free and we got moving. What a difference the sun makes. The shattered dome of Uwerau offered more loose rock, and after 27 hours without it, we reached water in the valley. We drank like fish.

With our packs on again we headed down-valley for our last camp. As with so many transalpine trips, we had started out with intentions, but what we received was something we hadn't planned on. We thought this trip was going to be about climbing Mt Manakau, but what we remember is the cold, the deep, bone-chilling cold.

OPPOSITE A gorge in the Hapuku River.

RIGHT Climbers approaching Mt Manakau.

OVERLEAF (LEFT The Seaward Kaikoura Range from near Mt Fyffe. The pointed (centre) skyline peak is Manakau, and immediately right is Uwerau. Our cold night out was on the ridge between them.

OVERLEAF (RIGHT) Climber returning from Te ao Whekere, the second highest peak in the Seaward Kaikoura Range, under a sky of lenticular clouds (hogsbacks).

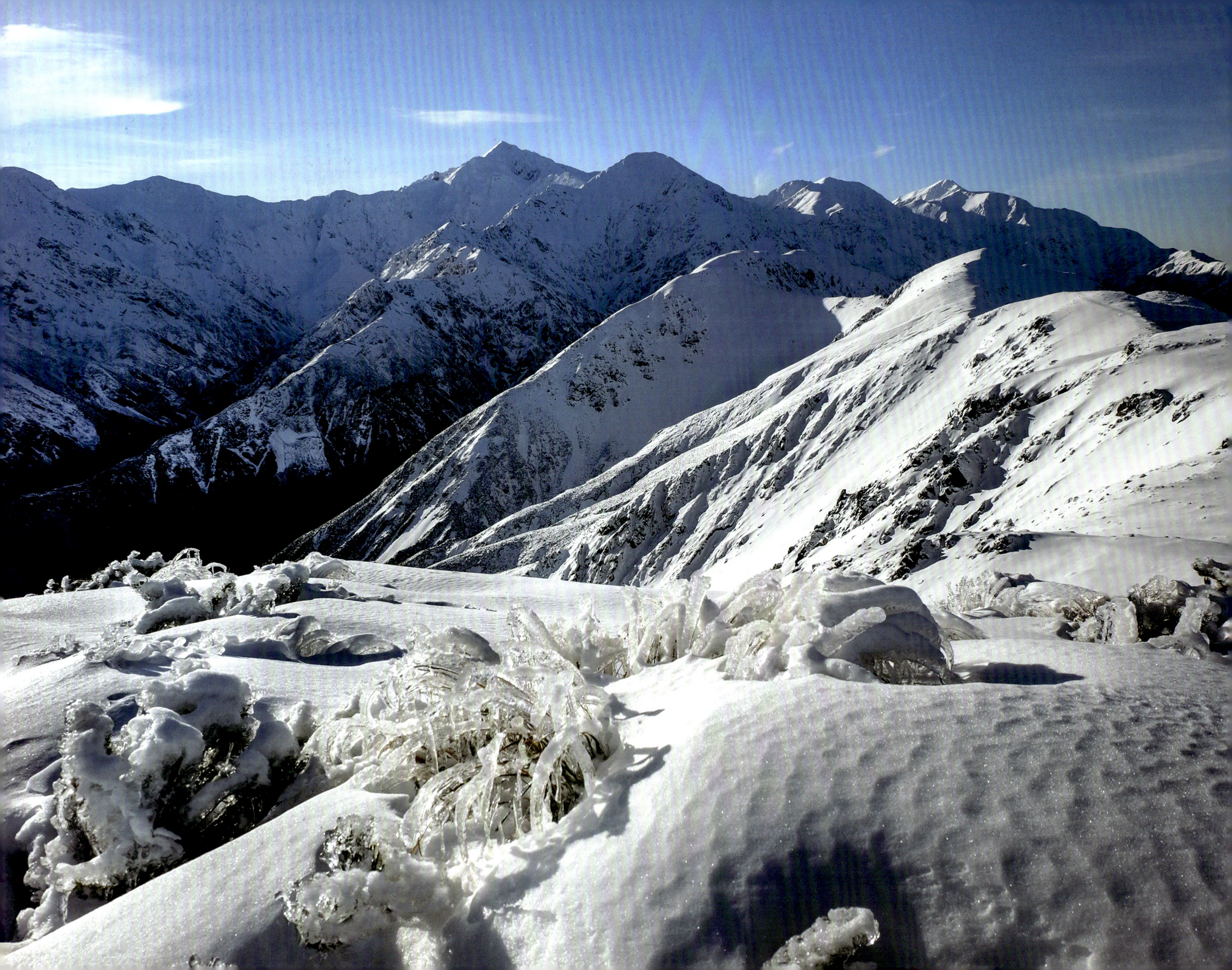

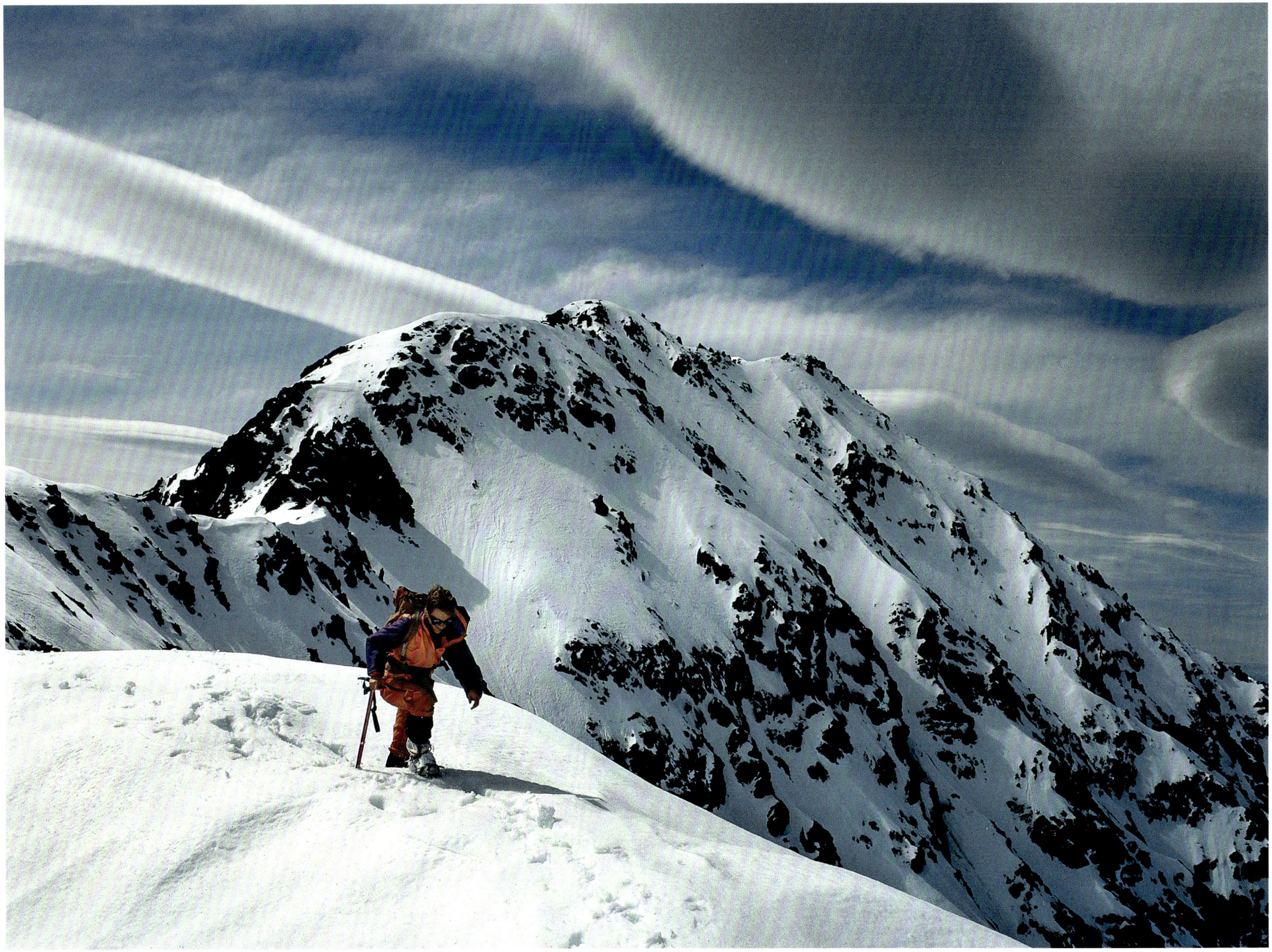

INLAND: TAPUAE-O-UENUKU CLASSIC

HODDER RIVER–MT TAPUAE-O-UENUKU–TRAIL STREAM– TOTARA STREAM–WINTERTON RIVER OCTOBER 1977

3 DAYS: 21–24 OCTOBER 1977
GS WITH JAN AND ARNOLD HEINE, PAUL AUBREY, HUGH VAN NOORDEN,
BEV THORNE (NÉE LONG), RICHARD STRUTHERS AND BOB HENDRY

At 2885 metres Mt Tapuae-o-Uenuku crowns the Inland Kaikoura Range, standing like a beacon on the hazy horizon between Wellington and Christchurch and attracting trampers and climbers alike.

Eight of us joined many other tramping parties heading away on the Picton ferry from Wellington, turning the boat into a fun party for three hours at the start of Labour weekend. At the Hodder bridge we crawled into a barn and slept on hay, looking forward to the adventure ahead.

Among trampers, the Hodder River is well known for its freezing water and its numerous crossings to negotiate. But the day was fine, and we stopped for lunch among the eroding hillsides before sidling up around a waterfall. Using a rusty waratah to hold the billy over the fire, we made a brew.

The sidle provided a break from the gravel riverbed and led us through scratchy scrub, with low tōtara lining the trail in places. In sheltered patches *Hoheria* (mountain lacebark) budded out of hibernation. Higher up, at 1440 metres, Tararua Hut appeared. Prior to the hut, four specific campsites were recognised in the upper valley on a provisional map drawn up by Nelson Tramping Club in 1949.

Proposals for a hut in the upper Hodder began in 1967, spearheaded by Graham McCallum of the Tararua Tramping Club. Plans were approved and funds allocated in 1969, but then it gets interesting: when the club went looking for a helicopter to transport materials, they ran into Gordon Howitt, a geologist organising mineral exploration for Kennecott Exploration, who had been on Arnold Heine's transalpine journeys in central Westland. They all had mutual friends and interests.

Kennecott needed a bigger hut, TTC agreed, and both parties, along with the Pitts who farmed the valley, worked to build the new Tararua Hut, which was finished by Easter 1970. Ray Molineux of the TTC designed it. I suspect that the new arrangement suited TTC and Gordon Howitt very well, while Kennecott footed much of the bill. Ten years later, when we were there, it was full to capacity and our party camped up-valley. In 1986, Marlborough Tramping Club built a second one, the Murray Adrian Hut, with twice the capacity. Marlborough now manages both huts.

Overnight the wind dropped and everything froze to the gravel, including boots and billies. As we climbed up, sunlight came down the slopes to meet us. Plenty of frozen snow made our travel fast in crampons, and we all ended up on the ridge between Pinnacle and Tapuae-o-Uenuku. (Paul and Hugh also climbed Pinnacle then followed the rest of us up Tappy.)

Near the top, the sheer size of the mountain becomes more apparent, with views reaching far and wide. It was a wonderful place to be, with intense sun and a freezing wind. Taking care with sastrugi ice, we headed back down again.

LEFT The energetic Hodder River flows fast and cold from a small gorge in the Inland Kaikoura Range. With over 80 crossings, the river can be more challenging than the climb.
OPPOSITE The summit of Tapuae-o-Uenuku is the skyline knob above and slightly right of the waterfall in Staircase Stream. This route is a common approach to the summit.

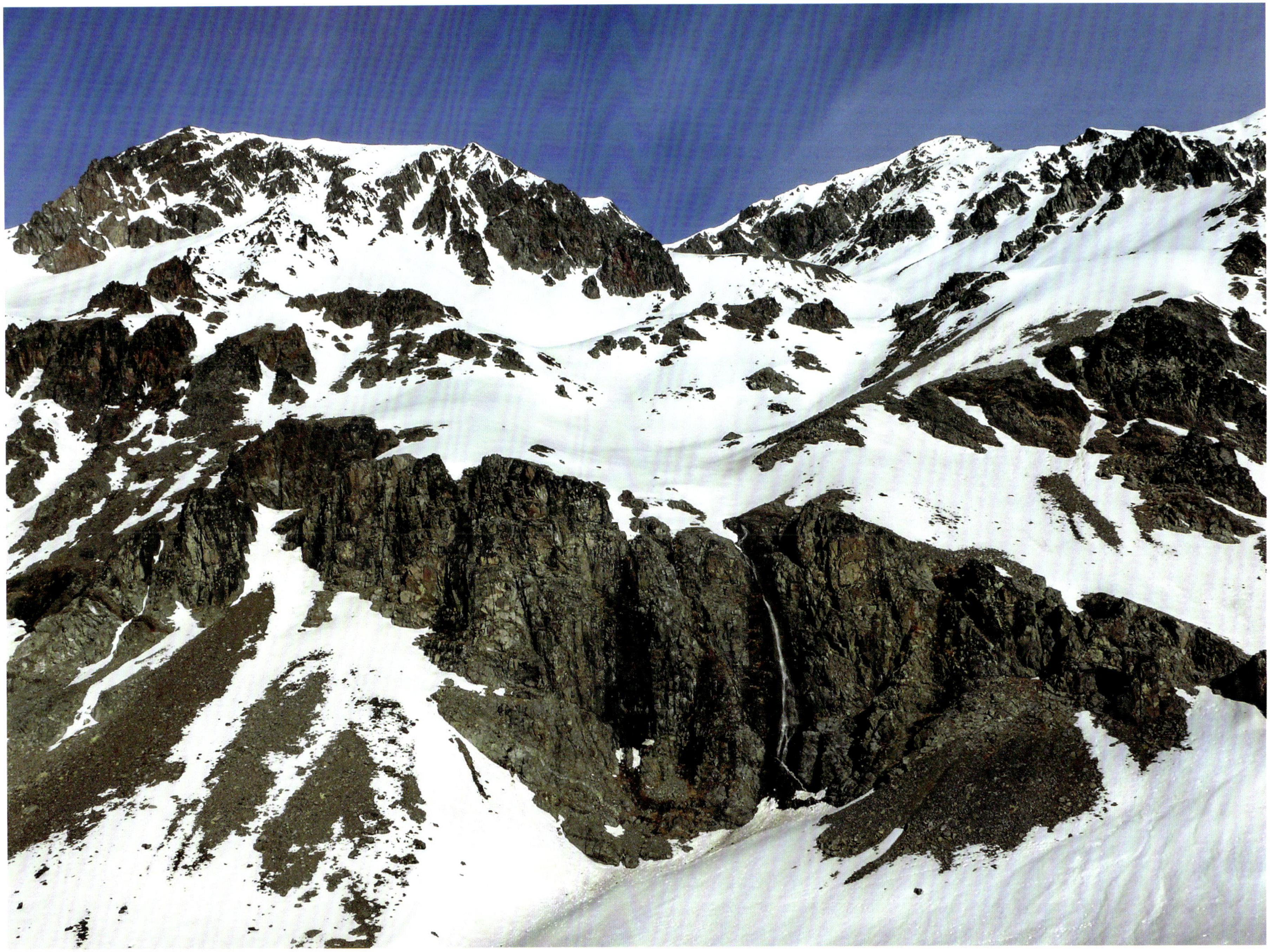

Paul and Richard also climbed Mt Alarm from where they sent out kiwi yodels. The first ascent of Mt Alarm was in 1928 by Tom Fyfe and I. Rawnsley, but the first winter ascent was in 1947 by I. Mackersey, T. Hills, G. Milne and W.G. Lowe. They came in up the Hodder then crossed the Inland Range to the Clarence River before also traversing over the Seaward Range to the coast. One of them wrote: 'Two sets of long woollen underclothing, long trousers, two shirts, a pullover and windjacket and two balaclavas failed to prevent the cold striking up from the snow through the floor of the tent.' In these ranges there is even a peak called Mt Cold.

Back at our camp, I chanced sleeping out, but Huey noticed and began to drizzle. I retreated to the tent. In the morning, under an indifferent sky, we picked an alternative route back out of the ranges. Initially we crossed the Red Hills before we glissaded steeply down to the head of Trail Stream. We were off on another adventure.

The head of Trail Stream took us over into Totara Stream, where travel became tricky. The high walls of the stream closed into a slit canyon that twisted and turned, made of rock as fractured as Weetbix. We could touch both sides at the same time and pull out any stone we liked. Jan wondered what an earthquake might do just there.

After a couple of hours, we were back in open travel, but there remained a very long slog down the isolated Winterton River through farm hills back to the Awatere and Hodder bridge. Long stony streambeds and then gravel farm tracks ground our feet away in our boots, burning them with blisters until they felt like tenderised meat. Just walking on them became an exercise in pain control. On a dry, dusty afternoon, it wasn't the cold that bothered us but blisters in the heat.

LEFT Beside the Hodder River.
OPPOSITE The northern faces of Mt Alarm.

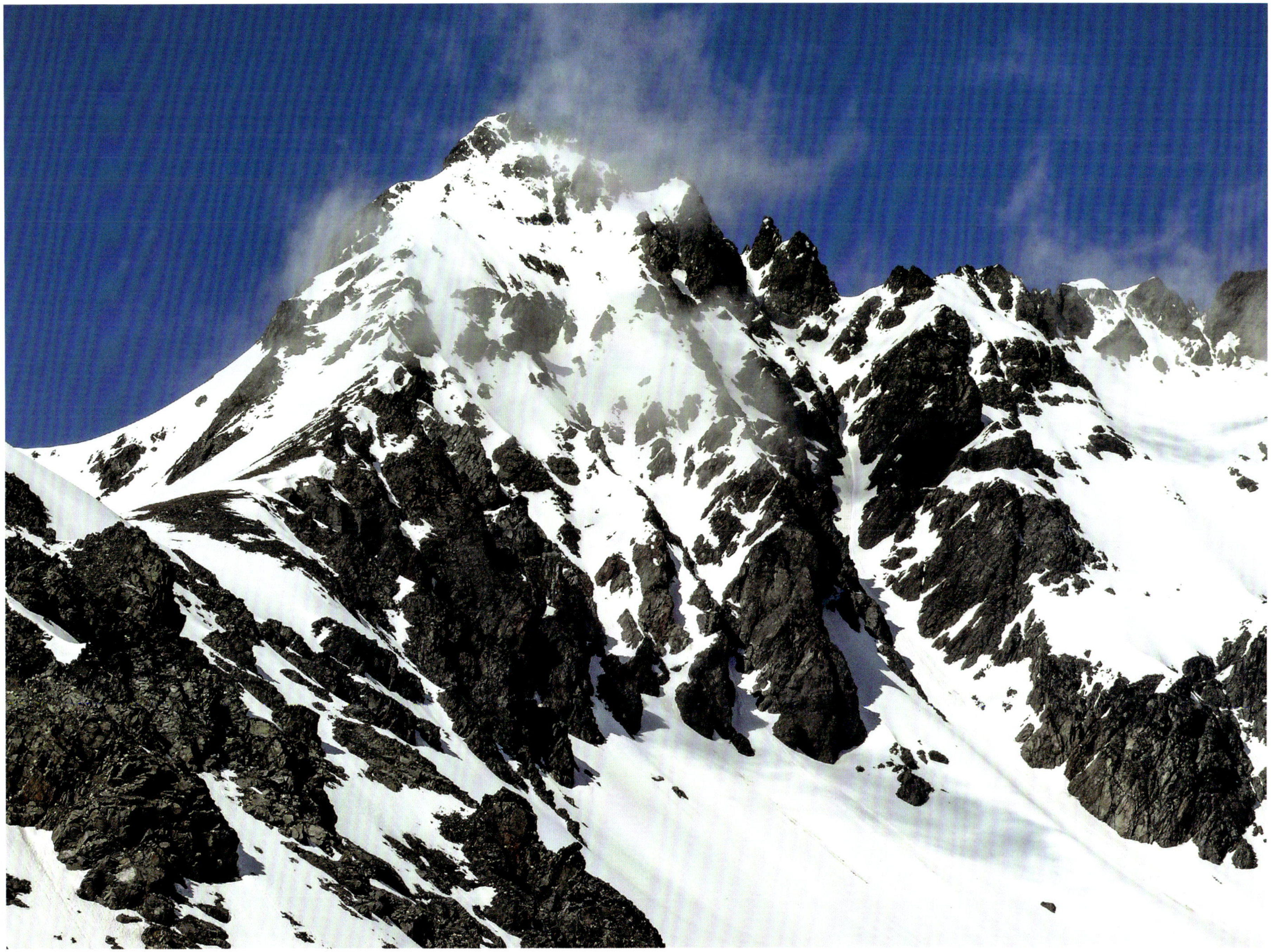

N

0 5 10 km

ALONG THE MAIN DIVIDE

< Kokatahi River

< Hokitika River

Ross

6

< Styx River

< Arahura River

< Taipo River >

Mt Rolleston

MAIN DIVIDE

Arthur's Pass

73

BROWNING RANGE

< Crawford Ck

Mt Learmont

Mt Rosamond

TOAROHA RANGE

< Toaroha River

< Kokatahi River

Mt Griffiths

Farquharson Saddle

) (Browning Pass/Noti Raureka

CLARKES PASS (1990)

DIEDRICHS RANGE

Mt Ambrose

Clarkes Pass

Mt Murchison

) White Col

< Waimakariri River >

< Hokitika River

Toaroha Saddle

< Park Strm

Hokitika Saddle

MAIN DIVIDE TRAVERSE ABOVE THE WHITCOMBE VALLEY

< Mungo River

Mungo Pass

Burnett Stream

Sir Robert Hut

Hokitika River >

Mt Bryce

ROLLESTON RANGE

Unknown Strm >

< Whitcombe River >

Frew Saddle

Mathias Pass

Canyon Creek Biv

Mt Young

Mt Williams

Moa Strm >

< Avoca River >

MAIN DIVIDE

Mt McWhirter

Mt Warner

CHRISTMAS AT SIR ROBERT HUT

Wilberforce River >

Mt Neave

Whitcombe Pass

Mathias River >

Rakaia River >

Lake Coleridge

MAIN DIVIDE

CHAPTER 4
THE WAIMAKARIRI TO THE HOKITIKA

A land of remnant ice, shingle and shattered rock, gnarly scrub and thick forest, this section of the Main Divide offers wonderful adventures for the moderately skilled. Samuel Butler called the western side 'that unexplored region of forest which may contain sleeping princesses and gold in ton blocks, and all sorts of good things'. In reality, the 'good things' for me include natural hot pools, small backcountry huts in neglected corners, and a network of rugged tracks and bridges, along with interesting ranges and craggy Main Divide peaks.

This is a region with a long human history. Nōti Raureka/Browning Pass was in use by 1700 and other passes such as the Whitcombe were also used intermittently by Māori. The Arahura Valley has long been an important source of pounamu. Then from the 1860s, gold prospectors, surveyors, geologists and farmers all explored the area. By the 1920s, recreation began to feature more prominently, and fledgling clubs such as the Canterbury Mountaineering Club (CMC) and the West Coast Alpine Club (formed in 1936) began their own exploration of this corner of the Southern Alps.

There are many fantastic trips to do in this area, supported by a wilderness-style infrastructure of huts and marked routes, maintained in many cases by locals. The Toaroha, Diedrichs, Newton, Browning and Campbell ranges and parts of the Main Divide itself all offer superb transalpine journeys. There is more infrastructure support here than many other regions in this book, but don't be fooled into thinking that makes it easy. There is a lot packed into this patch.

CHRISTMAS AT SIR ROBERT HUT

WILBERFORCE RIVER–MUNGO PASS–MUNGO RIVER– SIR ROBERT HUT–MATHIAS PASS–MATHIAS RIVER

8 DAYS: 21 DECEMBER–28 DECEMBER 1991

GS WITH BARBARA BROWN, SVEN BRABYN AND GAYLENE WILKINSON

Strong nor-westers and rain storming down the Wilberforce faced the four of us at the beginning of this week-long Christmas trip. Up-valley, the gravels of Gibson Stream led towards a narrow, rocky defile and waterfall, while high above on the Main Divide lay our first objective: Mungo Pass.

Once over, we followed Brunswick Creek down to the Mungo River, where the smell of sulphur led us to hot water snaking over the gravel. We levered rocks away with iceaxes and dug a pool. Later, under a starlit sky, our candlelight danced on the river shingle. It is quite magical to sink into hot water, surrounded by mountains.

Trampers, hunters and climbers such as Merle Sweney's 1935 Canterbury Mountaineering Club party have been enjoying these hot pools for many years. They are fuelled by earthquake faults, as are many others throughout Westland. These ones are recorded on a geological survey map published in 1907.

Up near the bushline on Homeward Ridge, slippery carpets of leaves fallen from mountain neinei crackled under our feet. Called Dr Seuss or pineapple trees by some, these are one of about 30 species of *Dracophyllum*, native to New Zealand.

At just above 1600 metres, we camped on a knoll in a flowering alpine herb field, where rock outcrops provided back rests and tarns provided water on a stunning summer evening. Location, location. One thousand metres below us the Mungo murmured in its bed, opposite lay the Toaroha Range, and up behind stood peaks on the Main Divide.

It was Christmas Eve. Others would be in frantic shopping sprees, chasing last-minute necessities, while the quiet mountains kept vigil. We'd been shopping beforehand and had red longjohns and jackets. A little secret. The handles of white shopping bags fitted over the ears allow the bags to give passable Santa impersonations. Well, if you really need a Santa at Christmas. In the mild evening air, dinner cooked over the primus, the steam slowly drifting left and right above it.

We kept the best of our goodies for Christmas dinner at Sir Robert Hut, and slept out under the stars in just our sleeping bags. Then all we did on Christmas Day was get up late, descend to the valley, and find the hut in the sun for lunch.

Sir Robert Hut, built in 1963, was put in the subalpine zone to cull deer from. There is no track to or from it and the valley below is gorged, so the hut has developed its own aura, and the logbook reinforces this. Only about 20 people signed it in the previous 10 years. The hut has recently (2017) been maintained by volunteer members of Permolat, an online group that maintain huts, facilitated by the Backcountry Trust.

Our Christmas dinner was a sumptuous affair. Decorations went up on local shrubs and we nibbled on starters, while new potatoes and other vegetables simmered in a billy over an open fire outside. We lay back in comfy hollows munching olives and slices of ham. Aroma from the musk tree daisy, *Olearia moschata*, wafted with the smoke from the fire. Barb made hats for us all from the upturned leaves of Mt Cook lilies (which looked kind of cute on Sven). Hakeke, *Olearia ilicifolia*, with its holly-like leaves, added a nice kiwi touch to the pudding decoration. Freshly brewed coffee and special chocolates followed. It's tough out there.

On Boxing Day it drizzled while we recovered, read paperbacks and looked at the map. We still had to cross back over the Main Divide again, hopefully from the head of Sir Robert Creek into the Mathias, before tramping down-valley and then across to the car at the Wilberforce. Tension can build when facing an unknown alpine crossing, especially when poor weather and lack of time combine. But we had time on our side, so we waited. Another brew, then another trip outside to give Huey a hand watering the plants.

John Pascoe had a great day out near here in the summer of 1930. Approaching from the Mathias Valley with R.R. Chester and A.H. Willis,

OPPOSITE: Christmas morning 1991 on Homeward Ridge, with three good friends. Where else would you want to be? Tussocky Frew Saddle is behind the camp, and Mt Frieda is to the left, high above the Hokitika headwaters.

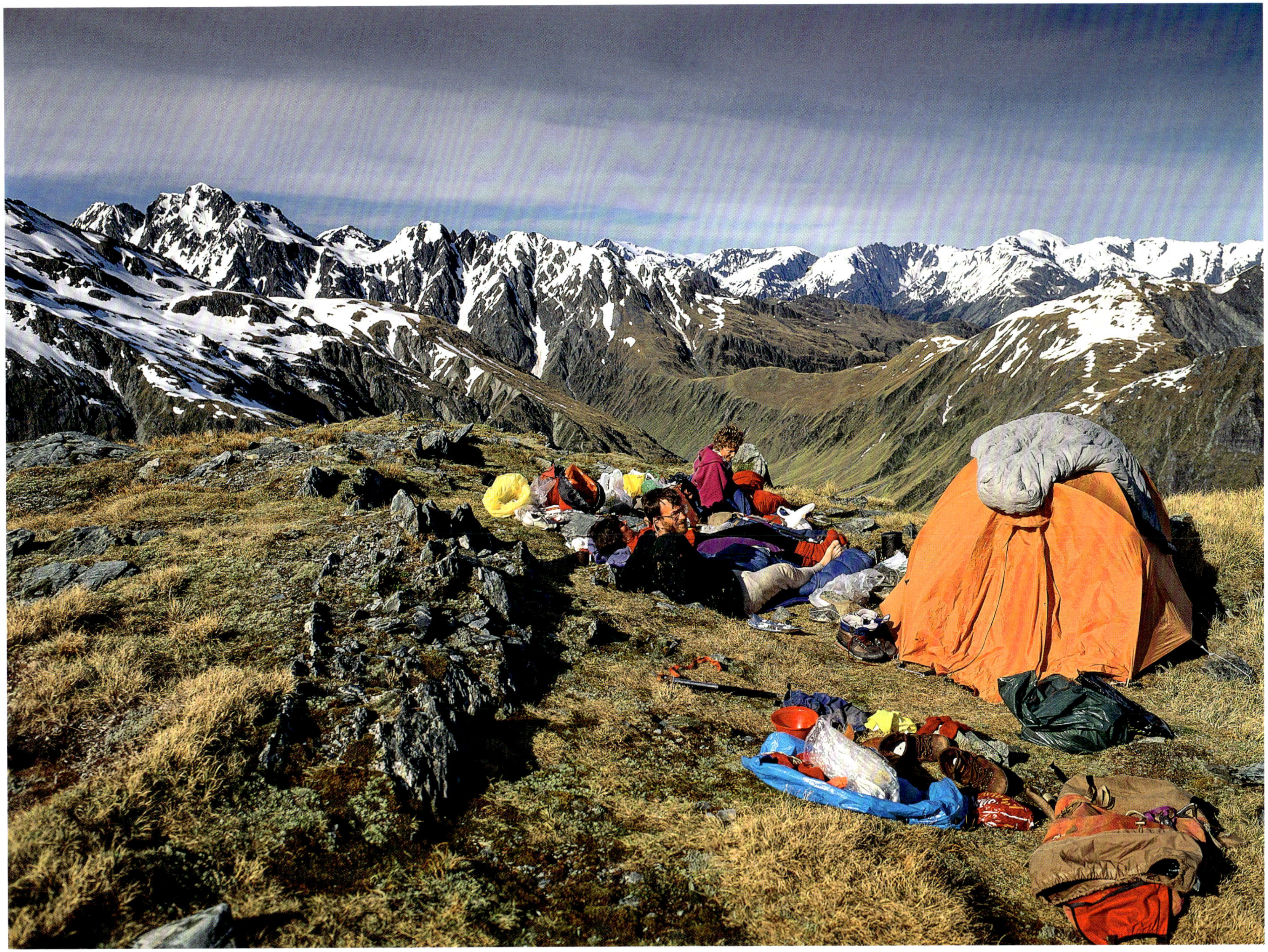

LEFT Sir Robert Hut, isolated and nestled above a gorge, with no track to or from it.

OPPOSITE Lake Browning/Whakarewa from above Hall Col. The Wilberforce Valley is to the right and the high peak is Mt Rosamond.

he scrambled up a steep spur on to the Main Divide. It was tough, they weren't impressed, and thus named the spur Treachery Ridge. But even so, before the day was out they had traversed 11 previously unclimbed peaks, beginning with Gerard Peak and finishing with Mt Bryce. That's living the dream.

Next day, despite mist and drizzle, we, too, crossed the Main Divide. In steep soft snow we reached the crest to drop down onto extensive snow avalanche debris in the head of a swollen Canyon Creek. With the canyon below impassable, we continued high over a spur on Monarch Hill to finally reach Canyon Creek Bivvy in the North Mathias at eight o'clock. Inside, we tucked up dry again, before the long tramp out to the Wilberforce. Small huts are just the best.

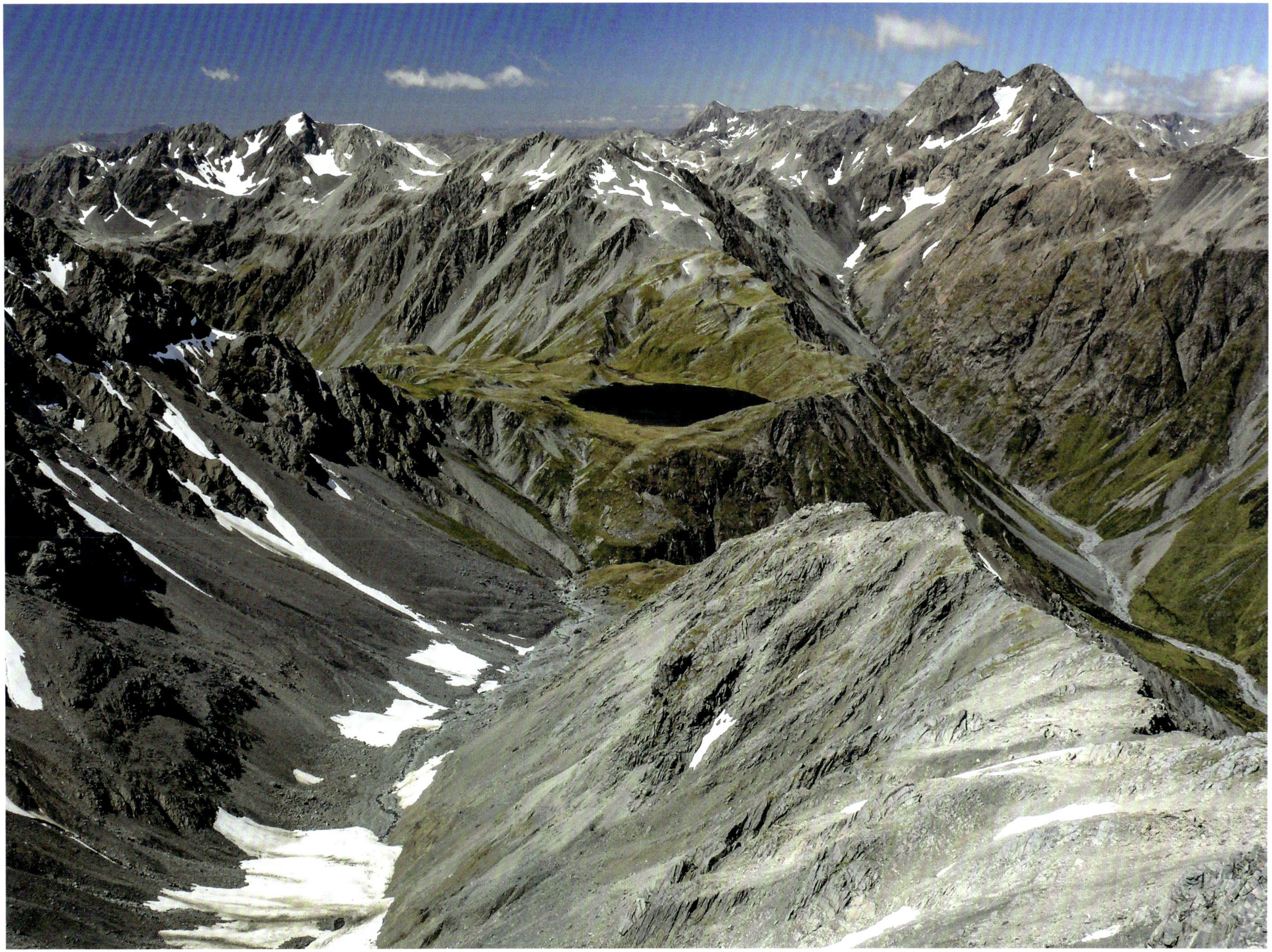

ALONG THE MAIN DIVIDE

STYX RIVER–ARAHURA RIVER–BROWNING PASS–HALL COL–
FARQUHARSON SADDLE–GRIFFITHS SADDLE & GLACIER–
CLARKES PASS–MT AMBROSE–THE RAMPART–PARK STREAM–
MUNGO RIVER–TOAROHA SADDLE–TOAROHA RIVER

7 DAYS: 3–9 FEBRUARY 2008
GS WITH LINDA LILBURNE AND BRYAN TUFFNELL

One of the best transalpine trips in this area threads along the Main Divide from Browning Pass to around Hokitika Saddle. This is largely a snow and rock trip, full of alpine basins and high passes with interesting little peaks to climb or bypass on the way.

Late in the day we made our way up a bush sidle track to Grassy Flat Hut in the Styx Valley. Inside, four others were already settled out of the drizzle. When the rain eased next morning, our party of three headed along the old pack track towards Harman Hut in the Arahura Valley, having lunch on Styx Saddle, with a slightly over-friendly weka also looking for lunch.

Considerable human history overlays the landscape around Browning Pass. Raureka, a Ngāti Wairangi woman from the West Coast, crossed Nōti Raureka/Browning Pass and, in about 1700, descended the Rakaia Valley. Further south, she ran into a Ngāi Tahu party who wanted to know where her pounamu came from. She showed them the route, with lamentable consequences for her tribe.

Gold prospectors, shepherds, surveyors and road-builders all lived and worked here from the 1860s. Parts of their benched pack tracks in the Wilberforce, Styx and Arahura remain. For a century, trampers and climbers have travelled here, too, with the (usually) three-to-four-day Three Pass Trip, from the Waimakariri River over Harman, Whitehorn and Browning passes to the Styx becoming a classic.

And of course some speed-tramped, with a 1947 Canterbury party undertaking it as an 18-hour day trip. Not to be outdone, Geoff Harrow, in a solo effort, cut two hours off that time, in 1948. Then in 1974, most of them wearing heavy leather Anson boots, John Visser, Les Jones, Chris Cox and Mike Spink completed the Three Passes, roadend to roadend, the fastest completing it in 9 hours 55 minutes. Speed-tramping is a whole genre in itself, and has synergy with today's mountain marathon/multisport industry.

For us, however, as we reached Browning Pass next morning, we ran into a cold easterly mist. It dissipated as we headed up through alpine herb fields to what's left of the Hall Glacier to Hall Col. Beyond, on the aptly named Retreat Snowfield, we dropped packs to head up scalloped summer snow to the top of Mt Learmont. When the Retreat was named by a CMC party in 1935, it flowed into streams on both sides of the Main Divide at Farquharson Saddle. Recession now means the remnant ice only flows to the west.

Farquharson Saddle was a spacious place with a wonderful ambience, despite all the gravel. We followed the Main Divide past a great campsite and tarn at 1800 metres on the way to Mt Keddell and Griffiths Saddle. A rock wren popped out of the rocks, squeaking hello.

We had a fantastic afternoon, as you can in such high places on a fine calm day. A gentle walk took us to the top of Mt Griffiths, before we dropped down the Griffiths Glacier, jumping slots and watching for bare ice patches. Then it was Clarkes Pass, Commodore Peak and Mt Ambrose's turn, just above Hokitika Saddle. To top the day off we slept among rock outcrops, tucked in our sleeping bags under a velvet black sky.

In the morning, an alert and excited herd of chamois pranced around in bright sunlight, kicking up snow. We continued past them over The Rampart towards the relatively steep and gnarly Commodore and Bastion ridges, where more rock wren were about. I'd been along those ridges before, but today we headed for Park Stream, the Mungo, and hot pools instead.

Sometimes certainties aren't. This time the pools just above Brunswick Creek were poor, and we chased hot-water seeps below Brunswick instead. Physics beat us. The water was hot – too hot – and we didn't have a cold source to get it right. As well, too much hot water was seeping away into the gravel.

However, there is more than one way to soak in the hills. We headed over Toaroha Saddle and down to the hot pool at Cedar Flat, on the bank of Wren Creek. This time we hit the jackpot with the added bonus of no sandflies or mossies. Very, very nice.

OPPOSITE Bryan and Linda in the head of Park Stream, looking across the Mungo Valley to the Main Divide and Brunswick Creek.

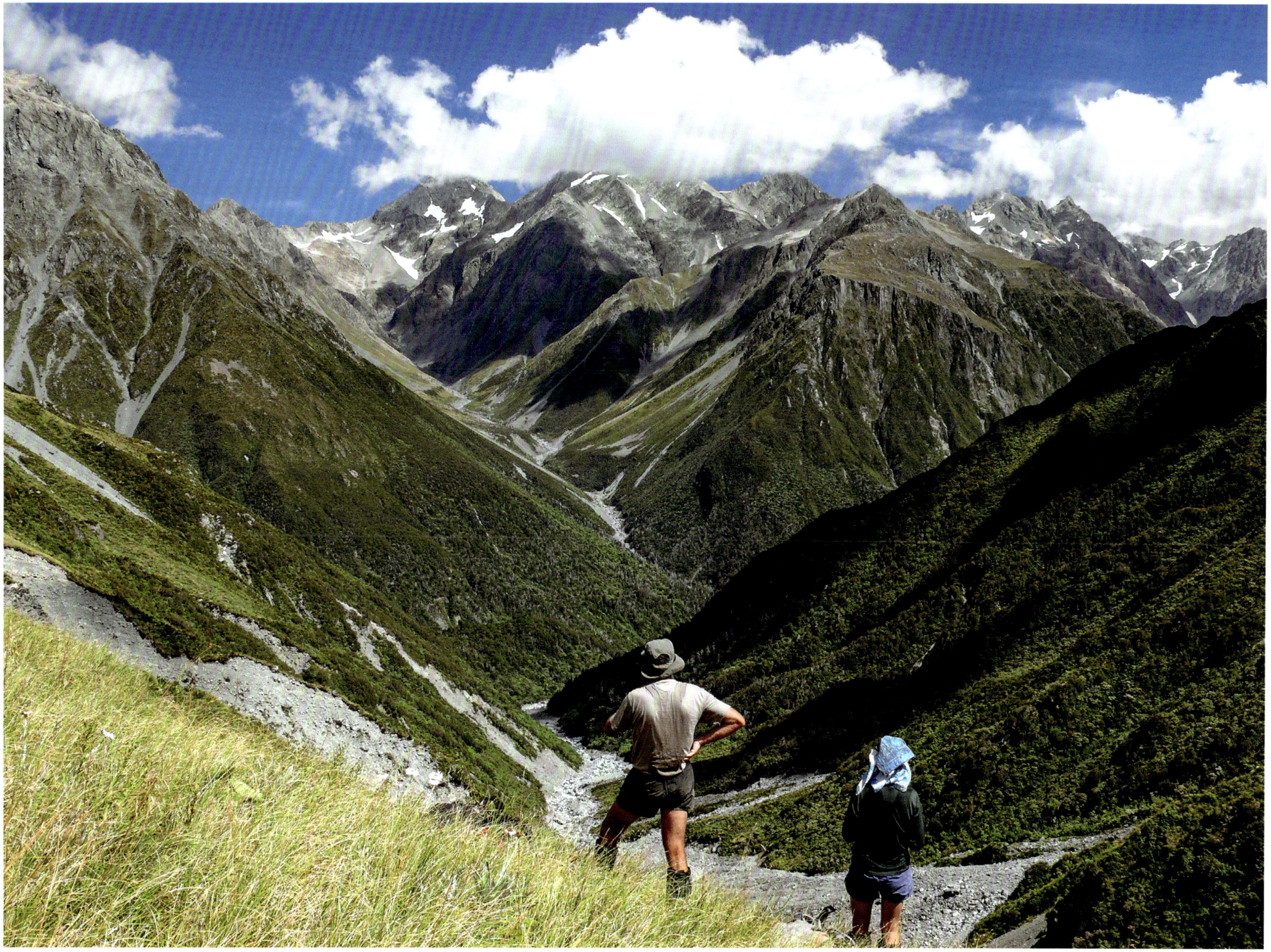

MATHIAS TO THE WAIMAKARIRI

MATHIAS RIVER–MATHIAS PASS–BLUFF HUT–MUNGO RIVER–
HOKITIKA SADDLE–GRIFFITHS STREAM–BURNETT STREAM–
WHITE COL–BARKER HUT–WAIMAKARIRI RIVER

8 DAYS: 18 NOVEMBER–25 NOVEMBER 2009
GS WITH ANDY DENNIS, ROB BROWN, COLIN MONTEATH AND ANDREW BUDD

This classic pass-hopping tramping trip began with a crossing of the Rakaia. Big river crossings can have a chilling effect and when planning trips, I try to get them over with at the beginning if possible, eliminating end-of-trip complications.

The Mathias gets little attention from trampers or climbers, and it has a remote feel about it. It doesn't have the scale of the upper Rakaia, but drains almost the same distance of Main Divide and has more scrubby forest in it.

After a look up-valley at Centennial Cabin, a cute, older three-bunk hut full of odds and ends, we returned to Mathias Hut for the night. Originally built in 1961 by the Rakaia branch of the New Zealand Deerstalkers' Association, Mathias Hut was rebuilt in 2007, with double glazing and wood burner.

Canyon Creek pours into the Mathias through a defile, where greywacke rockwalls rise for hundreds of metres. Deep in the canyon, some stream crossings among the boulders needed mutual support, then further up we climbed tussock slopes towards Mathias Pass.

There were government plans for a stock track over the Main Divide here in the early 1880s. Parts of it were benched, and some of the old track line high up on the true right of Canyon Creek still exists. But in one or two crucial corners on some bluffs, the formation has been eroded, currently making it impractical to use.

We camped just over the pass in fine drizzle. Morning brought more rain. We were, after all, in the Hokitika Catchment, which holds most of the New Zealand rainfall records. Almost 500 millimetres fell in one 12-hour period in 1994, and in the Cropp tributary of the Whitcombe River, in one consecutive 365-day period in 1997/8, over 18 metres fell, which is roughly the height of a six-storey building. This equates to another storey every eight weeks, all year. Eat your heart out, Fiordland: Hokitika is the rain capital of New Zealand.

We scurried down-valley through wet tussock clumps then low leatherwood, egged on by dripping grey shrouds, to arrive looking like drowned rats at the wonderfully rebuilt DOC Bluff Hut. With a fire going and lunch inside us, we began fluffing up warm dry nests, our enthusiasm to continue falling with the rain.

Some of us did go back to explore the tight little canyons we had passed, though. Where the river squeezes its way through sculpted bedrock I watched whio swimming on pools, shortly before the river cascades almost 500 metres down through bedrock and boulders to the Mungo.

I love the way colours in vegetation brighten in the rain. Leaves of leatherwood shine, bringing vibrancy, and the wet brings out the patterns and grain of rock like waves do to wet stones on a beach. As well, the water glows with the intensity of clear ice, blue like sapphire, full of subtlety.

The end of Conway Ridge below the hut opens in rock crevasses among the scrub and trees, and the track down weaves through bluffs in places. I remembered seeing goats down here on an earlier trip, but this day all we saw was rain.

The bridge was very welcome as the Mungo River was up, and so was Poet Hut welcome for lunch. Later, we sunk into the hot pools in the rain, still wearing our parkas. No point in getting wetter. Up at Mungo Hut we kicked the resident starling out, and over the evening were visited by kea, weka and tomtits. In 2015 Rob would lead a work party to restore and paint this four-bunk, ex-NZFS hut.

Hokitika Saddle was a very different place to the barren over-steep gravels of my last trip here. Now, copious snow from winter lay everywhere. Down in Griffiths Stream we camped in fields of flowering Mt Cook lilies.

The Wilberforce was fresh, and up a little with snow melt, so we reduced our crossings to a minimum in the morning. Another high crossing near White Col took us on to snowfields under Mt Murchison. We skiffed our way down through this alpine landscape to Barker Hut. The original hut was built in 1945 by CMC in memory of Neville Barker, a club member who died in the Italian Campaign during WWII. The club built this current hut in 1980.

Barker is one of those places where you're lifted out of the tussock to find a home in an alpine world. Striations in rock, ground by ice and gravel full of rounded, iron-stained pebbles, surround this hut perched on its knoll high above the valley.

Squeaking our way down into the White River branch of the Waimakariri River we chattered back to a pair of rock wren. A journey down this riverbed is always memorable for the mind-numbing gravel, but Andy kept me entertained most of the way to the road, enthusiastically recounting Icelandic sagas. It is always fascinating the range of talents and interests that trip-mates have.

LEFT Descending from Hokitika Saddle into the Griffiths branch of the Wilberforce Valley. Griffiths Saddle is to the left.

OVERLEAF (LEFT) The Hokitika River above Bluff Hut. The shaped bedrock, water and wet vegetation make the scene exquisite.

OVERLEAF (RIGHT) Colin, Rob and Andy crossing Canyon Creek on the way to Mathias Pass.

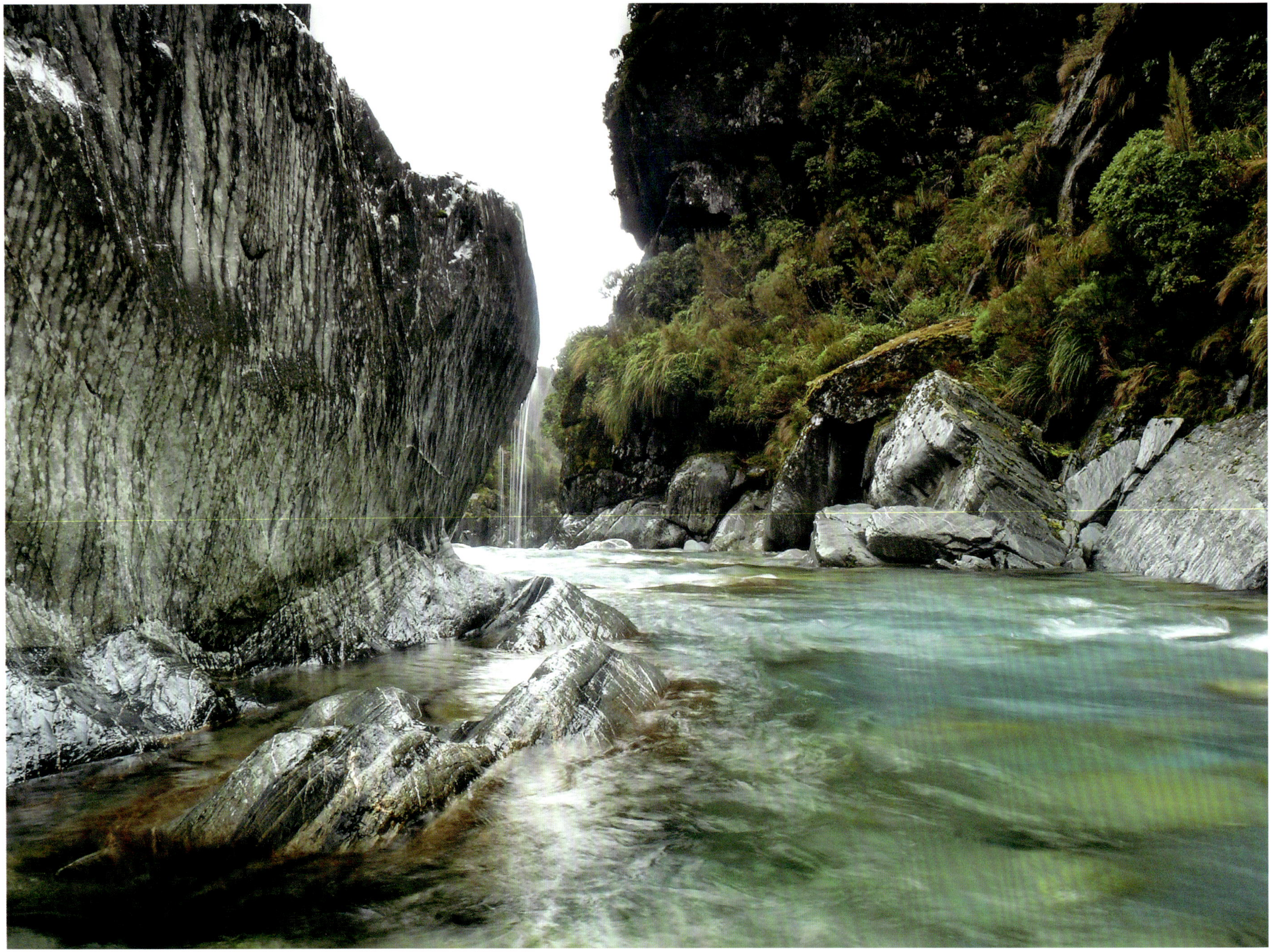

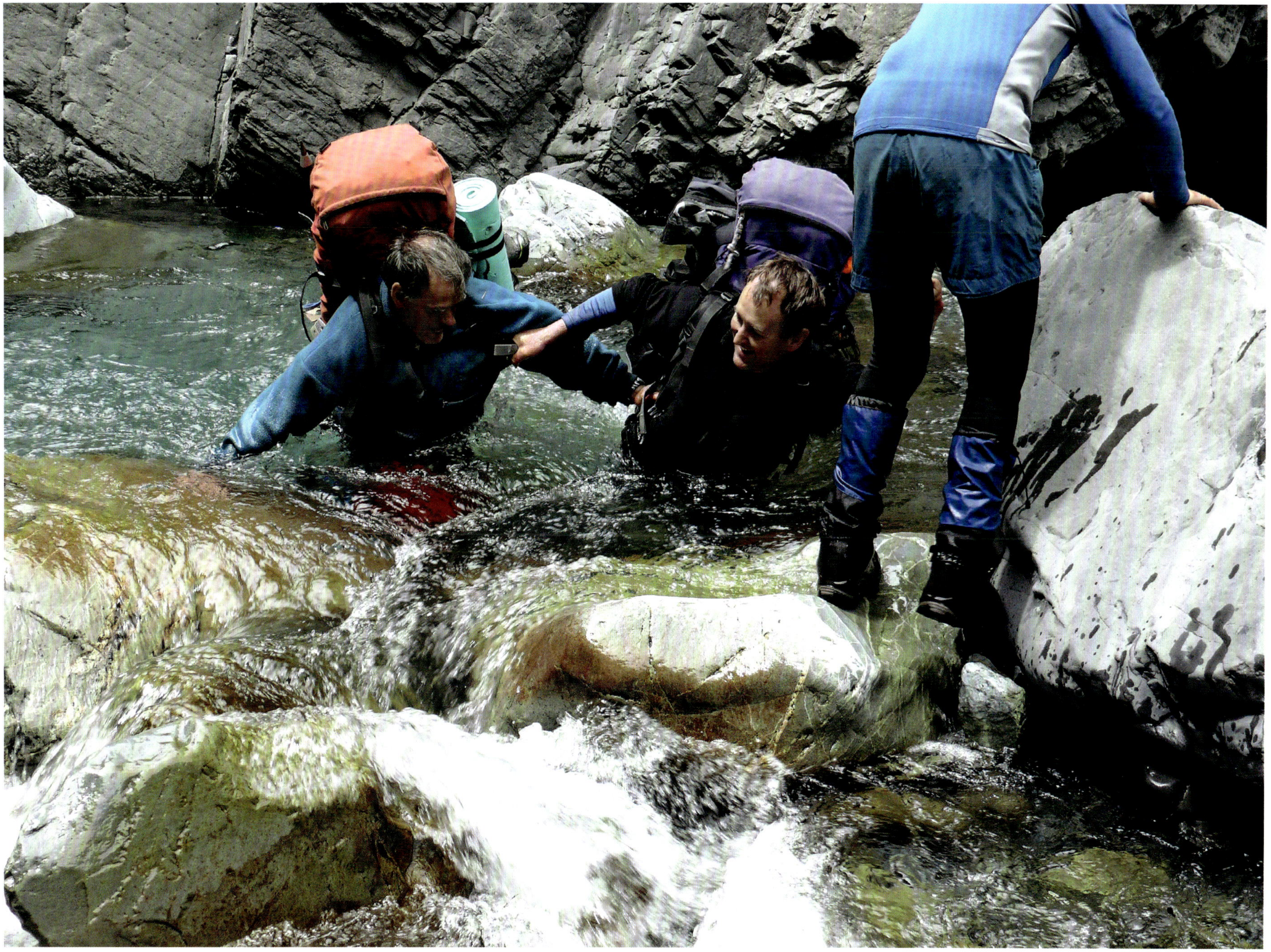

CLARKES PASS: WHAT COULD POSSIBLY GO WRONG?

MARCH 1974, GS WITH GRAEME LYTHGOE
SEPTEMBER 1987, GS WITH GAYLENE WILKINSON
APRIL 1990, GS WITH BARBARA BROWN

Sometimes a personal trauma develops around a peak or a pass or a river. There is often nothing particularly special about it in the bigger scheme of things, but one repulse turns into a failure, and then each time you return, for some reason or another, there's circumstances which conspire to create more difficulty than need be. Clarkes Pass has been like that for me.

The first recorded crossing of Clarkes Pass was by a Canterbury Mountaineering Club party of Ivan Tucker, Len Boot, Harry Andrews and Tom Beckett in March 1932. A couple of years later, Bert Cropp and Peter Phipps, with their two dogs, crossed the pass west to east. 'The Westland bush gave considerable trouble and the worst route was consistently chosen.' I can relate to that.

In 1974 Graeme and I had an enjoyable trip into the Kokatahi, although hookgrass featured to the extreme. It filled my hair and covered my legs and beard. Everything was smothered with the stuff. It was autumn, so other things compensated, such as the unexpected hot pool in the Mungo river-bed, full of clean water that was a perfect bathing temperature. Of course we stopped and made time to respect it. Then came Clarkes Pass. We slogged up through the scrub, with a cold easterly forcing itself over the Main Divide. It wasn't till we were up in the tussock that the venom of the graupel snow and wind, with the pass completely misted out, made us flag it away and return to the salubrious Kokatahi. It was bitter up there. Clarkes Pass remained a mission unfulfilled.

In 1987 I planned a trip to cross it, with Gaylene. The trip had been good till we reached Clarkes Pass. We had crossed Browning Pass in deep September snow, then had a rest day and fire at Urquharts Hut while it rained and snowed. To get back to the car we needed to cross the Main Divide again. We could've gone out down the Wilberforce, but then we'd have no transport as well as the hassle of getting the car back from the West Coast. Anyway, we were up for an adventure.

With a small improvement in the weather we headed up Griffiths Stream. Snow was deep and conditions were a bit dodgy getting to the pass, but we made it without incident. 3.30 p.m. Winter. But now it was snowing and a whiteout. We fumbled down into the basin, thrashed through leatherwood and sidled out onto a spur, because the creek turns into waterfalls. We already had enough challenges without waterfalls. Of course it was snowing down in the scrub too, and snow and leatherwood is a potent combination on slopes. But we got to the ridge. It just took time, and energy. And daylight. Being winter we were running out of that.

We pushed on, keen to cross the Kokatahi before we camped in case the river came up. Well, we didn't make it. But we tried. With torches out we bashed our way down, long after we should've stopped. In the end there were tears and then complete mutiny. By now we were both traumatised. It didn't rain much, the river never really rose, and we crossed the Kokatahi easily in the morning on our way out.

I hadn't learned my lesson. Barb and I had come up to Pinnacle Bivvy on the Toaroha Range in April 1990, then traversed wonderful tops to Zit Saddle. On our second day we dropped into Park Stream from near Mt Chamberlin, camping in the upper Mungo before crossing Hokitika Saddle the following morning. This time it was late summer, and the day had been good, but we had lost a bit of time sidling in and out of washout runnels getting into Griffiths Stream. So it was getting on when we reached Clarkes Pass and there was a warm overcast sky moving in. A nor-wester, and imminent rain.

Another race to the bottom. I'll spare the gory details a third time. Suffice to say, it was clear we needed to cross the Kokatahi to the track that night if we could. It began raining on the way down, and as the rain increased the light decreased . . . in the half-dark we crossed a rising river, and the only place in the wet we could find to camp was on the track. By morning the rain was torrential, the river in high flood, and we had a battle to get down-valley. We were only able to cross Meharry, Alice and Pinnacle creeks by clambering over collapsed trees with the water foaming like wild dogs under us. Boo Boo Hut further down the Kokatahi Valley never looked so good.

OPPOSITE Clarkes Pass on the Main Divide (left), from Whitehorn Spur.

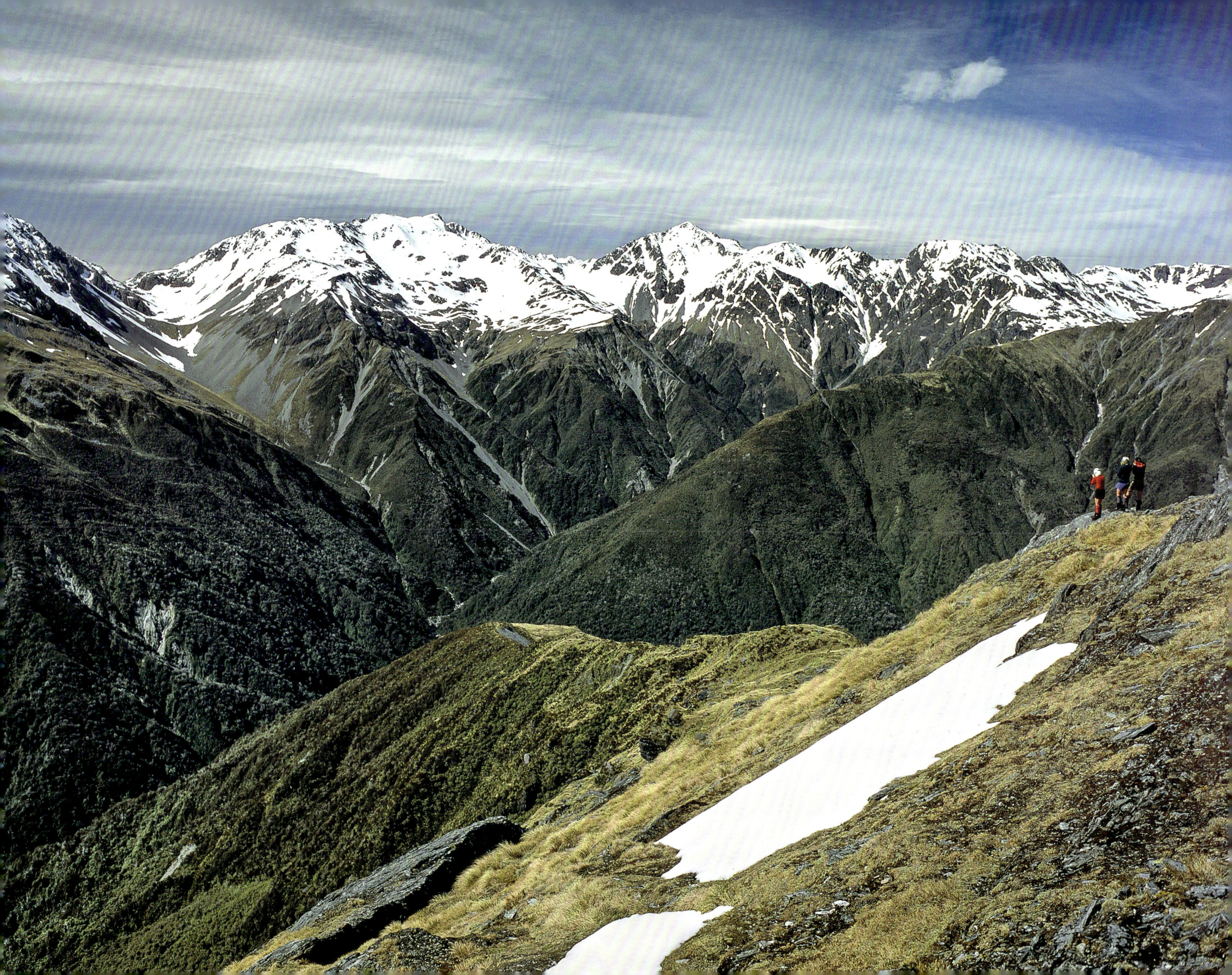

MAIN DIVIDE TRAVERSE ABOVE THE WHITCOMBE VALLEY

HOKITIKA VALLEY–FREW BIV–MAIN DIVIDE–WHITCOMBE PASS–WHITCOMBE RIVER

6 DAYS: 6–11 APRIL 2008
GS WITH FRASER MADIGAN

From some viewpoints, the slopes reaching back to the Main Divide above the Whitcombe River look like a tilted table top. It is a distinctive landform where, up close, many streams carve through that bedrock leaving incised canyons. Those Main Divide tops from Frew Saddle to Whitcombe Pass first caught my interest in 1970, but it wasn't until 2008 that Fraser and I headed up the Whitcombe Valley to Frew Hut to traverse them.

A hut of some sort existed near the Frew/Whitcombe junction as far back as 1907. In 1947 a replacement hut was built nearby at Tom Creek, and when that was on its last legs, DOC built the current 10-bunk Frew Hut closer to the original site in 2003.

I love idling through hut logbooks, reading about the wider whānau visiting the hills, and was fascinated to read an entry from 'Godfrey and Hamilton from the West Coast' who, on 31/1/89, had left Glenfalloch in the Rakaia at 6.40 a.m. and arrived at Frew at 5.15 p.m. the same day and were walking out. We sure wouldn't be travelling that fast.

Fraser and I continued to Frew Saddle Biv, then on across the headwaters of Harcourt Creek to camp just east of Kea Pass. Some of the rock wasn't very good. Button Peak nearby was described in 1950 by a CMC party as: 'A large heap of stones held together by fate and mutual goodwill, and giving the impression of imminent collapse.'

I'd also been here in 1982 on a trip with Mike Roberts. Part of that trip involved crossing Kea Pass from the Mathias to get back to the Whitcombe. The pass was steep and the September snow soft and deep.

Mike and I wallowed up in deteriorating weather and then a snowstorm, and were very pleased to reach Harcourt Creek and pitch our A-frame tent. We dropped to the valley next day via Lake Lyes, named after Percy Lyes who hunted this country in the 1940s.

Fraser and I traversed over Mount Young then descended south along the Main Divide. Under Mt McWhirter a line of bluffs created a small scrambling challenge, but we were soon on the summit and nearing the higher peaks. Fraser was good company and had a knack of interpreting the simplest things in the most outrageous ways. I spent half the trip laughing.

In a few places in the Southern Alps the bedrock has fractured into widening rock crevasses that lead to collapsing bluffs, giving a superficial impression of a rock icefall. It can end with rock crevasses that are metres wide and more than a dozen metres deep, sometimes over an extensive, confusing area. In some places, such as on an area of Destiny Ridge in the Olivines, eventually the bedrock bluffs out, and below, a jumble of massive blocks have collapsed on each other. Intriguing places. A smaller one of these areas exists just south of Chairmans Creek around the 1800-metre contour, and we examined it for a while, investigating deep breaks cutting through the rock. Some surface slabs had slid across the fissures, creating rock bridges.

That night we slept out just below the permanent ice on Mt Warner, watching the sun go down near Mt Evans. Later, the stars burned millions of holes into the black night sky with the cold, austere clarity which mountains invoke. At dawn, and still in the shade, we watched the bright sun turn Evans into a red and gold chameleon, feeling blessed just to witness it. Who could deny a spiritual connection to the mountains on a day like this?

The snow was frozen and we needed crampons on the old glacier ice as we wandered up Mt Warner and Bonds Peak. Nothing difficult, but it felt like the top of the world, surrounded in a sea of peaks with braided rivers snaking off into the Mathias, and green gutters cutting out to the west. Mt Warner has a couple of rock platforms on top, one of which had an old survey tripod, while Bonds Peak gave great views south along the Divide to Mt Neave, Lauper Peak and Mt Evans.

OPPOSITE Fraser on the Martius Glacier. The upper Rakaia and Arrowsmith Range peaks beyond. Mt Whitcombe (extreme right).

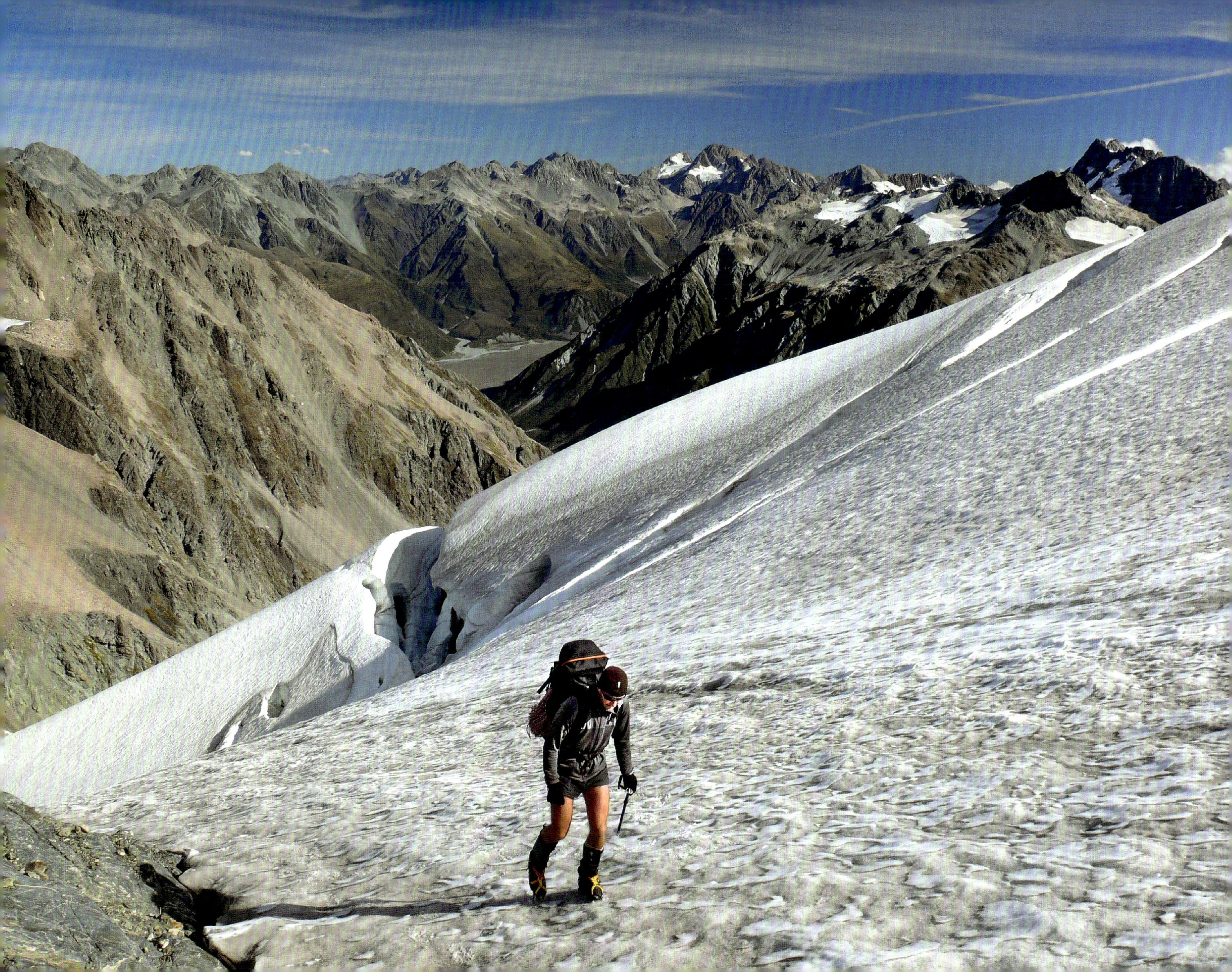

LEFT Frew Biv, built in 1957, above the Whitcombe Valley.

OPPOSITE Mt Neave on the Main Divide above the South Mathias River from near Mt Martius.

From here on water was a problem, being this late in the season, and travel was now mostly on boulders, wearing and slow. On our last night on the tops we slept out about 400 metres directly above Whitcombe Pass in the tussock by a little tarn.

Below us, at dawn, cloud poured over Whitcombe Pass into Canterbury.

As we had breakfast the cloud reversed, banking up in Canterbury but dissipating in Westland. We dropped to the pass and headed down the fine and sunny Whitcombe back towards the car.

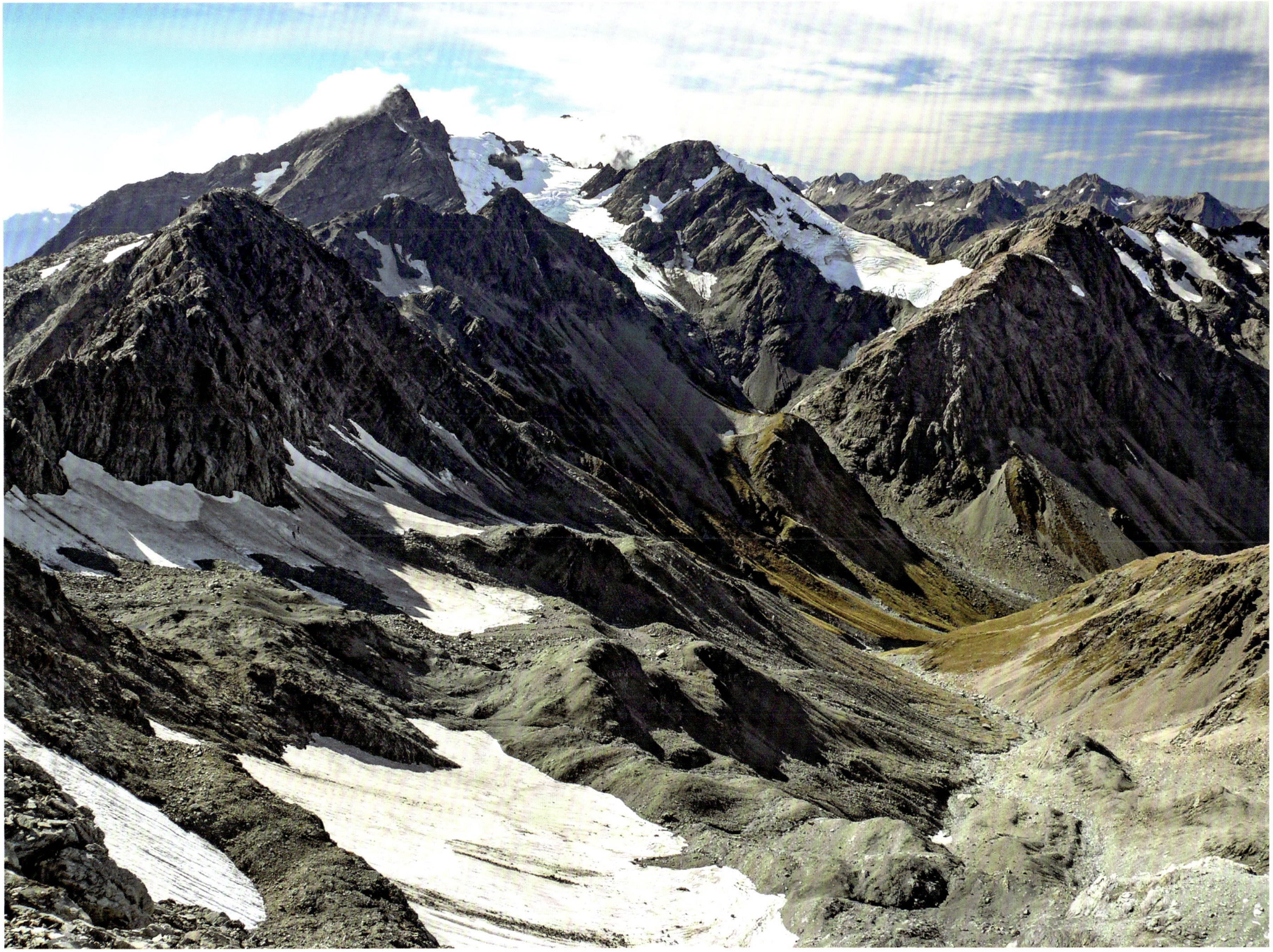

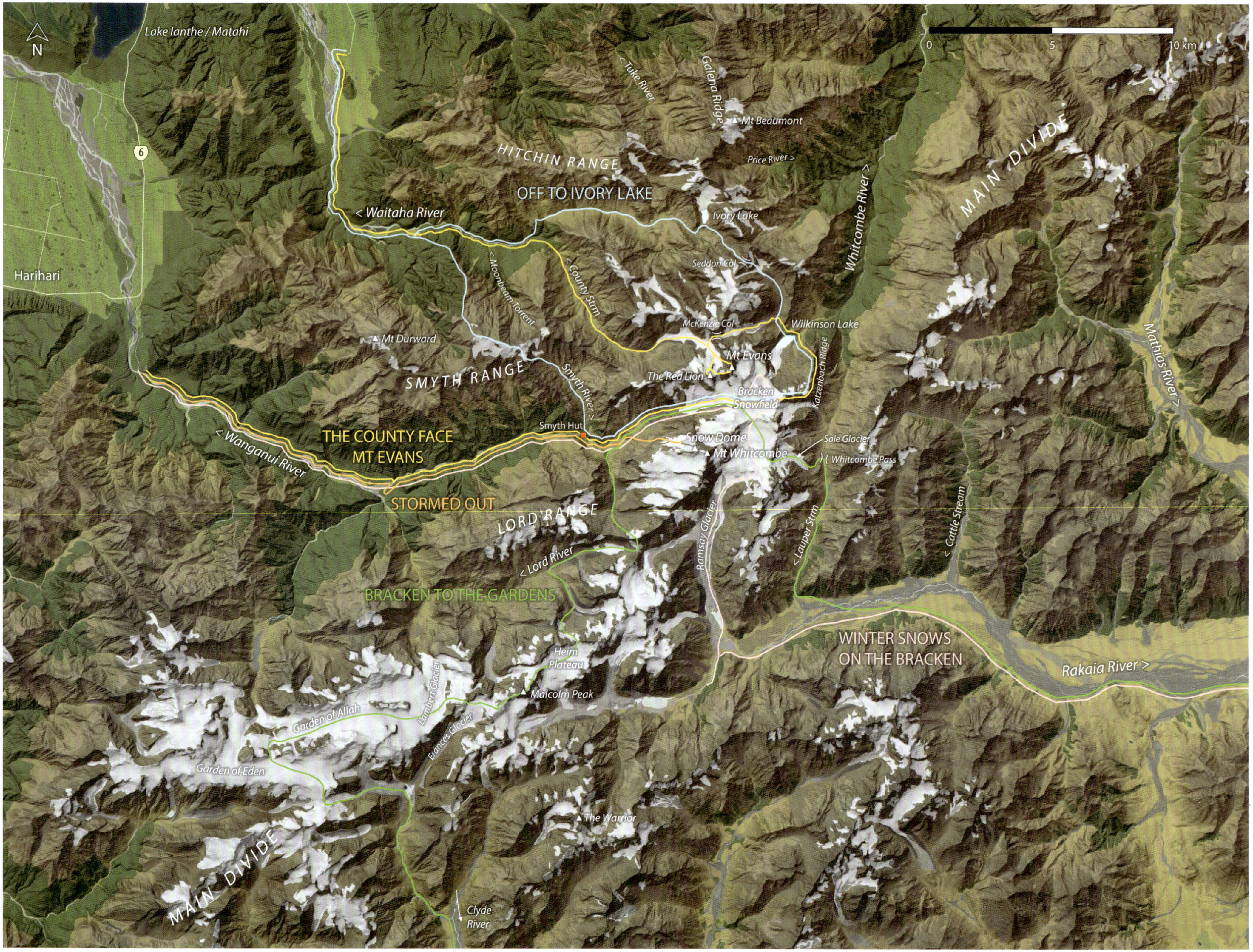

N
Lake Ianthe / Matahi
0
5
10 km
6
Harihari
< Tuke River
Galena Ridge
Mt Beaumont
Price River >
HITCHIN RANGE
OFF TO IVORY LAKE
< Waitaha River
Ivory Lake
Whitcombe River >
MAIN DIVIDE
Seddon Col
< Moonbeam Torrent
< County Strm
McKenzie Col
Wilkinson Lake
Mt Durward
Mt Evans
Katzenbach Ridge
Mathias River >
SMYTH RANGE
Smyth River >
The Red Lion
Bracken Snowfield
Smyth Hut
THE COUNTY FACE MT EVANS
Snow Dome
Mt Whitcombe
Sale Glacier
Whitcombe Pass
< Wanganui River
STORMED OUT
LORD RANGE
Ramsay Glacier
< Lauper Strm
< Cattle Stream
< Lord River
BRACKEN TO THE GARDENS
WINTER SNOWS ON THE BRACKEN
Heim Plateau
Rakaia River >
Malcolm Peak
Lambert Glacier
Garden of Allah
Frances Glacier
Garden of Eden
The Warrior
MAIN DIVIDE
Clyde River

CHAPTER 5
THE BRACKEN SNOWFIELD

The Whitcombe, Wanganui and Rakaia valleys all drain from a knot of country centred on the Bracken Snowfield and Ramsay Glacier, where the first major ice in the Southern Alps rises head and shoulders above lower peaks to the north. Here, peaks like Mt Evans and Mt Whitcombe throw out their challenges. In 1908 the Geological Survey published *The Mikonui Subdivision Bulletin*, with maps surrounding the Bracken that are especially detailed and accurate. This doesn't lessen the difficulties when travelling through this region, though, and its isolation remains one of its attractions. Iconic places like remote Ivory Lake remain intensely cherished personal journeys for many trampers and climbers.

From the 1930s, transalpine climbers, West Coast hunters, Canterbury mountaineers, the Alpine Club and various tramping parties headed into the Bracken Snowfield, Waitaha headwaters and surrounding wild ranges, exploring new routes and climbing peaks. Mt Evans was one of the objectives, but innovative parties went to all sorts of places, such as the 1938 crossing of Seddon Col to the Waitaha by Brian Mason, Austen Deans and Philip Willis. A year earlier, others had climbed Park Dome from the Wilkinson. But there were tragedies too, such as Norman Dowling's death while returning from the second ascent of Mt Evans in 1937.

The classic trip here involves a crossing of the Main Divide over the Bracken Snowfield. Probably the best approach is up the Rakaia then Sale Glacier to the Ramsay Neve, over Full Moon Saddle from the Bracken, then down the Evans Glacier and Wanganui Valley.

Plenty of people seek out challenges on these mountains, but the weather often interferes in difficult country like this. In January 2013, one party was four days late getting out due to a flooded Moonbeam Torrent. About the same time a major rockfall off Mt Evans travelled 5 kilometres down the upper Wanganui (and also 3 kilometres down County Stream) to form a dam and lake. This later breached during an extreme rainstorm, further scouring the Wanganui Valley. The mess has left travel far more challenging on boulders than it was. Debris swept both sides of Smyth Hut but the hut remains in good condition, as is the hot pool. You may need them. The Wanganui down to Hunters Hut can be a slog.

THE COUNTY FACE OF MT EVANS

WANGANUI–BRACKEN–KATZENBACH–MCKENZIE COL– MT EVANS–WAITAHA

7 DAYS: 5–11 FEBRUARY 1975
GS WITH IAN WILKINS

At 2620 metres, Mt Evans rises big and bold, looming over the Bracken Snowfield, and towering 2000 metres above Cave Camp in the Whitcombe Valley. It is a storm gatherer, and its wild buttresses have inspired transalpinists for decades.

On 1 Jan 1934, John Pascoe, Gavin Malcolmson and Priestley Thomson made the first ascent. Their climb, which began from near a rock bivvy at a height of 1000 metres beside Seddon Creek, was a 30-hour epic up steep slopes from the McKenzie Glacier and along the upper North Ridge. They traversed over to Red Lion Col, where they spent a shivery night. With the dawn they returned to camp via the County Glacier.

But like many transalpine climbs, that is only half the story. They had already tramped and climbed 40 kilometres from the Rakaia roadend, crossed the Main Divide and Bracken Snowfield, and been battered by bad weather. A snowstorm buried their tent and gear, forcing them to retreat, before they were finally able to reach the Seddon Creek bivvy eight days after leaving the road.

After the climb they returned by the same route. The whole trip took two weeks. Pascoe noted: 'Snowstorm on Katzenbach Ridge. Blizzard on Bracken Snowfield. Wind to gale force; no visibility; could not locate Full Moon Saddle; another forced camp pitched; miserable night . . . Tent badly torn; left it near Erewhon Col.'

I grew up reading accounts of epic adventures like this in club journals and was inspired to create my own. Ours was to be a lightweight, six-day transalpine trip up one West Coast valley, the Wanganui, crossing the Bracken Snowfield, circling and hopefully climbing Mt Evans, then coming out down the Waitaha Valley.

It was after six o'clock when we left the main West Coast road. With no torches (to save weight) we had to race to make it to Hunters Hut in the Wanganui Valley before dark. A couple of days later we ascended the Evans Glacier at the head of the valley onto the Bracken in a whiteout. Mist continued across the snowfield, and we felt our way down the Katzenbach Ridge on the other side. Loose, eroding moraine walls of gravel and boulders kept us looking over our shoulders as we descended to the Wilkinson lake shore. Ice still filled much of Wilkinson Lake then.

Across in scrubby Seddon Creek we poked around searching for Pascoe's bivvy rock (Bevernage Biv), found it, and lit a little fire. It was from near this bivvy rock that the first and second ascents had been made. We settled in for the night. I feel a deep satisfaction in doing things like this, such as finding places read about in earlier trip accounts. They're connection points in a wider transalpine community.

During lunch on McKenzie Col next day we watched rocks avalanche into the gully where we were to descend to the County Glacier. They were frequent and we didn't like it. Sometimes there is such an element of roulette in the mountains. Waiting for a lull, we went for it, and were down quickly, luck on our side.

Heading up the glacier, we found a campsite beside a boulder with veins of quartz crystals. We had left the primus behind to save weight, so with no vegetation nearby we cooked our dinner by burning our rubbish. That was a bit desperate. We'd also left the tent poles behind. With no floor, our single skin, A-frame tent was held up by a boulder at one end and an iceaxe at the other.

Morning saw us in crampons heading for the unclimbed County Face. Threading between large crevasses we then accessed the rock, which we climbed for much of the lower half of the face. Some of it was loose, but my diary noted some short walls of better rock too.

For much of the climb we left the rope on, climbing together, but belaying close under more difficult moves. Somewhere about half way, I put in a belay anchor, then backed it up with a jam nut. I yanked to test the nut. It failed, and hit me in the mouth, snapping half of a front tooth off. I could

OPPOSITE Sunrise lights up the bluffs on Mt Evans above the Bracken Snowfield. Full Moon Saddle is to the left.

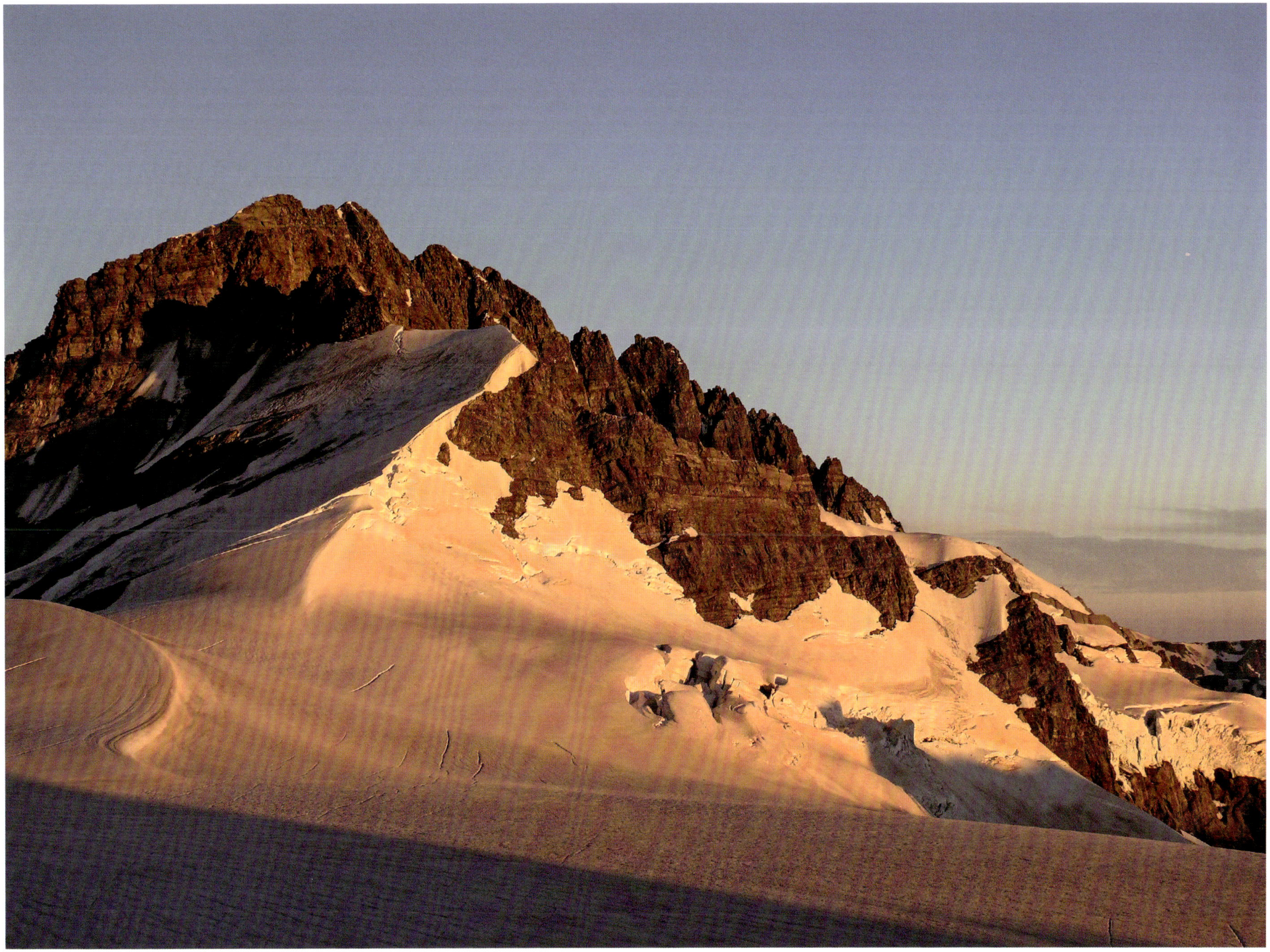

feel cold air through it, but fortunately it hadn't quite broken right through to the nerve – although it made eating and drinking from our one plastic teaspoon a bit tricky.

On the upper part of the face we front-pointed up a gully of hard snow before more rock led directly to the summit ridge between the high and low peaks of Mt Evans. Lunchtime. After checking out the summit cairn, we descended the ridge to Red Lion Col, then as an extra, climbed The Red Lion peak. With the sun getting low it was a glorious way to finish the day.

It was drizzling in the morning, but that didn't matter. We were headed down-valley, picking up tenuous Forest Service tracks in the Waitaha on our journey back out of the hills. However, mosquitoes had the last say. Leaving the Waitaha Pub in drizzle after dark, we settled into an old roadside milk-stand/shed to sleep. It didn't take long for the mossies to arrive. They whined all night and gorged themselves to bursting. I think a mossie App would make the best alarm clock ever. They certainly kept us awake.

LEFT Malcolm and Barb looking across to bluffs on Mt Evans from the Katzenbach Ridge. The Katzenbach provides a challenging route from the Bracken Snowfield to the Whitcombe Valley, or McKenzie Col and Seddon Col in the Waitaha.
OPPOSITE Mt Whitcombe and the Ramsay Glacier. Snow Dome rises to the right, behind. The upper Ramsay Glacier provides access to the Bracken Snowfield at Erewhon Col.

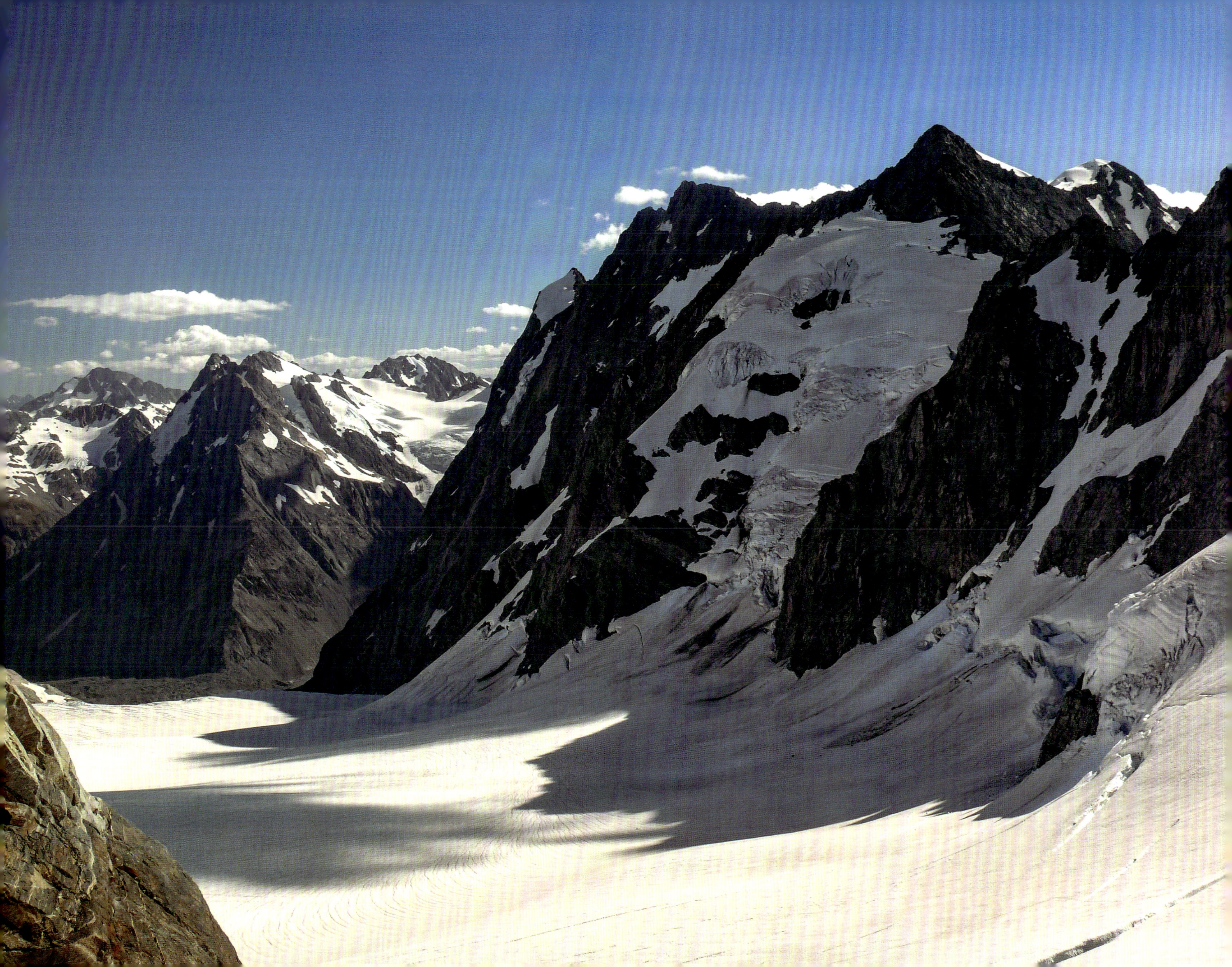

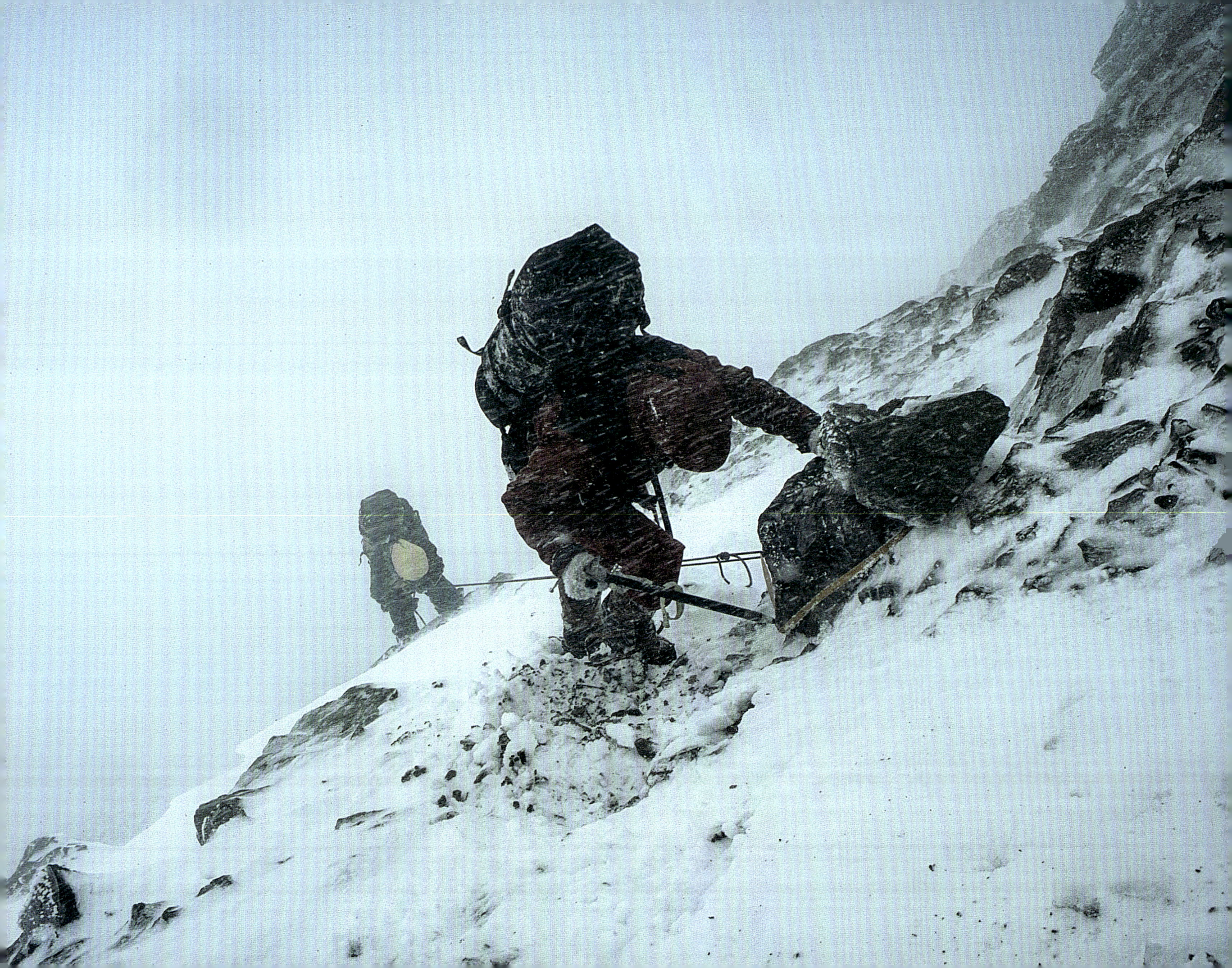

STORMED OUT

WANGANUI VALLEY–SNOW DOME–WANGANUI VALLEY

8 DAYS: 15–22 FEBRUARY 2003
GS WITH ERIC DUGGAN, JOHNNY MULHERON AND JONATHAN KENNETT

This was not what we had intended, and it was getting worse. All night the wind battered the bluffs, winding itself up into knots of brutal force that savaged the mountain like some out-of-control Leviathan. Rain hammered at every chance and we cringed into our sleeping bags, only too aware how fragile the tent was to this sort of violence. I've had several tents destroyed around me by storms – a new tunnel tent, a dome tent, several A-frame tents, and this was looking dangerously like being the next.

Four of us had come up the Wanganui River set on a transalpine trip that included Mt Whitcombe on the Main Divide and Dan Peak on the Lord Range. We were a strong crew with a week to spare, and it was summer. After two good days' travel, we had set up at 2200 metres on the north-west slopes of Snow Dome, next to Mt Whitcombe.

It had all been so promising.

As dawn approached, the intensity increased. Guy ropes wore out and fabric broke free. You have to attend to details like that or lose the tent. Outside, I grappled with a broken pole. Eric put more stones around the tent and Jonathan came out with pliers to tidy a splayed, broken pole end, so we could slip an emergency sleeve in place. We weren't dressed for it, and later I shivered back into the tent.

The wind continued to rage in the bluffs, becoming monstrous, becoming all-consuming, becoming ugly as it fought to destroy our shelter. We held our breath each time. Later in the morning it eased, and then began to snow. We thought it might clear now. Instead, the snow piled up, and on the second night at this spot the wind brought its violence back.

Darkness fell as the wind howled like a predator, the snow building up steadily. Morning brought another day of snowfall, but a few lulls, too. Far below we could hear the river, and even saw white-ribbon falls across the valley. Then it closed in again, and by our third night the tents were getting buried. This had the advantage of protecting them from the wind, but fresh snow was also loading avalanche slopes. Dawn was stormy again, but enough was enough, and discussion revolved around a plan to descend. Snow had reached the top of the tents.

Waiting till 11 o'clock in the hope it might clear a little, we began chopping the tents out of the snow and ice, and clearing frozen boulders from guys – a challenge in itself. Visibility was less than 10 metres, and the wind still roared. There isn't much leeway in situations like this. Hail drove at us out of the depths of storm cloud and wind below us as we stuffed gear into our packs and began our way down.

We called on everything we could, including Johnny's GPS. Wading in snow, we found the top of some slabs, our first reference point, and put in an anchor to abseil off. I went down, and while the others followed I went to investigate the next section. Total whiteout. A couple of steps, then a large area of cornice and the slope below avalanched under my feet. Oops. Be more careful.

Ice under the snow on a ledge between small bluffs made us belay the next piece. My diary says: 'Down, across, up and around and down to Jonathan's big cairn at the top of some bluffs.' Who knows where we went, but we were on track at that point. Now it was Jonathan's turn to set off a small, soft-slab avalanche, leaving a crown wall of about half a metre below him.

We took a different route. Another bluff. Not recognising where we had scrambled up, we tied two ropes together and abseiled down iced rocks into shrieking winds full of graupel. It wasn't very pleasant. We had been on the go for several hours and couldn't stop, but we knew we were winning and that is all that mattered.

As we got lower, under the clouds and down in wet vegetation, we started to laugh. Release. We all knew we'd gotten out of it by the skin of our teeth.

Lower down the Wanganui next day, more random outbursts of collective laughter pealed off the valley walls. So much for our confident plans.

OPPOSITE Descending from Snow Dome near Mt Whitcombe in a storm.

BRACKEN TO THE GARDENS

RAKAIA VALLEY–BRACKEN SNOWFIELD–LORD VALLEY–
HEIM PLATEAU–MALCOLM PEAK–FRANCES GLACIER–
LAMBERT GLACIER–GARDEN OF ALLAH–GARDEN OF
EDEN–CLYDE RIVER

8 DAYS: 21–28 FEBRUARY 1996
GS WITH BRYAN TUFFNELL AND DOUG LOWES

The Bracken Snowfield and the Garden of Eden are two snow plateaus separated by about 15 kilometres of wild mountains. Any transalpine trip that connects two big snow plateaus and traverses a significant peak on the Main Divide along the way is my cup of coffee.

A big fat anticyclone was coming onto the country when we headed up the Rakaia, crossing the river in two branches, and settling in for the first night at Lauper Biv. With bare feet on the moss, parakeets calling in the scrub, the subtle aroma of celery pine glades, a fire and the prospect of a great trip, I slept well.

In the morning we crossed Whitcombe Pass on the Main Divide and ascended moraine and ice up the Sale Glacier between cathedrals of rock standing silent and stark in the sun. Higher up at Erewhon Col we pitched the tent on a clear evening, expecting a sunny morning to follow. Instead, it was misty and snowing, forcing an initial detour.

With our backs to the weather we crossed Full Moon Saddle, jumped crevasses down the Evans Glacier, bashed through the scrub in the head of the Wanganui, then turned up Vane Stream on our way back towards the Main Divide. Opposite the Essex Icefall, boulders of blue ice lay scattered eerily on the gravel. We camped higher up under Mt Lord, among bluffs, herb fields and clear skies again.

Mt Lord on the Main Divide was a key trig point used by G.J. Roberts in 1881 to tie together the Canterbury and Westland land surveys. Strachan Pass is named after one of his assistants, Dan Strachan, and Dan Peak, likewise. They were people who revelled in the job.

From Strachan Pass we headed into the magical subalpine Lord Valley.

I like this place, hemmed in by rocky castles on the Lord Range, where all of the usual routes in and out cross high tops. Side streams from the Main Divide flow from gentle basins over cataracts as the river descends, culminating in the canyon of the Mad Water. Below here all hell breaks loose in the slit gorges of the Lambert. Even Charlie Douglas noted: 'Nothing but a blue duck could get either down or up it.' There's a challenge for someone.

Dan Strachan tried to descend it in 1880. When gorges repulsed him he returned back over the Main Divide. Then in January 1932, fresh from the first ascent of Mt Whitcombe, R.R. 'Boney' Chester and Alan Willis teamed up with W. Barnett with the intention of heading over Strachan Pass into the Lord Valley, sidling around past Blue Lookout and descending to the Lambert, then Wanganui Valley and out to the West Coast. Reaching False Blue Lookout, they mistakenly thought they were on Blue Lookout, descended, and things came unstuck:

'The following morning found us climbing through the upper branches of thick, sleet-covered scrub.' They headed further down towards the riverbed. 'Our boulder-hopping soon became impossible, as the river now ran into a steep gorge, and for thousands of feet on either side rose dense walls of bush. Seen on empty stomachs under rainy conditions, it was a most depressing sight.' They had only brought two days' food, and this was the second day.

Sidling through bush in the gorge soon became impossible so they headed straight up for about 400 metres until blocked by a bluff above. Chester climbed a tōtara trunk, and thought if they crossed two ridges they could descend a stream past the gorge. After much hard labour they reached the stream and descended bluffs and waterfalls to find themselves back at the river's edge on dark, still in the middle of the gorge. 'Tea consisted of one dried peach each, and two Oxo cubes in cold water, it being impossible to light a fire.' And of course it rained heavily overnight.

Before daylight they were off again. 'Our position was not too rosy, as we had no food left and not the strength to return the way we had come.' One hundred metres up they found themselves halted by a bluff. They considered abandoning their packs to try and sidle the cliffs, or alternatively stripping off

OPPOSITE Looking south-west from Malcolm Peak. The head of the Lyell Glacier is nearest left, with the Frances Valley behind. Mt D'Archiac is on the left, Aoraki Mt Cook centre, and Newton and Tyndall peaks rise above the Lambert Glacier to the right.

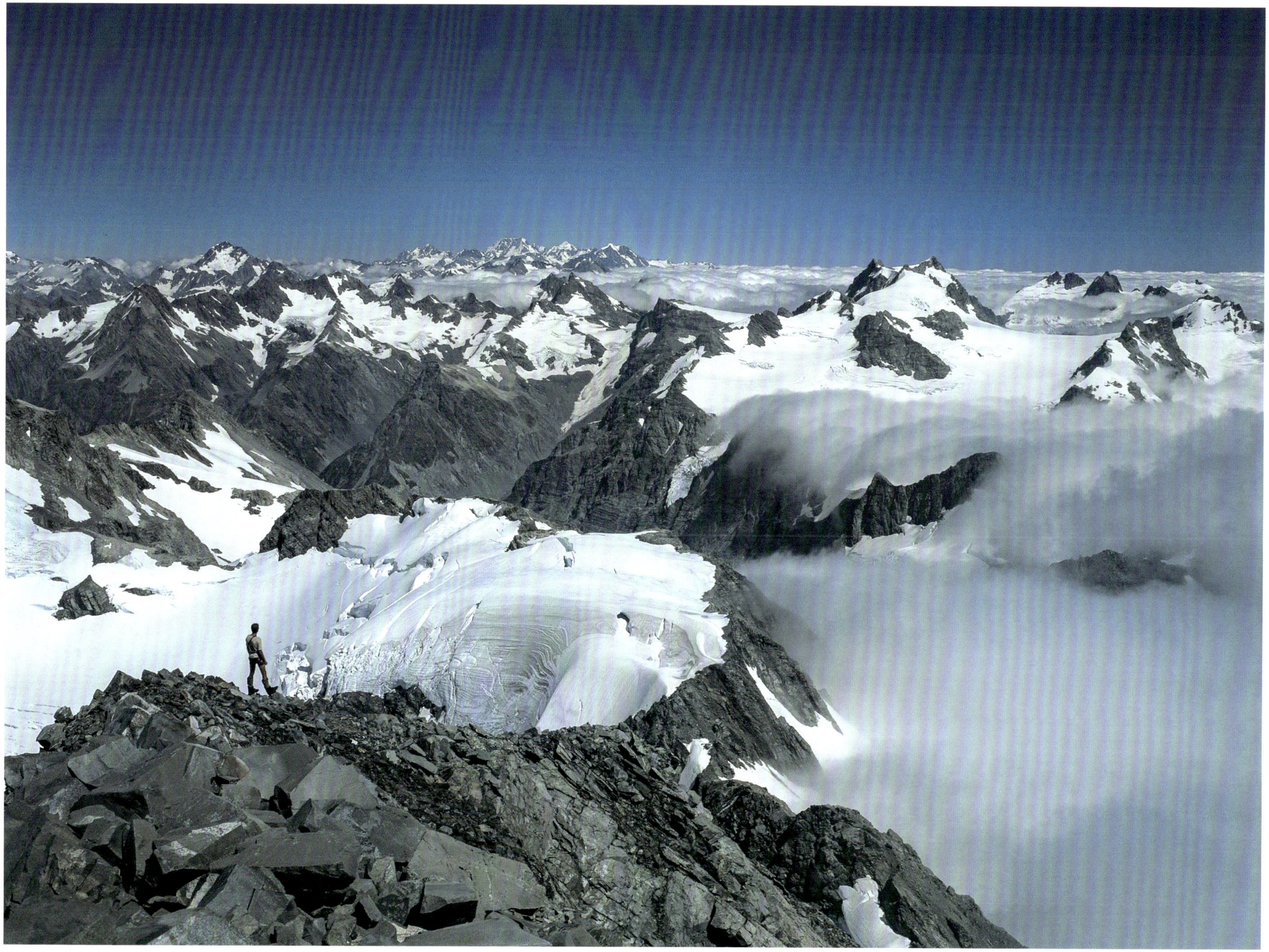

and attempting to swim the gorge, but, 'as it was a bit inaccessible to expect the Canterbury Mountaineering Club to build a memorial hut, we decided to postpone the attempt'. Instead, Chester made an attempt on the bluff with a rope on, succeeded, and on dark they reached the West Coast Road, very hungry and tired.

They aren't the last to have suffered while descending the Lambert. In an article titled 'Severe Punishment', Guy McKinnon describes a winter ascent of Malcolm Peak from the Rakaia in 2002, where he and Nick Moyle were tested to the utmost by deep, soft snow and cold as they battled their way out via the Mad Water and Blue Lookout.

For us, back in the head of the Lord Valley, we turned up the Swift Water, crossing stable red rock and herb fields, before sneaking through a keyhole under Blair Peak onto the Heim Plateau to camp on snow. Across the plateau the striking pyramid of Malcolm Peak presided, enjoying the last of the sun.

Malcolm Peak, 2512 metres on the Main Divide, was first climbed by Dr Teichelmann and his guides in 1911. They had camped in a basin under Mt Stoddart, followed up the Malcolm Glacier, and traversed the mountain from south to north, returning to their camp via the same glacier.

We travelled the other way with our packs, traversing north to south. The day was perfect, and I made the most of my medium-format camera. On the top we found a small container and bubbles of melted rock among the stones where lightning had struck.

Down towards Malcolm Col we received a wake-up call in gaping crevasses and dense mist sitting on the Frances Glacier. One crevasse ran from rock bluffs across to an icefall, and the only thing for it was to find a spot where collapsed seracs made a bridge. We belayed down the upper wall into the debris on our thin rope. Once across, we came out of the mist and had a clear run up onto Lambert Col, overlooking the extensive neve of the Lambert Glacier, Mt Lambert and its icefalls. What a grand place to be.

The rest of the trip was like that. Mountain scenery rising out of the glaciers, stunning places to be in as we wandered through the snow fields of the gardens of both Allah and Eden, then down off Perth Col into the boulders of the Clyde. Even they had a certain joy after a trip like this.

Crossing a major crevasse on the upper Frances Glacier, en route from Malcolm Peak to the Gardens.

OFF TO IVORY LAKE

WAITAHA–SMYTH RANGE–WANGANUI–BRACKEN SNOWFIELD–SEDDON COL–IVORY LAKE–WAITAHA

7 DAYS: 22–28 JANUARY 1990
GS WITH BARBARA BROWN AND MALCOLM GARNHAM

The Waitaha Valley is a wild and rugged place. High in the headwaters, beyond the bush and tussock, perches a little 'Shangri la' – Ivory Lake Hut, overlooking Stag Creek. It sits on flat, ice-ground bedrock just back from a plunging bluff, where alpine plants cling in crevices to flower brightly in summer. Behind the hut, Ivory Lake laps the shore, and behind, remnants of the Ivory Glacier cling to schist rock bluffs sweeping off the Lange Range. This place captures the heart, even in photos.

The trip began in rain after we had packed under a shop verandah in Ross, and it rained much of the way into Kiwi Flat Hut, where we of course had a brew. A break in the rain lulled us into keeping on, to camp in drizzle on Headlong Spur. Dismal really, and the firewood wasn't much better until Barb found some good dead *Dracophyllum*.

I've often found getting going rather than waiting for the weather to clear has given me a headstart on trips, and that's what happened here. By morning the sky was clear and we were already on top of the Smyth Range. For kilometres, this rolling hogsback of a crest, that touches onto 2000 metres, gave easy travel on a pavement of schist tiles weathered to within an inch of their lives. Ice remnants kept an alpine aspect, while far, far below, the Waitaha and Wanganui warbled in the depths. It's a serene place to travel in good weather, with incredible views.

Getting off was a bit trickier. Steep ravines and razorbacks carved into the range on both sides, and further east the crest deteriorated into a razorback of rotten rock as well. We headed off the Wanganui side of the range towards Smyth Hut via Smyth River, picking our way down from near Mt Barry. There is a hot pool amongst the river boulders just below the hut, and lying back I let the heat soak into my tired body. Perfect indulgence.

A new day led us into scrubby *Olearia moschata*, *coprosma* and *Neopanax*. At Vane Stream a whio appeared, pivoting around in pools as we continued up the Evans River onto the Bracken Snowfield in mist. Later, in upper Seddon Stream, a tributary of the Whitcombe River, a pair of rock wrens bobbed among the boulders.

Seddon Col proved a bit tricky. Both sides of the range were easy to access, but at different places, and in attempting to traverse between them I put myself in one of those compromising situations where going forward became impractical and getting back was just as bad. After some increased adrenalin and a lot of sweaty skin I extricated myself. Malcolm laughed. I did, too. Afterwards.

From upper Stag Creek we sidled across to Ivory Lake Hut. All afternoon we poked around in the sun, discovering willow herbs, snow marguerites in flower, and investigating moss flushes full of *Bryum* and *Fissidens*. Icebergs on the lake challenged us in to swim, but when we climbed onto them they ponderously turned turtle. It was cold work, but someone had to do it.

The logbook in the hut spoke of all sorts of adventures. Bryan Moore and Neil McDonald arrived in August 1989 from a bivvy on Erewhon Col via Red Lion Col, County Glacier and Reid Stream. Tony Gates, in his book *Worn Out Boots* noted: 'Only half a metre of hut roof protruded out from the ice, and after about half an hour's strenuous digging we found a hut window and saw that we had dug in the opposite end to the hut door. We couldn't enter.' They skied back to Top Waitaha.

That the hut exists at all is due to glaciologist Trev Chinn, who worked for the Ministry of Works in the late 1960s and chose Ivory Glacier as a research site. One of the hut's artefacts is a comfy armchair, Trev's Chair of Glaciology. More lately labelled the Chair of Recession, given how the Ivory Glacier has nearly disappeared, it is a favourite to pose in for photos.

On a fine morning we headed out down the Waitaha Valley, nearing the end of a wonderful week in the hills. Whio waved us goodbye from Moonbeam Torrent and later at Kiwi Flat.

OVERLEAF (LEFT) Ivory Glacier, Ivory Lake and Ivory Lake Hut, today. In 1990, icebergs bobbed at the hut end of the lake.
OVERLEAF (RIGHT) On Galena Ridge, between the Mikonui Valley and Ivory Lake. Mist and low sunlight often bring dramatic light. The schist rock here has the look of galena, an ore made up of lead sulphide. In this light, the name seems particularly appropriate.

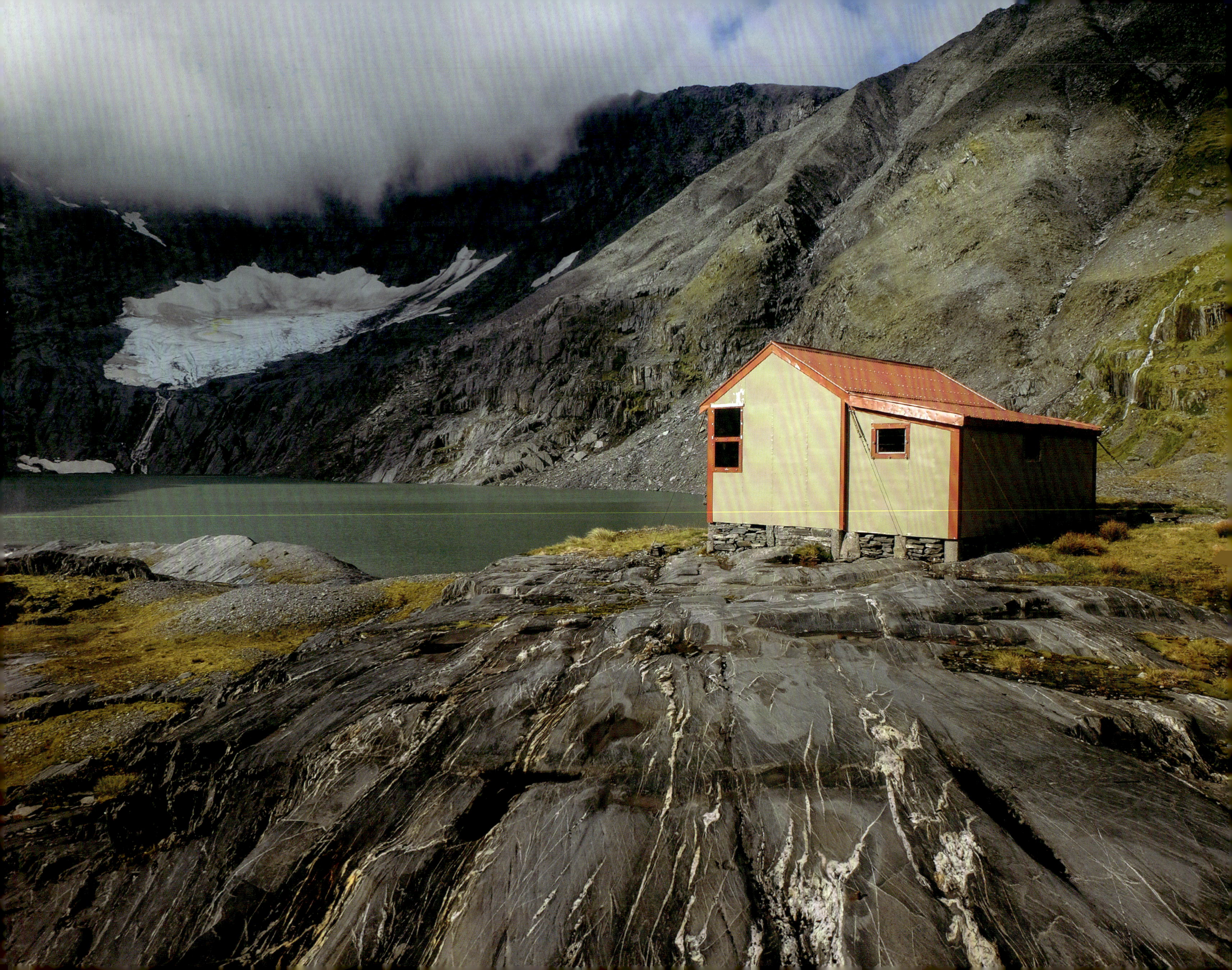

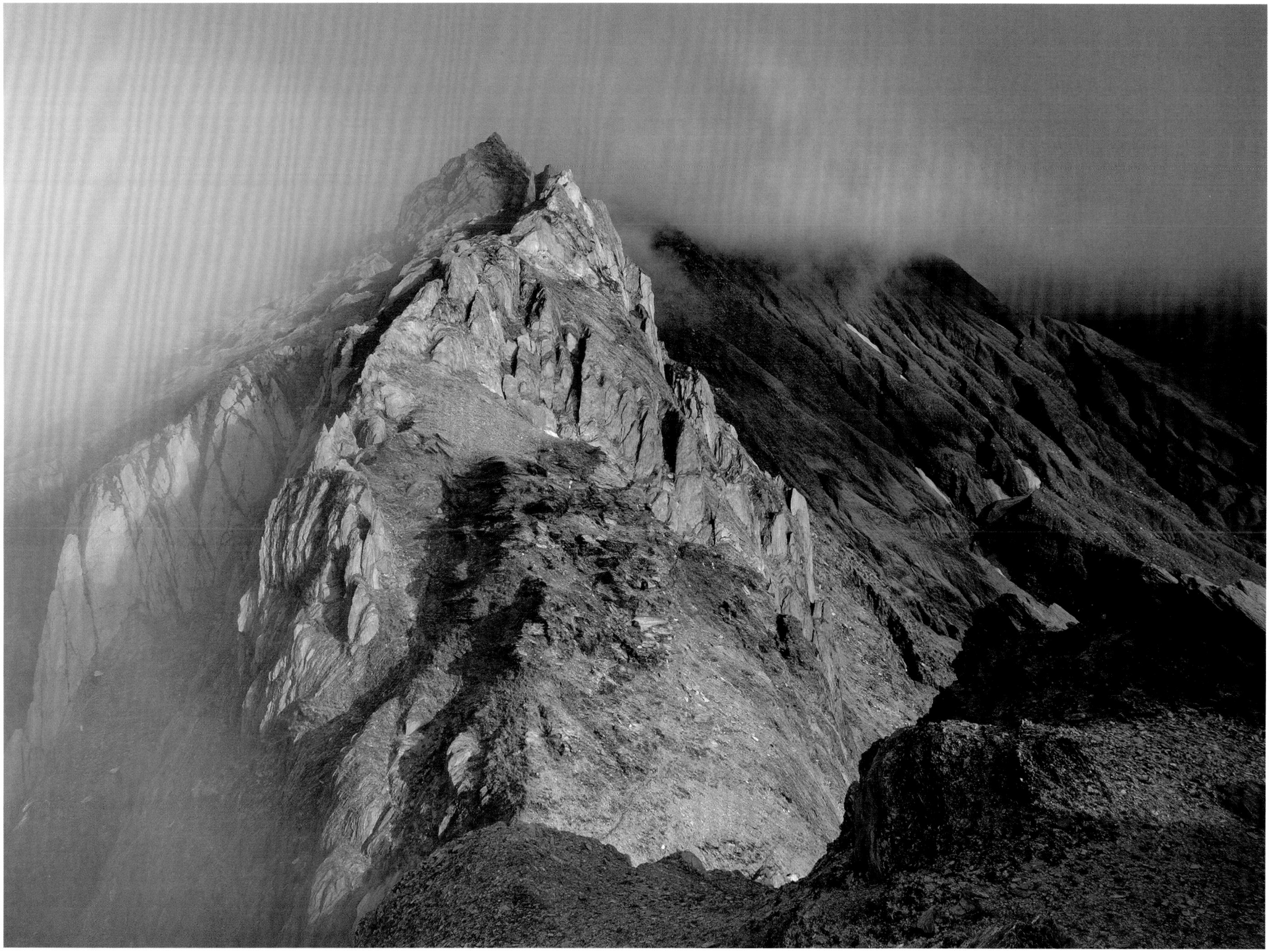

WINTER SNOWS ON THE BRACKEN

WANGANUI VALLEY–BRACKEN SNOWFIELD–RAKAIA VALLEY

7 DAYS: 12–18 AUGUST 1978
GS WITH HUGH VAN NOORDEN, STEVE BRUCE, MATT WARWICK AND
WARREN HERRICK

Winter truly transforms the mountains and the trips into them. Daylight hours shrivel in half, and the sun slinks down among the hills, leaving dampness to invade the land. The landscape is one of greasy rocks, lush mosses, wet logs, frost crystals and snow. Every year I relearn how short the days are, usually with a torch in my hand; how cold the water is; how good fires are and how stunning this new land looks, transformed by blankets of snow and frost.

The first night we camped at Hendes Creek in the Wanganui Valley under a heavy dew. Five fit young guys, excited by the challenge of a Main Divide crossing over the Bracken in winter. We romped up-valley, sidling Poker Bluff on the gravel at river level. Another bluff opposite Spar Creek wasn't so kind, and in one place the rope came out to cross a fresh slip where the run-out went straight into the river. But we were on a mission to reach Smyth Hut, which we did just on dark.

Above Smyth Hut the tracks fade, and we were on our own. Big boulders and scrub took over for a while, then we broke free into the gravels of the upper Evans Valley. Here the land remained frozen. No more water trickling, only dry barren rocks, ice and snow-avalanche debris. We made our way up the Evans Glacier in crampons, shaded by The Red Lion and then crunched on towards Full Moon Saddle at the lip of the Bracken itself. Four o'clock.

Half an hour later near Erewhon Col we strung up our blue tent close in against a small bluff and dug a small snowcave nearby to give us more room and add some insurance from the weather. But the night was fine, so I slept outside under an austere three-quarter moon. What a stunning, stunning place to wake up. All of eternity in front of my eyes, stars frozen in the blackness, and the ghostly shapes of mountains carved on the horizon. No need to get up for dawn photos on Mt Evans and The Red Lion, either. I took them from my sleeping bag.

Verglas coated the rocks in ice along the Main Divide. As the sun rose, it prised them off one by one to tinkle down in shards, clattering over bluffs and impaling the snow. The morning disappeared on what was meant to be just a quick look at the Wilkinson Icefall and spectacular bluffs on Mt Evans, but we lingered.

So, by lunchtime, when we went to investigate a quick climb of Erewhon Peak, cascading ice blocks made us think the better of it. The place was like a bowling alley. Instead, we romped over to the Amazons Breasts and took in the afternoon views from there.

With morning the weather changed to the west, it began to snow and we were soon engulfed in a whiteout. This was to be a trip of two halves. As the snow increased we packed and left, all on one rope. With no visibility we crossed crevasses and recent avalanche debris. The wind was now like a blizzard, and a depth of fresh snow added to the danger when in a gully bypassing the icefall.

Below this we could breathe easier, but deep soft snow on old moraine made travel hard work. Hopes of reaching Lyell Hut faded with the light, and we chose a campsite in the glacier centre, as far away from overnight avalanches as we could get. Snow continued to fall for the next two days as we floundered out down the Rakaia Valley, stopping a night at Lyell and another at Banfield Hut. With cold, wet feet for the last few days, some succumbed to drying socks in the oven, but the result was brown scorch marks rather than warm dry feet.

Winter cold can be something to reckon with. Steve had two toes that were swollen and black with frostbite, and when we arrived in Christchurch, he went to the hospital to check them out, and they admitted him. The possibility of gangrene isn't something to trifle with.

OPPOSITE Warren (left) and Hugh in the Rakaia Valley after crossing the Bracken, mid-winter 1978.

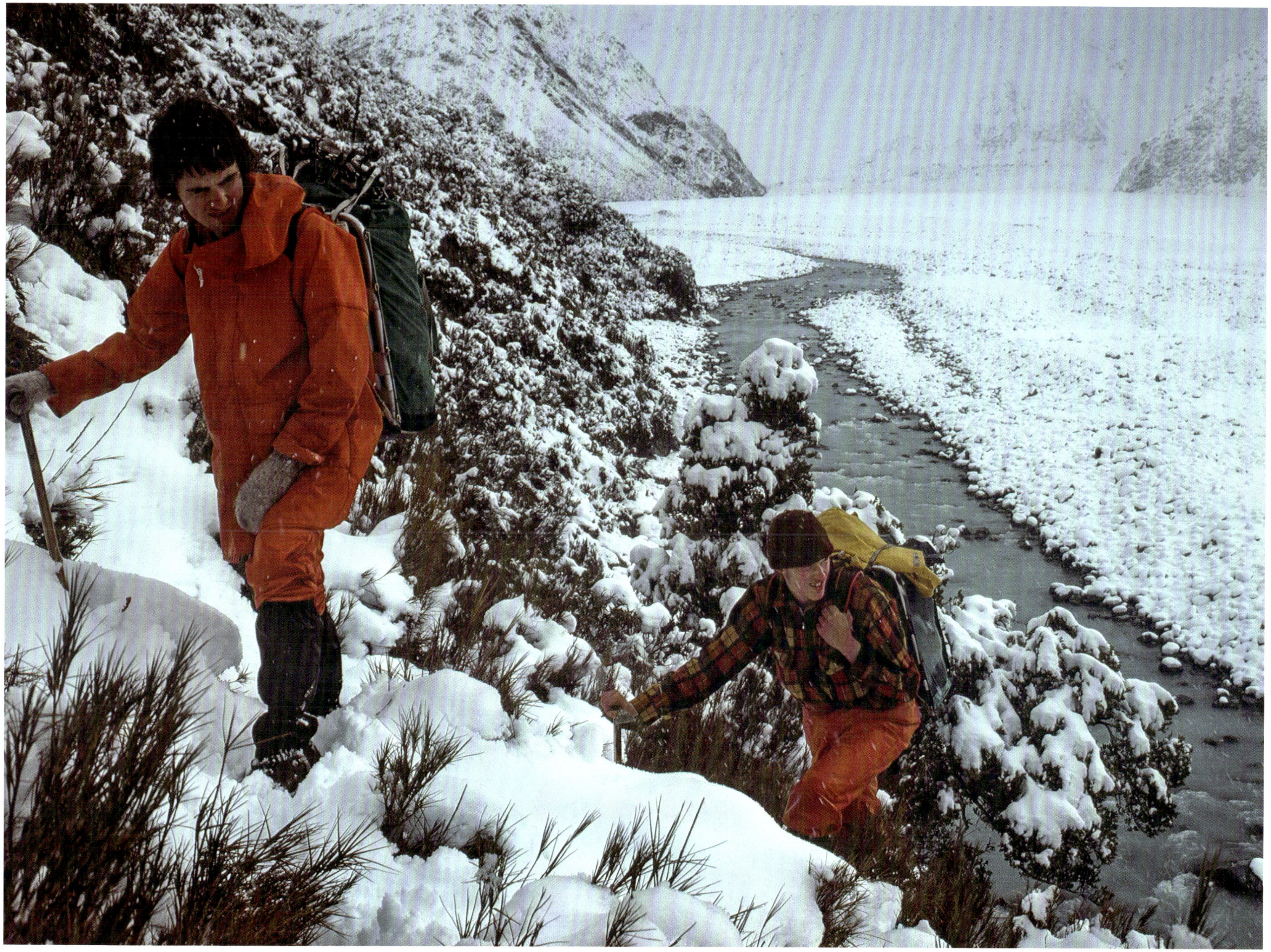

0
5
10 km
Harihari
Whataroa
< Poerua River
6
NORTH RIDGE OF MT KENSINGTON
WILLBERG RANGE
< Wanganui River
Hunters Hut
BIG DAY OUT
Blue Lookout
Camp Saddle
Dan Peak
LORD RANGE
MAIN DIVIDE
Ramsay Glacier
Strachan Pass
< Lord River
< Lambert River
Lambert Spur
Adams River >
Adams Flat
Mt Adams
ADAMS RANGE
Mt Kensington
Mt Lambert
Mt Stoddart
Malcolm Peak
Lambert Glacier
Frances Glacier
Garden of Allah
Newton Peak
Mt Tyndall
Mt Farrar
The Devils Backbone
Adams Col
Garden of Eden
STORM ON ADAMS COL
< Barlow River
< Whataroa River
The Great Unknown
Adverse Ck >
Perth Col
< Perth River
TO THE GREAT UNKNOWN
Scone Hut
< Perth River
Frances River >
< McCoy Strm
Havelock River >
Clyde River >
Whataroa River >
MAIN DIVIDE
Erewhon
N

CHAPTER 6

THE GARDEN OF EDEN ICE PLATEAU

The fabled Garden of Eden and Garden of Allah have captured the hearts and imagination of trampers and climbers for a century. These ice plateaus, situated on the western flanks of the Main Divide, are a magnificent region of wild valleys and isolated mountains that have been the backdrop to many transalpine adventures.

Together with the Lambert Glacier their icefields extend for 13 kilometres and range in altitude from 1600 to 2100 metres. Inspired names such as The Great Unknown, Angel Col, Satan Saddle, The Devils Backbone, Vertebrae Col and Gardens of Eden and Allah were given by A.P. Thompson, John Pascoe, B.D.A. Greig and others in the 1930s.

Dr Teichelmann and guides Jack Clarke and Alec Graham were probably the first onto the Lambert Glacier in 1911, during a trip that included ascents of Malcolm Peak and Mt Tyndall. They approached from the west.

Twenty-two years after, on 25 December 1933, L.K. Wilson and H.W. Cormack climbed both Tyndall and Newton peaks from the Clyde, via the Colin Campbell Glacier in the east. Between then and the late 1950s most of the surrounding peaks were also climbed, and transalpine journeys explored the Adams, Poerua, Barlow and Perth catchments. Many of these trips were epics, and some aspects of their inspirational stories are included in this chapter. Accounts of this history can be found in alpine journals and in *The Canterbury Mountaineer*.

The classic trip to the Gardens involves a crossing of the Main Divide, beginning in the east and finishing on the West Coast. From Erewhon, head up the Clyde Valley, then Frances River to the Wee McGregor Glacier and Perth Col. A snow sidle leads onto the Gardens from there. Many parties stay at Adams Col for a few days, climbing and exploring, before descending Adverse Creek to the Perth and following down the Whataroa. An alternative classic follows the route of the Big Day Out (see page 94), but, unfortunately, an essential bridge over the Lambert was recently washed away.

STORM ON ADAMS COL

WANGANUI VALLEY–LORD RANGE–CAMP SADDLE–
STRACHAN PASS–LORD VALLEY–LAMBERT GLACIER–
GARDEN OF ALLAH–ADAMS COL–GARDEN OF EDEN–
BARLOW RIVER–PERTH RIVER

18 DAYS: 25 DECEMBER 1971 TO 11 JANUARY 1972
GS WITH IAN WILKINS, COLIN JONES AND DAVE SOWRY

With high hopes and heavy packs we struggled up the Wanganui Valley near Harihari, and in rain the following day creaked across the river on a rickety cage to the old slab-walled Hunters Hut (now replaced), where two hunters and their fire made us welcome.

We planned to traverse the Lord Range, climb peaks on the Garden of Eden, then follow the main Barlow River from its source to the Perth and Whataroa. As we could find no accounts of the full Barlow being traversed from the Farrar Glacier, the trip had a touch of the unknown about it for us. Not quite Eric Shipton's *Blank on the Map*, but certainly a bit of exploring new territory for ourselves. I identify with Shipton's simple, lightweight, flexible approach to mountains: he rejected contemporary expedition dogma, and claimed travel is as simple or as complex as you choose, and the complexity comes from confusion between necessity and luxury. This, I think, still applies.

Our climb up through flax and scrub to the tops at the start of the traverse was brutal, carrying multi-day packs and climbing gear. The Lord Range has distinctive horizontal rock strata, making peaks on it look like castles. The highest peak, Dan, was first climbed by W.H. and R. Scott of Wellington in 1934.

We traversed through Camp Saddle and reached the Main Divide at Mt Lord. A few days later, under a sombre sky, we stood on the first of the big snow neves, the Lambert. From here, near-continuous icefields extended west through the Gardens of Eden and Allah.

A little adventure began for us here on New Year's Day, our eighth day of the trip. Dodging crevasses in thick, misty drizzle we followed our compass through Satan Saddle and down the Garden of Allah to near Adams Col as

ABOVE A young Ian Wilkins at the old Hunters Hut in the Wanganui Valley, 1971.
OPPOSITE: The dramatic southern slopes of the Lord Range.

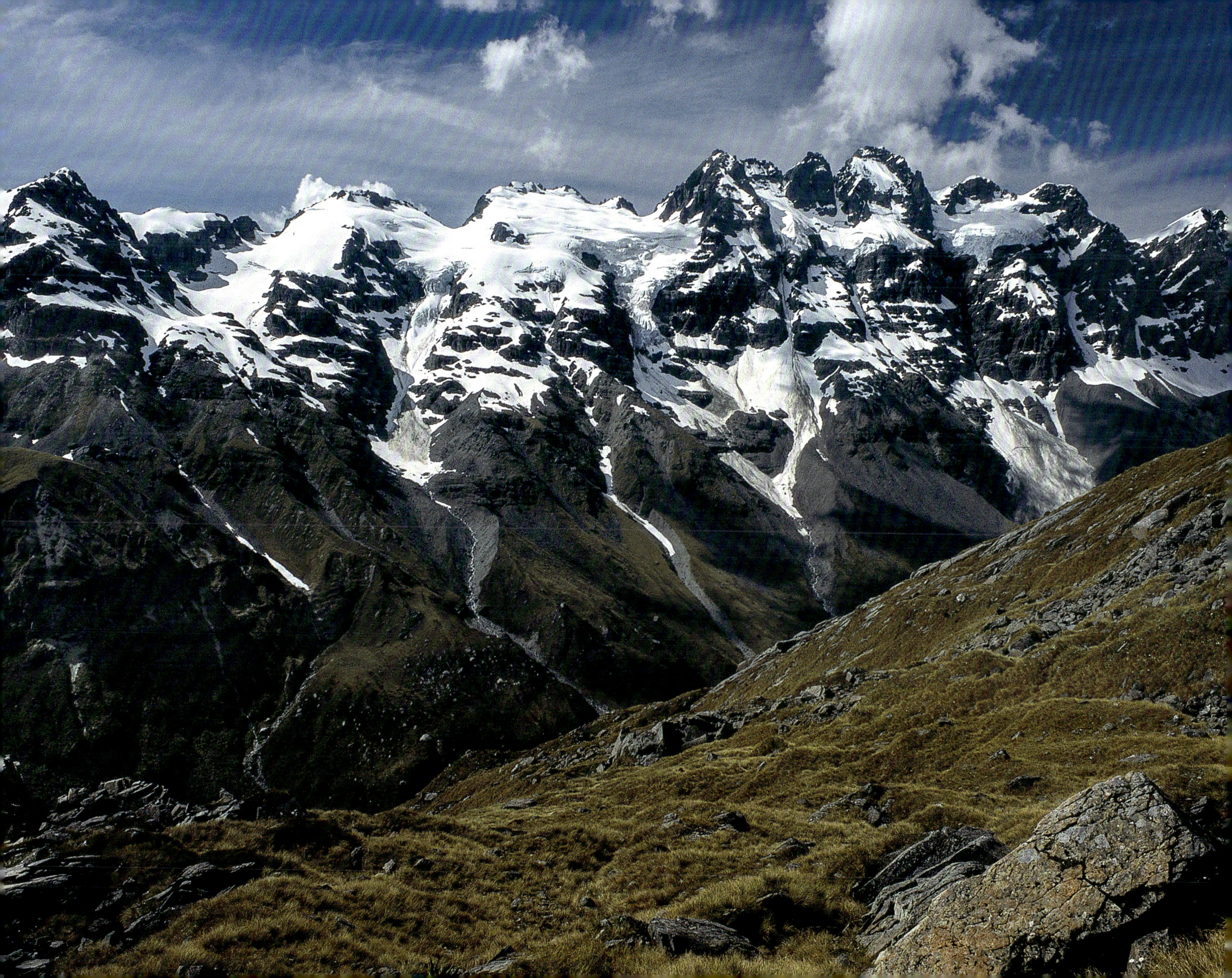

ice boomed and rumbled. Not sure where we were, we camped on snow. Our tent for this trip was an A-frame, single skin, nylon, four-person affair, with a single vertical pole each end but no floor. A tiny tarn many metres away provided water. It rained and blew and stormed through the night; in my diary I wrote 'existed'. But things were to get worse. While we were cooking a breakfast of rice and peaches on our pressure cooker, the snow became water-logged and suddenly our sleeping bags were soaked. Peering out the door revealed the tarn was now a lake.

In bare feet, clammy parkas and driving rain, we repitched the tent further up the snow slope, thinking we would be back inside in short order. But the storm wasn't having any of that. With the job half done a huge gust ripped out several guy ropes, making the tent useless. Wet and shivering, uncertain of our whereabouts and with only a day or so's food left, things were a little messy. We were by no means the first to have our tents trashed on Adams Col, though. Many parties have suffered a similar fate on the Gardens.

We clothed up and went looking for a snowcave site. With only iceaxes and billy lids to dig with, progress was slow. We managed, but not without frost-nipped toes that turned black and blue and later peeled like onions, bringing considerable tenderness. And those down sleeping bags still weren't dry after four days and nights shivering in them.

In the meantime, the weather eased, we retrieved our food cache for the second part of the trip and climbed some of the higher peaks: Newton, Tyndall, Guardian, and an anvil-shaped block near the summit of Lambert in freezing mist. We were certainly keen, given that it rained or snowed almost every day.

Ultimately, we resurrected the tent by tying pebbles into the fabric to make new guy attachments. These were tenuous, but they worked. We now said goodbye to our snowcave by setting fire to it with surplus white spirits. There is nothing so final or surreal as burning your snow home to the ground, flames licking out the entrance and the roof.

Heading west along the Garden of Eden, past Angel Col, we continued until the snow plateau began to peter out.

Back in the 1930s, glaciers were discovered and peaks climbed in a landscape where the extent of the ice and where it led was still being unravelled. If you look closely at the map supplied with the first edition (1939) of Pascoe's *Unclimbed New Zealand*, the Farrar Glacier and head of the Barlow River feeds into the Poerua River. It actually flows into the Perth, and this was later corrected on a reprint.

We crossed Vertebrae Col on the Devils Backbone with trepidation, and descended ledges through bluffs of loose rock to finally stand on the Farrar Glacier below. Around us the scene was grand desolation. Walls of broken schist, eroding slips from mountain to glacier, wild ice and ice tongues draining mountain walls greeted us. We only knew of a few parties who had ever been here in the head of the Barlow River, and none had gone far down-valley. For us it was the great unknown. We found a little grass flat at the end of the ice and camped.

When Canterbury mountaineers Stan Conway, Bill Hannah, Dave Parr and Ray Chapman descended off the plateaus into the head of the Barlow River in 1951, much of the main Barlow was terra incognita to them. Looking for a new route to the West Coast along the Adams Range, they became trapped by bad weather on the Siege Glacier and after days of wet struggle with storms they finally baled out over the range via the Escape Glacier. They named both glaciers in the process and I was lucky to chat to Ray in 2010 about his experiences there. Their trip sounded phenomenal.

We began our journey down the Barlow on boulders, stopping at some dead native broom for a fire and brew. Seduced by easy travel, we bowled on into a gorge and were suddenly playing around on slimy ledges, requiring the rope to get out. Scrub-bashing up greasy rockwalls can get precarious, and my arms were knackered by the time the angle eased off a few hundred metres up.

We reached the river again and camped on a sandbar at the confluence of the North and main Barlow rivers, after a mission that included using the rope to get past a tooth of rock on a bush rib. It was very satisfying to sit there by a fire in such a remote spot. Below us, the river curled into a gorge with 300-metre walls, so we crossed and sidled down the true left, using scrubby terraces and bush flats, where finding routes in and out of deep side creeks wasn't easy.

On our seventeenth day we reached the Perth Valley and made a deep boulder-crossing of the river. Our feet were munted, and the trip out wasn't fun, but for a party with an average age of just 17, we had had quite an adventure.

OPPOSITE Looking insignificant, two people traverse the Garden of Eden, with the Devils Backbone to the left.

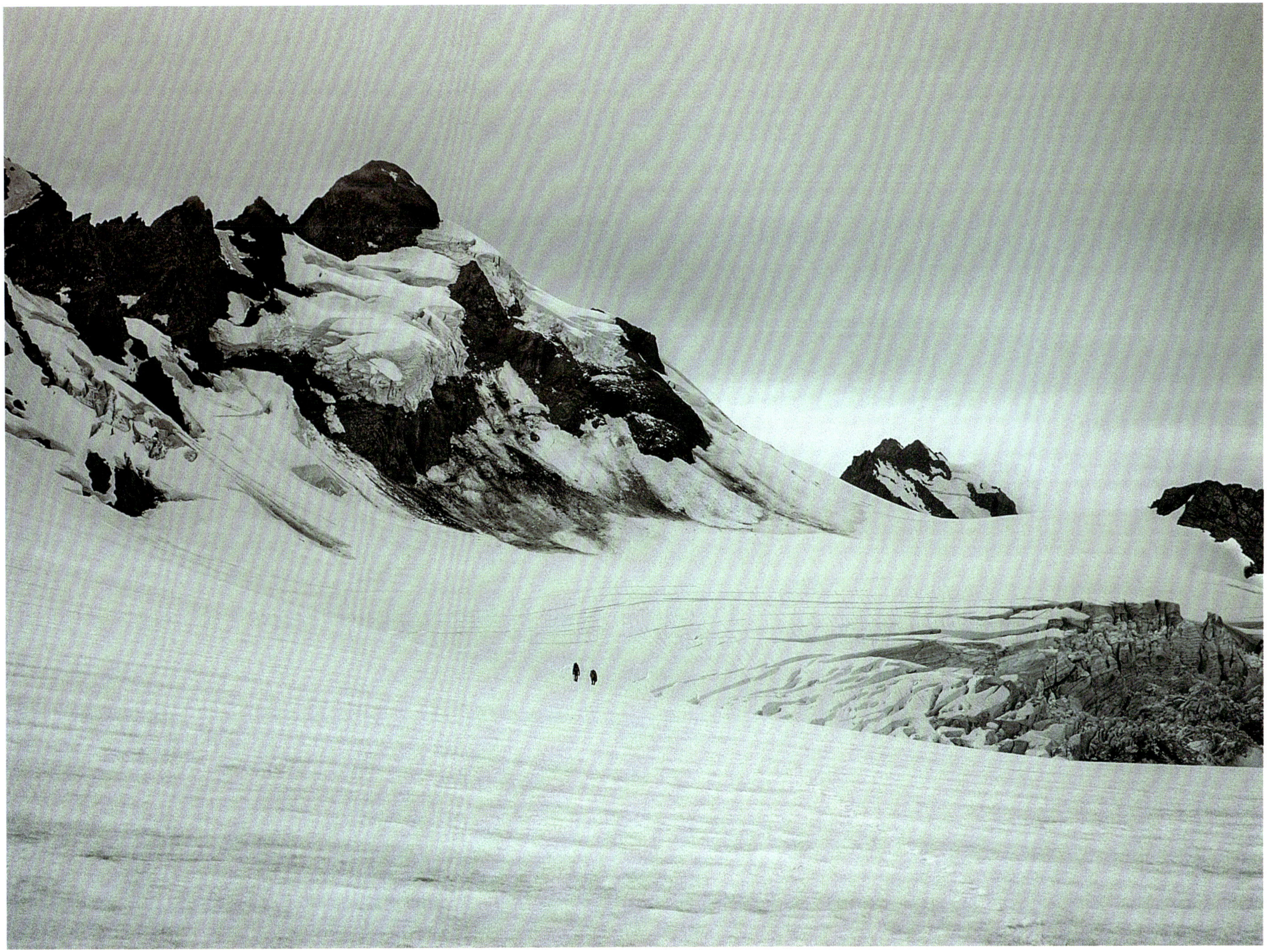

THE NORTH RIDGE OF MT KENSINGTON

WILLBERG RANGE–MT KENSINGTON–ADAMS FLAT– MT LAMBERT–LORD VALLEY–BLUE LOOKOUT–WANGANUI

9 DAYS: 10–18 DECEMBER 1974
GS, WITH LAUCHIE DUFF

When I arrived at Lauchie's flat in Christchurch, his Anglia De Luxe car, nicknamed Mrs Muffles, looked like Monty Python's Norwegian blue parrot: very dead. The motor was in a pile on the grass. This was our transport. With a confidence that was to stand us in good stead throughout the trip, Lauchie waved at it and said, 'I'm just putting it back together now.' I thought of the parrot shop-owner.

Driving through farm paddocks beyond the Poerua Valley roadend we ripped the muffler off, then realised we had to drive back to Harihari to get white spirits. We finally got away at 4.30 p.m.

Our main goal was the unclimbed North Ridge of Mt Kensington, but the Poerua Gorge was apparently untraversed too. A short way into it we abandoned that idea. Instead, we climbed out in a haze of sweat and supplejack vines. Over vines and under them. Through them and around them. Caught up in them. Lauchie getting ahead. Bugger them, and the mossy stones, and slippery logs, and the drizzle, and the whole West Coast . . .

About 300 metres up we stumbled onto an overgrown track. Higher, we struggled with belligerent scrub, reaching that strange free world of the tops at 10.30 p.m. and slept out, exhausted, 1000 metres above the river, with tiny snow patches for water.

The Willberg Range extends all the way to Mt Kensington and, in 1951, Arnold Heine, Gordon Howitt, Harry Stimpson from Hutt Valley Tramping Club and Jim Cruse of the Tararua Club traversed much of the range as far as Adams Flat, naming Avalon Peak and several other features. They returned from the Willberg tops via Adamsons Creek and the Wanganui.

Beyond Mt Ferguson on the Willberg Range we dropped into Exit Creek and the Willberg (North Poerua) River, enjoying the stony riverbed in dry, sunny conditions. Higher up, we reached the snows of the North Poerua Glacier and camped on the ridge at the head of it, where the last of the day's sun washed the snow with gold.

Up before dawn, we took a daypack each and stashed the rest of our gear away from kea. A little too well, as we would later find. Sidling Alpheus slopes, we scrambled around to the cold and shaded col at the foot of the 250-metre rock step that was the key to the North Ridge. Smooth, fine-grained schist confronted us, rising as a buttress.

At Easter 1963, Gordon Howitt and Alan Gill set out on a lightweight expedition to traverse Mt Adams and the Adams Range to Mt Kensington, then descend the North Ridge. They very nearly succeeded. They carried no tent or primus on their six-day trip, and had managed much of the North Ridge when they were forced off it, 'to descend approximately 1000 feet of exposed and difficult rock chimneys which finally put us on the South Poerua Glacier. . .'

It didn't look any easier to us. We roped up and started to climb from the col itself. Tenuous leads on flimsy protection made some moves a bit desperate, but having come this far we weren't about to give up. A smooth slab proved a bit too challenging in my old, worn John Bull boots. Instead, I went over to a corner on the left, and this gave enough ledges to get some height. However, the rock there was flaky and by the time I reached secure ground again my legs were flaky too, and my fingers were cramping. Despite these challenges, we got there. Piece by piece.

As it does on fine afternoons on the West Coast, cumulus cloud billowed up, reducing our world to a few metres. At the top of the rock step we were ready for our two o'clock lunch. By now we had cracked the most difficult part of the climb, and the rest of the ridge involved step-kicking in snow, some smaller rock steps and a sidle on snow to reach the summit at 8 p.m. Days like this leave you utterly wrung out and at the same time utterly exhilarated.

In gloomy drizzle we used the compass to head down onto the Arethusa

OPPOSITE Upper basins of the South Poerua River and the North Ridge of Mt Kensington on the skyline. The photo is taken from a camp on the Barlow/Poerua Saddle.

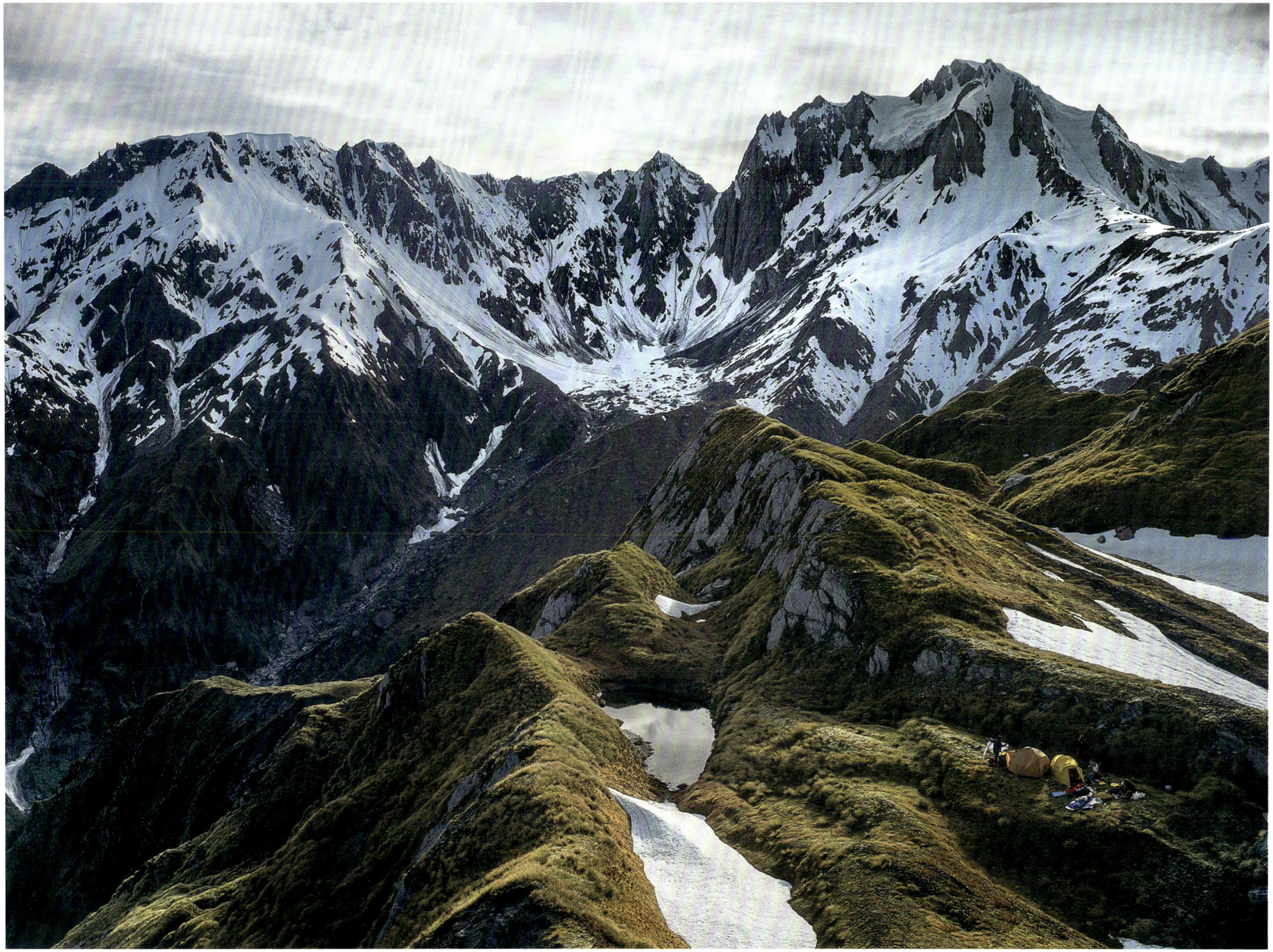

Icefall. With no tent, primus or sleeping bags, we dug two snowcaves in soft snow to pass the night. Why two? Because the first one leaked water so badly it may as well have been raining, and we had to abandon it. It was nearly midnight when we finished the second one, had muesli for dinner and crawled onto our foam mats.

In the morning we descended steeply into Alpheus Creek to retrieve the gear from our North Poerua camp. This proved easier said than done. Wandering around in a whiteout, we became more and more confused as to where our gear and food was. It seemed so obvious when we had hidden it. There was a lesson in that!

We found a bivvy rock down at Adams Flat and for two nights and a day we lay in it, watching the rainwater seep down the edges of rock and drop off little nodules into our billies. It was pleasant. Both of us were tired, sunburnt and happy to rest.

Then the weather cleared, *Celmisia* on the flat sparkled with dewdrops, and we were full of life again. Whio whistled at us from a creek; chamois did the same from a scree. Heading up onto the tops meant camping near a gravel col north of Mt Lambert. The following morning was perfect, giving me a wonderfully relaxed solo climb on frozen snow to the summit. I spread the map out. Twenty minutes later I realised it was still just lying where I'd left it, there not being the slightest breeze. (I have a friend who liked to conduct a candle test on summits. It was very simple. He lit a candle and if it could make it to a minute without being blown out, it was a fine day. Quirky, I know. Scientists can be like that.)

The first ascent of Mt Lambert in 1933 took Ivan Tucker, Len Boot, and Harry Andrewes over Strachan Pass, down the Lord Valley and up the Lambert River to the col near where we camped. We now followed their route in reverse down to the Lambert head flats and across to the Lord Valley. It wasn't plain sailing.

A metre-high boulder rolled away under Lauchie's boots in the steep, dusty gully leading down to the flats, spinning him down 3 metres. That unnerved both of us. Fighting our way through the scrub above canyons in the Lord and Lambert, we were eventually forced by bluffs into a crossing of the Lord River where it corkscrewed on bedrock and disappeared into a defile, only 100 metres above the Lambert forks.

Travelling up-valley at river level another bluff intervened, and we crossed again, this time swinging the packs between boulders on a rope flying fox. Without packs, we were able to jump. The excitement continued as we struggled through tunnels and chimneys along the true left. At the Mad Water we crossed the Lord for the final time, climbed onto the end of the Lord Range and followed the standard route past False and Blue Lookouts, leading to Benighted Creek and the Wanganui.

LEFT Mt Kensington's North Ridge above Alpheus Creek.
OPPOSITE The extensive neve of the Lambert Glacier, with Mt Lambert to the right.

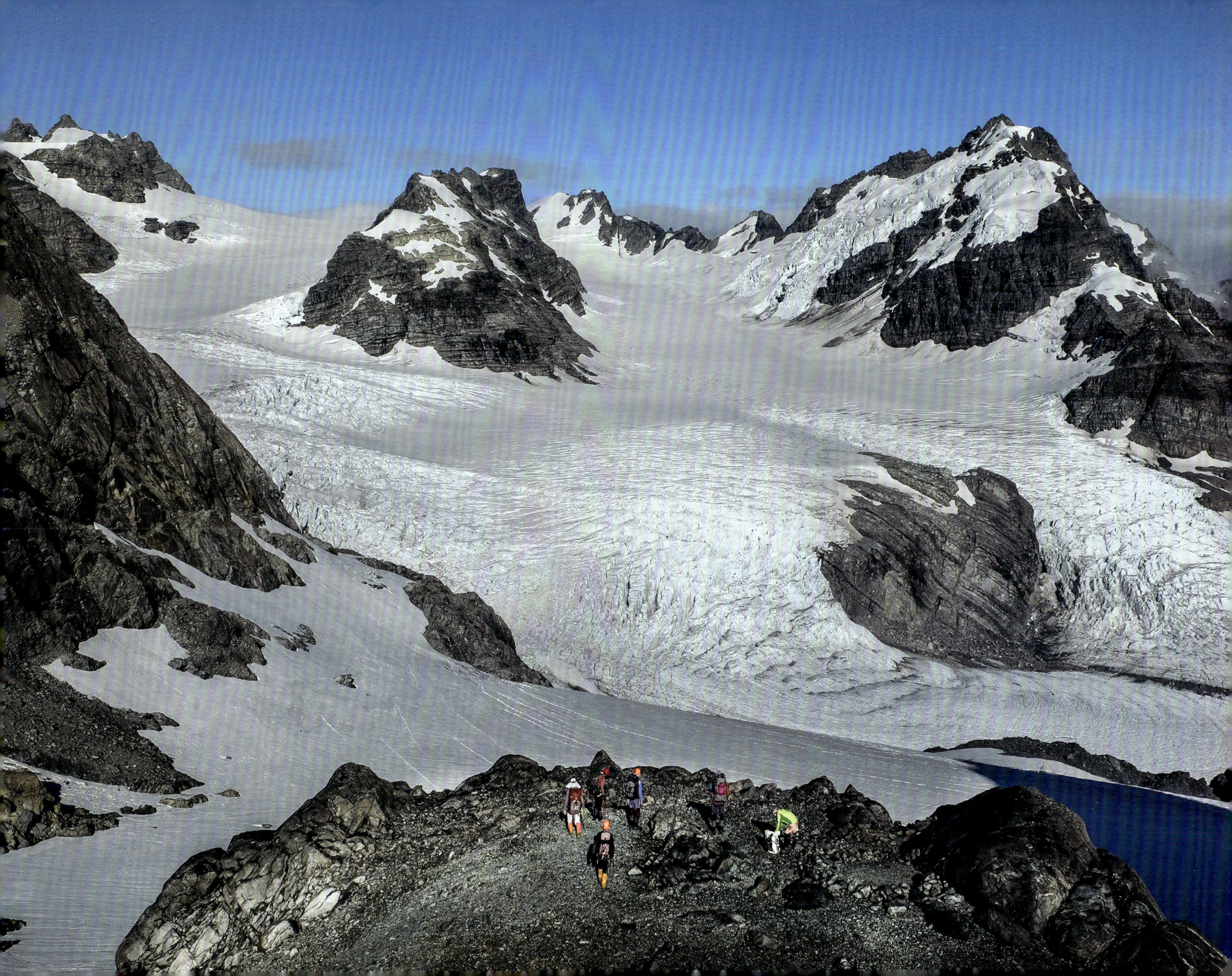

BIG DAY OUT

EREWHON–CLYDE–PERTH COL–GARDEN OF EDEN–ADAMS COL–GARDEN OF ALLAH–LAMBERT NEVE–LAMBERT SPUR–WANGANUI VALLEY

1 DAY: 20 FEBRUARY 2008

GS WITH PHIL NOVIS

Sometimes an idea will lodge in your brain and not let go. Could a crossing from Canterbury over both the Garden of Eden and Garden of Allah to the West Coast be done in a day? A lightweight, seize-the-day trip, sort of an alpine multisport, perhaps. I had considered attempting a one-day crossing of the Adams Wilderness since the early 1980s, when criteria around wilderness areas were being discussed. I've occasionally enjoyed a fast trip in the hills, as a personal challenge, but generally I prefer to take my time.

In my late teens I completed a two-day Schormann–Kaitoke via the traverse of the Tararua Main Range, involving about 6800 metres of climbing and 80 kilometres of rough travel. The proposed one-day Garden–to–Garden traverse requires about 2500 metres of climbing and is roughly 60 kilometres, much of it in alpine terrain.

An attempt from west to east foundered on the Lambert tops in the 1990s. Another venture in 2005 with Marcus Waters began shakily on a pitch-black night by torchlight when we almost headed up the Lawrence instead. That became a two-day crossing.

In 2008, I got it sorted. The night was mellow and the moon full when Phil and I climbed into our sleeping bags under the pines at Erewhon. But I lay awake, and two hours later, at 11.30 p.m., we were up again preparing to leave. A sleepless rest before a trip like this isn't ideal, however, just after midnight we were away, our feet rolling awkwardly on the greywacke rocks.

Trips like this need careful planning: a timetable to tick off, a minimal gear list, light food that can be eaten easily; boots, crampons and an iceaxe, light down-jacket, an EPIRB and about 30 metres of 6-millimetre nylon cord. No GPS.

The full golden light of the moon cast shadows at our feet as we focused, Phil's powerful LED headlight scouring the gravel for the best route. The Clyde and Lawrence were both easy to cross this late in summer, but darkness made us concentrate. With wet feet we passed Black Bluff and scraped to our first stop a little past Sinclair River. Three hours so far. At the Frances confluence we crossed to the true right, and further up, the odd scramble in scrub behind boulders made for an extra dimension in the dark. We reached the mudflat lake at about 5.30 a.m. and I lay down to recover. Overhead, predawn stars filled an inky sky, the moon having set, and the landscape outlines were stunning. Part of my soul lives in this place.

At the Wee McGregor Glacier we put on crampons and headed for Perth Col. The sun was up now, its warm light sweeping down Baker Peak. On the expansive Garden of Eden ice, we set sail for Adams Col. People appeared – the Stout party from Otago.

The sidle below Adams Col across to the Garden of Allah has changed in the last 40 years. Where we camped on creamy snow slopes overlaying ice in 1972, we now crossed gravel and rock. Soon we were on the Garden of Allah, where my lack of training for this trip began to show up as sore knees. We crossed Satan Saddle at noon and headed down into the Lambert Neve.

I love the airiness of the sidle from here – the Lord Range views, the Lambert ice rumbling now and then, and occasionally coming across pipits and rock wren. But the place is a black hole for time. It sped up, leaving us behind our time estimates. However, by the top of the Lambert Spur it was 4.15 p.m. We had clawed that back somehow.

By seven o'clock we had crossed the Lambert bridge, bypassed the hut, checked the Wanganui River and deferred to cross the cage instead. Time was still tight. By Hendes Creek we'd been in the dark again for an hour. It was 10 p.m. and I was a bit over it. Both Phil and I knew the Wanganui pretty well, but we still missed some track entrances back off the riverbed, and we didn't have time for this. Eventually the track led to the quarry and the carpark beyond.

We'd been on the go for twenty-three and a half hours. Despite sore feet and cramping muscles, we revelled in the satisfaction of getting there and being able to rest after our big day out. Wearing puffer jackets and tucked into big plastic bags, we drifted off, blissfully, into the sleep of the dead.

OPPOSITE The canyons of the Lambert Gorge, with Mt Stoddart high on the right.

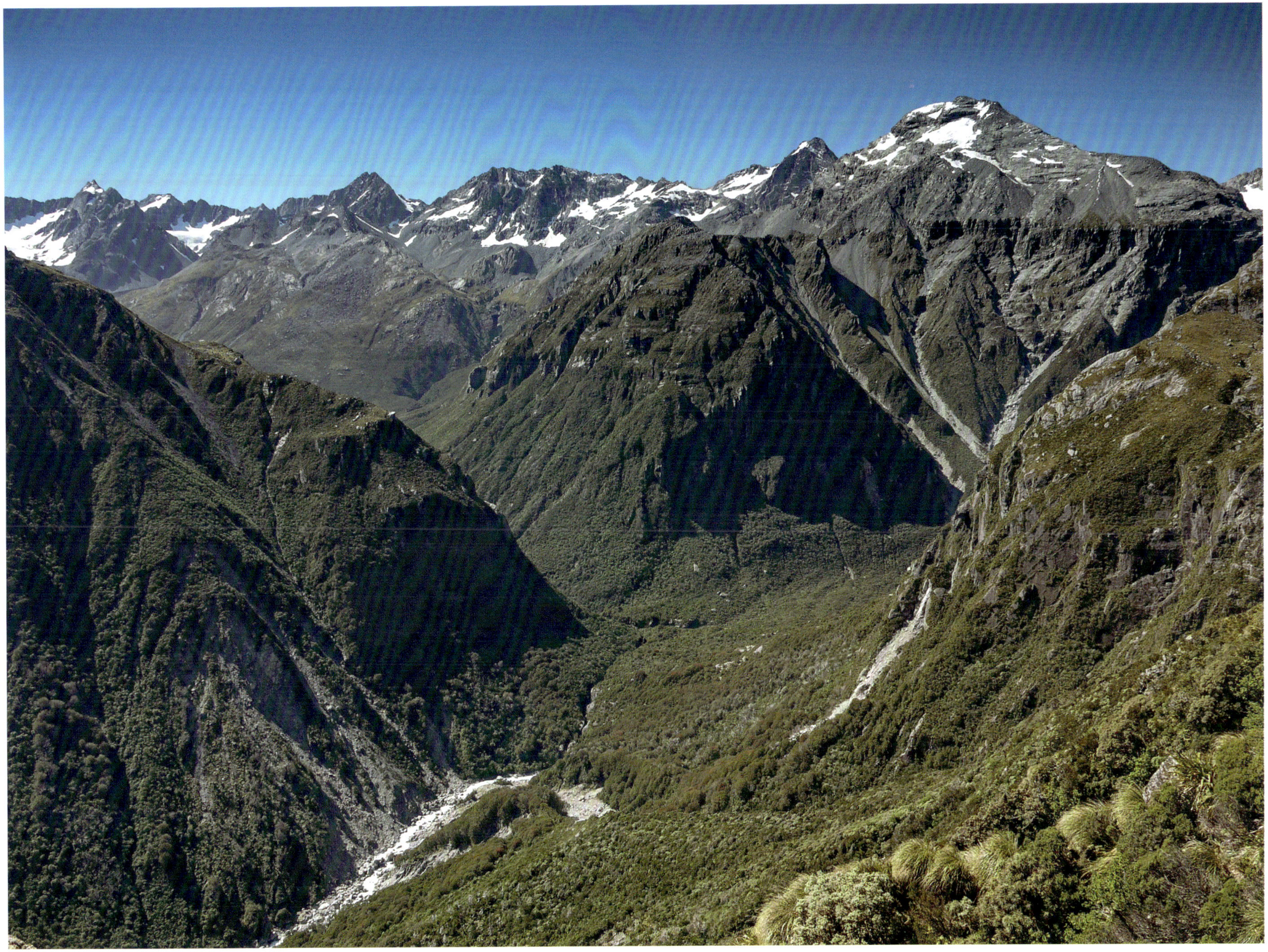

TO THE GREAT UNKNOWN

CLYDE–PERTH COL–GARDEN OF EDEN– THE GREAT UNKNOWN–PERTH RIVER

8 DAYS: 3–10 FEBRUARY 2013
GS WITH RAYMOND FORD, GARY HUISH, LIZ STEPHENSON, LAURAYNE DEVERY, KEVIN HUGHES, MERV MEREDITH, CHRIS LEAVER, RUTH BARRATT, KAREN KEITH AND AARN TATE

Over the years I have learned to be flexible with what the weather deals us on trips, and I try to tailor the days to suit. This is why on day two of an eight-day trip we had a rest day, tucked up dry and cosy in Watchdog Hut, watching the rain lash down. We had already crossed the Clyde River, and were well positioned to approach the Garden of Eden when it cleared.

The following day it did clear, and all went well until we met Agnes, who was still raging over the boulders. Agnes taught us not to take things for granted. Probing carefully, we linked up and were drenched by the time we were over. The Canterbury Mountaineering Club put a small A-frame hut here in 1939, but unfortunately it was flattened by avalanches in about 1969.

The route to Perth Col is fraught with loose stones and small crevasses, but we slowly made height to sleep out near the col on a frosty clear evening. It's exhilarating arriving in such places, and our campsite buzzed with the joy of it all and the promise of a fine day to follow. The sun rose directly onto our camp, thawing away the night, and making everyone glow.

On a day like this the Gardens are magical. Keeping together, we made our way past mounts Newton and Tyndall, Guardian and Farrar, went over to Adams Col – the scene of so many good and bad experiences for different alpine parties – and looked down across the extensive snowfields of Angel Col, towards Adams Valley and Mt Kensington.

A little history: In late December 1934, John Pascoe, Priestley Thompson, Gavin Malcolmson and Duncan Hall were the first to cross Perth Col from the Clyde to the Perth Valley. During the following days, they explored the Garden of Eden, which they named before descending the Perth to Whataroa. A year later, Pascoe, this time with H.A. McDowall, Merle Sweney and A.F. Pearson, travelled down through Angel Col to explore the Adams Glacier and valley. Theirs was a descent and exit of epic proportions, crossing Speculation Range to avoid the Eblis Gorge in the Adams River, only to find their chosen alternative, Hot Spring Creek, even more gorged.

Then in 1939, a Tararua Tramping Club Christmas trip of nine led by Don Viggers became the first to traverse the full length of the Garden of Eden, naming the Devils Backbone as they went. Two of the party also made the second ascent of The Great Unknown. The first ascent had been made by Paul Powell, Bonk Scotney and Jim Croxton only two days before, from the opposite direction.

And now in 2013, there we were under the Devils Backbone, a spine of peaks and rock that shadowed us towards The Great Unknown, beyond the end of the ice. During a recce from our campsite checking out tomorrow's route, I mislaid my iceaxe. Derision followed from most of the party. I tried bribery. Free chocolate to anyone who found it. The bribery worked, and Raymond found my axe. In the morning, I also mislaid my parka. Huey listened to my prayers, and it didn't rain for the rest of the trip.

In the final basins leading to The Great Unknown, rock wrens welcomed us, cheeping from the boulders. It's always good to see those little guys. The climb to The Great Unknown required care with route-finding, amongst the bluffs and snow shelves. We left our packs where we crossed to the Adverse Glacier, and we were on the summit by 3 p.m. Eleven elated people on a warm day with mist beginning to build. Beyond Adverse Glacier we dropped to tussock benches and bluffs, where some chamois were startled to see us.

Some of us found a tarn to swim in – no point in getting clothes wet, though. On dark we camped in Elizabeth Stream, having felt every wobbly step of the 1000 metres down from The Great Unknown. A lone kea commiserated. This was the first kea we had seen on the trip, a reminder of the decline this species is suffering throughout the Alps.

The descent to the Perth Valley next morning via Redfield Stream continued to test us. It isn't an easy route, and it had us scrub-bashing along steep slopes around three small falls and down boulders into the creek. In the headwaters, another two rock wren came to say hi, and on the way down, long-tailed cuckoos gave their familiar *zziiit* calls. Below, at the Perth, a whio gave us a whistle.

We camped on the riverbed and enjoyed a good fire, with every muscle complaining. We had had our casualties. A loose stone had hit Aarn in the leg, Merv hit his head and arm, and Chris developed a bad blister. A minor stumble while in crampons left Karen needing attention, but fortunately nurse Ruth was there to sort that. A bigger party does increase the chance of issues arising, but often this is compensated for by a greater range of skills in a group.

We were met just below Hughes Creek by Chrys Horn who had brought our transport to the West Coast, and the last night was spent beside the Whataroa, indulging in fresh veges and cheesecake.

RIGHT The sheer joy of being in mountains. Liz on Baker Peak at the edge of the Garden of Eden.
OVERLEAF (LEFT) The Garden of Eden ice plateau, a place of ambitious dreams and wild storms. Mt Farrar rises above the cloud, while Angel Col sits below it.
OVERLEAF (RIGHT) Ice crumbles into the head of the Perth Valley off the Garden of Eden. Down valley, the peaks of The Great Unknown and Little Unknown (to the right) guard the end of the ice plateau.

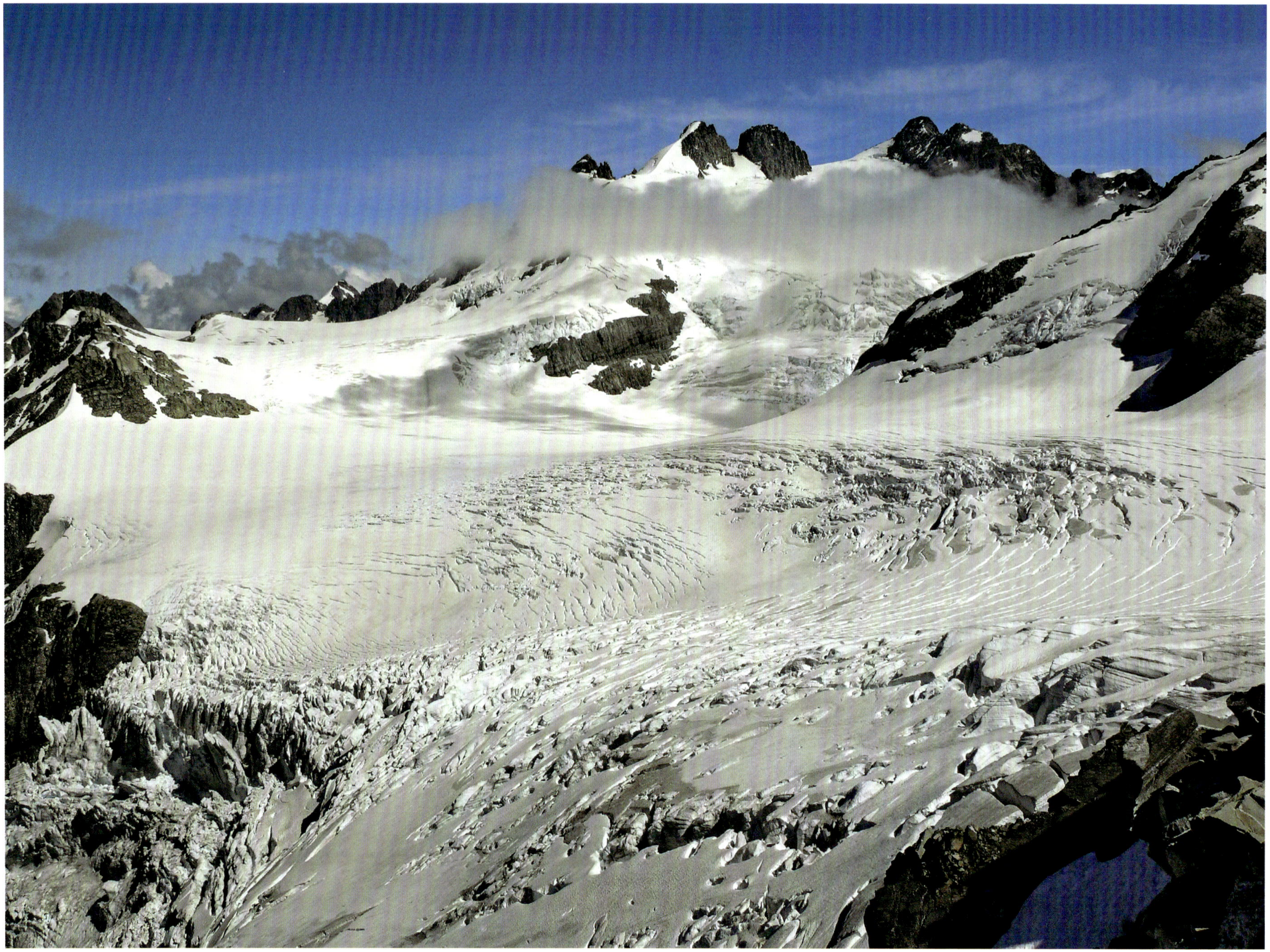

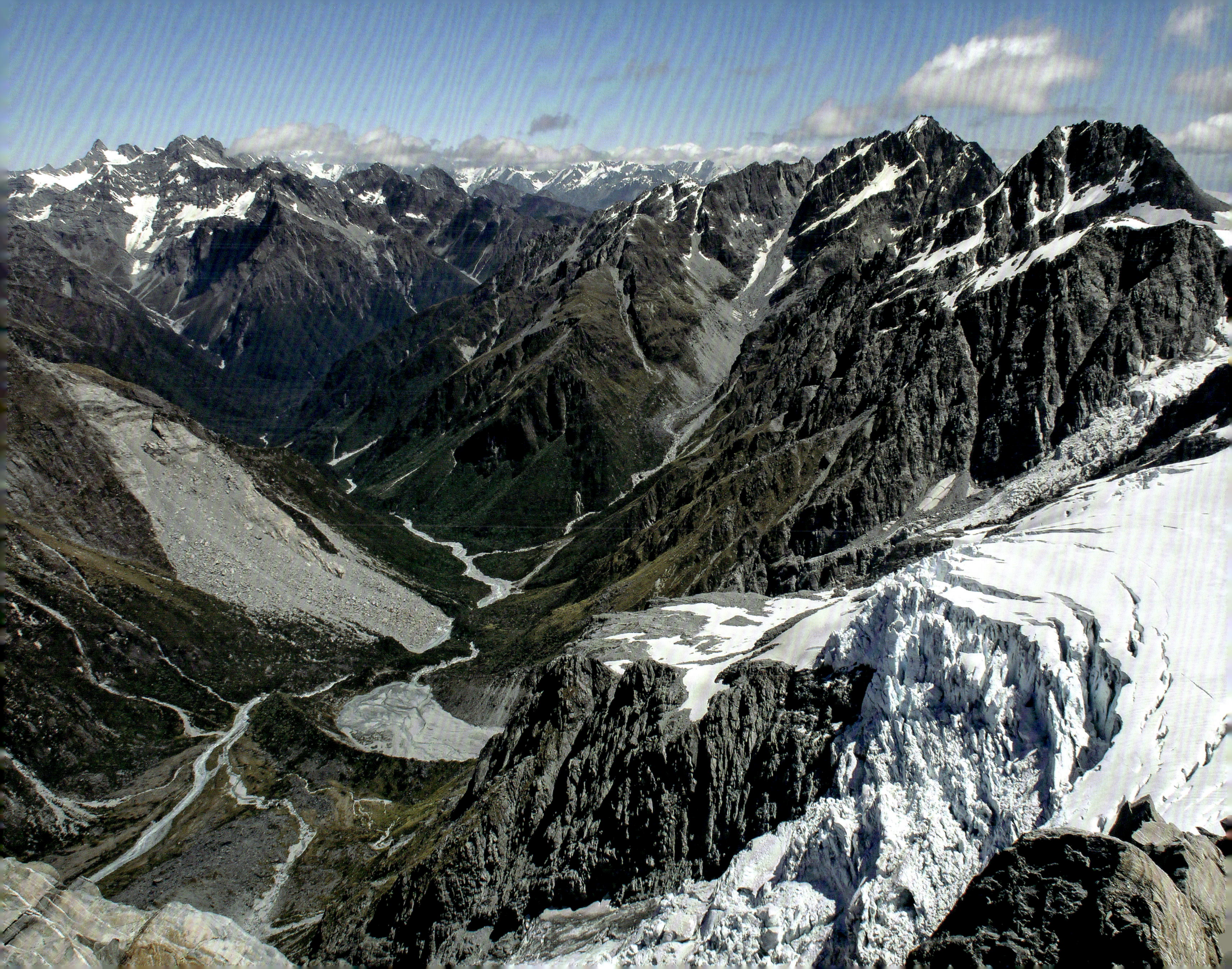

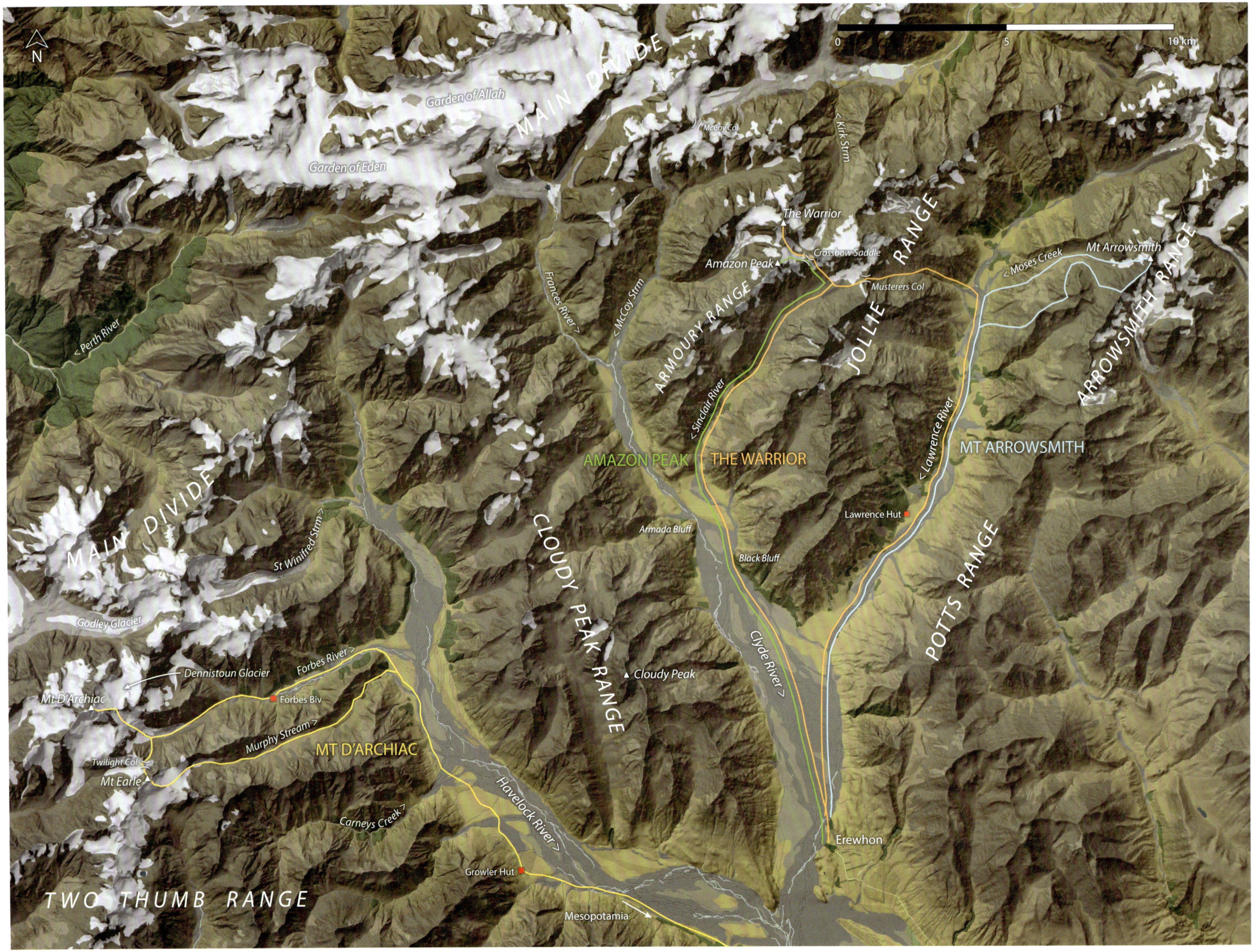

N
0
5
10 km
MAIN DIVIDE
Garden of Allah
Garden of Eden
Mccoy Col
< Kirk Strm
The Warrior
Crossbow Saddle
Amazon Peak
Musterers Col
JOLLIE RANGE
ARMOURY RANGE
< Moses Creek
Mt Arrowsmith
ARROWSMITH RANGE
< Perth River
Frances River >
< McCoy Strm
< Sinclair River
< Lawrence River
AMAZON PEAK
THE WARRIOR
MT ARROWSMITH
Lawrence Hut
MAIN DIVIDE
St Winifred Strm >
Armada Bluff
Black Bluff
CLOUDY PEAK RANGE
POTTS RANGE
Godley Glacier
Forbes River >
Dennistoun Glacier
Mt D'Archiac
Forbes Biv
Cloudy Peak
Clyde River >
Murphy Stream >
MT D'ARCHIAC
Twilight Col
Mt Earle
Havelock River >
Carneys Creek >
Erewhon
Growler Hut
TWO THUMB RANGE
Mesopotamia

CHAPTER 7
RANGITATA, THE MOUNTAINS OF EREWHON

The country in the headwaters of the Rangitata has a boundless scale to it. These are sharp, angular, dusty mountains of broken greywacke, where streams bustle tightly over wide gravel flats, knitting together in skeins to form major rivers such as the Clyde and Havelock. These rivers, and even tributaries like the Frances, are unable to be crossed for weeks at a time. It is a dry country of spiky speargrass (Peter Bain in a *Canterbury Mountaineer* article referred to a nearby area as 'Aciphyllastan', in reference to the Latin name for the speargrass genus), but it also has its charms. Little oases of mossy flats in the head of Sinclair River, alpine basins above the Lawrence, a turquoise lake in the head of Murphy Stream and, everywhere, rugged ranges full of interesting glaciers and mountains. Samuel Butler chose well to call his home here Erewhon.

Samuel Butler, Sir Julius von Haast, J.B. Acland, and others explored the region from the 1860s, with Haast naming Mt Arrowsmith after a London cartographer and D'Archiac after a French paleontologist. By the 1890s, mountain explorers such as Guy Mannering and J.R. Dennistoun were coming up with their own names (Couloir Peak, Terra Nova Pass) to add to the lexicon, as they travelled and climbed in the area. It wasn't, however, until the 1930s onwards that the Armoury Range and most peaks on it were climbed and named by Wellington or Canterbury mountaineers. These are all home mountains for the Canterbury Mountaineering Club, who have an Erewhon Branch in Ashburton.

There isn't really one classic trip for this area, but various options can offer great adventures depending on time, skill and the season. A good introduction for transalpinists is to head up the Clyde then Sinclair rivers to good camping flats below Crossbow Saddle. Both Amazon Peak and The Warrior can be climbed from here. An alternative return route can be picked over the south end of Musterers Col to Outlaw Stream. You can side the waterfall in Outlaw Stream on the true left, then continue down the Lawrence back to Erewhon.

THE WARRIOR

CLYDE RIVER–SINCLAIR RIVER–CROSSBOW SADDLE–
THE WARRIOR–SINCLAIR RIVER–MUSTERERS COL–
LAWRENCE VALLEY

3 DAYS: 10–12 FEBRUARY 2011
GS WITH PHIL NOVIS

Tucked between the Arrowsmiths and the Garden of Eden, the Armoury Range is themed around Shakespearean battles: Pistol, Bardolph, Scimitar, Spearpoint, (no relation) Battleaxe Col, Crossbow Saddle (more of that later), Outlaw, Renegade, Bandit, and two higher summits, The Warrior and Amazon Peak.

Virtually nothing was climbed in the range until December 1932 when, first Amazon Peak, then The Warrior, fell to S.A. Wiren, L.K. Wilson, H.W. Cormack and E.C.A. Ferrier. Having climbed the peaks, they then named them. Wilson is also credited with naming the range itself in 1934. For those prepared to do a bit of walking, it's a cracker little range for a long-weekend alpine fix.

I always enjoy Erewhon, leaving the car at the Jumped Up Downs, and heading up the shady track under pine trees beside *Aquilegias* and currant bushes. Then over the brow into the stark brightness of the Clyde, with its vast gravel bed stretching off towards Garden of Eden peaks crowning the Main Divide, well over 20 kilometres away. These are peaks that are often wisped with cloud like a fringe on one of the valley's Clydesdale horses. For me, it is a place filled with anticipation and memories that go back to 1969.

With the main river running hard and slightly murky against the bank near Erewhon, Phil and I were forced to cross a couple of times. Sinclair

LEFT The formidable Black Bluff in the Clyde Valley.
OPPOSITE Crossing the Clyde River with the Jumped Up Downs behind. Trips here are very dependent on river levels.

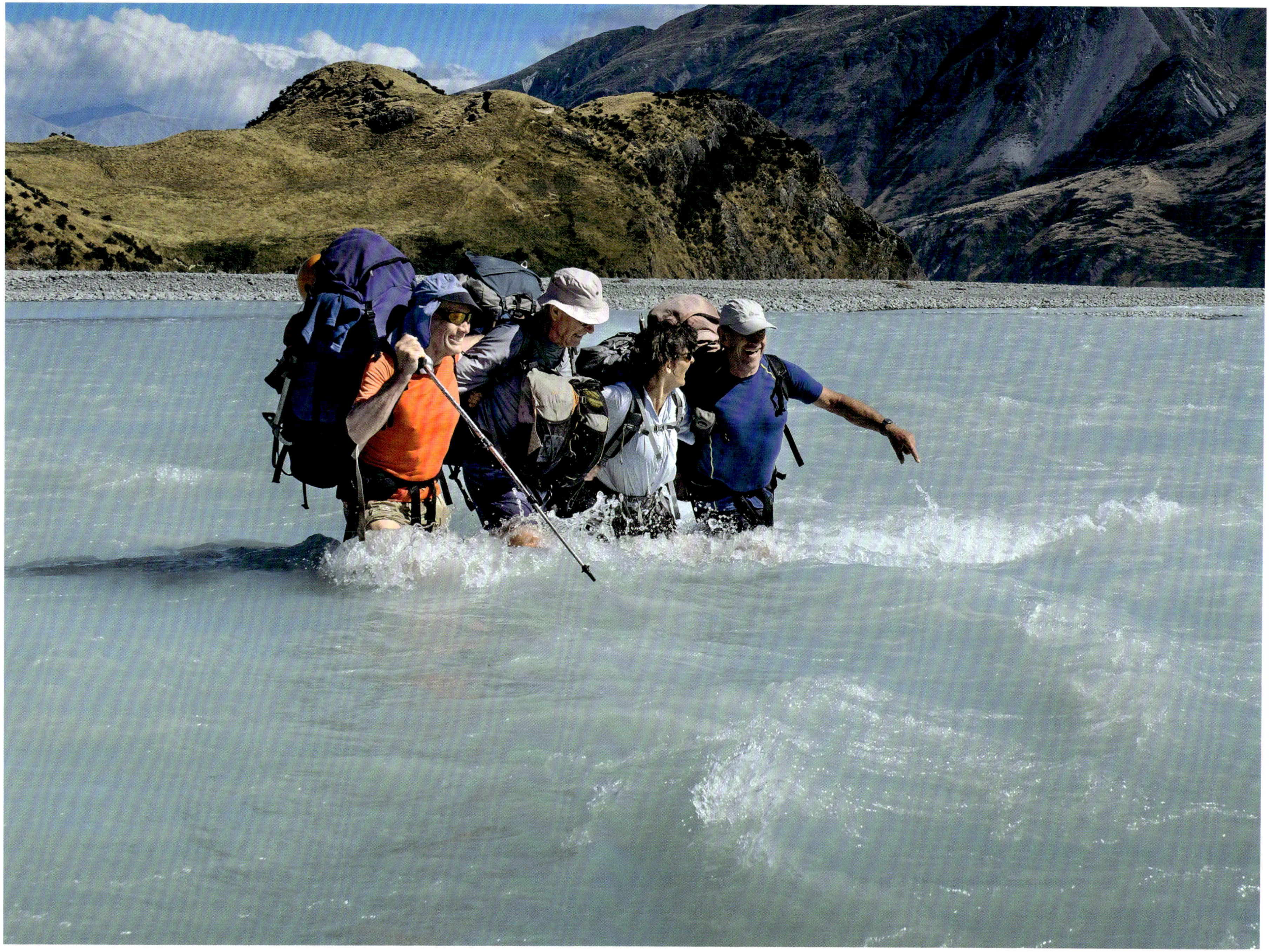

River, in comparison, ran clean and clear enough to bottle for overseas. Black Bluff, just below the confluence, looked tiny from downstream. Up close, its sheer walls of greywacke rose imposingly, leapfrogging 700 metres up towards the snowline without a break. It's a mean bluff.

Turning up the Sinclair, we bounced along on the boulders, bypassing matted scrub and sometimes speargrass with ease. Well up the valley there is an established rock bivouac, though the floor looks a bit lumpy and rain might get in. Much better than nothing, though. Up on gravel flats in the head, where gorgeous moss flushes glow green, we pitched our tent, not far from some tiny alpine lakes.

We were over Crossbow Saddle in an hour and a half in the morning, but then had to grope our way in mist towards Battleaxe Col, where the south ridge of The Warrior begins and rises to the summit. One of the challenges for mountaineering in February was getting off the snow on to the rock. Winter snows had long since retreated, and growing chasms which plunged into blackness between the rock and snow complicated things. We used the rope here. A faded sling around a chockstone told us others had had similar issues. Once on the rock we were away, scrambling as the mist cleared, finding the joy as we gained height. But it was joy tempered with much care. The rock was very broken and loose stones with a band of argillite partway up kept us concentrating and vigilant.

Phil led a lot of the way, scampering ahead then waiting for me to catch up. Once on top we had a look at the clean red slabs that show up so well from the Clyde. They looked very inviting. The north ridge, first climbed by John Nankervis, Hugh Fyson, Clayton Jeffery and Charlie Ledbrook in August 1967, looked to have more of that good rock, or what we could see of it.

During lunch I unfortunately managed to move a large rock, which crashed on to my finger – that happened to be draped over a sharp edge of rock already . . . leaving a very sorry cut finger to tape up. I've still got the scars. After an hour on top we descended the same route, on what was now a gorgeous afternoon.

And we weren't finished yet. Back at the tent we packed up and headed for Musterers Col and Outlaw Stream. We were keen to make a round trip of it, but we weren't sure the weather would hold till morning. The sun was splashing the higher peaks of the Arrowsmiths in brick orange as we crossed the col, offering spectacular views across the Lawrence. At 9.15 p.m. we called

OPPOSITE Phil crossing from the snow onto the rock of the south ridge of The Warrior.

RIGHT The Warrior, seen from the north-west.

it a day and snuggled into the tussock to cook tea. Blustery winds shook at us, but nothing was going to keep us awake.

Outlaw Stream, like many of the streams flowing into the Lawrence, sweeps down a broad open basin then cascades into a chasm, where waterfalls cut access. We sidled out on the true left and followed bits of animal trail through scrub and Spaniards before plunging down into the canyon immediately below the waterfall.

Out in the Lawrence we watched huge nor-westerly dust storms sweep down gullies and blast the whole riverbed. The air became so thick with dust that sometimes we could only see a few metres ahead. By the time we were at the Clyde our hair was full of grit, and we finished the trip with an essential swim. An unsettled sky was on the turn, and a storm was on its way.

AMAZON PEAK

CLYDE RIVER–SINCLAIR RIVER–CROSSBOW SADDLE–AMAZON PEAK–SINCLAIR RIVER–CLYDE RIVER

3 DAYS: 5–7 MAY 1989
GS WITH MALCOLM GARNHAM, BARBARA BROWN AND SVEN BRABYN

Sometimes a significant event will define an adventure. Memories coalesce, and it becomes *that* trip. *That*, in this case, was falling stones. We had come up the Clyde Valley with plans to climb Amazon Peak, a reasonably straightforward, if not taxing, weekend out, with an approach the same as for The Warrior. We camped on those same upper flats. Crossbow Saddle loomed above us, but we didn't know it had us in its sights.

All seasons have their own influence on the mountains. Late autumn is a time when the rocks are most exposed, and in much of the Southern Alps this often means loose falling stones. Couple that with concrete-hard snow slopes which accelerate anything falling on them at this time of year, and the danger is heightened. Sven decided not to join us for the climb and stayed in camp. It turned out to be good intuition.

As we cramponed our way up, a zinger stone bigger than a fist purred past us less than 10 metres away and 3 metres up in the air. It was the speed that impressed. If that connected, it would blow you apart.

From Crossbow, we dropped on to snow feeding the Kirk Glacier and followed this up to a col overlooking Billy McCoy Stream. From there, long snow slopes and a bit of rock-scrambling took us to the top. Nothing particularly difficult; just a wonderful thing to be doing on a fabulous early-winter day.

The descent was uneventful too, until we were descending that last 50 metres of shaded, bullet-hard snow under Crossbow Saddle. Not steep country, but the snow was polished hard. A sharp noise made us look up to see several boulders falling from the ridge above. Tense and concentrating, we tried to guess the trajectories of the larger ones, which were more than half a metre across. They were headed for us. Barb, being further back, managed to get out of the way off to the side, and to our good luck the bigger boulders flashed past between us.

A small stone hit Malcolm on the arm, but I was watching another random stone, a flying disc about 200 millimetres across and about 150 millimetres thick, that hit the ice running and had me in its sights. It was travelling like a bullet and each time it glanced off the ice it accelerated. It wasn't rising high. Too fast. It kept a low profile, humming its way down on a slightly curving trajectory. I was so exactly in its path that I tensed, standing legs apart on the ice, iceaxe in my uphill hand, deciding which side to jump in my crampons to avoid it.

I never got a chance. By the time I was making the decision the missile hit. All I knew was a stinging sensation on my inner thigh as it went between my legs, striking just a glancing blow, but grazing my leg and immediately bringing up a bruise. My iceaxe was completely blown out of my hands. I spun around looking for it. It was about seven metres below me, and then I did a double-take because I could also see my axe about seven metres below me, but in a slightly different place. It made no sense.

It slowly dawned on me. The rock had hit my axe, broken it clean in two, then blown both pieces between my legs as it, too, had rocketed between them. I had had the greatest of good luck. A few centimetres left, and my femur would have been pulverised. A few centimetres up and it would have been the family jewels. In the 1980s we had no PLB and just thinking about the pain potential made my eyes water.

We never quite know how we will react in situations like this. I talked. Gabbled, some might say. I knew how lucky I had been. But I had a lot of adrenalin to use up and I did it exercising my tongue, and giving thanks for being alive. Still, Malcolm had put up with that before, and so had Barb.

Back at our campsite, Sven had already packed and headed down, and we sped after him. My leg was sore and sensitive, but all I felt was fortunate. Dusk fell as we rounded under Black Bluff and continued down the boulders. In the distance the dark silhouettes of the tall pines at the Jumped Up Downs stood out, reassuring and familiar, Erewhon's sentinels at the roadend, but we all knew they were many kilometres away yet. Those pines play tricks on you in a riverbed as vast as this. But we got there. I still have bits of the axe somewhere in my gear shed.

OPPOSITE Amazon Peak (left) and The Warrior (right) from Musterers Col.

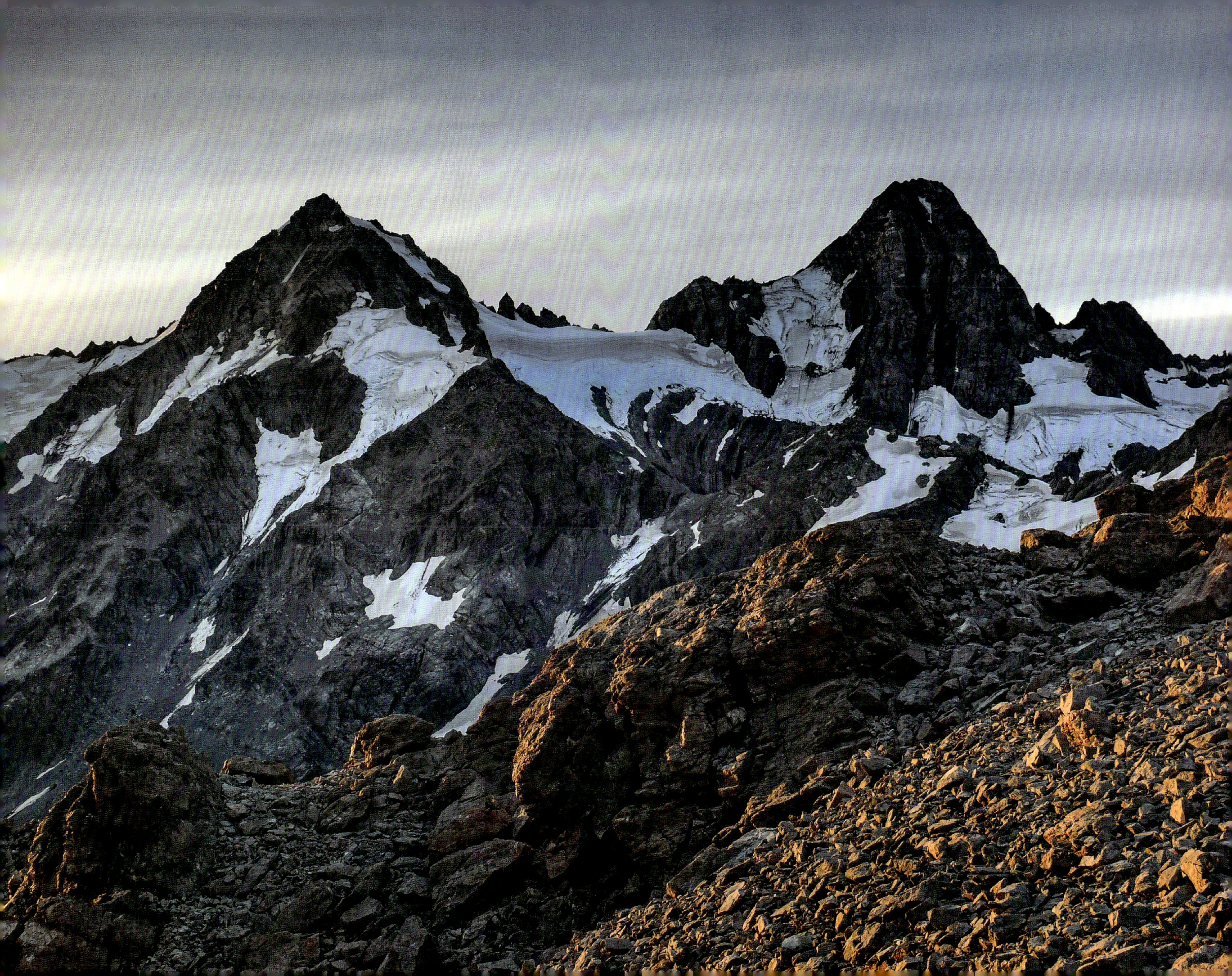

MT ARROWSMITH

CLYDE VALLEY–LAWRENCE VALLEY–MT ARROWSMITH TRAVERSE–LAWRENCE VALLEY–CLYDE

3 DAYS: 3–5 DECEMBER 2000

GS WITH JOHNNY MULHERON

The Arrowsmith Range is one of the mountain homes of the Canterbury Mountaineering Club, who built and look after two huts there, Banfield Memorial Hut and Cameron Hut. The relationship goes much deeper than a couple of huts, though, and many of their members over the generations have lived out some of their best and worst days on its summits and in its shadows.

Mt Arrowsmith is a peak on many a climber's bucket list, with them often climbing it from the Cameron Valley, but we opted for a route out of the Lawrence Valley. The mountain was first climbed by Hugh Wright and guide J.P. Murphy in January 1912 from the Lawrence, and then again from this side in April 1934 by CMC members D. Brough and L.R. Hewitt.

East-coast gravel approaches are renowned for their boring riverbed travel, however, our trip in was anything but. That's one of the great things about the hills – they can be a great place to yack. I didn't say much. It was a little like having one of those telephone calls where you go away and make coffee and come back an hour later and the other person is still going. Therapy can be like this, and time passed quickly.

Midway up the valley we found a dry, sheltered campsite and settled in, snug and toasty. The 1967 *NZAJ* described the south ridge as 'a good route', so we planned to climb it. By five the next morning we were away, heading up a spur on a side ridge and making things difficult for ourselves by climbing higher than we needed before swinging down into Moses Creek basin. The creek is named after Moses Rock, on the lip of the basin which, viewed from the valley, is a rock outcrop with a stream leaping from near the top of it.

Scree-bashing gave way to snow slopes that increased in steepness up towards the ridge. The route was fun. Nothing particularly difficult, but it kept us on our toes with a bit of exposure and the odd gendarme to negotiate or bypass. And it took us quite a while, but with over a kilometre of broken rock on a narrow ridge, this is not surprising – even if it was to us. It was 3 p.m. before we reached the summit, and views down as far as Aoraki Mt Cook and over to the Armoury Range kept us excited. What a wonderful place.

Looking for an easier way back, we picked slopes to the west, down onto snow, then into a saddle before glissading back into Moses Creek. By eight o'clock we were back at camp after 15 hours away. The day had been long, satisfying, and we were both knackered. Two thousand metres is enough climbing for one day. The evening was still and clear.

Feeling very much at one with the world around me, I dragged my sleeping bag into the open and slept out, listening to the sounds of the valley, smelling the grass and gazing at the impossibly distant stars, slowly unwinding across the sky. There is no greater peace than to drift off looking up at nature after a long, hard day, feeling toasty and comfortable.

Walking down the Lawrence next morning into a light southerly we stopped in the riverbed and stripped for a swim and clean up before arriving at the car. The runholder of the station had a trailer to manoeuvre on to the back of a truck, so we helped him out before heading back to town and to work for the afternoon.

OPPOSITE Mt Arrowsmith (right) and the upper Lawrence Valley from Musterers Col. Red Peak and North Peak to the far left.

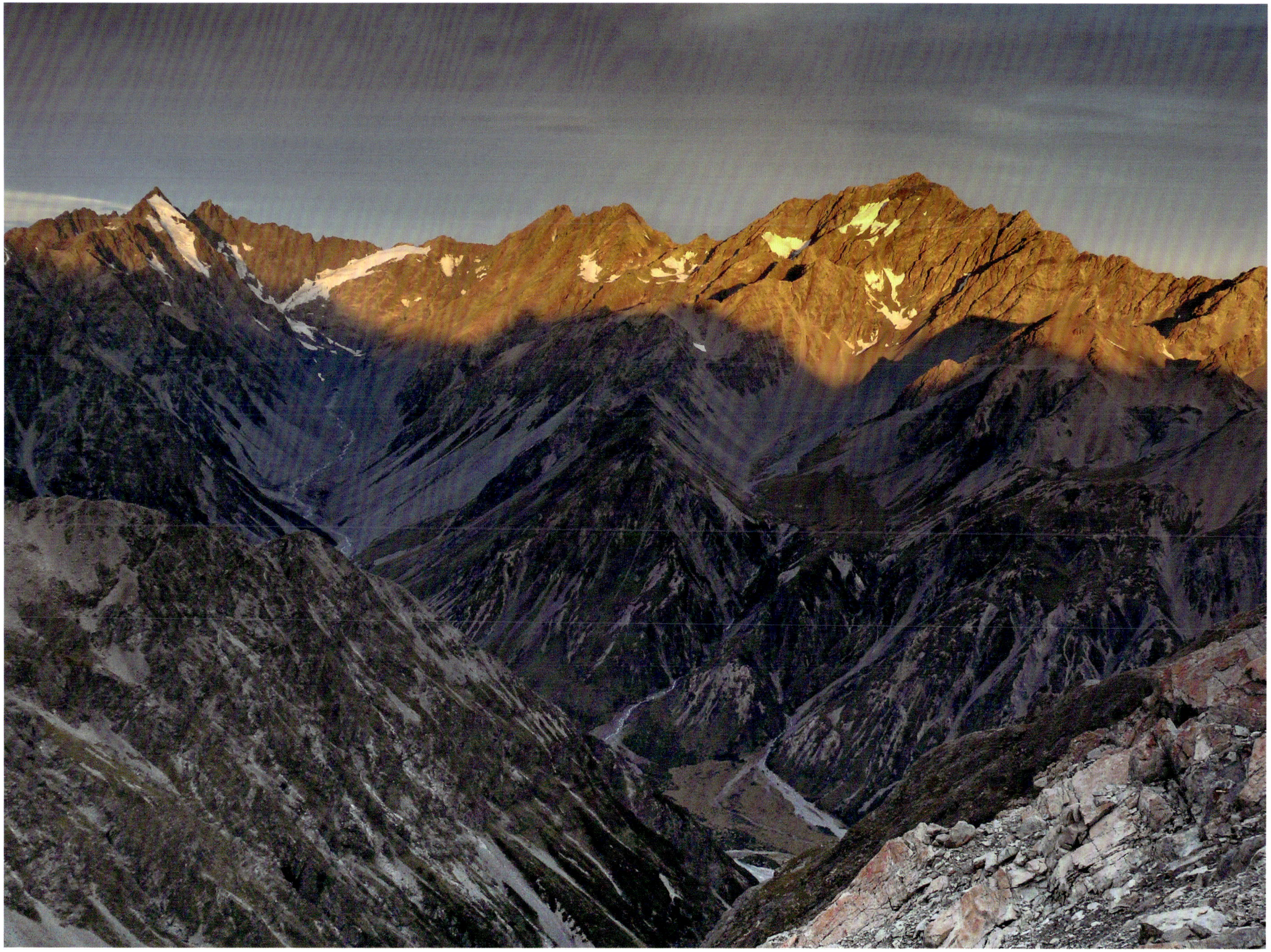

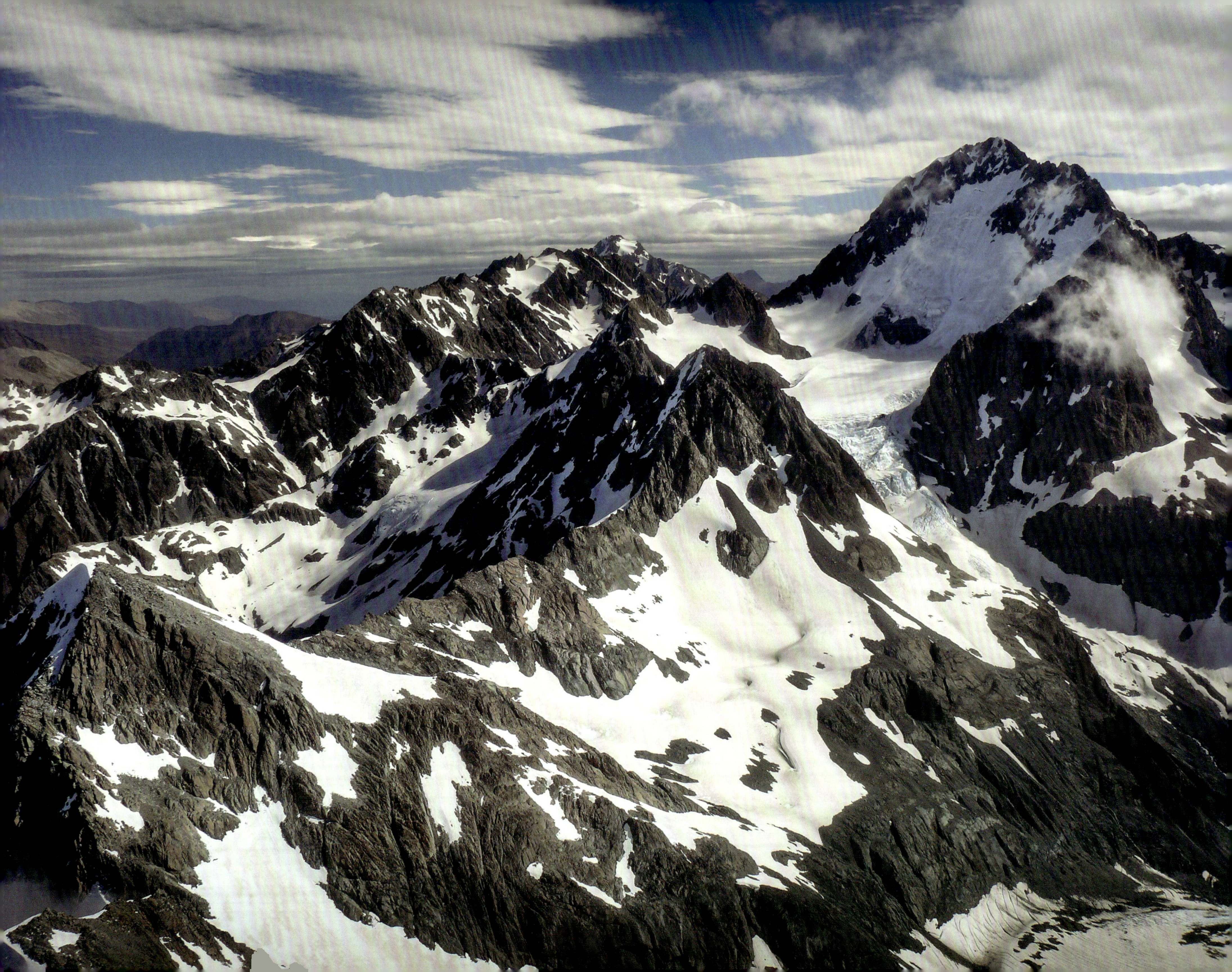

MT D'ARCHIAC

MESOPOTAMIA STATION–HAVELOCK RIVER–FORBES VALLEY–
MT D'ARCHIAC–TWILIGHT COL–MT EARLE–MURPHY GLACIER–
MURPHY STREAM–HAVELOCK RIVER

5 DAYS: 5–9 JANUARY 2002
GS WITH JOHNNY MULHERON

As you do before trips, we watched the weather closely. It wasn't promising. In the days preceding, rain had deluged the upper Rangitata, and the Havelock was still very swollen, delaying our arrival at Mesopotamia. Cloud hung on the peaks up-valley, and the listless wind hadn't changed from the west. The river wasn't able to be crossed, and alternative scrub-bashing and high sidles didn't appeal and would put our timetable back further. Laurie Prouting, who was at his airstrip beside the road, suddenly seemed a great way to jump-start the trip and we asked him to fly us to his airstrip at Growler Hut, a place many off-roaders drive to.

We lost the first hour listening to the dangers of climbing, the need for care, the need for . . . well, everything really. But eventually we landed at the Growler at 3 p.m. Bowling on up the valley like excited schoolkids we still had a bit of matagouri bashing to keep out of the river, but we finally reached Forbes Bivvy at 8 p.m.

In the best traditions of VUWTC, it was clear we needed a bit of professionalism for this trip so Johnny, who is quicker than me, began calling me guide. He, of course, could thereafter only be declared the client. And I have to say, in the good-natured way that banter can take over a trip, this little device kept both of us on our toes and doubled the fun.

Overnight the rain returned, easing to drizzle with dawn. The client in his sleeping bag slept on, but by lunchtime the rocks were dry. The guide raised the client and we left at 1 p.m. to put in a high camp at 1800 metres beside the South Forbes Glacier, slogging up the boulders before taking to the snow, then simple rock bluffs. Continuous mist returned, before tipping over into drizzle. And later rain. Still not promising.

At four in the morning the client still didn't think it looked good, with drizzle again. But by five, things were improving, and we started breakfast. Heading up the South Forbes towards the east ridge, we noticed that the big schrund across the upper glacier looked filled, so we headed up a steepening snow gully known colloquially as 'the Motorway'. Higher, we headed up rock, then back to the snow to the summit ridge. The day was calm, and blue sky competed about equally with the clouds, which continued to drift from the west and roll around on the Two Thumb Range. But we knew we had it in the bag, and we followed a narrow snow arête up to the summit at 1.30 p.m. The client and his guide shook hands.

D'Archiac is a little more demanding than many mountains. The first ascent was made in an enthusiastic manner by an irrepressible Jim R. Dennistoun with Lawrence M. Earle and guide Jack Clarke in March 1910. The second ascent in January 1933 by a CMC party of S.H. Barnett, Edgar R. Williams and Bruce Turner used the same South Forbes approach, climbing a small peak en route they named The Onlooker. On the descent, like the first 1910 party, they had a night out, and soon after midnight it began to snow.

It settled lightly on our sou'westers and capes, making movement undesirable. I have a very vivid memory of Edgar looking like an Indian squaw in his waterproof cape. He was sitting under a shelf of rock, head and all under the cape, feet in his rucsac [sic] and a lighted candle somewhere under his chin shining through the cape and casting a glow on the rocks and snow around, while in the background the drifting snow continued to pour through the gap like a mystic waterfall into nothingness.

They descended the Godley Glacier in snow and drenching rain, then circled the whole mountain, returning to their Forbes camp three days later via Separation Stream. Having been up it one evening in the past, Edgar Williams knew that the Separation led back to the Forbes. Now, in the same place at dusk, they named it Twilight Col.

OPPOSITE Mt D'Archiac and the Dennistoun Glacier from McClure Peak on the Main Divide. To the left, the terrain drains into the Havelock catchment and the Godley Glacier can be seen in the bottom-right corner.

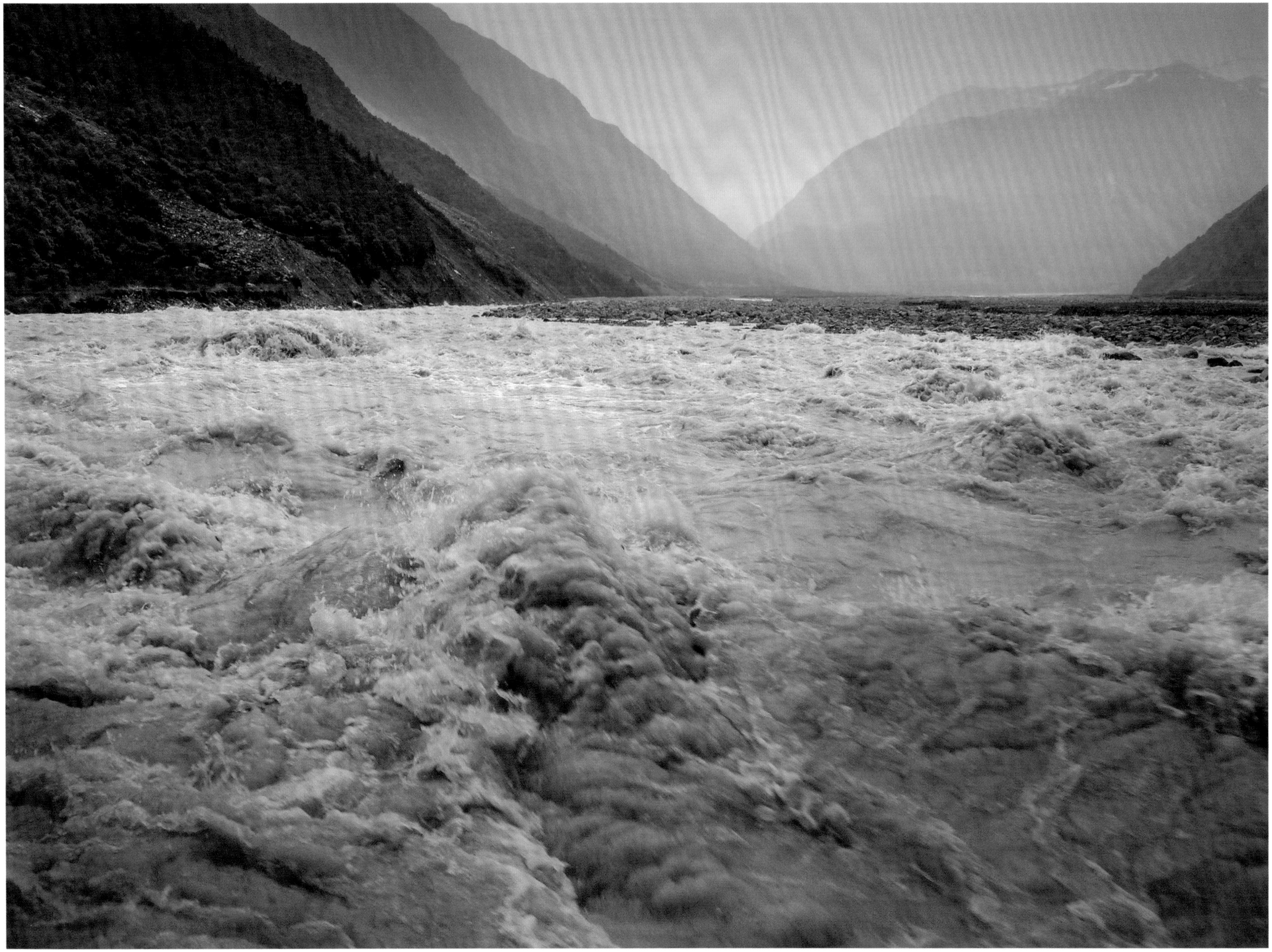

No night out for us, though. We were tucked up in our tent listening to rain again. There hadn't been much of a weather window. We had two days to get back to the car, and no self-respecting transalpinist wants to walk out the way they came in, so we also headed over Twilight Col, up Mt Earle and down Murphy Stream. Holes in the mist led us up a gully onto the Two Thumb Range at 2094 metres, where snow showers began. Climbing greywacke rocks, we were engulfed in mist then driving sleet, especially on the summit of Mt Earle. It was already 4.30 p.m., and the idea of another night high up wasn't at all attractive to client or guide. In this weather we were gunning for Murphys Bivvy. Murphy Stream turned out to be a magic place in the very head. Dropping out of the mist, we passed a stunning little lake before tipping down-valley into the tussocks. And then Spaniards and scrub, with an over-excited bubbly stream running through it. But especially lots of Spaniards.

Parkas had been pretty important on this trip, and the client was very enthusiastic about his brand new red Goretex one. By the time the bivvy was reached at dark we were both saturated through, and the gloss had gone off that new parka somewhat. It was returned as leaky, and the manufacturer replied that they didn't know what it had been used for, but it was full of micro holes . . . Spaniards have a lot to answer for.

The upside was that the bivvy was dry, with dry firewood and a fireplace. This is my idea of heaven after a full, wet, cold day. We relished it, letting our imaginations run wild with all sorts of outrageous guide/client claims. Meanwhile the dead sticks of aromatic mountain celery pine (*Phyllocladus alpinus*) on the fire scented the bivvy. Outside, the rain continued.

Not really knowing the route down-valley made us look around a bit in the morning, but with the odd subtle cairn here and there we managed to drop down into the gorge. Murphy Stream couldn't be crossed so we went further, to find a place lower down. Then it was all plain gravel-bashing back to Growler Hut, dodgy crossings over part of the Havelock, and a long slog back to the car.

LEFT The Clyde in high flood above Armada Bluff.
OPPOSITE *Celmisia* flowering in McCoy Stream.

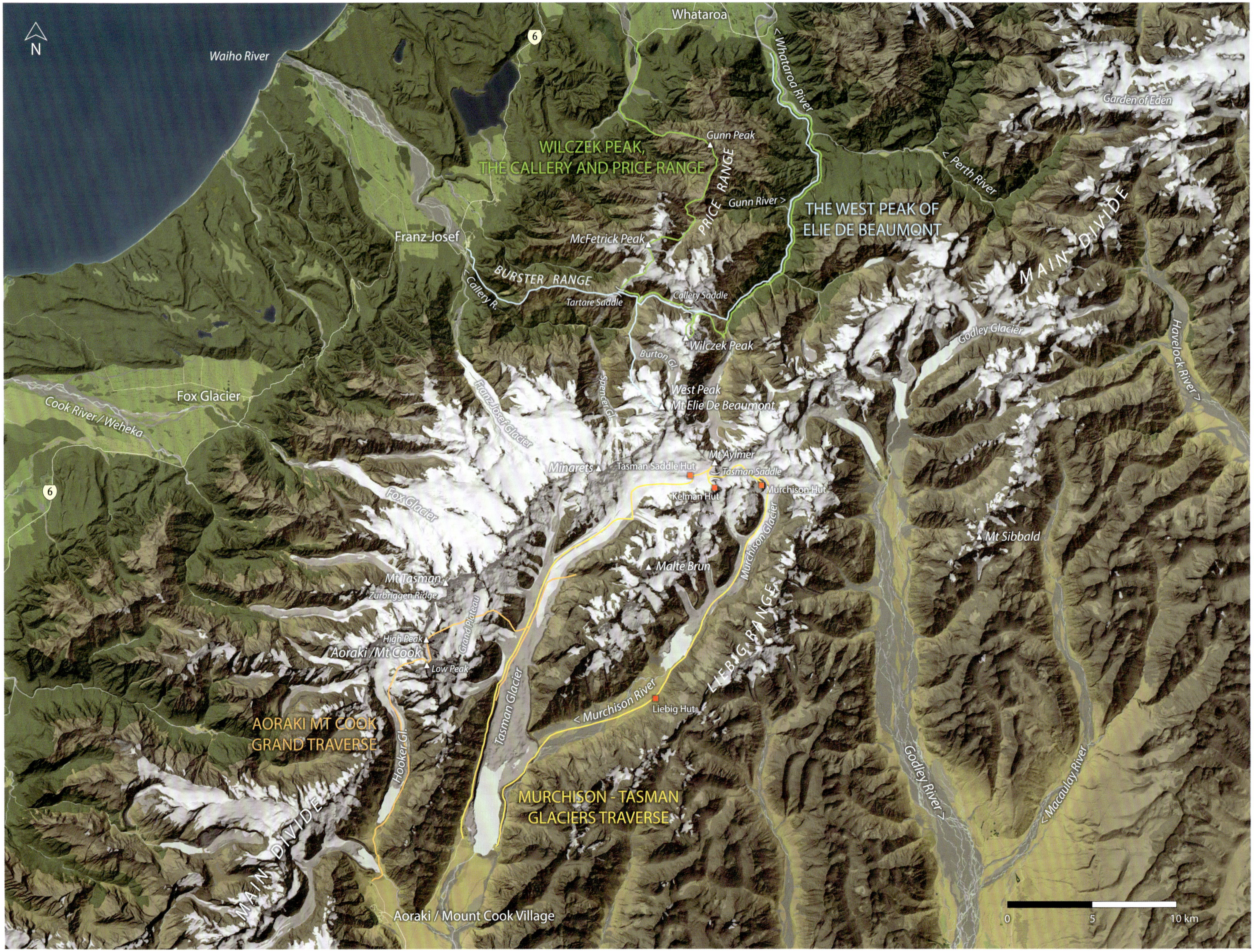

N
Waiho River
Whataroa
6
< Whataroa River
Garden of Eden
Gunn Peak
WILCZEK PEAK,
THE CALLERY AND PRICE RANGE
< Perth River
PRICE RANGE
Gunn River >
THE WEST PEAK OF
ELIE DE BEAUMONT
Franz Josef
McFetrick Peak
MAIN DIVIDE
BURSTER RANGE
< Callery R.
Tartare Saddle
Callery Saddle
Godley Glacier
Havelock River >
Wilczek Peak
Burton Gl.
Fox Glacier
Spencer Gl.
Franz Josef Glacier
West Peak
Mt Elie De Beaumont
Cook River / Weheka
Mt Aylmer
Minarets
Tasman Saddle Hut
Tasman Saddle
Kelman Hut
Murchison Hut
6
Fox Glacier
Mt Sibbald
Malte Brun
Murchison Glacier
Mt Tasman
Zurbriggen Ridge
Grand Plateau
LIEBIG RANGE
High Peak
Aoraki / Mt Cook
Low Peak
Tasman Glacier
< Murchison River
Liebig Hut
AORAKI MT COOK
GRAND TRAVERSE
Hooker Gl.
Godley River >
< Macaulay River
MURCHISON - TASMAN
GLACIERS TRAVERSE
MAIN DIVIDE
Aoraki / Mount Cook Village
0
5
10 km

CHAPTER 8
ELIE DE BEAUMONT TO AORAKI MT COOK

Between Elie De Beaumont at the head of the Tasman Glacier and Aoraki Mt Cook lie the highest and most glaciated peaks in the Southern Alps. With about 12 kilometres of white ice and another 12 kilometres covered in moraine, the Tasman Glacier is the largest in New Zealand. Further east the less-visited Murchison Glacier also begins in sparkling snowfields, but after about 7 kilometres the white ice slides under boulder-covered moraine that continues a few more kilometres before it, too, terminates in a glacial lake. Draining west and north from Elie De Beaumont, the Callery and Whataroa valleys have long ago lost much of their ice, but they make up for that in the fierceness of their gorges and their isolation.

Following an earlier visit to the Tasman Glacier with Julius von Haast, Edwin Sealy surveyed the Tasman, Mueller, Hooker and Godley glaciers in 1867, taking photos as he went. From the Godley, Sealy crossed what is now Sealy Pass into the headwaters of Scone Creek on the West Coast before returning; one of the earliest transalpine crossings of the Main Divide in the region.

A year after Green's near-successful attempt on Aoraki Mt Cook in 1882, the Lendenfelds travelled up the Tasman Glacier and climbed Hochstetter Dome. Various further attempts were made on Aoraki Mt Cook, but it was Kiwi amateurs Tom Fyfe, George Graham and Jack Clarke who first climbed our highest peak on Christmas Day, 1894.

Tom Fyfe later crossed Lendenfeld Saddle to the Whymper Glacier and Whataroa River, ending up with a poisoned leg at Greymouth Hospital, where his stories inspired the start of Dr Teichelmann's climbing exploration. Everything is connected. The Callery gorges became the province of miners after gold, and some of their names feature through this chapter.

My trip suggestion is up the Murchison Glacier, over Tasman Saddle and down the Tasman Glacier. Or vice versa. The crux is the Murchison headwall under Tasman Saddle, and advice needs to be sought over its condition before leaving. Crevasses often cut it off by January, and the snow slopes are subject to slab-avalanche conditions. Like many of the classic trips in this book, it is an alpine undertaking and requires mountaineering skills and gear, but is not particularly difficult. Some will balk at the moraine-bashing required. Treat it for what it is, allow time to enjoy the views, keep pack weights down and pick campsites carefully. It is still a great alpine area to visit on foot.

THE WEST PEAK OF ELIE DE BEAUMONT

CALLERY RIVER–BURSTER RANGE–BURTON GLACIER–
WEST PEAK OF ELIE DE BEAUMONT–CALLERY SADDLE–
WHATAROA RIVER

8 DAYS: 12–19 JANUARY 1977
GS WITH IAN WILKINS AND DAVE SOWRY

Peter Graham was once lowered on a rope into the depths of the Callery Gorge to get a gold nugget. He reported that it was so confined and dark at the bottom that he could see two stars in the middle of the day. We never found that particular spot, but the magic of the idea sowed seeds. I wanted to go there, and climb Elie De Beaumont from the west along the way.

Prospector George Park explored the Callery in 1888 and again in 1890 with his brother James. And it was gold mining that originally led Peter Graham into the valley in 1899. Later that year Dr Teichelmann asked to join Arthur Woodham and Peter Graham on their next prospecting trip to take photos. On that trip Teichelmann and Graham discovered that the real gold was the mountains themselves and two climbing careers were born.

From the Waiho confluence, in 1977, we followed the overgrown goldminers' trail along vertical green walls about 100 metres above the Callery River on the true left. About four hours in, we reached Big Beach, a small break in the gorge. There wasn't much human sign after that. We were on our own.

Across the river lay Mt Burster, and we headed up. A 1200-metre climb through West Coast scrub took half a day, with seven-day packs full of tramping and climbing gear. It certainly slowed us down. On the Burster Range we were in mist and drizzle, and every now and then buttresses would appear to block our way. Up close, there was always a way through, though.

Ian, Dave and I knew each other through the Hutt Valley Tramping Club, and we worked well together in this sort of country. The mist, which had kept us on our toes, began to break up as we approached Tatare Saddle, and the sky cleared. In the beautiful, still evening that followed, we found ourselves in the sort of place a transalpinist dreams about. The Tatare Valley and gorges muttered far below on one side, the Callery on the other, and sweeping views ran along the Main Divide from Elie De Beaumont to the Minarets. Talus paving, tarns, snowbanks, and alpine plants in flower surrounded our camp.

The following day we dropped into the upper Callery. At that time there were only clear, shallow, tiny lakes in the valley. When I returned in 2007, underlying ice had melted and left a much larger lake the colour of sludge, but that has changed yet again, and now the lake is a beautiful turquoise.

Back to 1977. From the head of the Callery we sidled our way up onto the Burton Glacier and set up a rocky camp in anticipation of a climb on Elie De Beaumont.

Night faded as we headed up boulders, then a snow couloir towards the Burton Ridge. Our route took us onto the upper Johannes Glacier, where big crevasses, some partly covered over, made us take care. When we had left camp, a few wisps of high cloud passed quickly over the sky. Now, a more

ABOVE The moraine-covered Burton Glacier drains the flanks of Elie De Beaumont. The Burton Ridge is under cloud to the right.

OPPOSITE On the Price Range tops, with the view from Gunn Peak of Fardowner Peak.

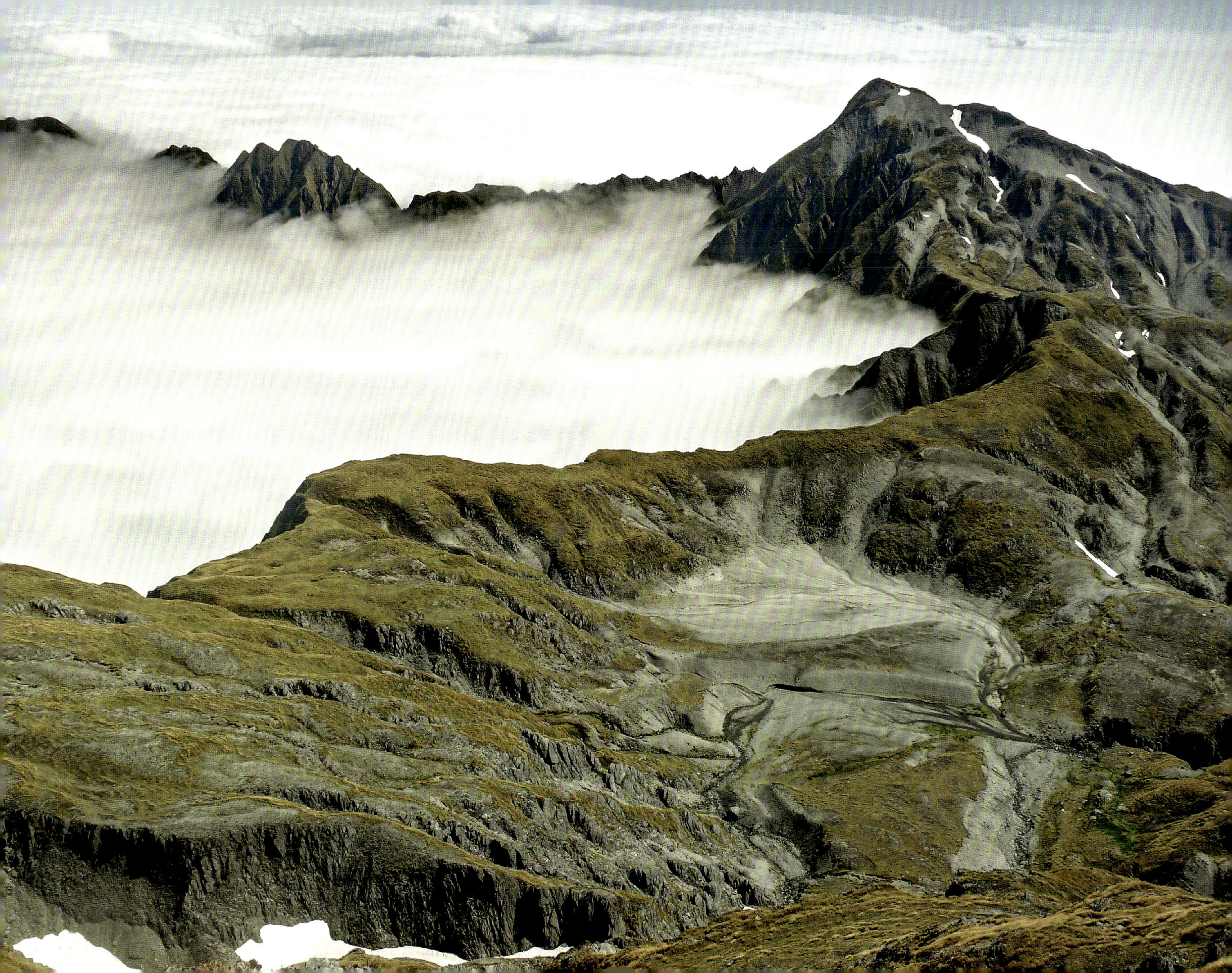

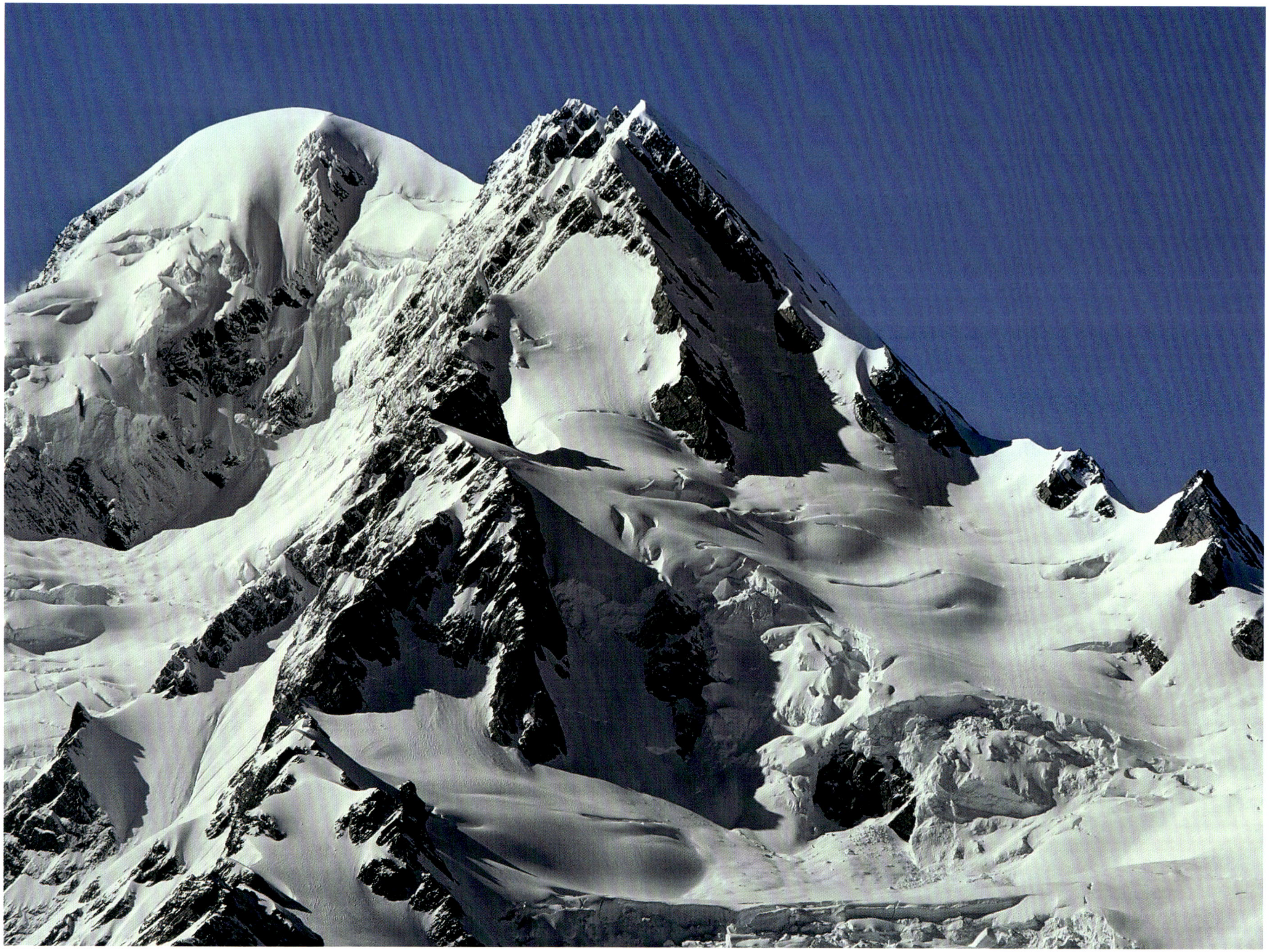

ominous steely grey sheet was forming, throwing hogsbacks ahead over the Main Divide and cold, unsettled wind gusts rattling on the snow. The upper 300 metres of the climb on exposed sastrugi-covered slabs led us to our summit, the West Peak of Elie De Beaumont, 3054 metres, at 11.30 a.m.

A storm was brewing, and we didn't linger as the wind started to shunt us around. We descended without the rope and were back at camp by three-thirty. Drizzle followed overnight and throughout the next day, as we inspected various bivvy rocks, including one marked The Monastery. It was cramped, had health and safety issues, and no close water. But it was shelter.

For us, it was now time to leave the Callery. Waving goodbye to a solitary whio, probably a juvenile male, we headed for Callery Saddle. A part-clearance saw us over, but mist thickened as we plunged towards the Whataroa. We ended up scrambling down uncomfortably steep ribs, and clinging to dodgy vegetation with no view and little idea whether we were in for a soft or hard exit. But we reached flatter ground and headed down-valley. It was now mid afternoon, drizzle was turning to rain, and the river still had to be crossed. Picking up a good track we hurried on, bursting into applause when a bridge appeared. Without that, we would have been sunk.

We stumbled into Butler Junction Hut, wet as shags and eternally grateful to find dry shelter. All night the thunder rolled, and lightning painted strobe effects around the hut. The rain fell in waterfalls as we drifted off, dry, warm and snug, enjoying the glow of fire embers. With the rain still drumming down next morning, we made it a pit day, kept the fire going, and felt smug that the walkout down the rest of the Whataroa was a breeze on a Forestry track. But that was for tomorrow.

OPPOSITE Elie De Beaumont, with the pointed West Peak and Burton Ridge on the skyline (right). Below is the Johannes Glacier.

RIGHT Deep in the Callery Gorge at Big Beach, about 2.5 kilometres up from the Waiho confluence. A few old mining relics lay buried amongst the ferns in 1977.

WILCZEK PEAK, THE CALLERY AND PRICE RANGE

WHATAROA VALLEY–CALLERY SADDLE–CALLERY VALLEY–MCFETRICK PEAK–PRICE RANGE

5 DAYS: 15–20 JANUARY 2007
GS WITH PHIL NOVIS AND BRIAN ADAMS

It was 30 years since I had been in the Callery, but I hadn't forgotten the fierce Maximilian and Tatare ranges that surround it. There had to be a nice little transalpine trip there somewhere. Phil and Brian were keen to check out the head of the Callery, I was fascinated by Wilczek and McFetrick peaks and a traverse of the Price Range seemed like a great way to finish.

On a mild, overcast evening we camped on a grass flat about an hour up the Whataroa. With packs for five days and a bit of climbing gear, three of us churned up the Whataroa, reaching Whymper Hut above the Whymper Glacier moraine in nine and a half hours. I was stuffed, and feeling a little sick. When Phil had finished cooking, he asked how he should serve. Brian suggested Phil fill his 2-litre icecream container then divide the rest between us. My stomach didn't care.

Getting up to Callery Saddle proved a bit troublesome. Somewhere around 1500 metres we ended up having to abseil down a slab to get onto a more practical route. You shouldn't need to do that, especially on a fine morning. Once on the glacier under Callery Saddle we left our heavy packs for the afternoon and headed up with basic climbing gear onto the Maximilian Range, grabbing the opportunity to climb Wilczek Peak on our way across.

West Coast mist was beginning to swirl and boil, but we still enjoyed some limited views. Approaching the peak from Whataroa snow slopes, we traversed over onto the Callery Glacier on the way back. In the summit rocks we found a small rusty can tucked away that was very likely the one D.A. Carty's party left with a note on the first ascent in December 1937. Carty ran some great trips into this area in the 1930s, inspiring many others with his enthusiastic *New Zealand Alpine Journal* accounts and maps.

By 5 p.m. we were back at our packs and heading over Callery Saddle. Sidling down and left, to avoid steep rock slabs, we scrunched our way under icefields into the head of the desolate grey Callery, with its walls of broken rock. The mist followed our tracks down. A couple of Southern black-backed gulls wheeled overhead, upset at being disturbed. Many alpine lakes have a pair of resident seagulls, and their strident cries in the distance added to the vastness of the place. Sometimes they nest on the lake shore.

Fine gravels in a sheltered bay at the lower end of the lake made a wonderful campsite. Mist hung quietly over us when I went to bed outside. Later, drizzle made me seek the shelter of the tent. Sleeping out is always a gamble.

The mist softened overnight, leaving holes of blue sky. From Tatare Saddle we climbed to McFetrick Peak, dodging slots and schrunds on mostly good snow travel. Just over a kilometre further, we dropped into the head of the Gunn Valley, and headed down to more friendly tussock flats under Mt Cloher, where there were lots of comfy campsites.

A decaying high-pressure system left the tussocks wet with drizzle for our climb up to the Price Range in the morning. The Price Range tops were magical, with wide flat basins tiled in schist plates, scarps off to the side, and short tussocks and carpet plants interspersed with outcrops. Snow banks lay about and our views from Gunn Peak extended all the way back to the Main Divide. From Fardowner Peak the range drops wildly down as razorbacks into a sea of subalpine scrub, but we weren't going that way.

West off Gunn Peak lies a detached spur of flat tussock tops, separated by steep crumbly rock and eroding gutter creeks. We went that way. Our last night was spent beside a fire on the tops, camped by a tarn where frogs called. Mist hung in curtains around us, like shutters on the window. No views.

In the morning we headed down a scrubby spur expecting the worst and it delivered, but the suffering was cut short when we stumbled onto a lightly marked track. Hallelujah! One thousand metres lower and we were out of the cloud beside Darnley Creek, heading down flats in the Waitangitaona River to the road.

OPPOSITE Phil (left) and Brian at our campsite in the head of the Callery River.

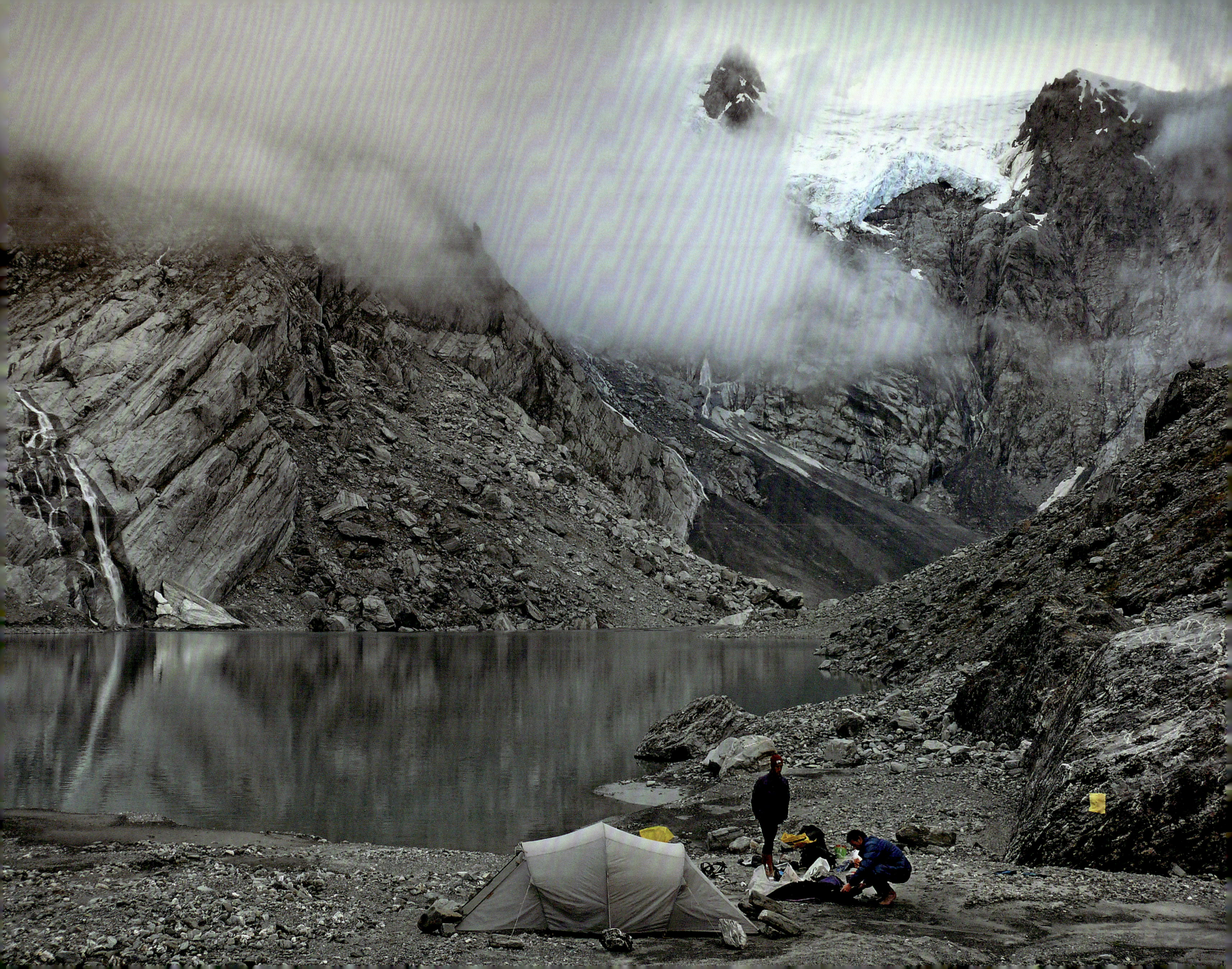

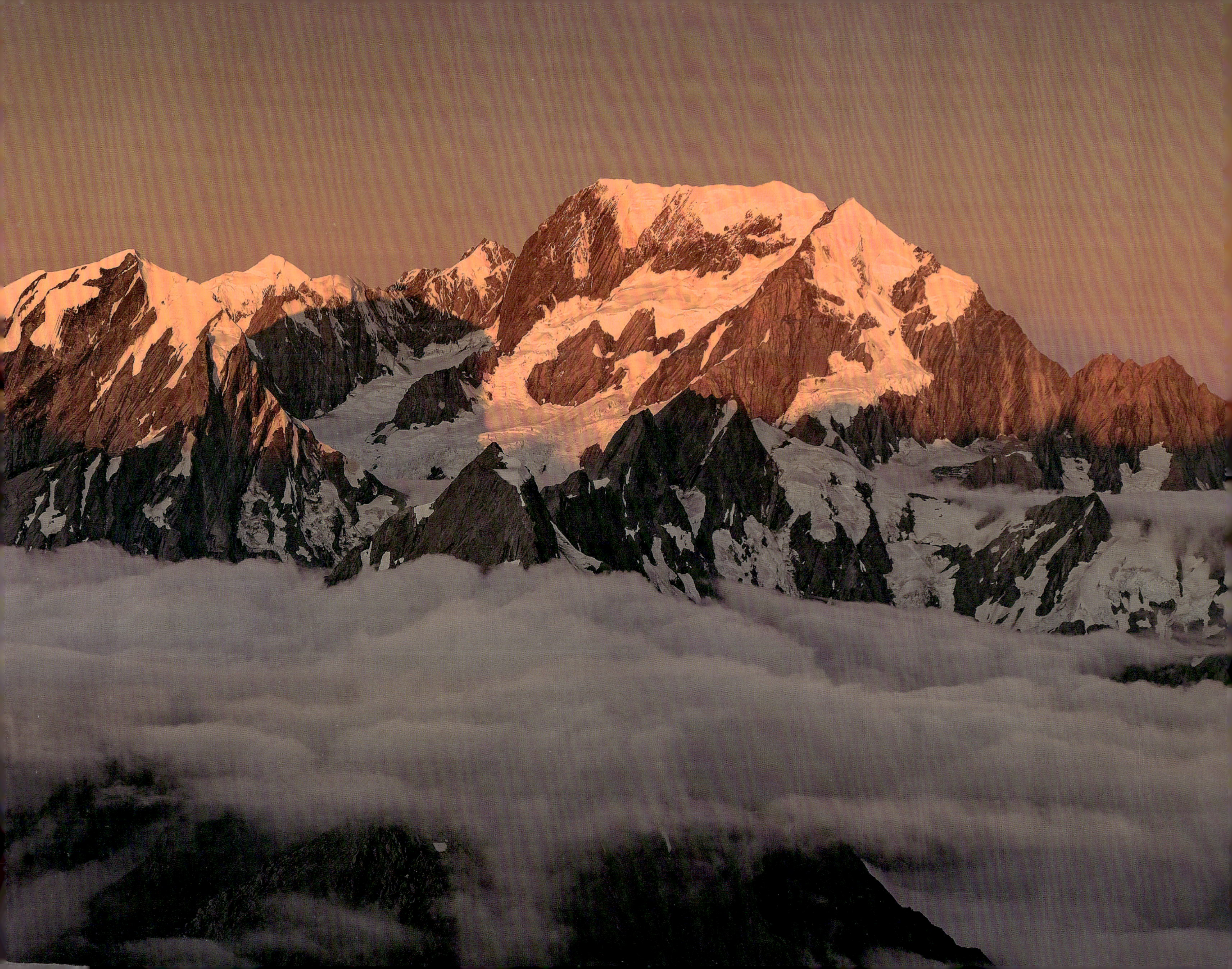

AORAKI MT COOK GRAND TRAVERSE

TASMAN GLACIER–PLATEAU HUT–ZURBRIGGEN RIDGE–HIGH PEAK TO LOW PEAK–PORTER COL–HOOKER GLACIER

3 DAYS: 23–25 FEBRUARY 1985
GS WITH DAVE BAMFORD

The Grand Traverse on Aoraki Mt Cook can be seen as the highest transalpine trip in the country. Most people who enjoy rock and ice aspire to climb Aoraki Mt Cook at some point. I was no different, and at Dave's suggestion we cooked up a plan to traverse over the Mt Cook Range after a snowcraft instructors' course based at Beetham Hut, in 1985.

Dave and I had a bit of history together and it was good to be back in the mountains with him. In 1973 five of us had been caught by bad weather on a climb near the summit of Mt Hyades (3078 metres) overlooking the Northern Patagonian Icecap. Building an emergency snowcave, we spent seven cold nights trapped, with no sleeping bags and virtually no food, before self-rescuing on the eighth day. It was quite an epic, and we reflected back on it as we headed across the Tasman Glacier and up Haast Ridge.

Both of us were fit, and we arrived at Plateau Hut mid afternoon. Others lay around on the rock nearby, sunbathing and melting snow. We packed for a big day out. The alarm went off shortly after midnight, and we crept around with our head torches, getting our gear and breakfast together. Soon we released the door and greeted the frozen air outside, under the sort of stars that are so sharp they burn into you. Crampons on, rope up, prusicks on and we were away. Making our way through black air we headed across the Grand Plateau, en route for the big slots at the base of Zurbriggen Ridge. Dave did a great job navigating in the dark, and we were well and truly warmed up by the time we arrived there.

OPPOSITE Sunset on Aoraki Mt Cook from the Sierra Range.

Conditions were good. Nice firm snow, and we hummed along, climbing together, and making good time. It was turning into a very enjoyable day. By dawn we were well up, and watched the sun light up Mt Tasman while sitting at the Summit Rocks. We had had the place to ourselves on Zurbriggen Ridge, but now other climbers who had come up the Linda Glacier appeared. We followed them up the last rope length or so onto the summit, where knobs of sastrugi stretched out towards the wind. Sastrugi can be dodgy stuff in crampons. It is so easy to catch and trip. But both of us were feeling good, and the Grand Traverse was on. Dave led off with me belaying.

The summit ridge is an airy place, dropping off quickly in all directions. The first Grand Traverse of Cook had been done by Freda du Faur, with guides Peter Graham and Darby Thomson, in January 1913, travelling in the opposite direction to us. Theirs had been a 20-hour mission – a fantastic effort without crampons.

Our descent off the high peak was not difficult but it is very exposed. We belayed and took care. A year or so later I heard of Rob Hall parapenting from the summit on a day when there was no wind. To fill the sail he had to run down the icecap. That is commitment.

Dave and I traversed steadily along New Zealand's highest 1.5 kilometres of ridge, enjoying the unique views that seem to stretch to the earth's curve away across the Mackenzie Basin. A kea eye's view of lakes, the hot brown grasslands, mountains, glacier ice and glacier gravel were laid out like a scale model. Back behind us, the darker forests of the West Coast rolled into haze and the ocean was very, very far below.

We were going well. Passing over the Middle Peak we descended towards Porters Col. Phil Doole and Mark Inglis spent two weeks up here in a schrund, referred to as Middle Peak Hotel, before being rescued by helicopter in November 1982. After Patagonia, we could commiserate with that.

From Porters we traversed out to the Low Peak, then headed down towards the upper Empress. There was a déjà vu moment here, when we found ourselves caught in thick afternoon mist above icefalls. Patagonia had begun with a whiteout. Above icefalls. We looked at each other, stood around waiting, and laughed. But we got our clearance and were able to descend the north west couloir to Gardiner Hut, tired, happy, and ready for a brew. (Gardiner Hut once sat on Pudding Rock, a gateway to the upper Hooker Glacier and the western faces of Aoraki Mt Cook. The hut was built in 1934 and named after

LEFT The Hochstetter Icefall. Haast Ridge, which we used as a route to the Grand Plateau, is on the right.

OPPOSITE The summit ridge of Aoraki Mt Cook, as it was in 1985.

climber Katie Gardiner, who helped fund it. In July 2014 it was hit by a rock avalanche and the remains removed by DOC.)

The descent off Pudding Rock in the morning reminded us we were still in the mountains, but the wander down the ice, then the moraine of the Hooker Glacier allowed us to unwind and reflect.

The first winter Grand Traverse had only been done 13 years before, in June 1972, when Keith (Limbo) Thompson and Bob Cunninghame, both based in Dunedin, grabbed a weather window and headed up to Gardiner Hut. They climbed to the Low Peak and Porters Col before putting the rope on, Thompson belaying. Dinner-plate ice, which tends to shatter, gave way on Cunninghame about 5 metres above Thompson, and he fell, smashing his helmet and later his glasses. Sleeping out on the Middle Peak with the temperature on Cunninghame's thermometer -27°C, they had trouble managing the primus, and resorted to eating cold chicken warmed by their bodies. Reaching the summit in candle-calm air the next day, they descended the Linda Glacier to Plateau Hut to complete a memorable first ascent.

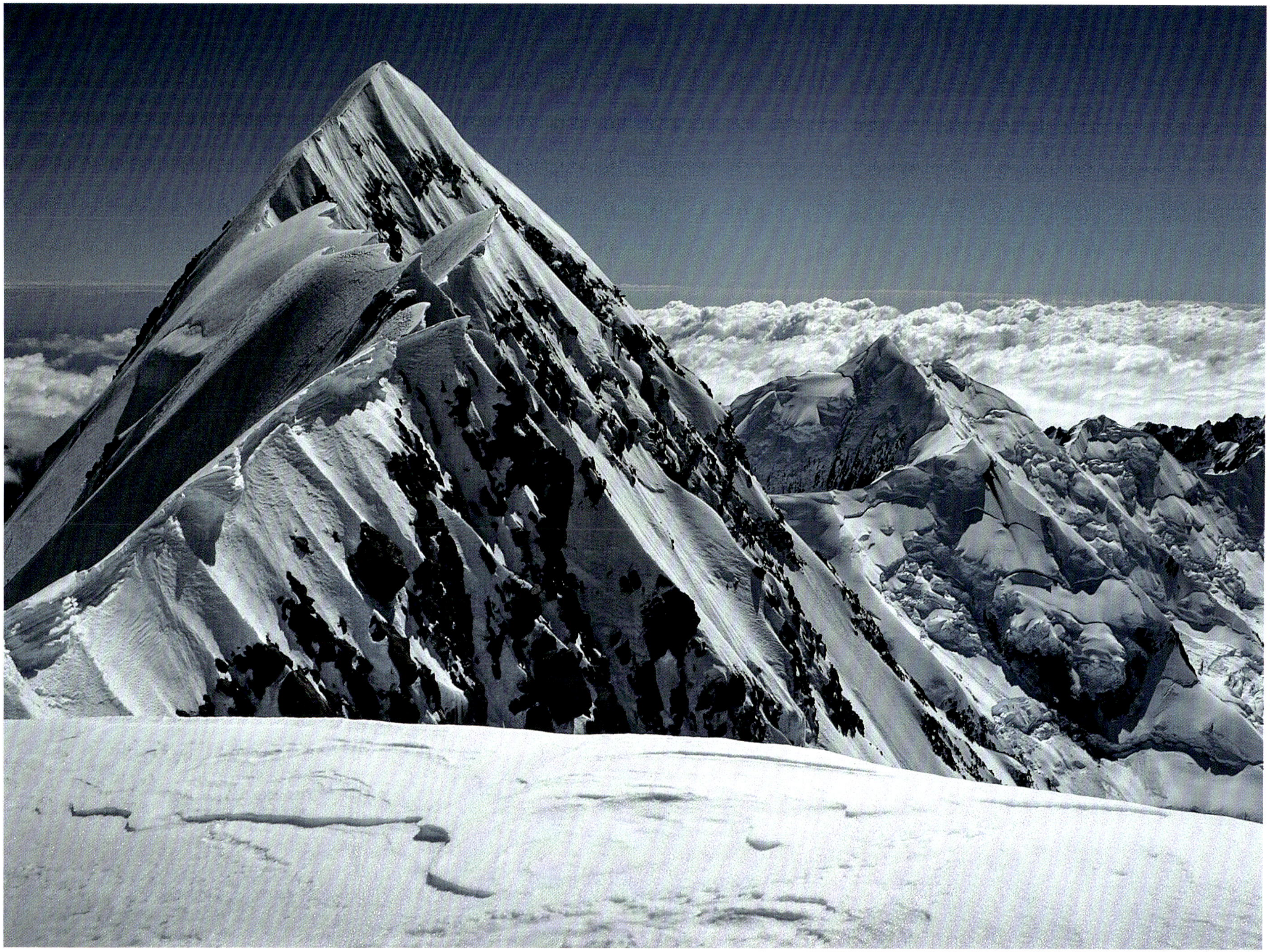

MURCHISON–TASMAN GLACIERS TRAVERSE

MURCHISON VALLEY AND GLACIER–TASMAN SADDLE–TASMAN GLACIER

8 DAYS: 4–11 FEBRUARY 2017
GS WITH AARN TATE, RAYMOND FORD, GARY HUISH, LIZ STEPHENSON, JOHN ALLAN, CHRIS LEAVER, GAYLENE WILKINSON, TONY LAWTON AND ANGELA GRIGG.

Every year, for the last 10 years, I've been leading a trip to a major alpine area in the Southern Alps for the Peninsula Tramping Club. We've been on trips from the Bracken Snowfield to the Olivine Ice Plateau, and many in between. We are not an especially fit or fast group, and we aren't into serious climbing, but what the 10 of us have in common is a love of spending time travelling in the mountains, enjoying campsites and good company in spectacular places under our own steam. These trips have been some of the best in my life, bar none.

It is always nice to settle into the first campsite, watch the evening draw down, and be immersed again in the hills, feeling like you have come home. We were camped on Murchison River flats, tucked under the moraine ridge that blocks off the Tasman Glacier from this mellow, neglected, attractive corner.

Last time I was in the Murchison we had crossed the river with little fuss, but somehow it wasn't like that this time. The swirling quick-silver surface had us linking up and crossing channels from island to island, with each crossing becoming more serious. The final channel carried most of the flow, and we groped our way across to a land of grateful smiles and cold legs.

Liebig Hut, tucked on a tussock and scrub flat under the Liebig Range, was built by the New Zealand Forest Service in 1965. Aoraki Mount Cook National Park took it over in 1979 then closed the hut in 1999. Fortunately, others understand the cultural value of these places. When Australian Barry Armour died in 1998, he left a significant bequest to restore and maintain it, which Doug Henderson Building carried out in 2000. We spent a wonderful day here with Ben, an English hunter, sheltering from the rain while a front passed.

As we cruised along the lake edge in the morning we noticed two paddlers on the far side amongst the ice floes. That looked very fun. Beyond, we sucked it up and headed out onto the Murchison moraine. When we reached the white ice, it was already 5p.m., but we eventually made Murchison Hut, where it snowed overnight.

The following afternoon we continued. The crevasses on the Murchison headwall leading up to Tasman Saddle didn't look to present any real problems, and as this was the crux of the trip, the snow was in good shape, the weather was fine and we were all still pretty fresh, we chose to head on up.

It would mean arriving late at Kelman Hut, but we could camp if needed.

We zig-zagged up, finding easy lines around all the crevasses except the top one at the rollover, where we put in a belay. Conditions can change quickly in the mountains, and we were now in a whiteout with a cold persistent breeze, but it didn't matter. We were over the saddle and on the Tasman Glacier. Kelman Hut sounded great. Inside, we found Bill Atkinson and Taichiro Naka, instructors with a group of eight or so climbers. They welcomed us and offered some of the copious hot water boiling on the stove. Just what we were after.

Usually on these PTC trips we find a peak to wander up for a view. Nothing too challenging, something accessible, something to stand on, breathe in the air, and survey where we had come from and were going to. Mt Aylmer was perfect.

By the time we were approaching the summit, cloud in the west obscured the Whymper Glacier in the head of the Whataroa for a while, but then it cleared enough to see directly down almost 2000 metres, and across to Brodrick and Mannering peaks along the Main Divide. What a stunning place to be.

Next was a visit to the people down at Tasman Saddle Hut. The hut sits on a spectacular bluff of greywacke rock set in the upper Tasman Neve. Kelman Hut was built to replace it, as Tasman Saddle Hut was seen to be geologically unstable. But you can't trust the mountains, and now it seems Kelman is at threat from rock instability, and Tasman Saddle Hut lives proudly on.

Circling back to our packs we curved down the glacier and headed for a night at Darwin Corner. Several helicopters had thudded up-valley during the day, and now, below Tasman Saddle Hut, a plane carved across the snow with

OPPOSITE The Malte Brun Range across Murchison Lake. Aiguilles Rouges (centre) and Malte Brun behind to the right.

127

LEFT A group from Peninsula Tramping Club on Mt Aylmer, at the head of the Tasman Glacier. The Minarets are behind to the left.

OPPOSITE Tasman Saddle Hut perched on a bluff in the upper Tasman Glacier.

a load of tourists, scattering Aarn and one or two others like sheep.

Lower down we found an abandoned snowplough being transported by the ice, while above us the faces of Douglas Peak and Mt Haidinger frowned through swirling streams of cloud. This Tasman Glacier was a spectacular corridor of ice to walk down, but in places the surface was quite cut up, making us concentrate on our route finding.

After several hours on the moraine we called it quits near Garbage Gully, the old exit route off the moraine, to reach what was the Ball Hut road. There was flat shingle, running water, wonderful views, and on such a fine night it was somehow fitting to be still beside glacier ice.

We also used our poo pots. There is a lot of angst and concern about human waste in the mountains and rightly so. DOC, the NZAC, and many others have supported a carry-out-your-own initiative at Aoraki Mount Cook in recent years, and DOC publicise and sell bags and pots for the purpose.

Huts of course have toilets, but we were keen to do the right thing when camping. When we reached Ball Hut next morning, most corn-starch bags disappeared into the loo, but one or two ended up somehow still full once we had walked out. There followed some interesting conversations at the Visitor Centre, when it became clear they had no place to dispose of them.

'You can dispose of them at Twizel.'

'We aren't going to Twizel.'

I won't upset your dinner by saying what happened.

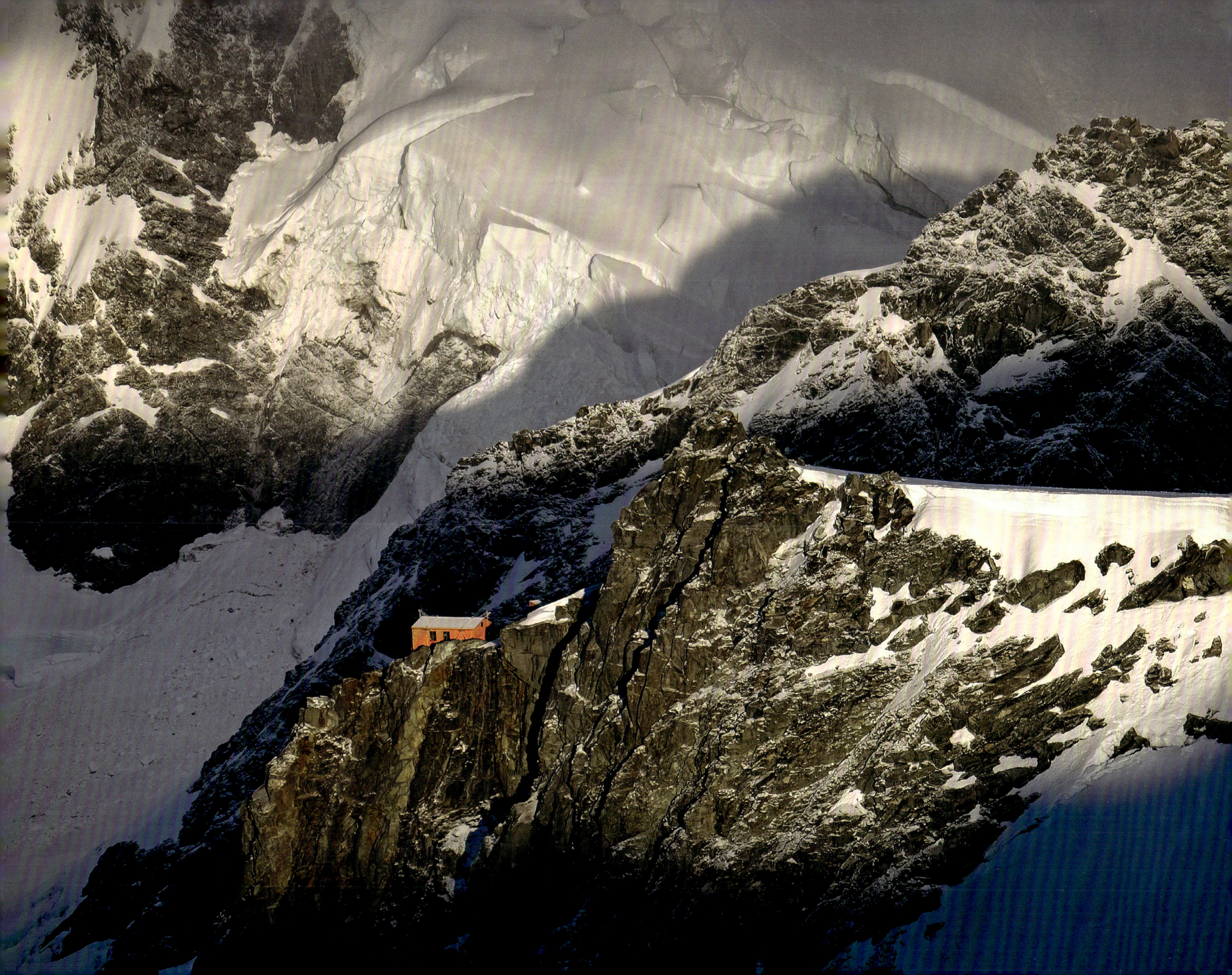

N
6
Mt Fox
< Karangarua River
Bullock Ck >
< Cook River / Weheka
Craig Peak
Fox Glacier
THE NAVIGATOR
ACROSS THE BALFOUR RANGE
< McKenna Creek
Balfour Gl.
BALFOUR RANGE
Mt Tasman
< Cook River / Weheka
COPLAND RANGE
Whales Saddle
La Perouse Gl.
NAVIGATOR RANGE
< Architect Creek
Lyttle Peak
Aoraki / Mt Cook
Mt Copland
Gulch Glacier
La Perouse
Baker Saddle
< Copland River
Strauchon Gl.
Darkwater Saddle
MT SEFTON
< Ruera River
< Jungle Creek
BANKS RANGE
Welcome Flat
< Copland River
MAIN DIVIDE
Scott Creek
THE SIERRA RANGE AND DOUGLAS NEVE
Hooker Glacier
Cassel Flat Hut
Conical Hill
Horace Walker Gl.
Welcome Pass
< Douglas River
Blizzard Peak
Douglas Neve
Mt Sefton
< Makawhio River
BARE ROCKY RANGE
McGloin Peak
< Karangarua River
Harpers Rock Biv.
0
5
10 km

CHAPTER 9
THE BALFOUR, NAVIGATOR & SIERRA RANGES

Majestic views of Mt Tasman and Mt La Perouse from the West Coast have inspired trampers and climbers for generations. Between those peaks, big buttressed ranges bash their way down to the edge of the Alpine Fault, and squeezed between them, the remote Balfour and La Perouse glaciers feed the gorges of the Cook River system. The Balfour Range stands in the middle of it all, stretching up to the Main Divide at Mt Teichelmann. Further south, the Navigator Range runs parallel to the Balfour Range and borders the Copland Valley while, across the Copland, the serrated Sierra Range marches up past Welcome Flat to Mt Sefton. It is spectacular, wild, difficult country.

Many of the transalpine journeys have reflected this, right back to the gold-miner journeys in the 1860s of Harry the Whale, Tony the Greek and German Harry over Whales Saddle on the Navigator Range into the upper Cook valley. More recently, in 1979, John Nankervis, Dave Bamford, Phil Grover and Barry Kivell ran a 15-day transalpine climbing trip to the Cook River. They climbed Lyttle Peak, then moved to the La Perouse neve to climb the South Face of Drake and the Balfour Rib on Tasman, then from the Gulch Glacier they climbed La Perouse, followed by Mt Copland from the Strauchon Glacier. It is a place in which some stunning wilderness adventures have happened, and the alpine journals contain many of them.

A classic trip heads up the Copland Valley and climbs to Welcome Pass. An ascent of Mt Sefton can be made from here in favourable conditions. Continue across the Douglas Neve and descend the Horace Walker route to the Douglas Valley, before traversing tops to Conical Hill and descending to Regina Creek. This remains difficult alpine country, not to be taken for granted. Exit down the Karangarua Valley.

ACROSS THE BALFOUR RANGE

MT FOX–CRAIG PEAK–BALFOUR GLACIER–BALFOUR RANGE–LA PEROUSE GLACIER–WHALES SADDLE–ARCHITECT CREEK–COPLAND VALLEY

7 DAYS: 24 FEBRUARY–2 MARCH 2002

GS WITH JOHNNY MULHERON AND ERIC DUGGAN

The Balfour has long been synonymous with wilderness climbing, and some brilliant trips have been done in this area. Back in 1948/49, Earl Riddiford, Bill Beaven, Norm Hardie and Jim McFarlane crossed the Fox Glacier, snowcaved on Katies Col, accessed the upper Balfour Glacier and climbed Mt Silberhorn and Mt Tasman before descending to the floor of the Balfour Glacier. Packing all their own food and equipment, they then crossed the Balfour Range, seeing a herd of about 90 chamois on the way, climbed La Perouse, dug a snowcave in the upper La Perouse neve to attempt Mt Dampier, and tried crossing the Navigator Range near Cuttance Col. In deteriorating weather on their sixteenth day they headed out down the Cook River.

Our trip was somewhat more modest. Cutting south across the grain of the country from the Fox Range we traversed the Balfour Glacier, the Balfour Range and La Perouse Glacier in the head of the Cook River, but we didn't ascend any peaks. We crossed the Navigator Range at Whales Saddle, coming out down the Copland Valley.

First, we climbed onto the Fox Range, where an Israeli guy offered us a brew. He was the only person we saw all trip. Despite being February, the weather was cold, and further along at about 1600 metres where the tussock turned to shale and rock, heavy mist turned to drizzle, then rain. Bugger. With freezing fingers, we camped between Craig and Sam peaks, but by morning the sky had cleared, a heavy frost covered everything and the mountains burned bright white across the horizon.

Between McKenna Creek below us and the Balfour Glacier lay a ridge of bumps and hollows that A.P. Harper called The Hen and Chickens, on a visit to the Balfour Glacier in the 1890s. We descended that ridge, then dropped off the side down steep slopes onto the Balfour. Some climbers dream of journeys that culminate in a summit. I dream of all sorts of hidden, remote, inaccessible places to visit, and sometimes that is a summit, sometimes it is a place like this. For me there is a joy in reaching and experiencing the ambience of such a place. It sucks into my bones.

Not that it was a *pretty* sight. Rolling cloud hung low off the peaks and the glacier was a mess of eroding ice, covered in gravel debris. Dirty creeks picked their way out of ice tunnels, flip-flopping down towards the glacial lake. Between the ice and the cloud was a desolate landscape of collapsing moraine walls and strips of scrub desperately clinging on while being dragged down, relentlessly, into the glacial decay. But the sheer starkness of the place gave it a scale and beauty of its own that equally attracted, repelled and excited me.

Rock strata on the Balfour Range dips towards the north west. The southern faces are generally steep, shady gullies of damp, crumbling schist. At other times, snow couloirs and slopes would be useful, but that seemed unlikely, it being late February. We chose a route that climbed up opposite McKenna Creek and crossed the range about 200 metres west of 1792 metres. This committed us to climb bluffs covered in ferns, then a scrub bash with our old friend leatherwood from Tararua days, before better going on tussock and rock took us to the crest of the Balfour Range. Two o'clock.

Now the fun began. Mist had gathered, and looking over in the gloom, nothing looked attractive. Pinnacles and walls of loose rock below hemmed a steep gully in, but at least the first section looked doable even if it didn't look particularly healthy. We put on harnesses and got the rope handy. There were some bedrock waterfalls we could climb down. Some we abseiled, lowering the packs separately and leaving a sling behind, but at the last nasty drop we sneaked out to the side down a parallel gully. The Cook River crossing at the lake outlet was chest deep and we all felt a little munted by the time we camped beside the Gulch Stream at 8.30 p.m.

The following day we attempted La Perouse. Waking at four, we battled through miles of flax and scrub in the dark to reach the tussock at dawn. This was the standard approach to La Perouse from the west, a route originally

OPPOSITE: Mt Tasman and the Balfour Glacier on the left. Balfour Range on the right, with Aoraki Mt Cook above.

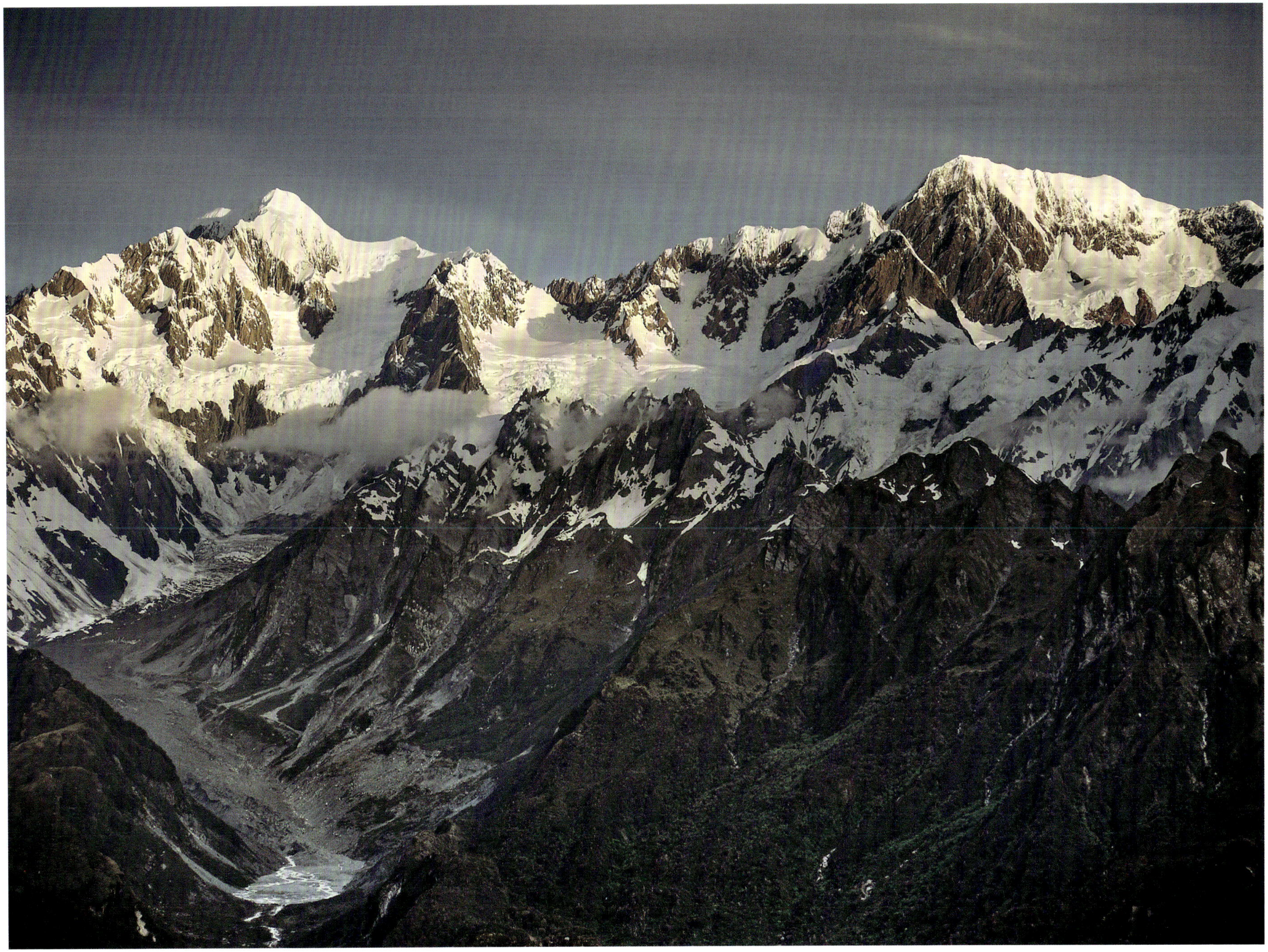

pioneered by Dr Teichelmann, H.E. Newton, R.S. Low and A. Graham in 1906. But at a little over 2000 metres, with the weather and our energy deteriorating, we gave it away.

That night it rained heavily and continued to do so all next morning. We listened to weka prowling around in the scrub, calling across the valley. Over by the river bank, big glistening waterdrops curved purple flower sprays of native broom (*Carmichaelia* sp). We rested and studied the route notes of a friend, Tony Gates, who had also been in the Cook.

The climb out of the Cook towards Whales Saddle on the Navigator Range had a steep little kick in the tail near the top. We rewarded ourselves with lunch, and later headed down Architect Creek to camp on lower flats of *Raoulia*, beside *Olearia* shrubs almost as big as trees.

Dead *Olearia* burns well, and soon a fire crackled along under the billy. About then it started raining again. We had obviously used up all our fine weather. Later, a fireworks display of lightning, thunder and heavy rain set in. This was a command performance and we were in the dress circle. At times, the orchestral precision was literally breathtaking. We cowered in our sleeping bags, a little too close for comfort. By morning, hail had settled around the tent.

Both Johnny and Eric were members of Victoria University Tramping Club, a proud institution running Lost Sheep Tours Ltd. I'd been assured that their chief guide offered breakfast in bed on the last day. 'Sleep in and enjoy the river's murmur.' I waited. And waited. And waited. At ten o'clock nature called, instead. You can't always believe the advertising.

It stopped raining for 40 minutes at lunch time, so we optimistically packed up and headed out down the true right of Architect Creek. Huey noticed, and rain began again. The pleasures of bush-bashing have an inverse relationship with age, but we reached the Copland and the roadend later that evening. What a magnificent country we live in.

LEFT Getting off the Balfour Range on the La Perouse Glacier side.
OPPOSITE The Cook River and La Perouse Glacier. The Balfour Range (left) under cloud, Mt Tasman on the left skyline, Aoraki Mt Cook (centre), and Mt La Perouse, slightly below and to the right.

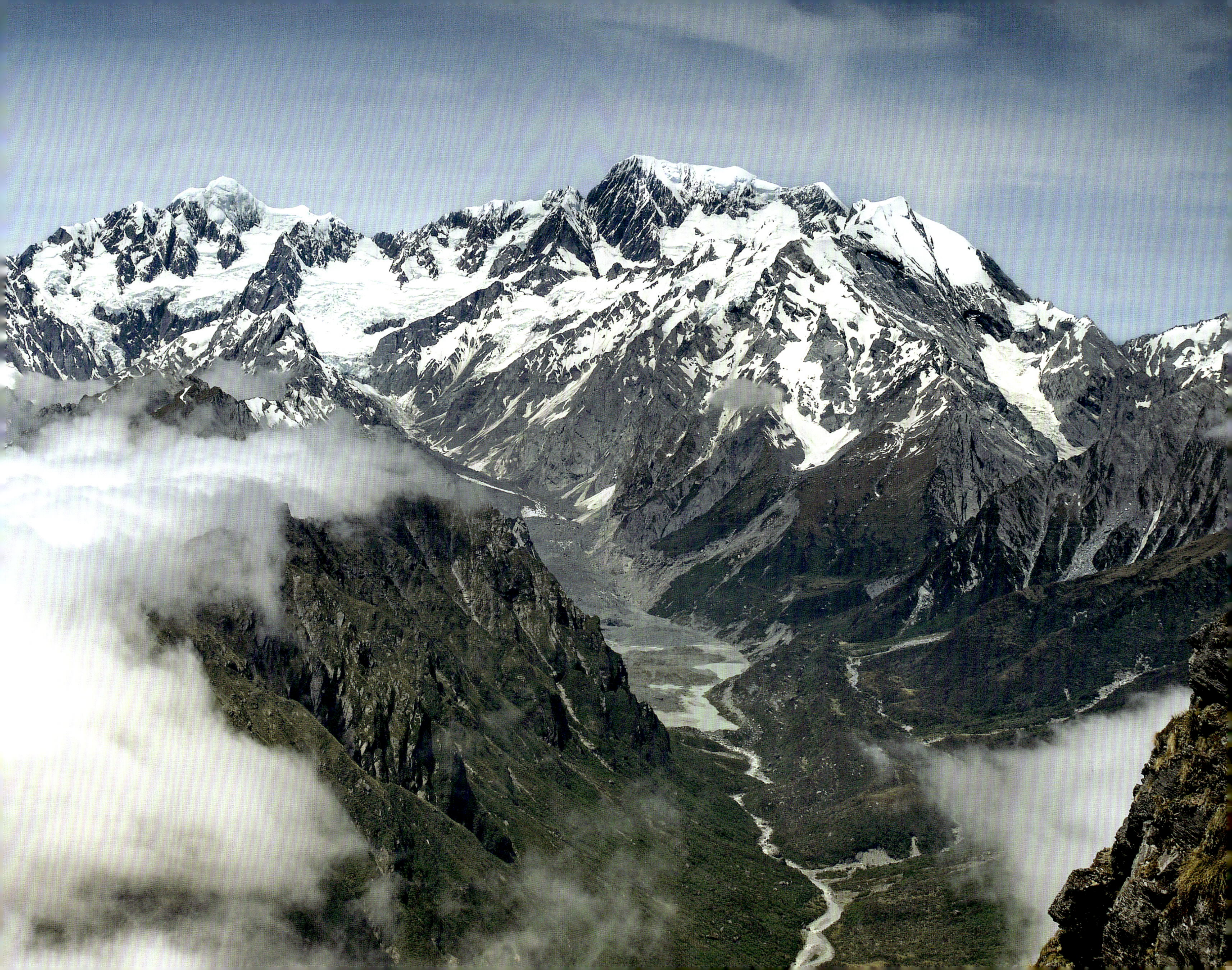

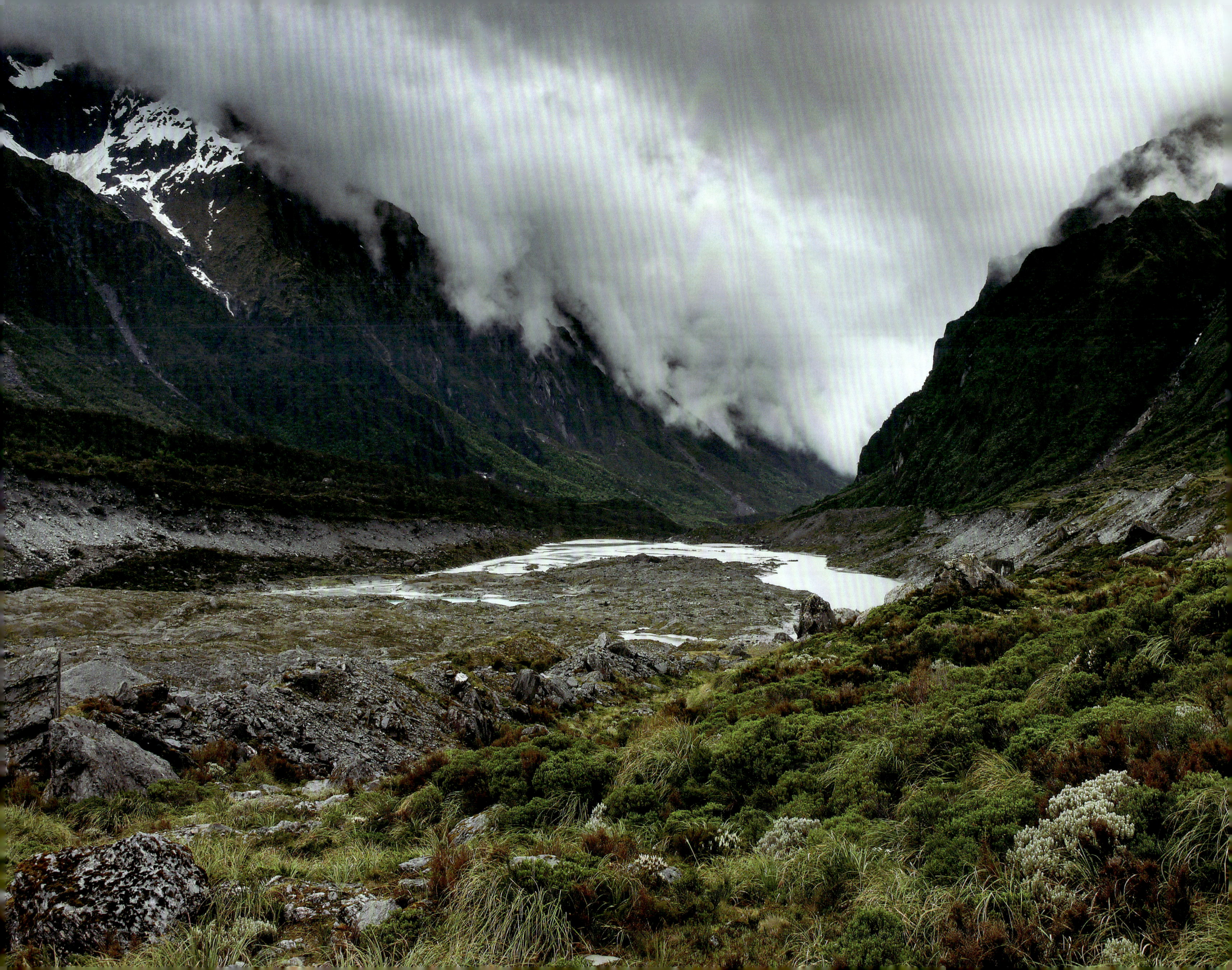

THE NAVIGATOR

BULLOCK CREEK–NAVIGATOR RANGE–DARKWATER SADDLE– STRAUCHON GLACIER–BANKS RANGE–COPLAND RIVER

7 DAYS: 3–9 JANUARY 2015
GS WITH ROB FROST

Tasman, Malaspina, Vancouver, Dampier, La Perouse: five navigators immortalised as peaks on the Main Divide in close proximity to each other. It is fitting, then, that a range rising up from the west and finishing on one of their summits should be called the Navigator Range.

Even the start was an adventure for us. Three friends working at Fox Glacier came along to enjoy the 1200-metre grovel up Bullock Creek past a waterfall and thick subalpine scrub to camp with us in the tussock on the end of the range. Views unfolded across the Cook River all the way from Mt Tasman to La Perouse; there were tarns to cool off in, and later, under a bright moon, a chorus of frogs. The other three had arranged to be flown back down in the morning, but I couldn't help thinking the walk up and flight down was back to front.

I always love getting going on tops at the start of a trip, feeling fresh and fit. Some gnarly stretches kept us on our toes, and travel was steady but not fast. Dry West Coast fog collected, forcing hide and seek with the ridge, and sometimes giving alarming perspectives. Whales Saddle loomed up at 6.30 p.m., so we found a place for the tent and lit the white-spirit stove. Below, we could see the route up from the Cook Valley.

During fog clearances, we had seen the sweeping slabs of Lyttle Peak further along the range rising in front of us. This is a mountain with style. Mary Roberts and Dora de Beer, with guides Alec Graham and Tom Sheeran, thought so too, reaching the low peak in February 1931. Later that season, Sheeran came back with George Bannister to make the first ascent of the high peak.

From Whales Saddle, evening sunlight swept up that beautiful smooth

LEFT Fingers of jungle mist creeping up the Cook Valley.
OPPOSITE The Strauchon Lake and Valley. The Navigator Range (left) finishes on Mt La Perouse (centre). To the right, Aoraki Mt Cook stands behind Baker Saddle.

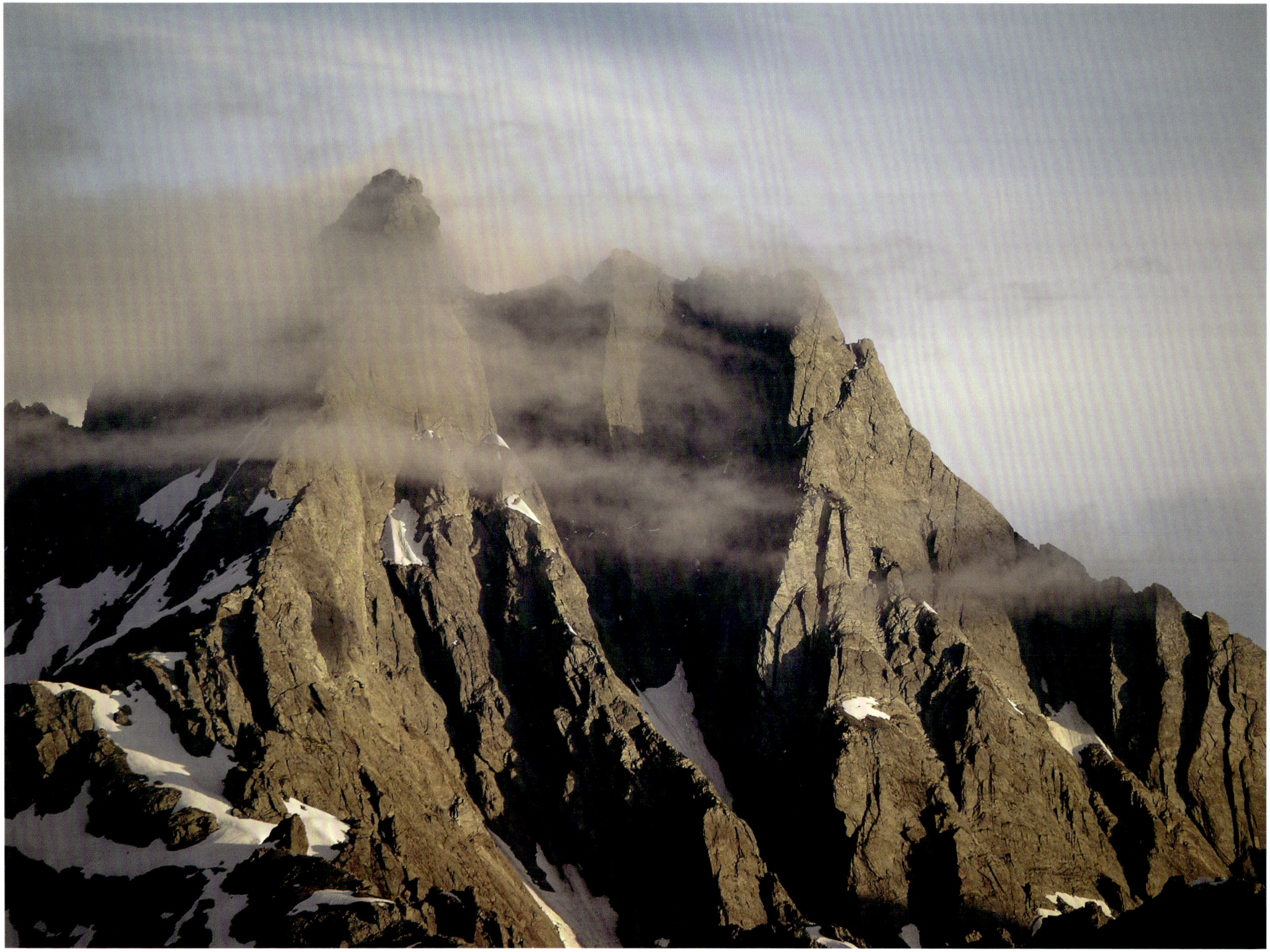

rock to the summit. It was only in April 2014 that these slabs were first climbed by Pete and Steve Harris. Both the rock and the line looked inspiring.

Our morning began with a detour right under the slabs, before regaining the range north of Lyttle Peak. High cloud and misty fingers prowled around as we dropped into a basin above the Cook then climbed out towards Dent Noire in thick wet mist and drizzle. Later we camped on a narrow earth shelf below one bluff and above another, which wasn't the flashest place to be next morning when we were shaken awake by an earthquake.

An easy ridge of snow wound over The Nick, and on to The Fang. Hugh Wilson and Paul Grocott made the first ascent of The Fang in February 1967, while Dent Noire and The Nick were first climbed in 1969 by Wayne McIlwraith, Maurice Conway, Walter Fowlie and Stewart Bain.

From The Fang we looked east to a ridge of gendarmes and rock so rotten it could be eaten like Weetbix if you had an appetite for it. It remains untravelled. Instead, we headed down Crumbling Ridge, where we needed a couple of abseils to get into the Ruera. Complacent herds of tahr were busily chewing their way through the tussock and subalpine scrub. They looked at us, decided they were busy, and went on feeding. That night we slept in the head of the Darkwater, watched over by more tahr and chamois.

Next morning the Strauchon Valley from Darkwater Saddle, with the slabs of La Perouse, Unicorn and Dilemma rising ahead, was glorious. Thoughts of climbing Mt Copland beside us faltered, and instead we investigated Strauchon Lake and Glacier where there were more tahr. One posed just a few metres away, with one horn missing and a coat that was moulting. It looked like I felt.

Up-valley, the Navigator Range descends to Cuttance Col before sweeping up with a flourish to La Perouse. Cuttance Col has only been crossed the once by G. Howitt and J. Jackson in 1952, as the rockwalls down to the Gulch Glacier on the far side are wildly bluffed. The ridge on to La Perouse from Cuttance Col was first climbed in 1953 by A. Cunningham, A. Witten Hannah, and Tom Barcham, a friend I had been to the Indian Himalayas with.

We photographed Unicorn and Dilemma from the Strauchon Glacier as the sun set, then headed down to camp on flats by the lake outlet. When we left the Strauchon for the Copland Valley next morning it was in true transalpine style – by climbing up over the end of the Banks Range. From there it was another trip down the Copland and out.

OPPOSITE The sunlit slabs of Lyttle Peak drain into Architect Creek.
ABOVE On the Navigator Range. The Fang is the rocky peak on the right, showing through the mist.

MT SEFTON

KARANGARUA VALLEY–DOUGLAS VALLEY–DOUGLAS NEVE–MT SEFTON–WELCOME PASS–COPLAND VALLEY–STRAUCHON VALLEY–BAKER SADDLE–HOOKER GLACIER

12 DAYS: 22 DECEMBER 1974–2 JANUARY 1975
GS WITH ERICA LAW

Sefton. Who hasn't stood at the Hermitage and looked up at mist or snow plumes streaming off the summit ridge and felt the call of Mt Sefton? For our trip we chose to approach from the west, not up the usual route from the Copland Valley but from the Karangarua and its big tributary the Douglas River, and neve.

Trip adventures often began right from the city, back in 1974. I caught a train to Greymouth; slept on the beach but it rained, so I was on the road fairly early. The rain eased as I hitched past the Waitaha River. Erica, from VUWTC, was at Fox Glacier to join me. In typical hot, overcast and humid weather this close to Christmas we spent the first afternoon on the old cattle track heading up the Karangarua towards Cassel Flat. We didn't quite make it, giving in at a superb little campsite just before.

Sandflies and mosquitoes chased us across Cassel Flat in the morning to the wire cable and cage crossing of the Karangarua to the side stream of Regina Creek. The track up Regina left most of the route to the imagination. I think we found about four markers. But still, we found the three-wire bridge and the start of an old blaze up to Conical Hill, and it all helped.

The Douglas Valley was originally called the Twain, after 'cleft in twain' because the valley looked like it had been hacked out with an axe, creating a steep and deep ravine. A.P. Harper's map to accompany his book *Pioneer Work in the Southern Alps*, published in 1896, calls it the Twain, and marks the gorge impassable.

Conical Hill had cut the worst of the gorge out for us, but from Conical Hill we descended back to the river and choked in deep, prickly shield fern, logs and boulders under a cover of shrubby, deciduous *Hoheria*. Their fresh apple-green leaves spoke of summer. The day was fine, and as we wallowed, glimpses of beautiful clean bluffs would appear high on walls around us, reverberating with weka calls. Tired and worn out, we camped at 7 p.m. We repeated the effort the next day.

The head of the Douglas is a tremendous place. Leaving our packs at the door of Horace Walker Hut, we continued up to Lake Douglas, to drink in the vastness of the valley walls, watch the waves lap, and listen to ice rumble off the Douglas Neve, while kea and seagulls wheeled high overhead. Tomorrow we would be up there.

Christmas day was spent on the climb up the Wicks Glacier to Wicks Col, then traversing icefields to camp on exposed ledges near Welcome Pass at an altitude of 2400 metres. Far below, the Copland River murmured.

There wasn't much of a frost so the snow was still soft when we left at six-thirty on Boxing Day morning to climb Mt Sefton. From here it is a snow climb, steepening for the last 300 metres, and with big crevasses to navigate through along the Douglas Neve. For Erica and me, it was a wonderful day out, traversing a neve that crumbled away regularly in icefalls into the Douglas Valley from where we had come. On top we found a little dachshund soft toy tied to the rock, an update on the traditional rock cairn or tin. It hadn't been there too long yet, judging by the leather skin condition.

On the first ascent in 1895, E. Fitzgerald and M. Zurbriggen left a note in a bottle tucked into the rocks close to this summit. During the climb they had a near-fatal accident when a boulder knocked Fitzgerald off, injuring him and leaving him hanging 2 metres lower. Zurbriggen was only just able to hold him.

The western route we climbed was first pioneered from the Copland Valley in 1912 by L. Earle, B. Head, J. Clarke and A. Graham. A year later it was used as a descent route on the first traverse of the mountain. This was a gutsy climb full of adventure by Freda du Faur, P. Graham, and D. Thomson. Du Faur's account is well-worth reading, both for the climb up the east ridge and also their descent to the Copland, where mist and route-finding in heavy crevasses slowed them, and the last two hours among the rough terrain of Scott Creek were in the dark by candle lantern.

We returned to the Douglas Neve in soft snow on a mellow afternoon, and next morning I followed Erica up Scott Peak for a last look over the Douglas kingdom. Unlike now, Scott Creek proved a straightforward route down to the Copland then, often over big boulders, and we sidled the big

RIGHT Sunrise on the east face of Mt Sefton, seen from the Annette Plateau.
OVERLEAF (LEFT) Mt Sefton at the head of the Douglas Neve.
OVERLEAF (RIGHT) Mt Sefton and the Sierra Range, with Welcome Pass on the right. Rob surveys it all from above Darkwater Saddle.

waterfall on the true left down a slight shelf on bedrock with bits of scrub.

We brewed up for lunch among river boulders before crossing the Copland River just below Jungle Creek, our proposed access to the upper Strauchon. Jungle Creek proved more obstinate than expected, but we got there. Now, a substantial lake replaces the lower Strauchon Glacier, but back in 1974 delightful bright-blue tarns dotted the ice moraine.

The upper Strauchon has an isolated appeal, and we enjoyed a couple of days here in unsettled weather before moving on over Baker Saddle, in sleety showers. Plugging down soft snow over ice in crampons, we descended onto the Hooker Glacier and weaved through a mess of crevasses before climbing up to what was still there then: the barrel-shaped Gardiner Hut (see chapter eight, Aoraki Mt Cook Grand Traverse). We were among people again, including the Gledhill brothers, who had been entranced by rock routes on Mt Unicorn and Dilemma Peak, which overlooked the Strauchon.

On our last day we descended the cables bolted to the rock, abseiled onto the lower glacier and headed for the fleshpots of Mount Cook village.

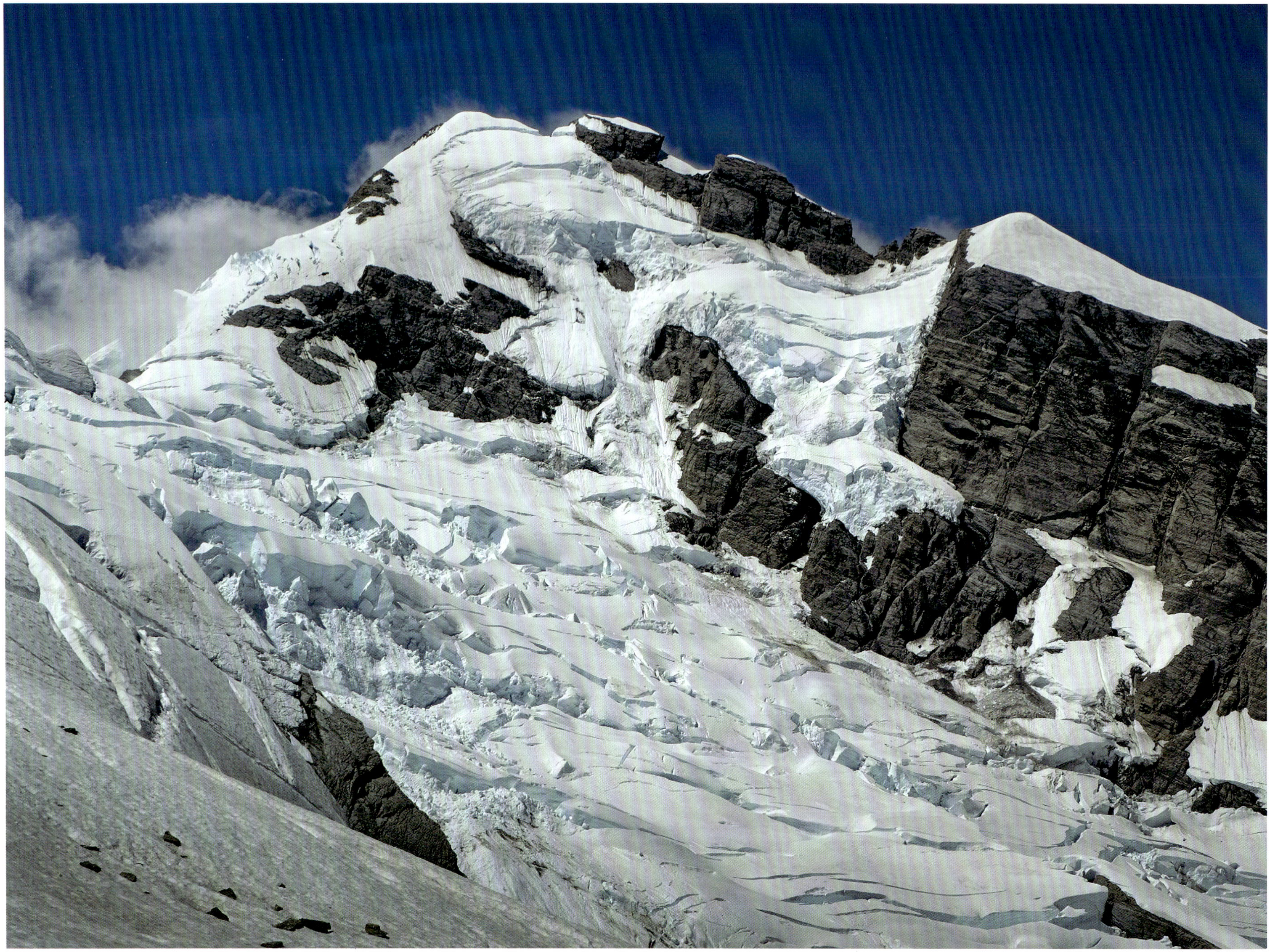

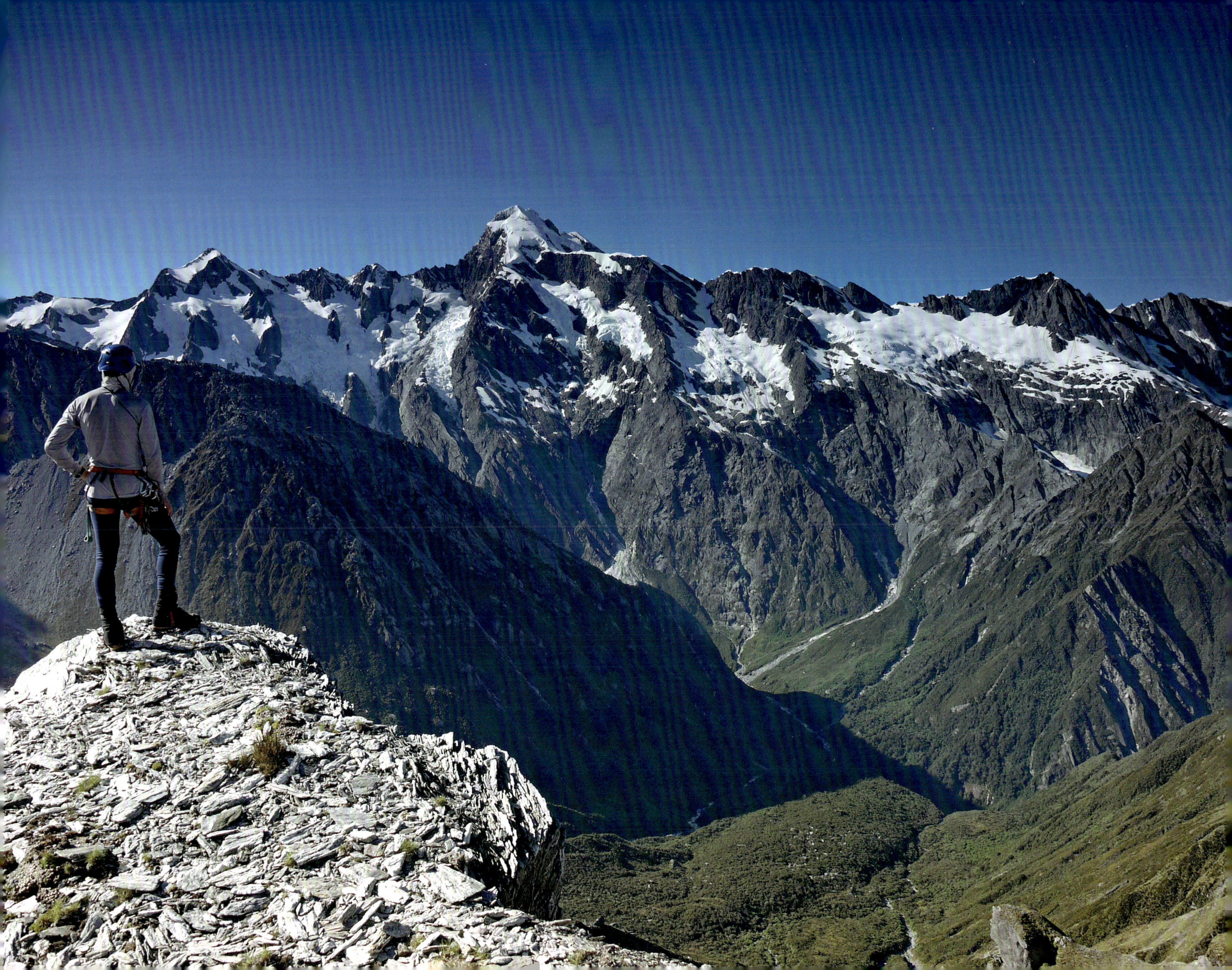

THE SIERRA RANGE & DOUGLAS NEVE

COPLAND VALLEY–WELCOME PASS–DOUGLAS NEVE– DOUGLAS VALLEY–KARANGARUA VALLEY

9 DAYS: 6–14 FEBRUARY 2016
GS WITH GARY HUISH, CALUM MCINTOSH, RAYMOND FORD, CHRIS LEAVER, KEVIN HUGHES, MERV MEREDITH, AARN TATE, JOHN ALLAN, GAYLENE WILKINSON AND TONY LAWTON

Friendships developed in the hills are often close and strong; small parties and challenging circumstances encourage this. For a party of 11 to bond tightly is less common. When it does, though, magic happens. We were a varied group with differing abilities and ages ranging up into the 70s. By the end, we shared an openness and connection that embraced the mountains by day and the stars by night. The weather helped. I slept out eight straight nights in a row.

The trip began with a two-hour wander up the Copland Track in the late afternoon before camping in the riverbed. A mellow, lazy, dry February afternoon where, as the sun sparkled down through shrubby leaves and flax, we lit a fire and cooked our first dinner. Not even the sandflies stirred.

Further up at Welcome Flat we lowered our gaze from the Sierra Range. Immense, clean rock bluffs frowned down from a jagged row of rock shards, one of which was appropriately named Splinter Peak. Behind it lay the Douglas Neve where we planned to spend a couple of days before continuing the crossing to the Douglas and Karangarua valleys.

The following night we tucked up on shingle talus in the head of Scott Creek, having climbed 1300 metres above the Copland River. The vaulting bluffs of Splinter Peak rose another 700 metres above. Wreaths of mist had formed in the bluffs as we climbed, but with evening, these had melted like ghosts, trailing away into thin air.

Frost woke us, and later, on crisp crampons, we threaded between crevasses up the Tekano Glacier to Welcome Pass, and on to the Douglas Neve.

We roped up to make our way over towards Lucy Walker Pass through a rolling landscape of ice and big crevasses, then camped in the icefields on an exposed rocky knoll, where the setting sun drenched surrounding snowfields in gold then pink. Those tents, with clear views of Mt Sefton higher on the knoll, made some rather extravagant claims about their exposed real estate. Others knew better.

This trip wasn't out to climb mountains, but Blizzard Peak (2435 metres) nearby, became an objective. It has some history. In January 1935, three climbers, Johnson, Scott and Russell, had quite an adventure here on a very staunch first crossing over the Douglas Neve and Sierra Range in a storm. At one stage, in blizzard conditions, they found they had made the first ascent of a small peak. They named it Blizzard. Our ascent would be a small tribute to them.

Scott Russell wrote: 'Memory of the next 8 hours is blurred. Sudden gusts tore us off our feet, throwing us on our faces. Visibility never exceeded a few yards. . . . for the first time I felt that detached indifference towards my own actions which is engendered by exhaustion: mind and body were severed, they became separate entities . . .' Still in the storm, they reached the range crest and crossed, unsure where they were until lower down when chips cut by an iceaxe allowed them to locate a rock bivouac near the bushline. Later the following day they reached Welcome Flat. The crossing took its toll, with Johnson spraining his ankle badly on the descent, and Archie Scott's legs swollen and showing signs of frostbite.

No such problems for us. From the sunny summit of Blizzard Peak we made our way down snow slopes north of Pioneer Peak to camp in an eagle's eyrie above the Douglas Valley. A couple of rock wren bobbed around in welcome.

The head of the Douglas Valley is a grand place, a fitting tribute to Charlie Douglas. We swam in the lake, visited Horace Walker Hut, and camped on flats downstream. Next morning, we took the high sidle out towards Conical Hill. Once we were back up on the tops, sitting in tussock, a muffled rumble alerted us to an extensive rockfall that swept across our route of the day before, kicking up a huge dust pall. Mountains can be very lax with their health and safety standards.

A hot descent to Regina Creek next day had us skinny-dipping again. We enjoyed emerald pools, river boulders, dappled sunlight, and the serenity of a

RIGHT A wonderful place to be on a calm, clear night. Camped near Lucy Walker Pass on the Sierra Range.

OVERLEAF (LEFT) Blizzard Peak above Lucy Walker Pass.

OVERLEAF (RIGHT) The Horace Walker River on its way down into the Douglas Valley. The high peak largely clear of snow to the left is The Gladiator, while Red Deer Col is centre right.

summer day under Westland forest. Another fire, another brew at lunchtime. After a week on the tops, it was blissfully refreshing to have a swim in a clear bush creek, entertained by the fluid notes of kaka.

We cranked our way across the cableway one at a time to Cassel Flat Hut, before wandering down to camp opposite the Copland Junction. A full circle. Gaylene got a fire going and the evening air filled with the scent of river flats.

Later, Aarn sang us a song he wrote on his traverse of the Southern Alps. As I snuggled into my pit for the last sleep a kaka chortled and a morepork started up nearby. Perfect.

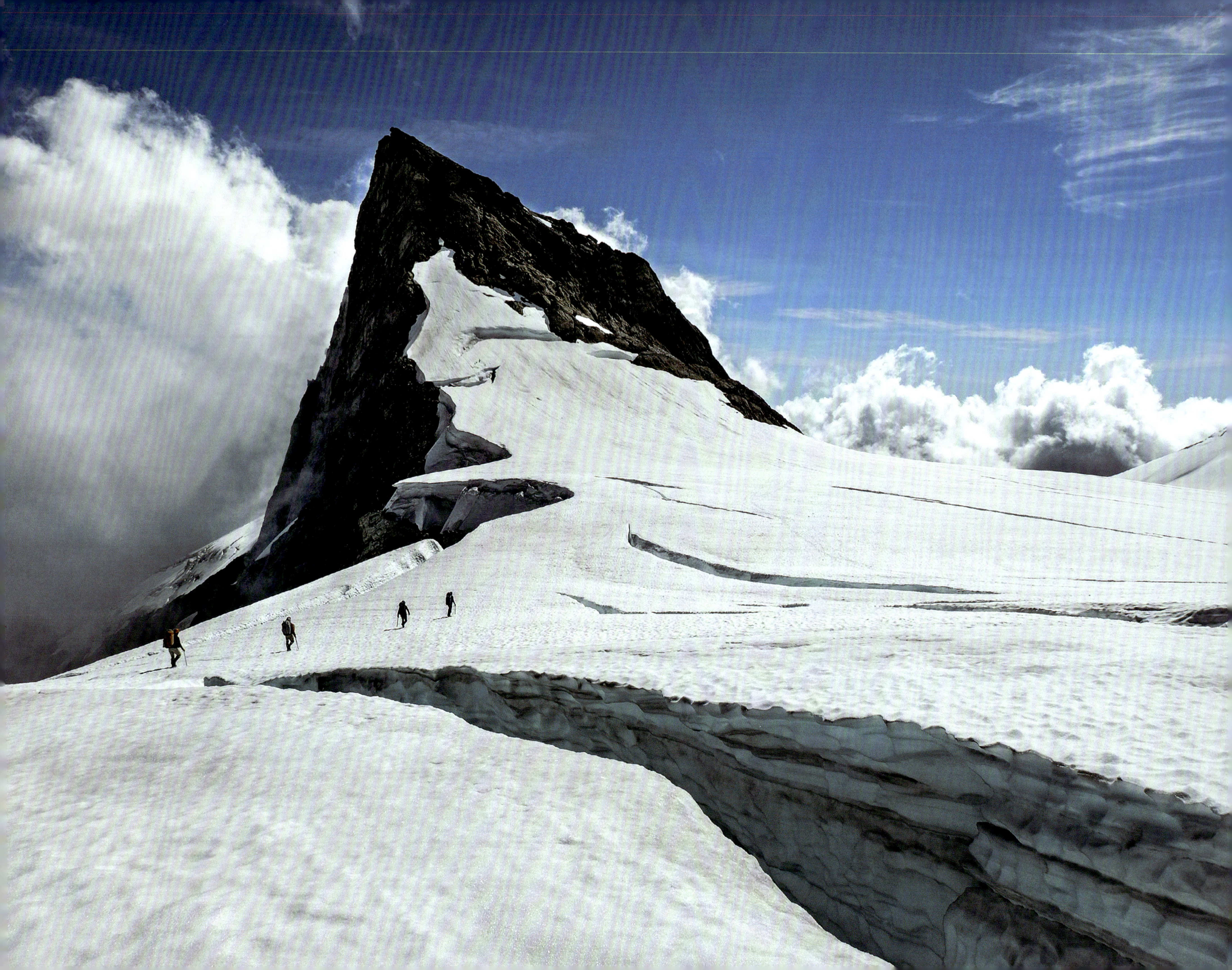

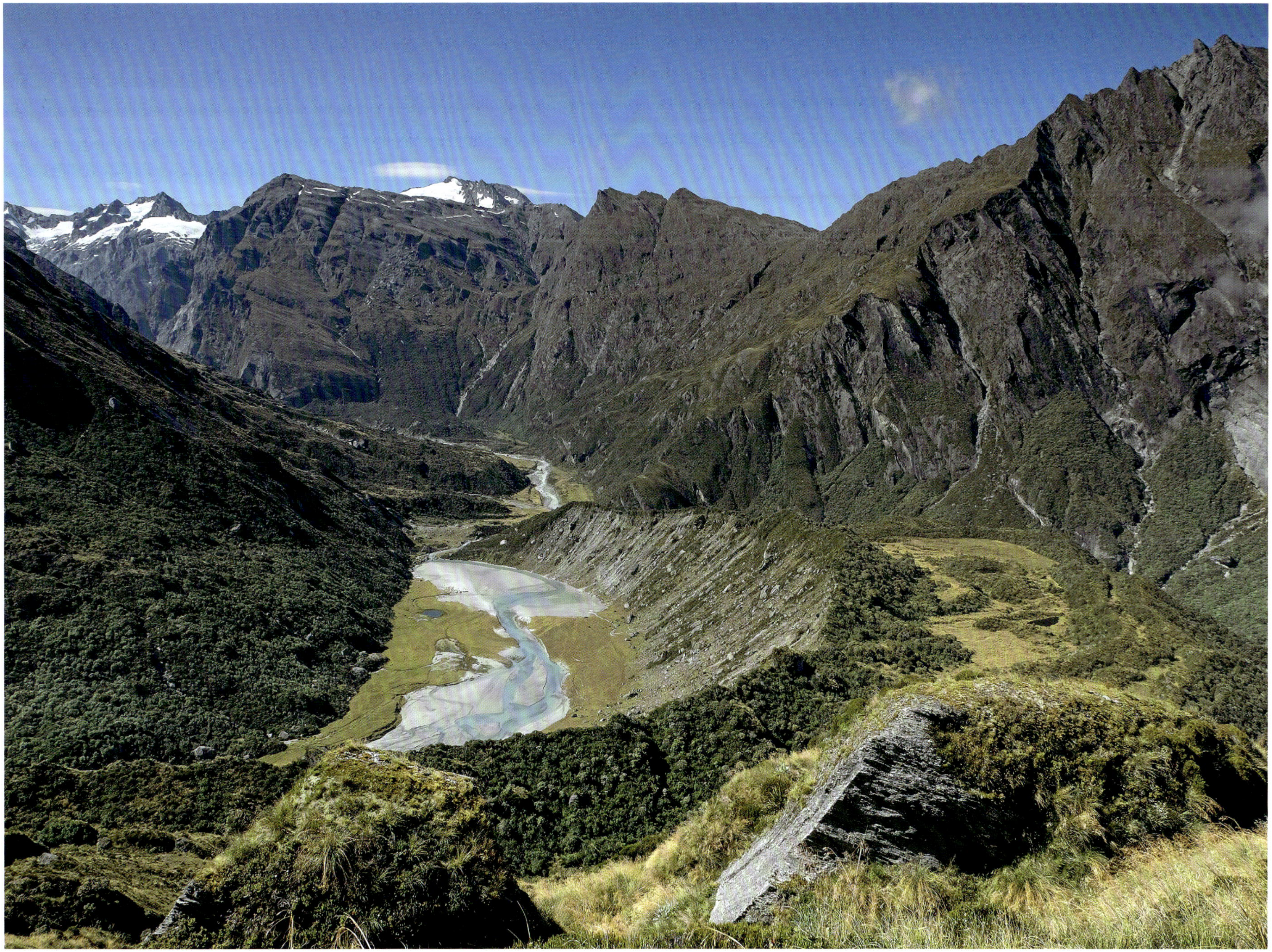

N
6
SCISSOR SLABS TO
THE MAKAWHIO VALLEY
< Karangarua River
< Copland River
KARANGARUA - FETTES PEAK - MAHITAHI
< Makawhio River
< Jumbo Creek
BARE ROCKY RANGE
Mt Sefton
< Paringa River
< Mahitahi River
BANNOCK BRAE RANGE
< Karangarua River
The Gladiator
Harpers Rock Biv
Douglas Pass
< Troyte River
Fettes Peak
Scissors
Aoraki /
Mt Cook
Village
< Morse River
STRACHAN RANGE
< Edison River
Mueller Pass
SEALY RANGE
MAIN DIVIDE
OTOKO - MARKS FLAT - MOERAKI
< Otoko River
Valley of Darkness
Zora Canyon
Mt Dechen
< Moeraki River
< Paringa River
< Tunnel Creek
Mt McCullaugh
Mt Hooker
< Landsborough River
Lower Otoko Pass
Zeilian Pass
Marks
Flat
Mt Ward
Zeilian Creek >
Elcho Col
< Clarke River
Toetoe
Flat
SOLUTION RANGE
< Hopkins River
< Dobson River
THE SOLUTION TO
MT HOOKER
Creswicke
Flat
MAIN DIVIDE
Mt Strauchon
< Haast River
0
5
10 km

CHAPTER 10
THE HOOKER WILDERNESS

Tucked in a knot of mountains west of the Mueller Glacier, the Landsborough River begins less than 7 kilometres from the Hermitage and reaches the sea over 100 kilometres later at Haast. On its way it has some fine scenery to look at, with the Main Divide on the left, and the Hooker Range and its peaks Fettes, Strachan, Dechen, and of course Mt Hooker itself, to the west. From these isolated western giants come other ranges: the Strachan, the Bare Rocky, and Bannock Brae; ranges that have probably still not been fully traversed along the tops. McGloin Peak has only had one ascent.

It is an unforgiving part of the world from valley floor to the tops of the mountains, and out of which the Karangarua, Makawhio, Mahitahi, Otoko, Paringa and Moeraki rivers flow.

Surveyor Gerhard Mueller and Charlie Douglas mapped much of the Landsborough in the early 1890s. A.P. Harper and Ruera (Bill) Te Naihi explored the Karangarua, upper Landsborough, the McKerrow Glacier and the upper Douglas (Twain) Valley during 1894 and 1895. Charlie Douglas began with them but returned home due to failing health. Tom Fyfe and his protégé George Graham also crossed into the Landsborough in 1894, this time over Fyfe Pass from the Mueller Glacier, and since then a century of great transalpine trips have criss-crossed the whole area.

A classic transalpine trip into the Hooker Range begins up the Paringa Valley, crosses to subalpine Marks Flat in the upper Clarke, then crosses Lower Otoko Pass before descending the Otoko River. There are many possible variations, including starting in the Moeraki, or crossing Brodrick Pass to Lake Ohau, or an ascent of Mt Hooker, but the basic trip is a superb journey through untracked isolated wilderness. It requires good bush skills as well as mountain and river competencies, along with a good summer forecast.

SCISSOR SLABS TO THE MAKAWHIO VALLEY

SEALY RANGE–SCISSORS PEAK–LANDSBOROUGH VALLEY– TROYTE RIVER–MAKAWHIO RIVER

6 DAYS: 27 JANUARY–1 FEBRUARY 2006

GS WITH PHIL NOVIS

Phil and I planned to cross from the Hermitage into the head of the Landsborough, continue across the Hooker Range, Troyte River basin, over the Bare Rocky Range, then out down the Makawhio (Jacobs) River. It would be a wonderful journey if we could pull it off.

After chatting to a group at Barron Saddle Hut we camped near the old Three Johns Hut site, where tiny pieces of debris were a poignant reminder of the intensity with which the wind can blow here. Four friends in a Wanganui Tramping Club party were sheltering in the hut on the night of 30 January 1977 when guy wires failed in extreme winds and the hut was lifted and blown over a bluff on the Dobson Valley side. Fenella Hut in the Cobb Valley is named after one of the four killed, Fenella Druce.

On a beautiful morning we cramponed across slopes to the Main Divide south of Scissors Peak and looked into the slab walls and great gravel gulch of Rubicon Torrent. Heading into Westland off the Main Divide is always special. It spells adventure, but you never quite know the nature of it. This is not a particularly easy route with packs, nor is it particularly obvious. Using the rope at times, we carefully picked our way down.

I love the description A.J. Scott gave of this crossing in December 1934 on their way to Fettes Peak: 'The slabs were indecently bare; abnormally advanced conditions were general in the Alps this season . . . With packs averaging 70lbs, we were frequently in unhappy positions as the declivity is severe, and in many places only friction grips are available. Two of us found our breeches somewhat draughty for the rest of the day.'

Later, in about 1946, Norm Hardie, Jim Mcfarlane and David Hughes crossed, descending the Landsborough, climbing Mt Dechen by a new route, and crossing Brodrick Pass to Lake Ohau. Hardie also gave his name to an alternative crossing near Fyfe Pass, called Hardies Gut. However, one suspects Hardie didn't like the name much. It isn't mentioned in his autobiography *On My Own Two Feet*. In 1971 Graeme Dingle and Jill Tremain travelled up the Landsborough on their winter traverse of the Southern Alps, only for Graeme to be swept 300 metres down in an avalanche close to the route we used. Winter is a hard season in the mountains.

In February it was hot, dry and dusty, and once down we flopped into an alpine lake for a swim. Seldom had life felt so good. Across the Landsborough, Mt Townsend reared up. Bill and Don Beaven, Murray Spencer, John Gummer and Earle Riddiford made the first ascent of this peak in January 1947 on a 15-day climbing trip beginning and finishing at the Hermitage.

We crossed the Hooker Range near Mt Townsend next day and gingerly descended a slabby gully towards the Troyte. Don French had sent me notes on this crossing, while others offered comment on crossing the Bare Rocky Range. Sharing route notes has long been a tradition in our backcountry culture, encouraging a sense of community and spider webs of information second to none. The Troyte River was named by A.P. Harper in 1894.

Rock wrens and pipits welcomed us while we had lunch and looked at the map. Crossing the Bare Rocky Range ahead had a few more challenges with wild bluffs and waterfalls disrupting old snow cones. A route used by others once or twice looked very ugly with little snow this late in the summer, so we went looking for a different way up. We found one about a kilometre to the north, though it wasn't easy, either, and a lot of searching without packs was needed before we linked it all together. A waterfall provided a challenge to get past and an exposed but exhilarating knife-edge ridge finally took us to Highland Pass and a route down to the Makawhio. We had made it.

Moments like this are special. It is quite an achievement reaching a remote corner of the Alps that is very hard to access on foot, and if you are into isolated places, it can give the same sort of buzz as reaching a tricky summit. We enjoyed the ambience of the place.

OPPOSITE Phil descending the Scissor slabs into Rubicon Torrent. The pointed centre peak across the Landsborough Valley is Fettes Peak. The snow peaks further left are Dechen (left) and Strachan.

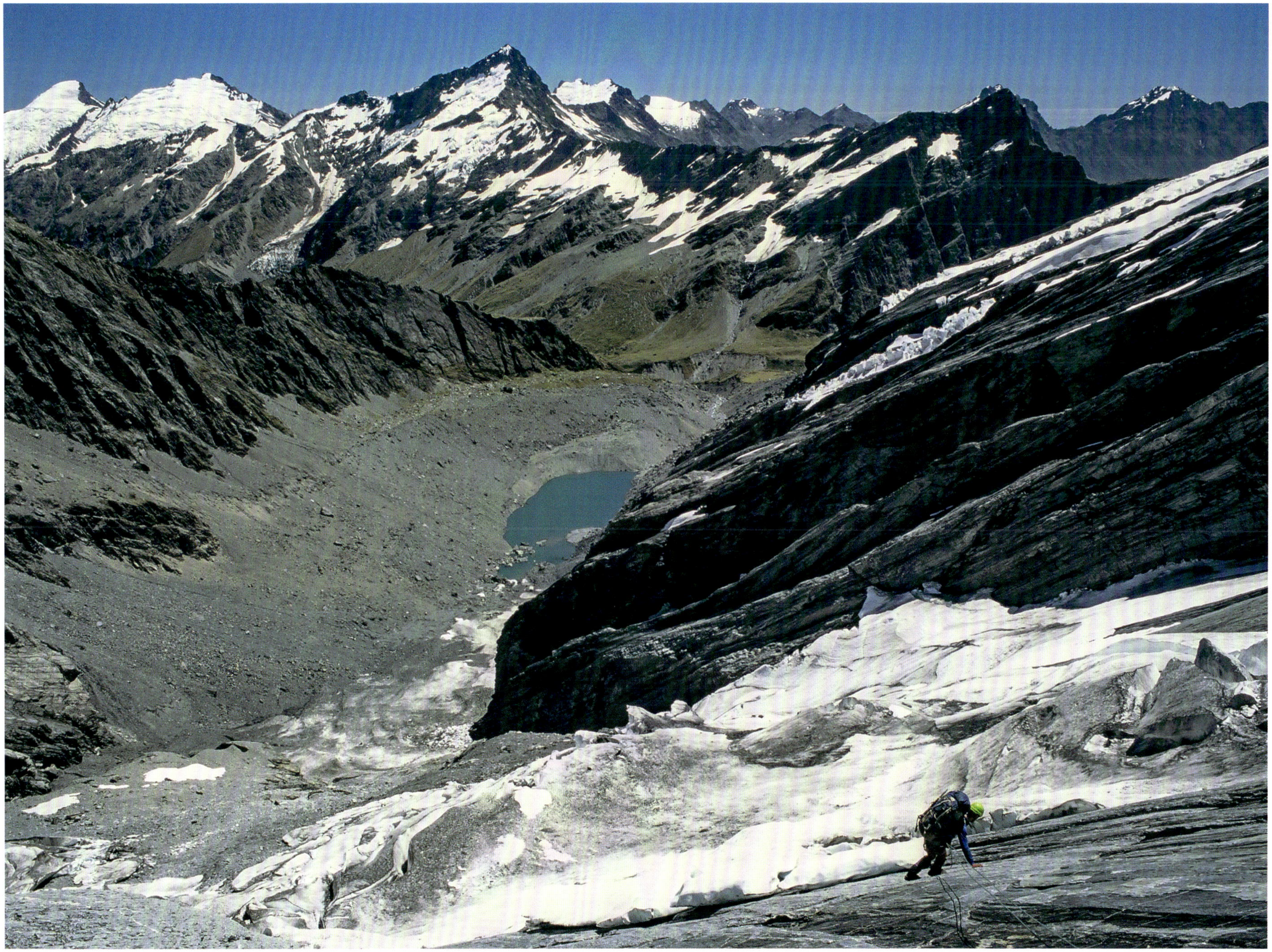

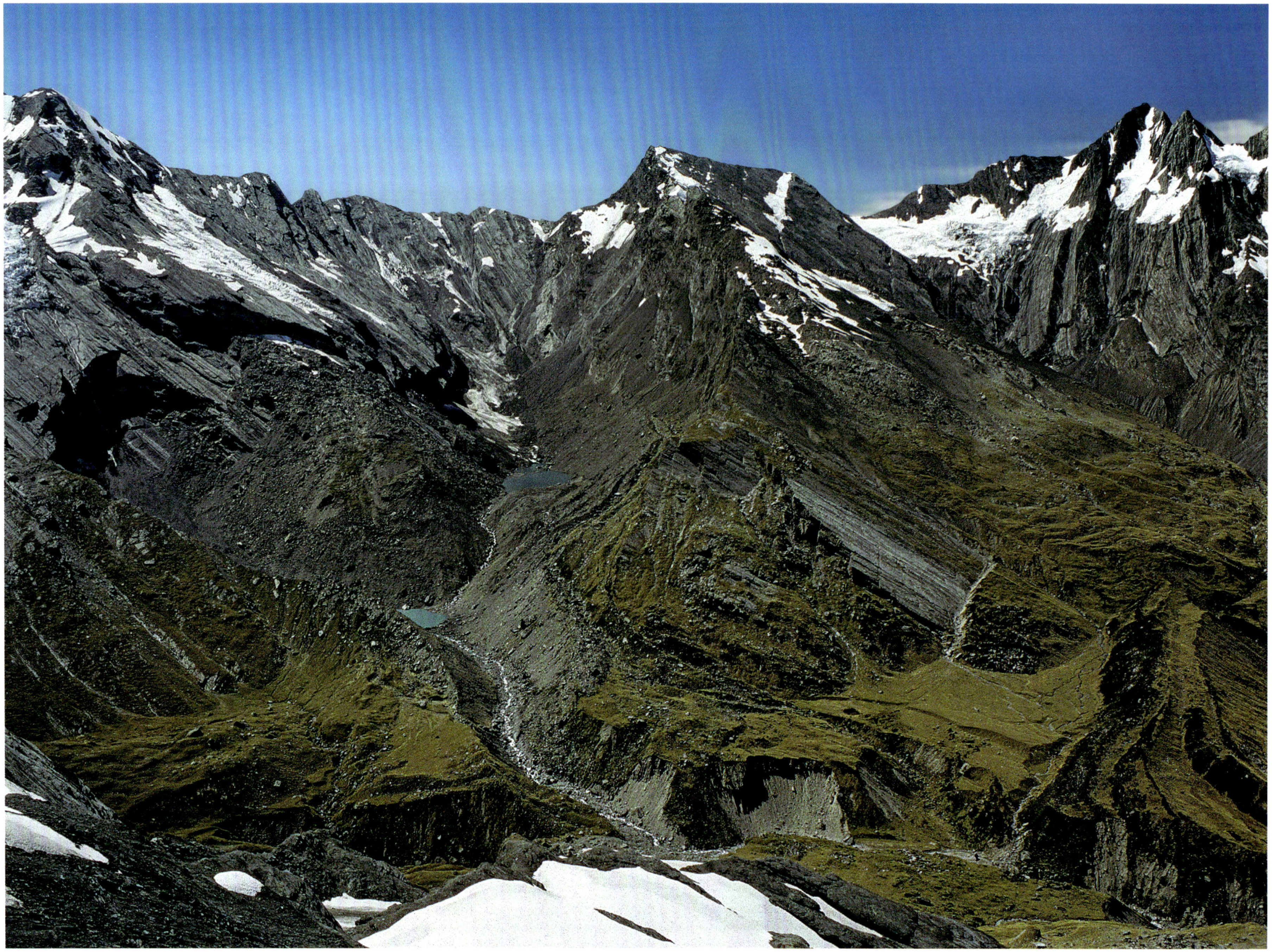

Once confronted, the dragons of the Makawhio turned out to be not much different from other nearby valleys, and we struggled with scrub, wet bush, river boulders and forest sidles. In the headwaters, though, down as far as Relief Flat, the sky was clear, and offered spectacular views up to Fettes Peak, on to the Bannock Brae Range, the Bare Rocky Range, and especially around the clean rockwalls of White Hummock and McGloin Peak. There will be some stunning trips there for someone one day.

One of the other enduring memories of the Makawhio was the wildlife. Whio appeared on the river regularly (about 16 to 20 in total), chamois families suddenly popped up among river boulders, and deer sauntered past on the other side of the river twice. Unfortunately, there was a lot of possum sign too, and palisades of dead rātā stuck out starkly on bluffs above the river. Lower down, we smelt several goats before we saw them, and several times kaka swung out, calling over the valley. In the riverbed, we saw one or two stones of aotea, a rare rock containing a blue/green mineral called kyanite, which is unique to the area. The Makawhio is a very special place.

OPPOSITE The head of the Landsborough River from the Hooker Range. Slabs leading into Rubicon Torrent are left of centre, Mt Burns is extreme left, Mt Spence, centre, and Black Tower, with its sweeping rockwalls, on the right.

RIGHT Jagged Spur on the Bare Rocky Range, from the Makawhio Valley.

KARANGARUA-FETTES PEAK-MAHITAHI

KARANGARUA VALLEY–THE GLADIATOR–DOUGLAS PASS– HARPER ROCK–LANDSBOROUGH VALLEY–ZORA CANYON– FETTES PEAK–MUELLER PASS–MAHITAHI VALLEY

12 DAYS: 3–14 FEBRUARY 1991
GS WITH JEFF HALL AND BEN UNDERHILL

The Karangarua is big country, with wild walls of scrub, high, vaulting rock bluffs and tough tops. It has long been a favourite for hunters and transalpine parties.

We started up the Karangarua with substantial packs, scrambling through the gorges and bluffs in mid valley on a track that was sometimes easy and sometimes crossed greasy rock slabs, where streams tumbled down between bluffs. Further up at Lame Duck Flat, under a sombre ceiling of low cloud, we came across a rusty old hut, and later another at Christmas Flat.

Both flats were named by A.P. Harper. Heading up from Baking Oven Creek to Mt Howitt we crossed over Gladiator and descended to Douglas Pass on the Hooker Range. Here we took the chance to spend a night at Harpers Rock Bivouac and watch the ice crumble 500 metres off the edge of the Douglas Neve onto the glacier below. It is a stunning spot.

As was the head of the Landsborough under Karangarua Saddle the next day. Back in 1894, Harper walked off this saddle straight onto the McKerrow Glacier. Now, the glacier has retreated up-valley and we were crunching down the fine gravel flats of a lazy Landsborough looking at sheer slabs 300 metres high. The ice has steadily been retreating from here for over a century. By the time we reached Zora Canyon it felt like we had been going for that long, too, and we were looking forward to Mueller Pass and Fettes Peak.

Fettes Peak was named by Charlie Douglas after his uncle who founded Fettes College in Edinburgh. Christopher Johnson had been a pupil at Fettes College and was very keen to be on the first ascent. With Archie Scott and Scott Russell, he achieved that in January 1935, placing his old school hatband in the summit cairn they built. Just two days later and approaching from the Mahitahi Valley, Marie Byles and Marjorie Edgar-Jones, accompanied by guides Harry Ayres and Frank Alack, made the second ascent.

Both parties were rather shocked by the timing. Marie Byles wrote, 'It was rather like Scott arriving at the South Pole to find that Amundsen had arrived there first, only this time it was 'Scott' who got in first . . .' Coincidences like this have happened in other places, The Great Unknown peak in the Garden of Eden being one of them.

Beginning up a gully from the Zora we traversed over 2190 metres and climbed Fettes on a crisp day that provided exciting views across the Landsborough. By the time we were on top, though, afternoon cloud curled up out of the north-west, offering only fleeting glimpses in that direction.

We did see the peaks at the head of the Zora Glacier. When Douglas and Mueller carried out a reconnaissance survey of this country, the subsequent map in 1887 had two peaks marked along the Bannock Brae range near Fettes Peak: Query and Doubtful. It then became doubtful whether Query Peak was marked in the right place, and this raised a query as to whether Mt Doubtful was either.

In the 1930s, Marie Byles and party had difficulty making sense of the map topography here – it was wrong – coming to the conclusion that Query Peak and Mt Doubtful, rather than being the two low peaks marked on the survey maps, were actually the considerably higher, unnamed snow peaks at the head of the Zora Glacier. This also made sense to mountaineers Norm Hardie and friends in the 1940s, and was corrected on a map published in *The Canterbury Mountaineer,* 1958/59. However, Lands and Survey-contoured mapping, both imperial then metric, continued to place them on lower peaks along the range.

Following Byles and Hardie, James Thornton and Nina Dickerhof have been unravelling this yet again and, following their submissions, the New Zealand Geographic Board officially accepted in November 2017 that Query Peak is 2259 metres and Mt Doubtful is 2245 metres at the head of the Zora Glacier. LINZ has updated the current maps.

The conflict between these previously mapped positions on the Bannock Brae Range versus the head of the Zora is easily resolved when the current maps overlay the old map. The exact positions of peaks were triangulated by theodolite from the coast and other places. Later, the positions of the ranges and headwaters were sketched in, and in this area the topography was drawn incorrectly, as a comparison with what the modern maps show. On the other hand, the triangulated positions, relative to the other main peaks in the area, Dechen, Fettes, etc, line up exactly with the peaks at the head of Zora Glacier. A very small mistake on an otherwise complex mapping feat by Mueller.

Crossing Mueller Pass into the Mahitahi, we sidled out high in the tussock on big old deer trails, dancing with the valley and cagey about dropping down gravel creeks into the scrub. We had to eventually but found lines that led us down through most of it without too much scrub bashing.

The Mahitahi is a rough little valley in places, but it is mainly boulders and scrub that interfere with travel. Near the Edison confluence we stumbled on the collapsed remains of an old hunting hut, mellowing down amongst the moss. I always enjoy coming across little signs of past eras in the hills, and I wondered who the dedicated hunters were who built it and about those who travelled through using it. There's no smoke in this chimney now, though. Even isolated valleys like the Karangarua, Mahitahi, and Landsborough have a rich history and all we have left are a few sparse remains tucked among the mosses and prickly shield ferns.

Lower, we tried cutting across a bush terrace rather than following the river. This can often cut corners travelling down a valley, but not this time. As we drifted away from the river we ended up among boulders, gullies of fern and slow travel. All in all, a stuff up. Wiser, we stumbled back to the riverbed. Lower still, we picked up an old 4WD track and followed it out to the Condon's farmland and SH6.

RIGHT Jeff at Christmas Flat Hut, Karangarua Valley, 1991.

OVERLEAF (LEFT) The view of the upper Landsborough from high on Fettes Peak. Baffle Ravine is on the right. Mt Burns pokes out from the cloud on the upper left, while the Fettes Glacier is below left.

OVERLEAF (RIGHT) Boulder travel in the Mahitahi River near the Edison junction. Rātā are flowering.

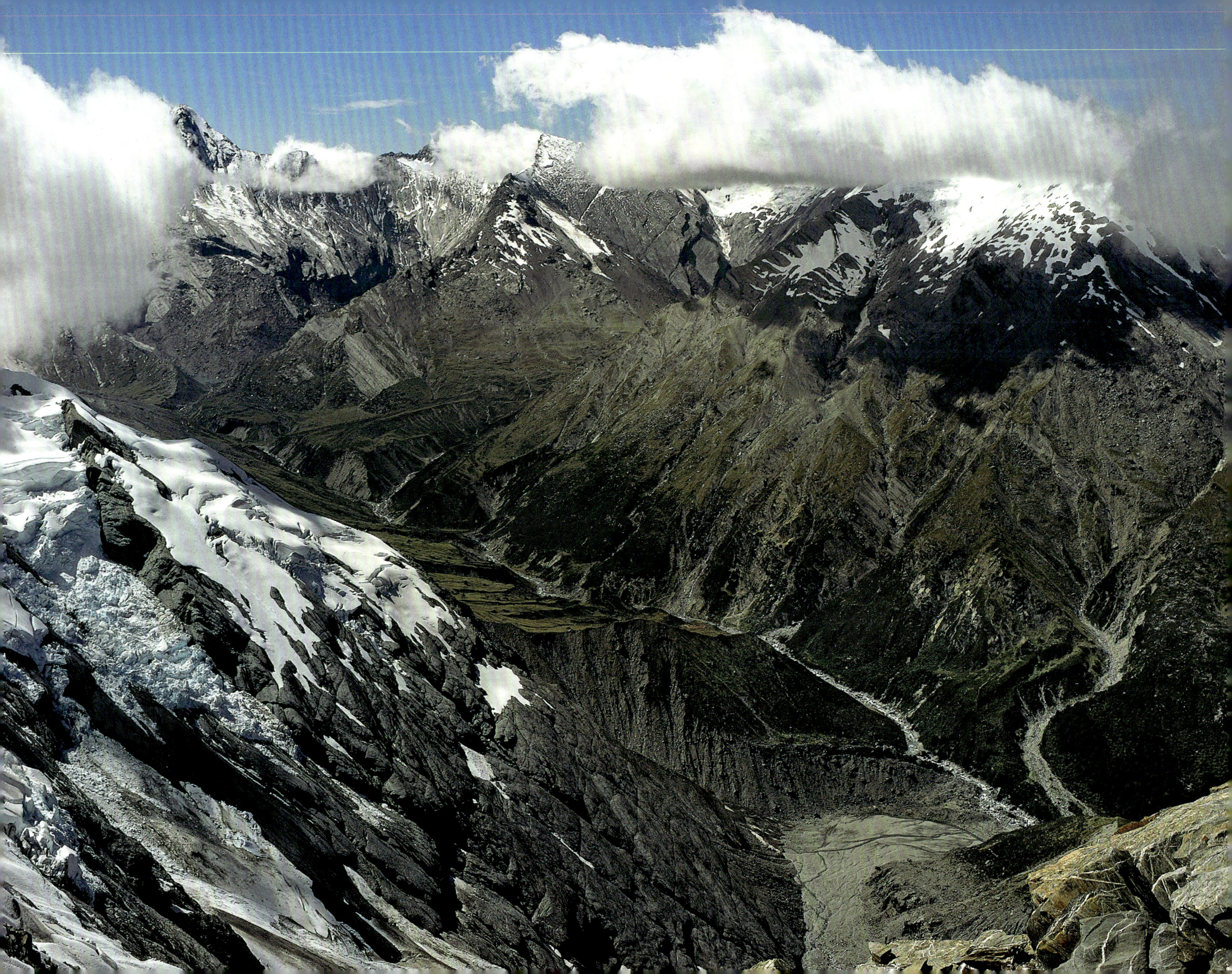

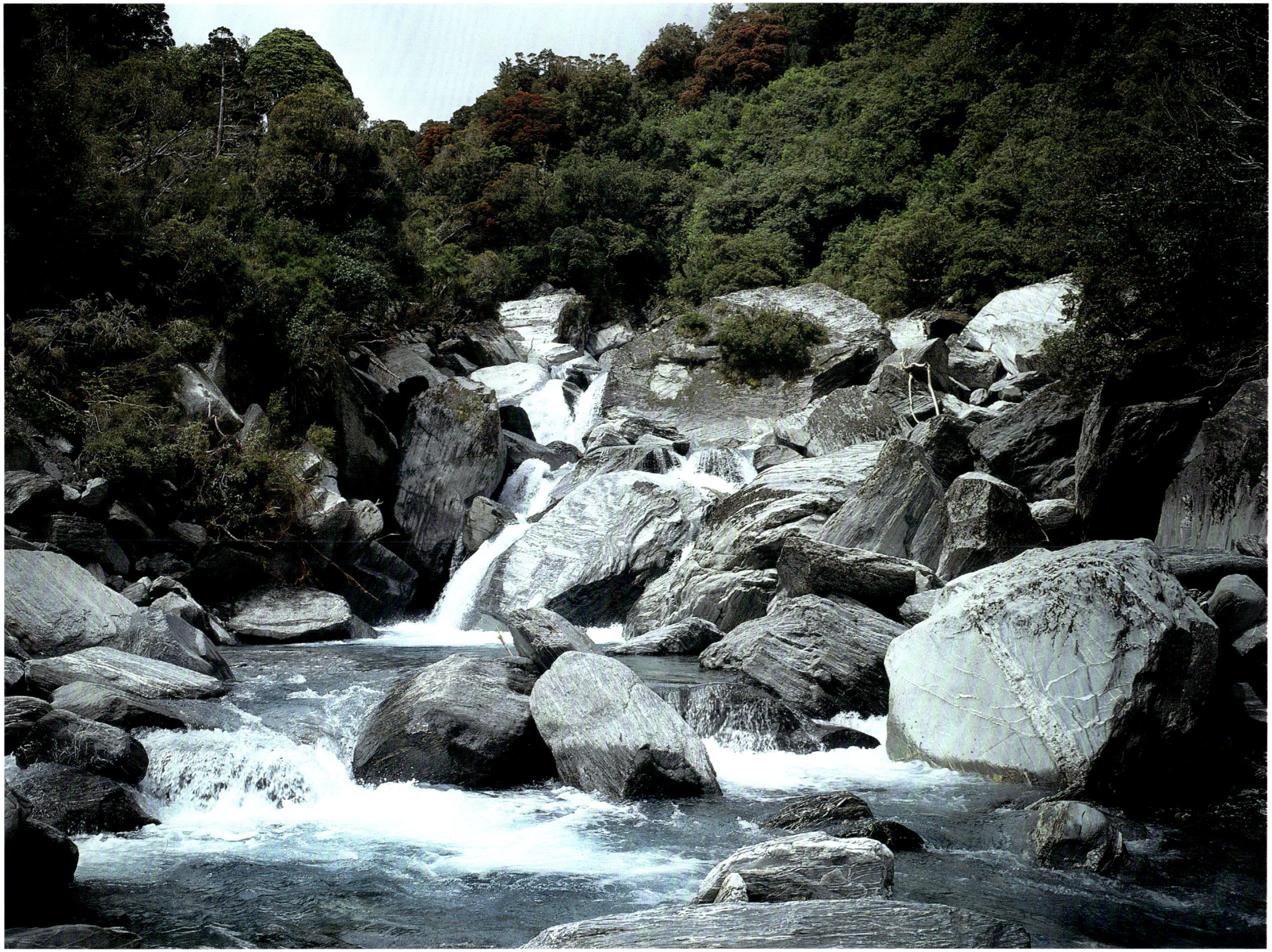

OTOKO–MARKS FLAT–MOERAKI

OTOKO VALLEY–LOWER OTOKO PASS–MARKS FLAT–
MT MCCULLAUGH–CLARKE RIVER–ZEILIAN PASS–
MOERAKI VALLEY

13 DAYS: 26 DECEMBER 1968–8 JANUARY 1969
GS WITH DICK CORIN, JOHN MACDONALD, IAN MACDONALD, IAN COLLIGAN, BOB HENDRY, ROSS COOPER, IAN LATHAM, PETER FULLERTON, MURRAY FEIST, IAN THORNE, TIM OMUNDSEN, ANNE RICHARDSON, SUE BROSNAN AND ROBYN KELTON

Early experiences in the mountains often leave sharp memories. This Hutt Valley Tramping Club Christmas trip of 15 people was my first extended trip in the Southern Alps, and where I climbed my first peak. The whole journey was a fantastic experience that encouraged me to seek out further remote and wild places.

A party that was mixed in age, gender and experience, we began in the Otoko branch of the Paringa River. To be fully self-sufficient for two weeks required very careful planning to keep the weight down. Virtually all food was dried, prepared for the whole party, and sealed in plastic. So, a breakfast bag might be porridge, with separate bags inside of dried fruit, milk powder and sugar, all carefully weighed. A couple of people would be responsible for breakfast, (and dinners) and we all took turns. That may seem like a hassle, but I don't remember it that way. Basically, it meant only being on cooking duty a couple of times a week. Hardly onerous.

The Otoko is a rough river, with stumbling, scrambling travel where, in the lower reaches, we took long detours past fierce stinging nettle (*Urtica ferox*) lying in ambush. The sandflies and mosquitoes attacked at every stop, and we used repellent liberally. Rough cattle trails gave way to deer trails, and then to scrubby forest. Our party battled on, assaulting boulders for a way through – big boulders surrounded by scrub.

Each night we chose campsites carefully and lit a good fire to cook over. This provided a focal point for the evening, and hours were spent in the fire's communal warmth, chatting about the day behind and the days ahead.

Within the party there was a lot of knowledge. Dick, the leader (or ringmaster as he was termed), had been a culler at one stage, and several other people had strong outdoors backgrounds. I was in good company and absorbed everything.

In the 1960s, Christmas trips like this were run by many tramping clubs. It was a wonderful way to celebrate both Christmas and New Year with lots of like-minded friends, and an attractive alternative to the frenzied buying, eating and drinking fests these celebrations have become. But the reason for long trips at Christmas was also much more pragmatic. In the very structured world of employment at the time, Christmas through to New Year was the only extended period in the year many could get off work.

In the head of the Otoko at that time lay an extensive lake with walls of rock rising straight out of it towards Mt Dechen. Reaching the lake, we had to cross the outlet. Using a rope for safety, we crossed one at a time, each of us up to our waists in the icy water. (Now the lake is a gravel flat.)

Turning south, the trip caravan climbed out of the Otoko over snowfields of the Lower Otoko Pass and descended to Marks Flat in the head of the Clarke River, using the rope again to get down a bluff.

New Year's Eve saw us camped at the bush edge overlooking flats of red tussock and midnight was marked by a rifle shot. Marks Flat is a captivating landscape deep in the Hooker Wilderness, with Mt Hooker rising to the north. On the following rest day, a keen hunter stalked around the flats looking for a deer, much to the entertainment of the rest of the party, his secret location well marked by Paradise duck alarm cries and kea squawking. But we did have venison a few times on the trip; a nice extra to complement the dry food.

From Munro Flat, lower down the Clarke, four of us climbed Mt McCullaugh (2266 metres). Peter Fullerton was in charge, and we headed up through dry beech forest to the bushline and camped. An early start soon saw us on the firm snowcap heading towards a final summit scramble. Views unfolded from Aoraki Mt Cook to Mt Brewster. This was my first ascent of a glaciated peak in the Southern Alps, and I loved it.

Alternating between flats and gorges, the party later continued down the Clarke to Rough Creek Hut and camped. We used the hut as a welcome shelter from the rain on a rest day, feeding the fire as it fed us brews. The hut is now gone, and last time I was there only the door could be found, propped against a tree.

RIGHT When descending into the Landsborough from Elcho Pass, the Hooker Range rises up across the valley. Snowy Mt Dechen (centre), rocky Mt Elliot, and Mt Strachan, further right.

OVERLEAF (LEFT) On Marks Flat. A unique and magical place.

OVERLEAF (RIGHT) Morning mist in the Clarke Valley below Monro Flat.

The last leg of the trip included climbing over a shoulder into the head of Zeilian Creek. From there we crossed a pass into the Moeraki Valley and later camped below Pegmatite Creek. One of the instigators of the trip but unable to go was club member Dr Jim Finch, a scientist who worked at the DSIR Gracefield. Jim was after flaky muscovite mica from pegmatitic rock, sourced from this area, for his theory that the hue in mica might be an indicator of specific minerals. With a bit of looking and good luck we found him some.

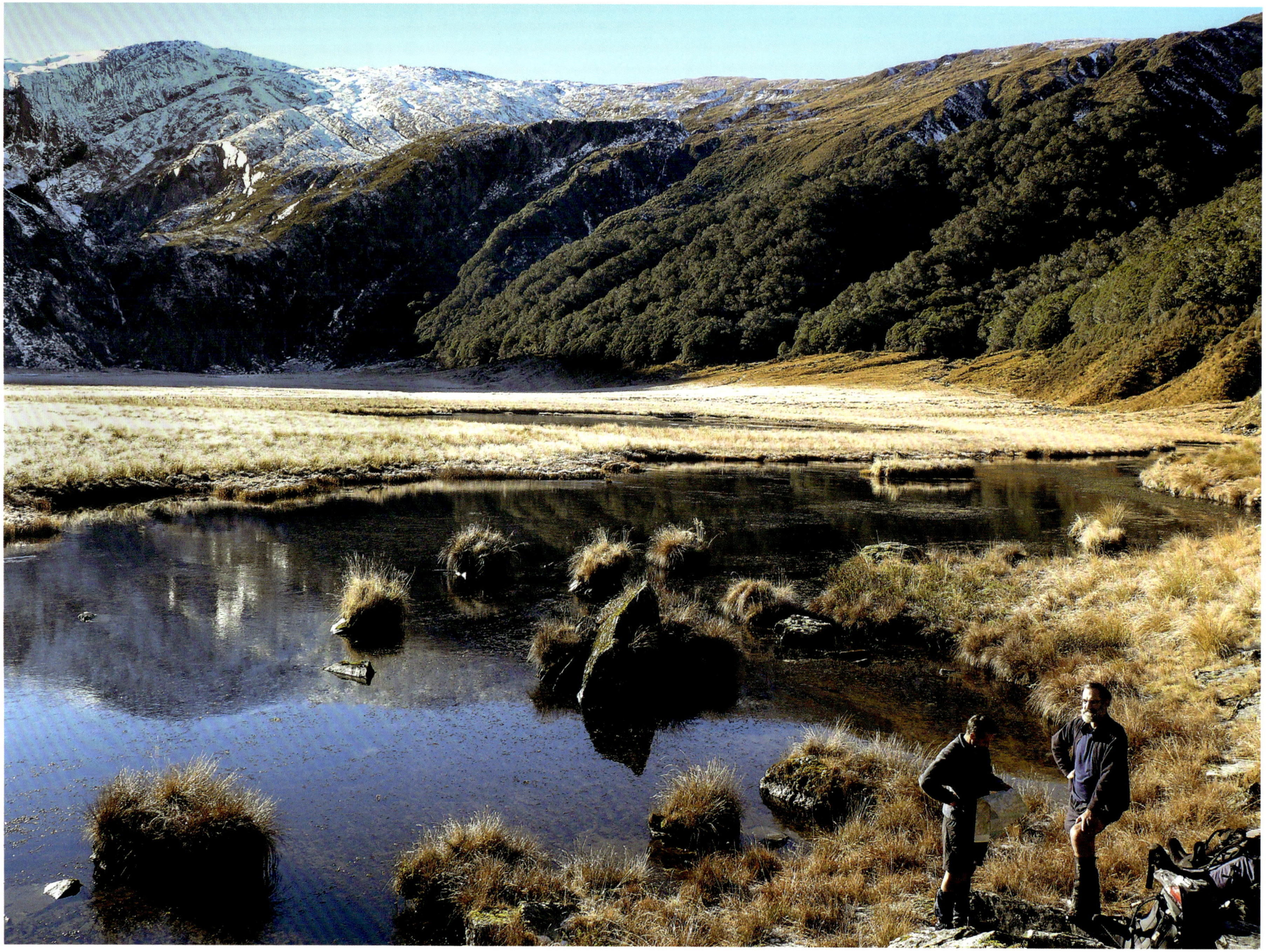

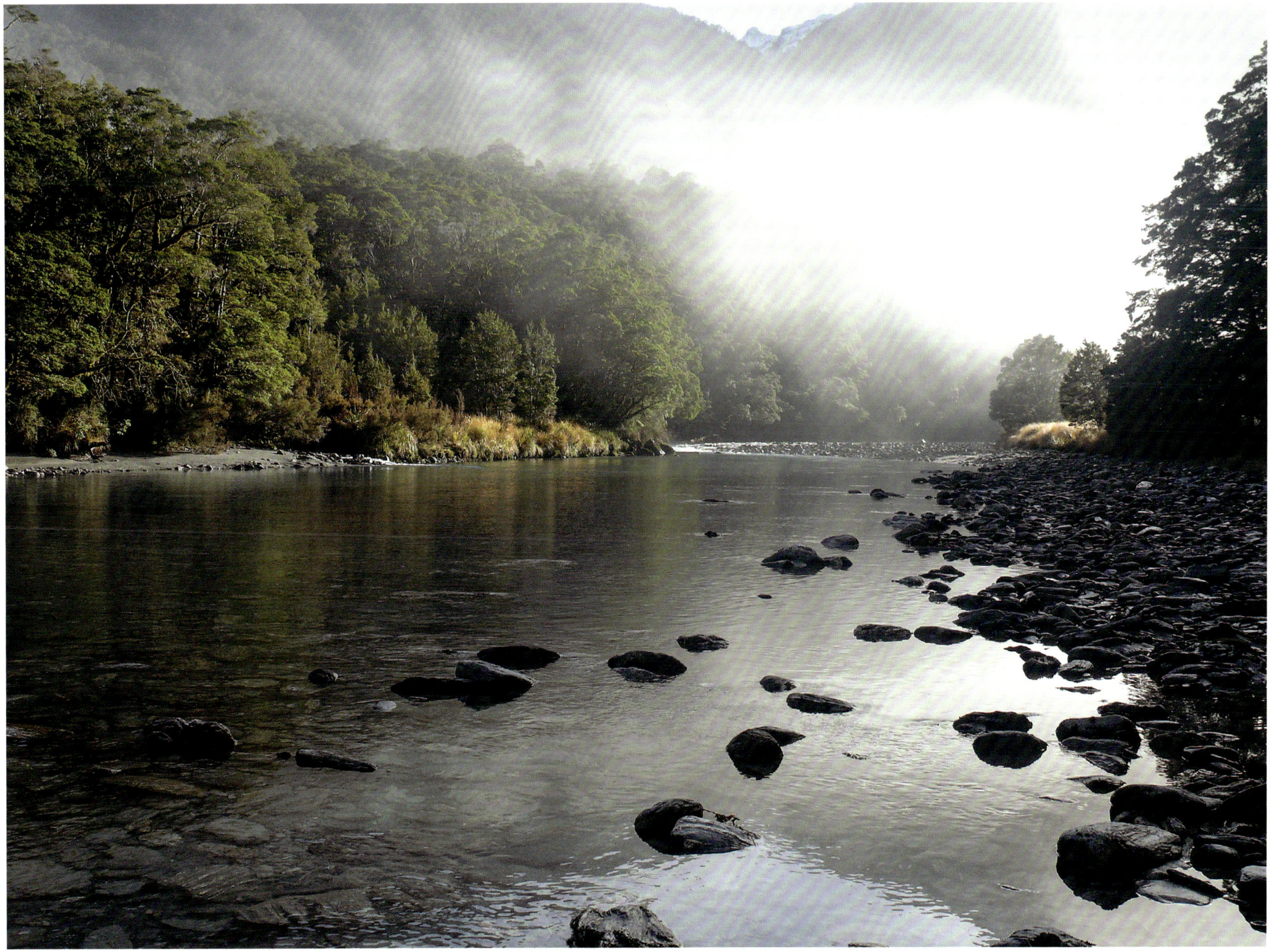

THE SOLUTION TO MT HOOKER

MOERAKI RIVER–CLARKE RIVER–SOLUTION RANGE–MARKS FLAT–MT HOOKER–MCCULLAUGH CREEK–PARINGA RIVER

11 DAYS: 22 DECEMBER 1996–1 JANUARY 1997

GS WITH BARBARA BROWN, DAVID GLENNY AND SVEN BRABYN

Mt Hooker, viewed from Pleasant Flat on the Haast Highway, is the epitome of a wilderness mountain. Thirty years after my first trip around it I went back, but this time we approached it from the Solution Range. An old cattle track led us into the Moeraki Valley and we bowled along listening to kaka and brown creepers. Mistletoe flowered profusely, its parasitic roots suckered onto the branches of silver beech trees. Now there were two huts in the valley, and a good track. By the end of the day we were settled into Middle Head Hut with the fire crackling.

Crossing into Zeilian Creek involved much of the same scrub-bashing through prickly shield fern and *Hoheria* as it did previously, and we tucked under a handy boulder out of the rain in our bright PVC parkas for lunch.

Down in the Clarke Valley we caught glimpses of chattering kākāriki and kaka, while the sharp roll of mohua sounded in upper branches. On the river, whio bobbed in front of us.

Opposite Rough Creek we began climbing through beech forest towards the Solution Range. On the midslopes where it steepened, rātā–kāmahi forest took over before handing back to silver beech near the bushline.

On this trip, David was our botanist, Barb studied entomology, and we all had an interest in natural history. Being aware of what is around in the environment adds whole levels of interest to trips, and as A.P. Harper noted, 'Observation is the foundation stone of bushcraft.' Some plants indicate winter avalanche paths; others indicate damp ground, such as the umbrella mosses (*Hypnodendron* spp). *Rhacomitrium* spp, on the other hand, usually offer dry campsites.

We hit the Solution Range where the range itself emerges from the forest. The day was hot and dry, so at the first large tarn, David and I plunged in for a swim. Beyond Mt Solution a section on the range is eroded. We sidled rock and scree on the Clarke side before reaching good tussock-going again and descending to the enchanted Marks Flat. Marion Scott, writing in the *New Zealand Alpine Journal* in 1937 described it this way: 'Kea Cliffs guard an inaccessible Lost World of a plateau well-watered by tarns; Marks Flat is a remote secret little plain where the Clarke rises, and from where it escapes by a very steep rock gorge.'

Marion Scott was viewing it from a spur above the flat, and from there she and Dora de Beer, along with their guides Joe Fluerty and Chris Pope, climbed a new route on Mt Hooker, on what has now become the standard approach from Marks Flat. Sven and I used this route to climb the mountain, too, and were surprised to find two guides and their friend on the Hooker Glacier. We had wondered who owned the duffle bag zipped up at the rock bivvy. It's not the sort of gear you walk very far with.

ABOVE Sven on the Hooker Glacier above Marks Flat, approaching Mt Hooker.
OPPOSITE The impressive southern faces of Mt Hooker rise above the clouds.

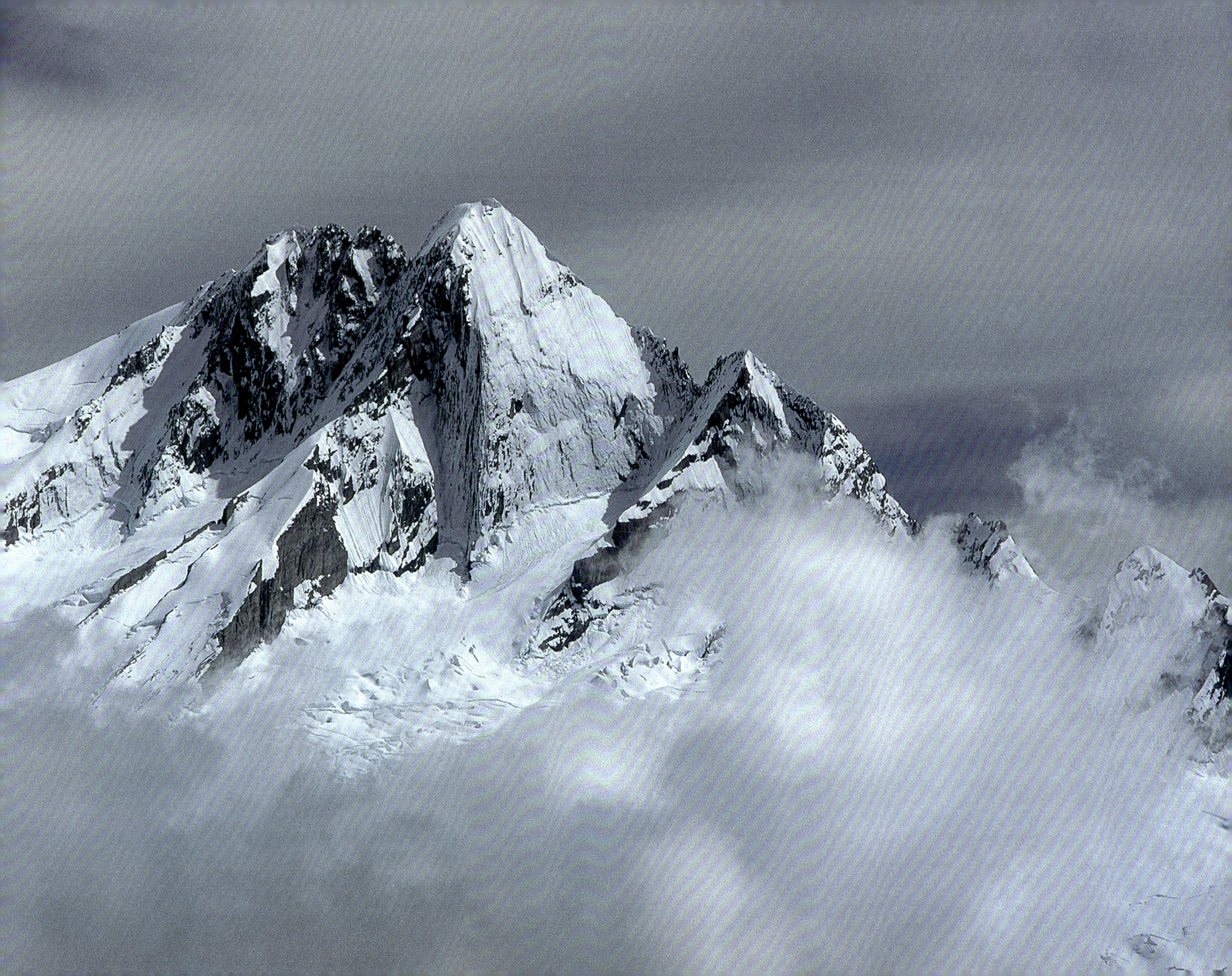

LEFT Snow falling on the Moeraki River.
OPPOSITE Paringa River, near Tunnel Creek.

Hooker by this route is not a particularly difficult mountain. The trick is really about good route-finding, and we were on top by 11.45 a.m. Our gear was as low tech as the others was high. We simply used 30 metres of 7-millimetre cord, a harness, prusicks and a few karabiners. And I'm going to claim that this was probably the first ascent of Mt Hooker in lace-up rubber gumboots. They were good khaki Paraflex ones, mind you, and I was careful when using them with my crampons, but rubber gummies none the less.

To use Marion Scott's description of the view: 'Next to us were the beautiful snow slopes of Dechen and the extraordinarily wild country of the Otoko Valley, stark uncompromising grey slabs of rock.' Once back down, Scott's party celebrated the climb with plum pudding. We enjoyed whisky and cake, thanks to the guided party.

Crossing the Hooker Range from McCullaugh Creek into the Paringa Valley took us past one of my favourite bivvy rocks at the bushline above Tunnel Creek. This big slab of rock, like an open cockleshell on its side, faces on to a tussock flat, with enough room for half a dozen people to sleep on flat ground underneath it. Tucked in one corner is an open fireplace.

On New Year's Eve we slept in Tunnel Creek Hut, too tired to hang around for 'Auld Lang Syne' or even hear the odd mosquito. But I was certainly enchanted by the whole Paringa Valley, with its emerald pools and forest.

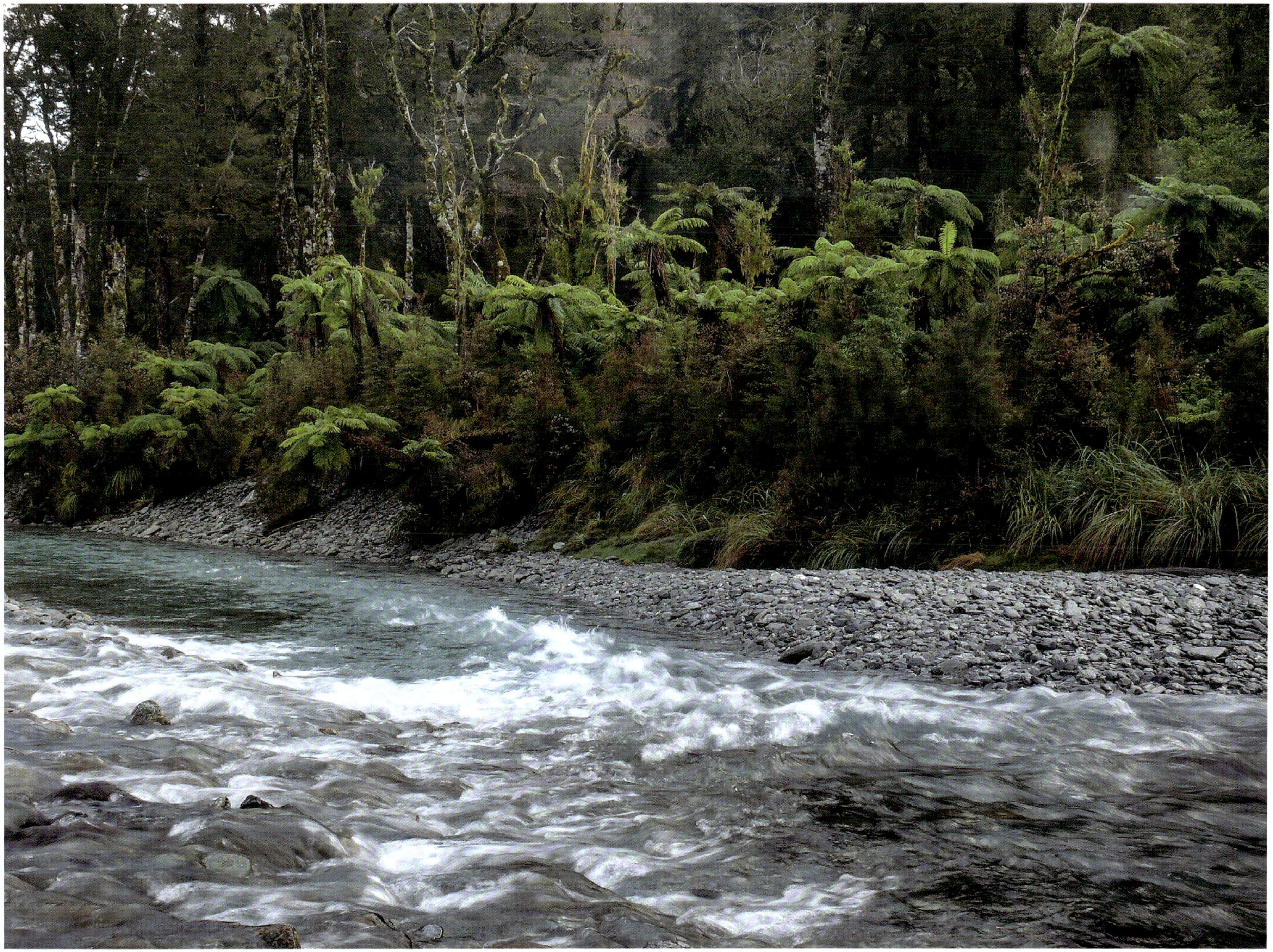

Jackson Bay
N
0
5
10 km
SELBORNE RANGE TRAVERSE
SELBORNE RANGE
Mt Selborne
< Turnbull River
< Okuru River
Burke River >
6
WINTER WILDERNESS
Haast Pass / Tioripatea
Souter Peak
Ngatau River >
MAIN DIVIDE
Maori Saddle
Jackson River >
Waiatoto River >
< Mueller River
Siberia Saddle
Blue River >
Mt Dispute
< Te Naihi River
Stewart Pass
Gillespie Pass
MOIRS MISSION
Mt Alba
Newland Pass
Siberia Valley
Young River >
< Drake River
Leda Peak
Mt Castor
Newland Strm >
Makarora
Arawhata River >
< Waiatoto River
Mt Pollux
< Makarora River
Wilkin River >
Wilkin River >
THE DARK SIDE OF THE DIVIDE
Pearson Saddle
Rabbit Pass
Ruth Ridge
Volta Glacier
Mt Aspiring / Tititea
< East Matukituki River
MAIN DIVIDE
Lake Wanaka
6
Lake Hāwea

CHAPTER 11

FROM THE OKURU TO THE WILKIN

Extending south and west from Haast Pass, this region is off many people's radar. Interlocking valleys of beech forest like the Okuru, Mueller and Te Naihi, with their attractive grass flats, fierce slot gorges and boulder cascades, are separated by craggy schist ranges like the Drake, Selborne and Browning. While many of the peaks don't go much above 2000 metres, some reach over 2500 metres in the south (Mt Castor and Mt Pollux), and there are remote icefields, glaciers, and difficult alpine rock ridges, such as between Souter Peak and Mt Dreadful. It's a place with a bit of everything wild, including sudden thunderstorms and lightning. Eastern valleys like the Blue, Young and Wilkin are mostly more mellow, and have huts and tracks where the scenery is attractive, but access to the Main Divide tops is seldom easy.

Many captivating names, such as Eyetooth, Mt Victor, Mt Achilles, Uproar Gorge, Presto Defile, Hailstorm Gully and Greasy Gully, go back to the survey days of Charlie Douglas. Otago climbers (OSONZAC, the Otago Section of the New Zealand Alpine Club was formed in 1930) explored and climbed most peaks here, almost invariably from the east. Mt Castor was first climbed from the Wilkin River North Branch via Chasm Pass, and Donald Glacier in 1937 by C.C. Benzoni, L.W. Divers, R.R. and G.L. Edwards, and D.C. Peters. Mt Doris (2010 metres) was climbed by Bob Craigie and party in 1948. Between these dates, most other Main Divide peaks were also climbed. In the west, much of the history belongs to hunters, who lived, flew into and tramped this country from the 1950s onwards.

There are some excellent and often staunch trips to be had in this region, where resilience and skill will be needed. The Young–Siberia–Ngatau–Okuru–Blue offers a great trip to get a measure of the area, and although it may seem like only three pass crossings, there is more challenge in it than that. Siberia Saddle is steep and difficult on the east, the Ngatau is untracked and the Okuru is slow travel with big boulders and tricky bush navigation. The upper Blue Valley has charming flats and steep mountains.

SELBORNE RANGE TRAVERSE

WAIATOTO RIVER–SELBORNE RANGE–MT DISPUTE–LEDA PEAK–WILKIN RIVER

10 DAYS: 28 DECEMBER 2011–6 JANUARY 2012
GS WITH ROB FROST, CLAIRE GIBB, YVONNE PFLUGER AND TIM CHURCH

The Selborne is a 20-kilometre 'aerial highway' sandwiched between the Waiatoto and the Mueller rivers, running south from near Okuru to near Mt Alba above the Wilkin Valley. I'd talked with Rob in the past about the Selborne. Now he invited me to join him and some Alpine Club friends on this major range-traverse.

To avoid a deep and difficult river crossing, we took a Waiatoto jetboat to Long Beach at the base of Selborne Spur. As we repacked on the riverbank once the boat had gone, I looked at the others and realised they were all half my age, and they were probably twice as fit too. This was a big trip, and I started thinking I might be lucky to get out of this alive.

With 10-day packs it was a bit of a slog up Selborne Spur, but our stops in the bush were enlivened by inquisitive kaka. On the tops we camped near a tarn and enjoyed a little scrub fire with a brew. On wet rock outcrops we discovered beautifully camouflaged, knobbly leaf-veined slugs, over 100 millimetres long.

Trips like this require a fair amount of faith and persistence to carry through. It took us six more days to travel south to the Main Divide, and all of them were strenuous 10-hour days or more. Some nights we camped right on the range, on knobs such as 1819 metres. The rocks were a bit rough but watching the sunset's rays playing with South Westland mountains from Mt Aspiring to Aoraki Mt Cook was magical.

On New Year's Eve four of us snuggled high up on Presto Spur overlooking Greasy Gulch (don't you love those names!) with just our sleeping bags. We even had a little Baileys Irish Cream to celebrate. Waking in the dead of night I watched the universe wheel its way inexorably across the blackness, the pinhole stars burning with intensity. In places like this the enormity of the mountains can be overwhelming, but lying there looking skyward, the mountains and all of planet Earth turned into a speck.

Friends Warren Herrick and Steve Bruce crossed the Selborne Range near here, from the Te Naihi to Quail Flat in the Mueller, during an epic traverse of the Southern Alps on the western side of the Main Divide from Lake Te Anau to St Arnaud in 1980.

Our days were filled with challenges and highlights, sometimes both together. Always, we were looking for a route past the next obstacle. Sometimes it was obvious. Other times it wasn't, and we dropped packs to investigate, scrambling up walls and setting up anchors to belay from, such as a wall just south of Mt Calliope. But that's the fun, sorting little problems, having adventures, with the next obstacle rising up on the range in front. After that, an airy traverse took us along a ridge of slabs and tussock to a saddle before the climb to Mt Dispute. Having found water, we camped there. This was our sixth night on the range, and so far I'd slept out on five of them. We were very lucky with the weather.

Kea were few and far between, but rock wrens showed up in twos and fours everywhere. The reality of what these guys face up here came home sharply when, high on Mt Dispute, we looked back to see a stoat rubbing his back on a tiny bank of snow about 40 metres away. I couldn't believe my eyes. It was cute and entertaining with its flips and flexibility, but left dread for the future of those rock wren.

Higher on Mt Dispute we belayed one or two sections where things were steep and exposed, on blocky schist full of quartz veins. I'd been on Mt Dispute a couple of times before and reassured the others it was all very easy up near the top. Turns out I've got a dodgy memory. Romping down snow slopes on the other side, we cut across the upper Te Naihi on to the Main Divide near Mt Achilles and camped by a big tarn, before dropping into the Wilkin River North Branch on our way out.

Our last night at Kerin Forks Hut was shared with a warden whom I recognised as Ivan McLauchlan, a friend from the Otago section of the NZAC. Ivan was scoping out a retirement home funded by hut fees, but he did provide a free breakfast of delicious brown trout. What a way to finish a fabulous trip.

RIGHT Claire and Rob near Mt Selborne, looking across the Turnbull Valley.
OVERLEAF (LEFT) A cold camp on the Main Divide above the Te Naihi.
OVERLEAF (RIGHT) Rising like a blade; the Selborne Range towards Mt Dispute.

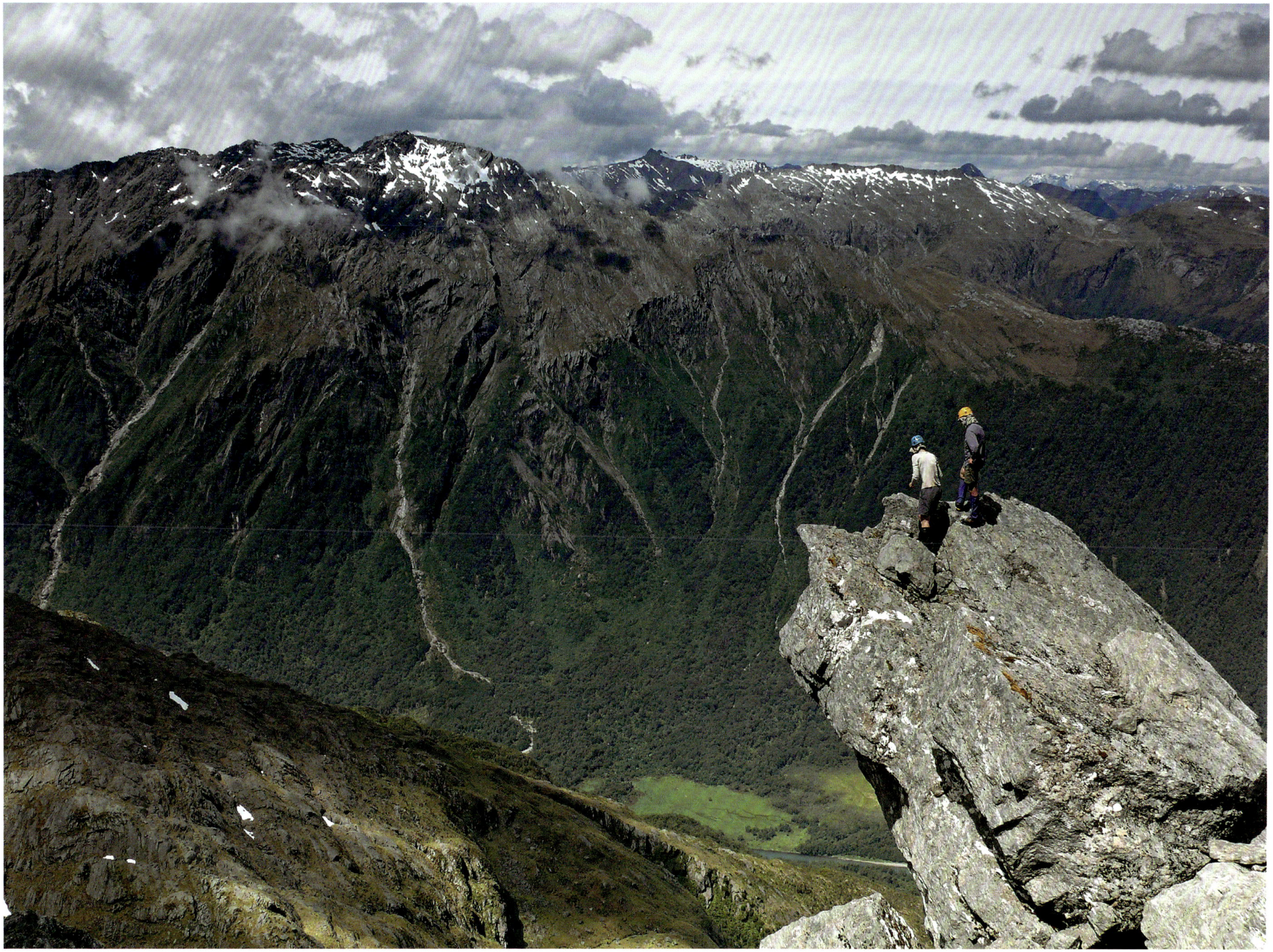

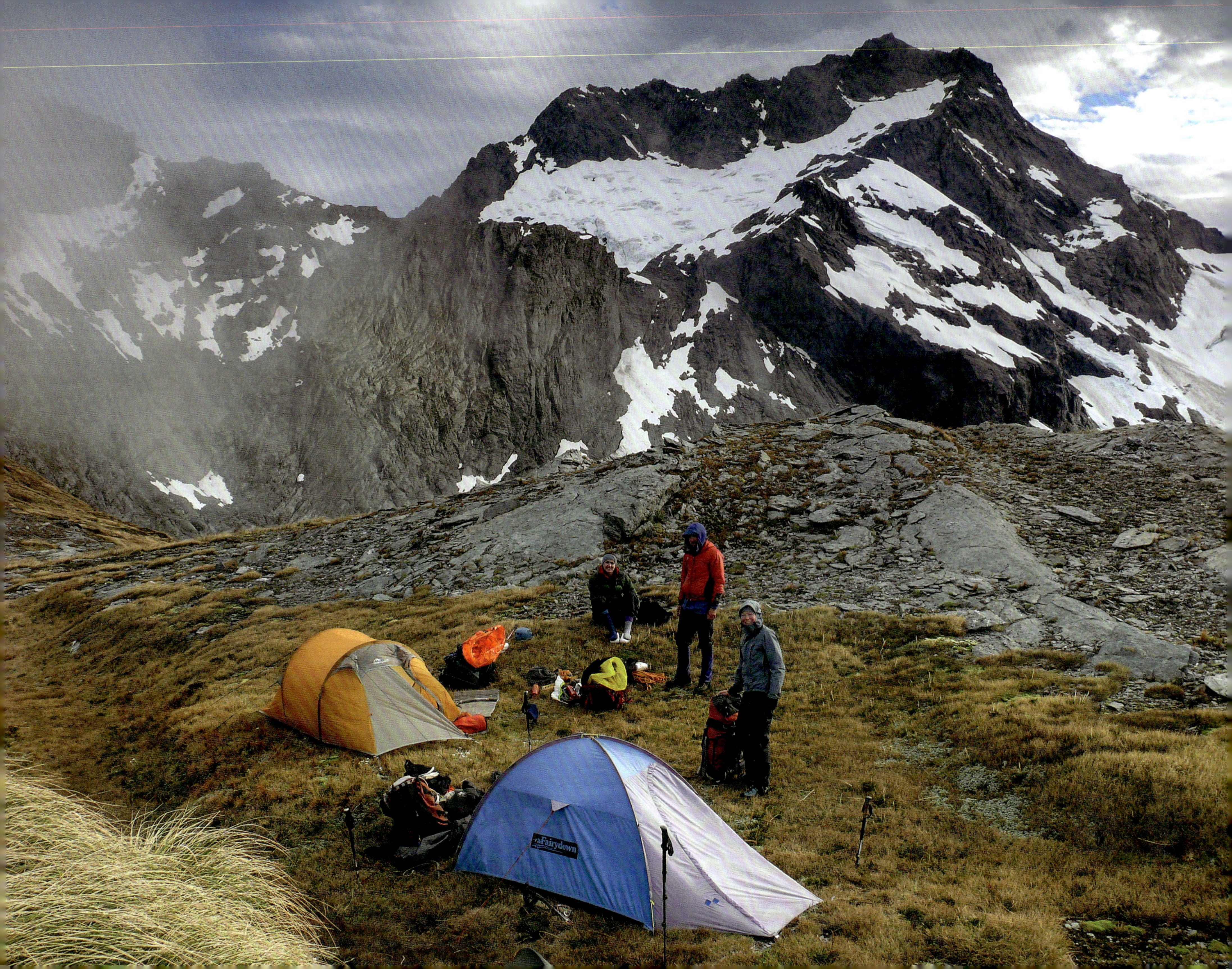
Fairydown

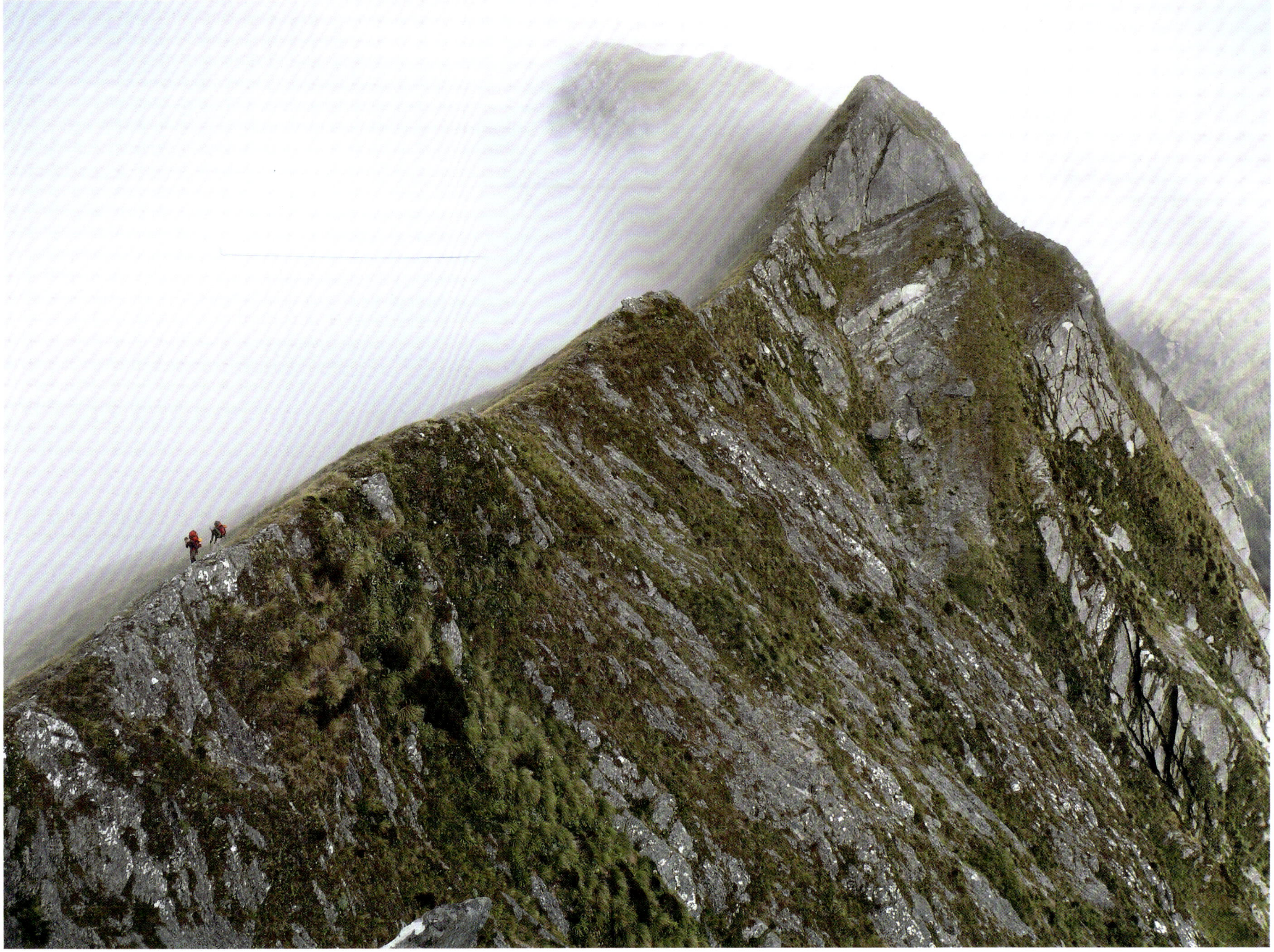

THE DARK SIDE OF THE DIVIDE

WILKIN VALLEY–NEWLAND STREAM AND PASS– TE NAIHI RIVER–DRAKE RIVER–MT CASTOR–WAIATOTO RIVER–VOLTA GLACIER–RUTH RIDGE–EAST MATUKITUKI

9 DAYS: 3–11 FEBRUARY 1979

GS WITH MATT WARWICK

North of Mt Aspiring/Tititea there is a block of mountains surrounded by icefields that includes Pollux and Castor mountains. Both peaks are normally climbed from the east, but we chose to try Castor from the west, on a mountain journey that would cross the Main Divide twice.

Matt and I took a jet boat up the Wilkin River to Kerin Forks, and in 1979 that cost us $9 each. About 2 kilometres beyond, we left the valley tramping track to cross the Wilkin River and swing up into Newland Stream, beginning with a sidle past a waterfall on the true right. Bashing through prickly shield fern and *Hoheria* under a partial canopy of silver beech set the scene for much of our forest travel. For the next week there would be no easy tracks to follow, but this was part of the attraction.

Newland Pass on the Main Divide looked more daunting than we'd expected, and we slept out under a boulder at the mercy of nocturnal kea. Just about asleep, then 'rustle rustle rustle' as they began pulling at the sleeping bag with their beaks. By three in the morning their game had become a bit tiresome. Kea have a persistence gene that sometimes jams on 'open'.

Sidling onto the Axius Glacier we headed towards Mt Alba, but steep rock in an approaching storm took away our enthusiasm. Instead, we headed for the lake outlet and then traversed across steep snow slopes to Te Naihi Saddle, which Charlie Douglas had arrived at in a snowstorm many years before. He hadn't had good views, and neither did we as we stood in mist looking for routes down.

In drizzle and on wet schist we picked our way with heavy packs through a grey world where a slip wasn't an option. A world of mushy rock and peeling slabs was dimming with the daylight. The rain became heavy and a waterfall lower down nearly called our bluff. Like rats looking for a new home we scurried on down unlikely routes to the safety of tussock below. Then we found a little miracle. Under a big bluff a few hundred metres on, there was a cave, a dry cave, a big commodious cave with a gravel floor. Sometimes heaven comes in small parcels. We settled in, while outside the rain poured down all night and into the next day. As it eased, we ventured out to find rock wrens on boulders near the entrance.

Fortunately, crossing over the Drake Range proved less challenging than Te Naihi Saddle, although the route up was steep and we had to poke around bluffs on sloping shelves to pick our way down the other side. Obligatory scrub tore at us as we descended, until at last we reached big flats in the head of the Drake. Interestingly, in 1950, deer hadn't spread to the Drake Catchment. By the 1960s and 1970s, the place was overrun with them.

From a camp beside an unnamed stream draining Pickelhaube Glacier we set out to climb Mt Castor. With almost 2000 metres to climb, we knew this would be a big day. Steep bush and scrub landed us on the wide open slabs of Pegasus Peak, an outlier from Mt Castor.

Back in 1950, Graham McCallum, Beryl Matthews, Tom Barcham and Ashley Cunningham of the Tararua Tramping Club did a marathon three-week Christmas trip to this area. I knew Graham McCallum and was to join him and Tom Barcham on a climbing expedition to the Indian Himalayas a few months later, but for now I was simply in awe of their trip in here.

They had explored over Newland Pass, climbed peaks on Mt Alba, traversed into the Drake, climbed Sombre, Rosy and other peaks before crossing the Waiatoto River, climbing onto the Haast Range and traversing it from Fingals Head to Aspiring. They climbed most of the peaks on the Haast Range along the way, including Stargazer and Aspiring itself. Then they exited down the Matukituki Valley to Wanaka. Part of their intention was to map the area in detail, and this map is included in the 1951 *Tararua Annual*. En route they made several first ascents and named several mountains and glaciers, including Pegasus Peak, which was named by Beryl Matthews on their first ascent.

Continuing across the western slabs of Pegasus Peak ourselves, we found our way onto the Pickelhaube Glacier and followed it to the Main Divide. Abrupt walls fell away towards the pale glacial waters of Lake Lucidus in the North Wilkin. As we climbed towards the summit of Mt Castor we pitched a couple of rope lengths, with an eye to the exposure below, but the climbing wasn't difficult. Wraiths of mist swirled around the summit, limiting views from the warm rocks.

As we returned across the Pegasus slabs, I remembered reading that the TTC party had camped here by a tarn at about 1500 metres. It rained on them all night, all the next day, then on the second night the weather turned southerly and before midnight when the guy ropes all broke, they wrapped themselves in the wet, frozen tent canvas. 'We spent a most miserable night, the wind cutting right through the sleeping bags, chilling us to the bone. . . . At the first flush of dawn, we bundled gear into packs and struggled into semi-frozen boots, shivering violently all the while.'

Getting off that perch down through bluffs and short slippery tussock in those conditions would have been very challenging. We, fortunately, returned to camp after 13 hours away and lit the fire. In the morning we would descend the Drake River through Guardian Gorge to the Waiatoto River, cross it, and head up-valley.

The lake in the head of the Waiatoto is a special place. We reached the mossy flats at the lake outlet on a fine morning. It is flanked by walls of rock and ice rising to the crest of the Haast Range, while Mt Aspiring towers at the head of the lake and almost 2500 metres above it.

An ice avalanche interrupted the vastness, roaring its way down a thousand metres of bluffs, right into the water. Twelve years after our trip, in 1991, about half a million cubic metres of rock fell from Stargazer into this lake, forcing 6 million cubic metres of lake water into a tsunami that reached 15 metres high, transforming the valley and affecting it all the way to the sea.

We climbed out. Our route up onto the upper Volta Glacier had a few curly steps in overlapping schist slabs, and we roped one section. Dreams of a day or two on the Volta dissipated as hogsback clouds and a brisk westerly developed. An earlier adventure getting off the Volta in a storm made us make a beeline for Ruth Ridge. It was almost dark when we began belaying down, and we had our torches out before we found somewhere to pitch the tent at about 1500 metres.

With the first daylight hours we picked our way through rain into the East Matukituki and the track down Bledisloe Gorge, in a race to get across two river crossings. Leaves and debris bubbling on the water showed the river was rising, but we made it, to then plod our way out. Back in the hills, fresh snow covered the tussock and westerly clouds hid everything else. There is a time for everything, including getting out of the hills. We'd already had a storm on this trip.

ABOVE The route to Newland Pass from Newland Stream follows tussock ribs, then rock and snow up to the col under Mt Alba.

OVERLEAF (LEFT) Matt on the summit of Mt Castor.

OVERLEAF (RIGHT) From Mt Dispute across the head of the Te Naihi catchment. Mt Alba to the left, and Lake Axius, centre.

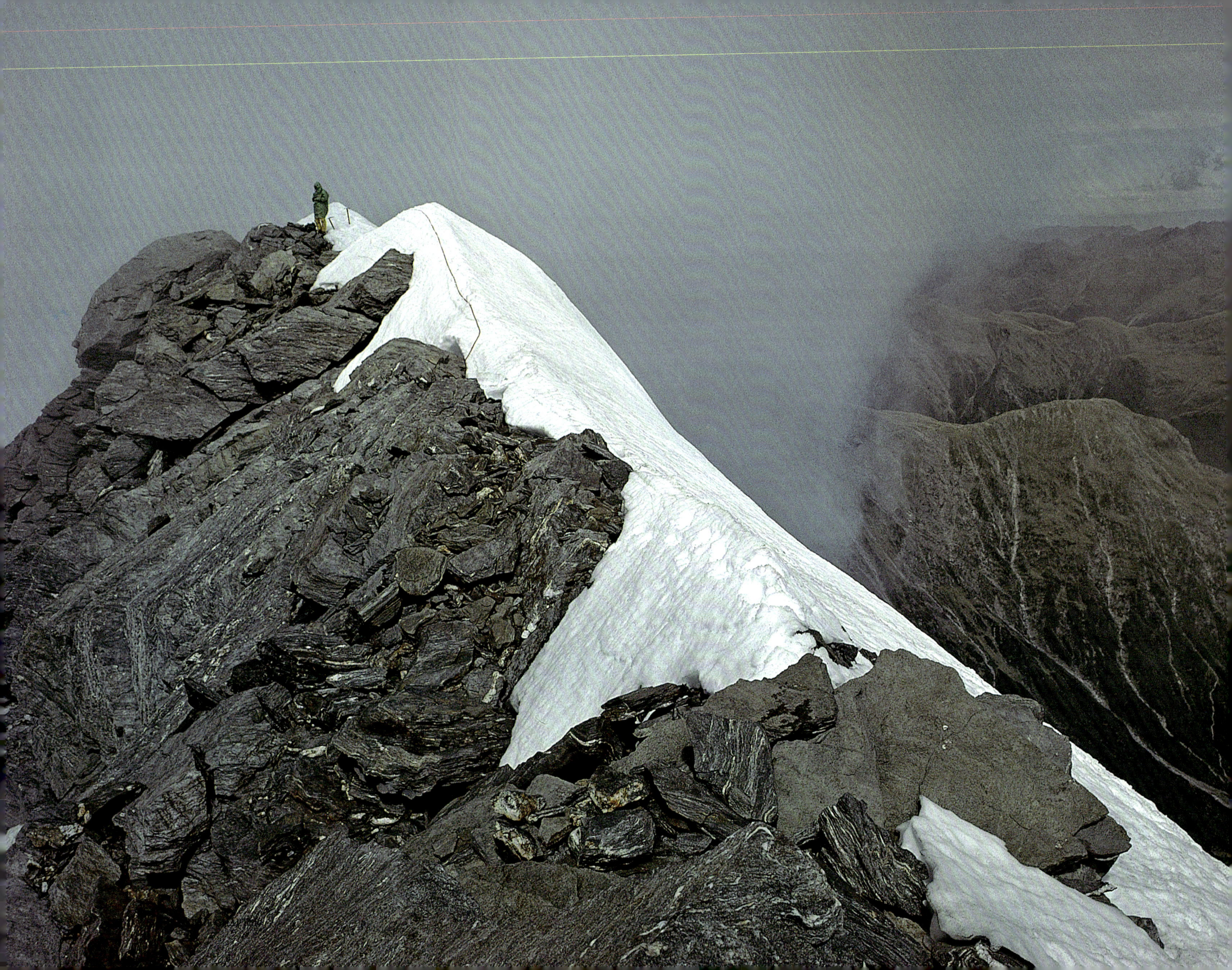

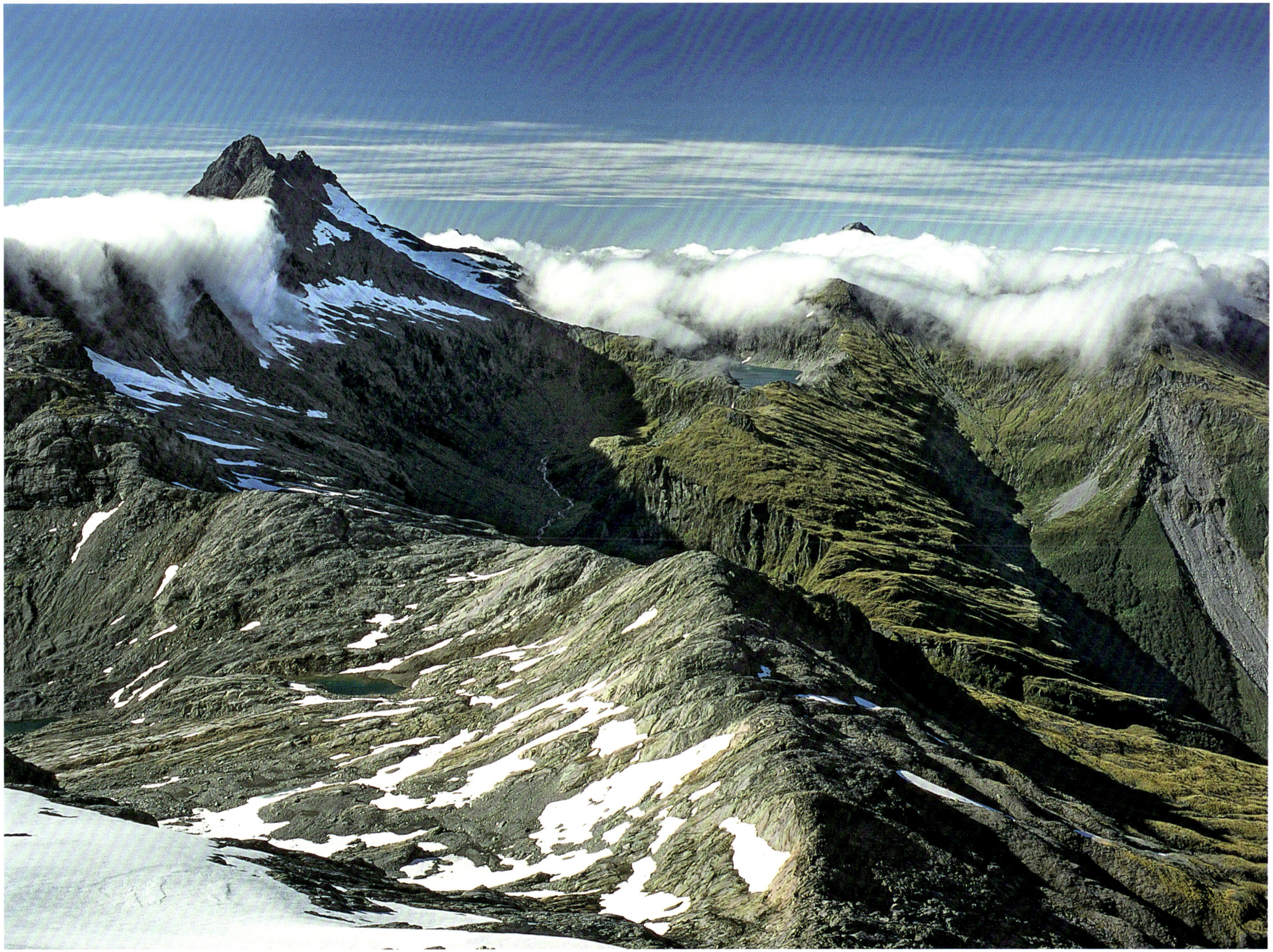

MOIRS MISSION

WILKIN VALLEY–LEDA PEAK–TE NAIHI HEADWATERS–
MUELLER HEADWATERS–STEWART PASS–SIBERIA VALLEY

6 DAYS: 26 FEBRUARY–3 MARCH 2001

GS WITH PETE BARNES

When rewriting *Moir's Guide North* it was difficult to find any information on, or anyone who had been over, Stewart Pass on the Main Divide. The pass separates the Mueller Valley near Okuru from Siberia Valley in the Wilkin catchment. So, I decided to invite Pete Barnes on a trip to see what it was like. Pete, possibly to his later chagrin, said yes.

And so it came to pass that we ended up camping by Lake Castalia in the head of the Wilkin. The clear waters of the lake are tucked in under huge walls of rock topped by snowfields and icefalls. Scree opposite leads partway up to the snowfields on Leda Peak, but there is an exposed awkward spot at about 1400 metres where an outward-facing slab needs to be crossed, with a wall above it. By 11 a.m. the next day we were past it. For me, that meant another route description for the guide personally checked out.

Mist caught us up on the Main Divide, and we dived off into the upper Te Naihi, aiming for a bivvy under a bluff in the very head to avoid the rain. I don't normally carry a mountain radio because I find they interfere with the dynamics on trips. One of the pleasures of being out there is that a party tends to get wrapped up in its own little world in the hills. However, on this trip we had one for backup and the forecast.

The Main Divide leading up to Mt Achilles is an idyllic place, a high traverse on open tussock, past tarns and gorgeous campsites above tremendous bluffs to the east. From Achilles we scrambled along the Divide descending little bluffs and earth clumps to Newland Pass for a look, before returning. Then it was down into another upper tributary of the Te Naihi, this one giving access to the head of the Mueller, where we camped on a gravel flat by Lake Dispute at about 1600 metres.

It was a campsite with atmosphere, but the flavour of the place dropped steeply away when it began raining again overnight, and water began seeping through the gravel. Sadly, we'd seen a better site for rainy weather, too, but no, it wasn't going to rain . . . the forecast had said so. In the afternoon, torrential rain fell, the wind blew hard and we dug water channels with our iceaxes. However, on dark, it cleared and turned cold, and the second of March was fine, frosty and icy as we wandered up Mount Dispute in the sun again.

We were at a crossroads. To complete the trip we either needed to descend the unknowns of Stewart Pass or head back the way we had come. I went and had a look, decided it was feasible, and we ended up on Stewart Pass with our packs at four o'clock. But I'll probably never be back.

The descent began easily enough, linking scree and snow patches until we were far enough down not to want to return. Then it became more challenging on smooth slabs, where we belayed a couple of pitches to a gully, which turned into a gut. Next, a boulder blocked that, needing an abseil to drop over it.

This was getting messier than expected, and by the time we climbed onto a steep, narrow prow of eroding avalanche snow it was nearly dark. Stopping wasn't an option, though. This section was a funnel for all the loose debris on the walls above, and we needed to be out of it. Torches on, we cramponed down a steep, hard snowbank back into the gully and eventually found somewhere to sleep under a small overhang sheltered from any rockfall.

It's times like this you really appreciate dinner. We didn't have much food left, but one of us, who shall remain nameless, had been saving a can of fish for this dinner. Unfortunately, the label had come off, and when it was opened the fish had all swum away and it was instead tomato sauce . . . but we were too tired to care.

Thick mist greeted us in the morning and we put off leaving in the hope of seeing where we were going. Eventually we left, anyway. We dropped out of the mist and cramponed down a long old fan of winter snow-avalanche debris. We were down. After this, the trip down-valley through scrub seemed pretty mild. Below the forks, the long grass flats of Siberia Stream began. We strode down to Siberia Hut and then the short distance down to Kerin Forks at the junction with the Wilkin River.

OPPOSITE Pete in the head of the Mueller Valley, with cloud spilling over Stewart Pass up to the right.

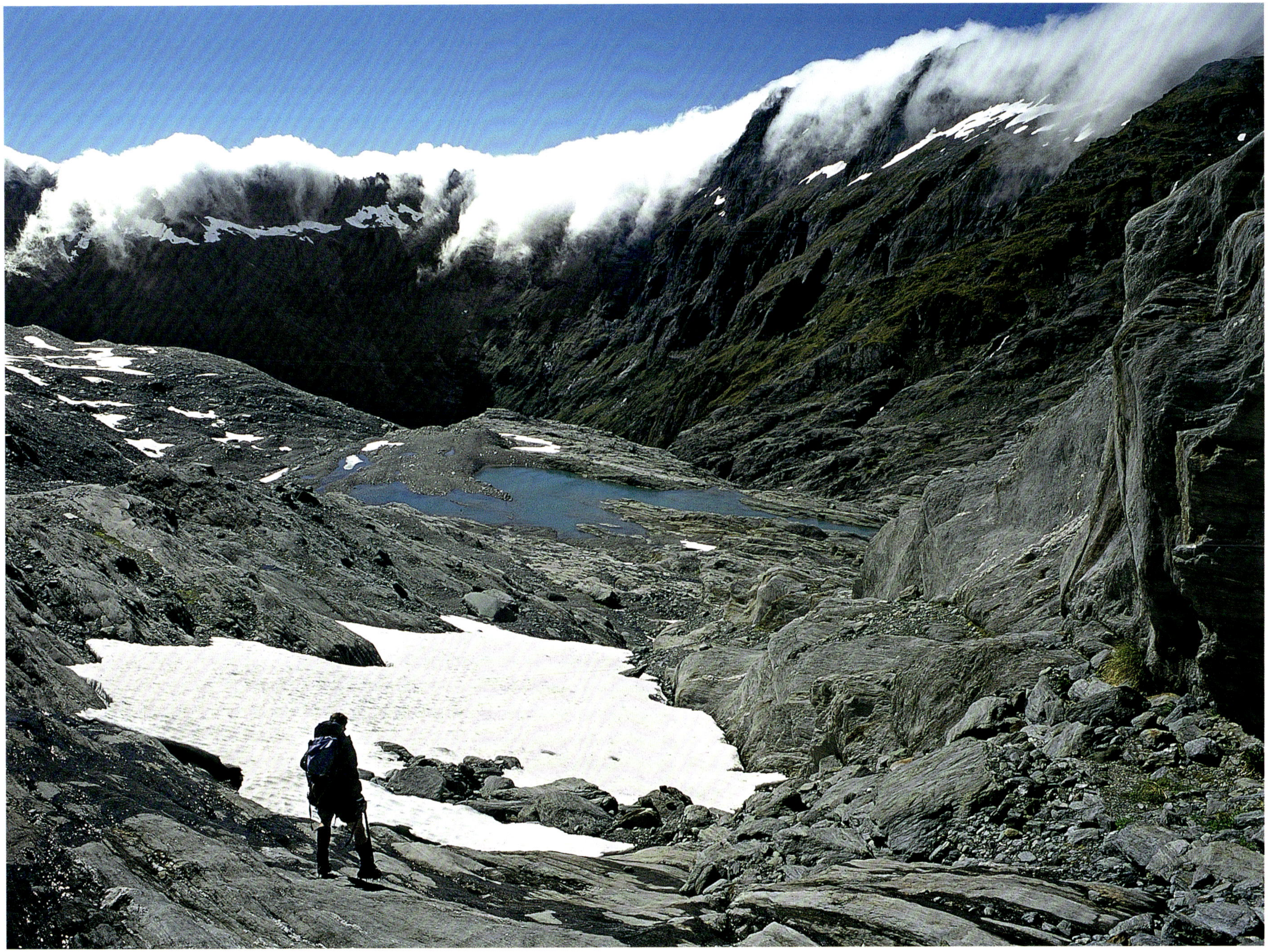

WINTER WILDERNESS

YOUNG VALLEY–GILLESPIE PASS–SIBERIA VALLEY–SIBERIA SADDLE–NGATAU VALLEY–OKURU VALLEY–MAORI SADDLE–BLUE VALLEY

8 DAYS: 22–29 AUGUST 1974
GS WITH IAN THORNE

For all sorts of reasons, some trips stay vividly in my mind even after 45 years. The weather, the company, a major winter trip in the Southern Alps, or the surprise at finding obscure, quiet places. Or it may be the cold, the dry, deep cold that freeze-dries beech twigs and makes them good fire material.

Anyway, a trip that remains vivid and one I look back on fondly was spending my twenty-third birthday crossing snowy Siberia Saddle on the Main Divide in perfect winter weather.

Leaving Makarora, Ian and I buried our boots into the bitterly cold water of the Makarora River and came out onto the Young track to warm up. On the flats at the North/South forks, frost crystals made the snow look fluffy, but we found a dry spot in the sun to eat our cabin-bread lunch. There was a Forest Service hut there then.

As we climbed up towards Young River South Branch, winter's frozen magic covered the land, making for strenuous step-plugging in mature snow. When stopping for the night, we used our rope to throw over dead branches and bring them crashing to the ground, for firewood. Fire kept us warm as dark descended.

The track into Siberia over Gillespie Pass is virtually a highway now, but back then much of it wasn't obvious, particularly under snow – deep snow, with avalanche paths in the gullies. Bullocking our way to the top of the pass through soft, unstable snow took much of the morning and afternoon.

In Siberia Valley next day we found a tiny hunter's hut and squeezed in. It had been snowing heavily all morning, and we retreated into our sleeping bags with books to read. The hut belonged to local hunter and helicopter pilot Alan Duncan, whom I met six years later when working for Mount Aspiring National Park at Makarora. He had come in then to tell us that South Young Hut had been avalanched off its foundations and was in the creek 50 metres away, which was rather challenging for us park staff. There's no such thing as permanence in the mountains.

Next morning was fine and frosty, so Ian and I got under way again. Siberia Saddle isn't particularly difficult, but the route needs good judgement higher up. It is shaded, steep and exposed near the crest, and in the snow conditions we certainly needed our crampons and iceaxes. Most of the ridge was corniced, and we climbed above the saddle to access the only break through it. Reaching the Main Divide here was like a revelation. Sparkling snow crystals disturbed by our boots were glittering like flecks of gold in the sun. Far off, the distant sound of water falling in the forest accentuated the winter silence.

Taking our time, we ambled down towards the Ngatau River, part of the Okuru catchment, me counting my birthday blessings. On this northern slope the radiant sun warmed us, and we stopped at the scrubline for a lazy lunch.

Down at the river, tall poles of silver beech lined the bank, and within minutes we had found our campsite for the night. We had expected to descend into dark and cold, wet Westland bush, but instead found ourselves on a tinder-dry forest edge of *Dicranaloma* moss flats merging into grass fringes, with all the wood we could burn – dry, crackly, and ready to go. How many times have I dreamed of finding such a campsite on wet miserable nights in the bush. Pleased with our day, we revelled in the pleasure of it.

Morning was just as pleasant. No dew, no clouds, and the sun arrived at breakfast. Ian had a fire going and the billy boiled. The clear river was low and easy going in places, and the forest relatively open. Winter was a good time to be here, but our enthusiasm boiled over when we had a quick swim. It wasn't really that warm.

We swung right when we reached the Okuru confluence, back towards the Main Divide. Up the Okuru the boulders became progressively larger as we gained height, and we finally camped just down from Princes Creek on a sand-flat surrounded by more crackly firewood. Towards the Main Divide, peaks ripened in the setting sun.

For the second night in a row we didn't put the tent up, electing to lie under the stars just in our sleeping bags. After rice and prunes for breakfast, we left at nine o'clock. We travelled up most of the Okuru in the riverbed, with a few short sidles. A low river and dry conditions certainly helped.

From the snowed-up top flats we climbed easily to Maori Saddle on the Main Divide, reaching it after four in the afternoon with the clouds, but things looked very steep on the other side and under snow. Uninviting. We scouted around. Not much option from where we were and little daylight to faff around, so we got the rope out and belayed three or four pitches steeply down to old avalanche debris. Then, once we were down, we discovered a sneaky route on the south side of the saddle that is a walk in the park. You get that.

Night was drawing down in the head of a valley that doesn't get much sun in winter. The Blue River is well named and it was cold. Frosted snow covered the prickly shield ferns, and we headed for the first patches of silver beech, exhilarated at the ease of running over firm snow. We made it by torchlight, and again slept out under the stars on a bed of grass under the trees, warm in the radiant heat of fire embers. Up on the ridges the snow glinted in pearl frost.

The Blue is a gorgeous valley with big walls and a series of grass flats interspersed with mostly short gorges. A simple track follows the valley down, crossing near the North Branch to avoid a deeply incised gorge. Instead, the track climbs above the gorge and then meanders out over quiet bush terraces. This is a place I especially love. Under the tall, mature forest of silver beech, kaka call in the canopy, screeching and chortling, while parakeets and brown creepers chatter in groups.

RIGHT Ian on Gillespie Pass, August 1974.

OVERLEAF (LEFT) The upper Ngatau River.

OVERLEAF (RIGHT) The head of the Blue River is attractive country. The peak on the Main Divide opposite is Mt Topsey, named after Charlie Douglas's dog.

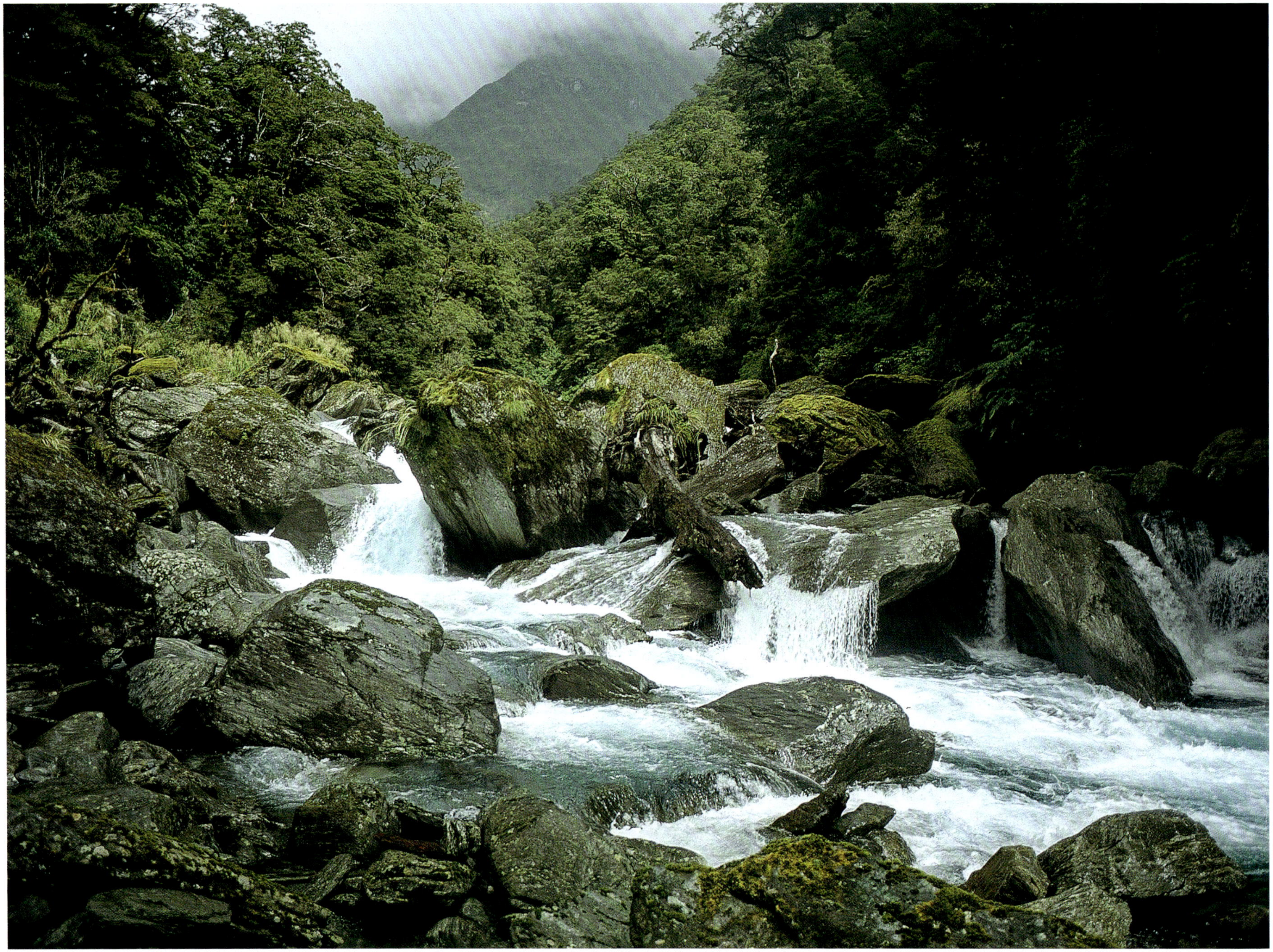

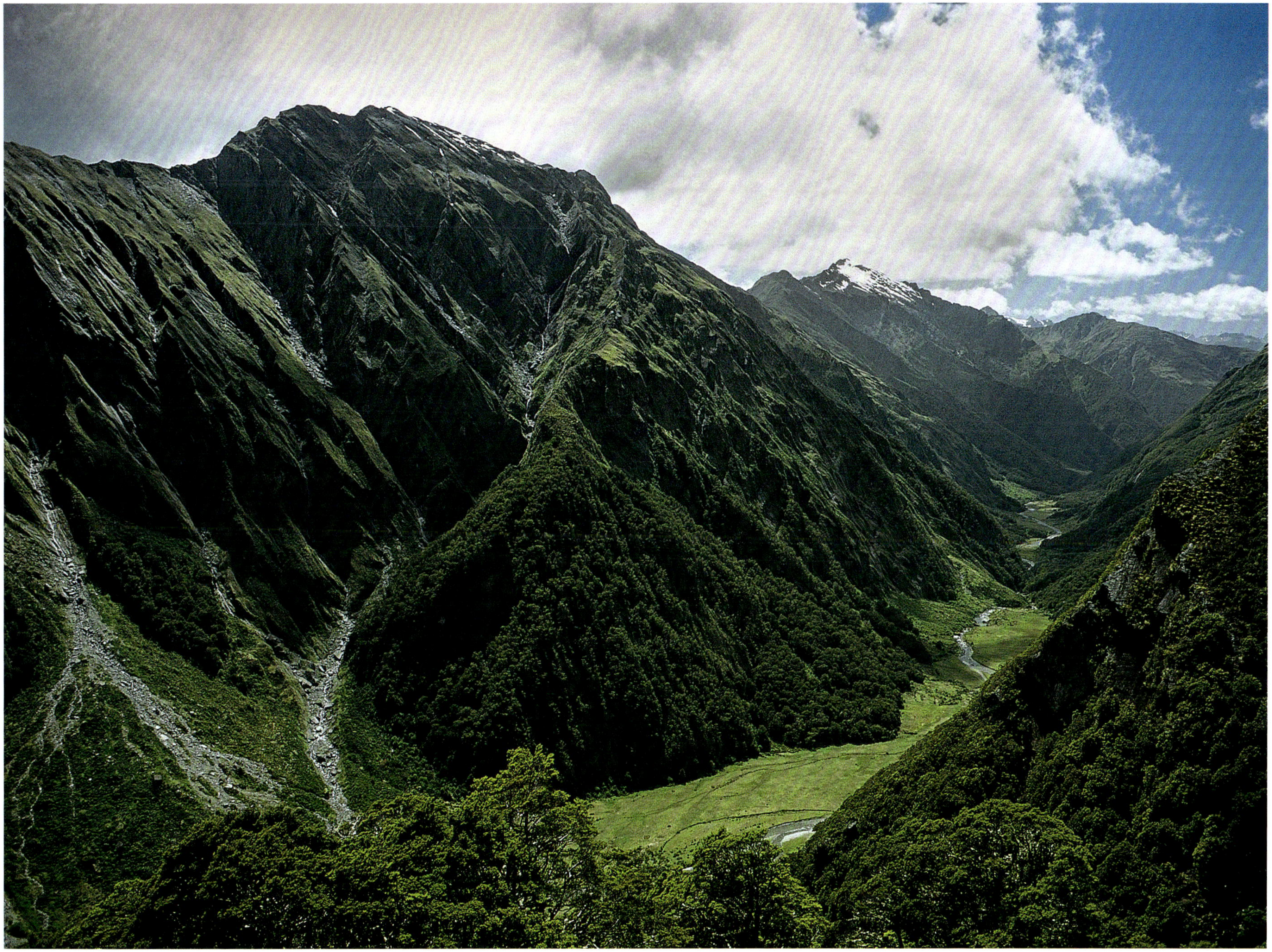

N
0
5
10 km
HAAST RANGE TRAVERSE
NOT ROCK SOLID – AN EROS ENCOUNTER
VIVA LA VOLTA
MAIN DIVIDE
HAAST RANGE
OLIVINE RANGE
Lake Greaney
Jackson River >
Waiatoto River >
Waiatoto Saddle
Cascade River >
Gerard Knob
Mt Castor
Fingals Head
Wilkin River >
Arawhata River >
Corner Post
Moonraker
Pearson Saddle
Cloudmaker Lake
Beauty Ridge
Rabbit Pass
Purity Glacier
Glacier Dome
Stargazer
Waipara River >
Volta Glacier
Eros
Colin Todd Hut
Wilmot Saddle
Mt Ionia
Mt Aspiring/Tititea
< Rainbow Stm
Bevan Col
Bonar Glacier
Waipara Saddle
Kitchener River >
< East Matukituki River
Arawhata Rock
Arawhata Saddle
Rob Roy Peak
Dart Glacier
West Matukutuki River >
Lake Wanaka

CHAPTER 12
THE HAAST RANGE, VOLTA GLACIER & MT ASPIRING

The narrow Haast Range snakes its sinewy way from the Haast–Jackson Bay road to reach the Main Divide at Mt Aspiring. The Waiatoto River draining the Volta Glacier carves a deep canyon along one side of it to the east, and the Arawhata, although more spacious, does the same to the west. The Waipara Range to the south-west, where the isolated peaks of Ionia and Eros lie, is sandwiched between the Waipara River and the upper Arawhata. All of this country is big and bold, and usually approached from the Matukituki Valley, with the popular Bonar Glacier approach to Mt Aspiring being used by most climbers. Access to the Volta Glacier is much trickier.

The Waiatoto is forever linked with the 1891 survey by Charlie Douglas, his dog Betsy Jane, and his canoe *The Surveyor General*. Teichelmann followed up the Waiatoto in 1908 to attempt Mt Aspiring but instead ascended Glacier Dome on the Volta Glacier. Major Bernard Head, with guides Jack Clarke and Alex Graham, were the first to climb Mt Aspiring in 1909 from the Bonar. But the greatest stories of mountain adventure in the area are recounted in alpine journals from the 1930s and 1940s when the OSONZACs (Otago Section of the NZ Alpine Club) made the Matukituki Valley part of their home base, building Aspiring Hut and exploring their way through the Aspiring country. Paul Powell's books about this area are well worth a read and show his real connection and identity with these mountains.

In this area I have chosen the trip up the East Matukituki River, over Wilmot Saddle to the Volta Glacier, around Beauty Ridge to Pearson Saddle, then back down the East Matukituki Valley as a great transalpine journey.

Good alpine skills and equipment are always necessary here, as are competence on very steep ground, and a fine forecast in summer. The Volta is not a place in which to get caught out.

HAAST RANGE TRAVERSE

ARAWHATA VALLEY–LAKE GREANEY–HAAST RANGE–
MOONRAKER–COLIN TODD HUT–MT ASPIRING–
BONAR GLACIER–BEVAN COL–WEST MATUKITUKI VALLEY

9 DAYS: 26 JANUARY–3 FEBRUARY 2002
GS WITH BARBARA BROWN, JOHN OMBLER AND DAVE CAMPBELL

Over the years some have been inspired by a holistic approach to climbing mountains, choosing a journey that begins near sea level, possibly traversing a range, and culminating in an ascent of a major mountain. Aat Vervoorn climbed Mt Tasman via the Fox Range, Johnny Mulheron and Jonathan Kennett climbed Mt Tasman from the sea, literally up the Fox Glacier to the summit and all the way back to the sea again. There are many such examples.

It is a classic transalpine style, and doing these sort of trips through the 1930s, 40s and 50s produced the well-rounded, capable mountaineers who then had an answer to whatever overseas mountain ranges would throw at them. It is no coincidence that so many kiwis did well on international expeditions at the time. These were the kinds of people Shipton and Tilman related well to.

We, too, were inspired by this approach to the mountains. Something with a bit of style and fun, where commitment, mountain skills and resourcefulness were required. A travelling mountain adventure.

John Ombler proposed this trip at a post-meeting dinner in Wellington where we had been in different camps arguing over backcountry huts and tracks. Red wine had mellowed both of us. John had been a shooter for helicopter pilot Alan Duncan on venison-recovery operations along the Haast Range. As well, John's father, Stewart Ombler, made the first ascent of the highest peak on the range, Mt Stargazer (2352 metres), in December 1935, along with Harry Stevenson, Doug Dick, Scott Gilkison and Jim Dawson, from Otago.

The full traverse, from the Jackson Bay Road all the way to Mt Aspiring seemed a great idea, although 35 kilometres is a long way to travel on rugged mountainous tops, especially in Westland. Paul Hellebrekers dropped us at the stockyards near the Arawhata Road bridge, in beautiful weather, and that is a good way to start on the Coast.

That night, having lost kilos of water on the way, we slept at the bush edge on Thirsty Ridge. Never was a ridge so well named. The northern end of the Haast Range contains an 11,000-hectare tokoeka (Southern brown kiwi) sanctuary, where dedicated local people working with DOC regularly maintain stoat traplines from the valley floor to the crest of the range. It is a big job. There are only a few hundred Haast tokoeka left.

Watching for kiwi probes, we sidled across to Lake Greaney, had a look at the locked DOC kiwi hut, then continued over dry tussock under overcast skies towards Mt Duncan. Duncan was our first high point and we were keen to see what lay ahead, but cloud skulked around the summit. As we scrambled down chunky schist to tussock again, the sun shone into the valleys, and by evening at Waiatoto Saddle the skies had cleared. For the first time we could see the scale of the challenge, with the Waiatoto and Arawhata rivers disappearing 20 and 30 kilometres into the distance, and Gerard Knob rearing up in a prow – our first obstacle to negotiate just along the range.

Gerard wasn't alone. Under Datamos there were more bluffs to traverse, near Mt Grant there was another set, and more again near Hyperia. Sometimes these needed the rope for pack-hauling or security, and all of them were tricky little climbing challenges to navigate on the way through. Under Fingals Head, permanent ice had largely gone, leaving parallel ribs of freshly shorn rock exposed between lines of snow to walk along.

Being on such a high, narrow range emphasised our height above the two rivers, and we roosted with kea in the evenings in some exhilarating spots. After a swim in a tarn one afternoon we tucked into the tussock by a little scrub fire, then slept out under a full moon, next to bluffs that fell all the way down to the Waiatoto. In weather just as calm the next night near Hyperia, we sat on clean rock outcrops above the Arawhata, watching the sun descend behind the Olivine Range while we ate dinner.

In 1971, Gilbert van Reenen and other students on a Forest Service

OPPOSITE Looking south towards Waiatoto Saddle with Gerard Knob in the cloud. Waiatoto Valley (left) and Arawhata (right).

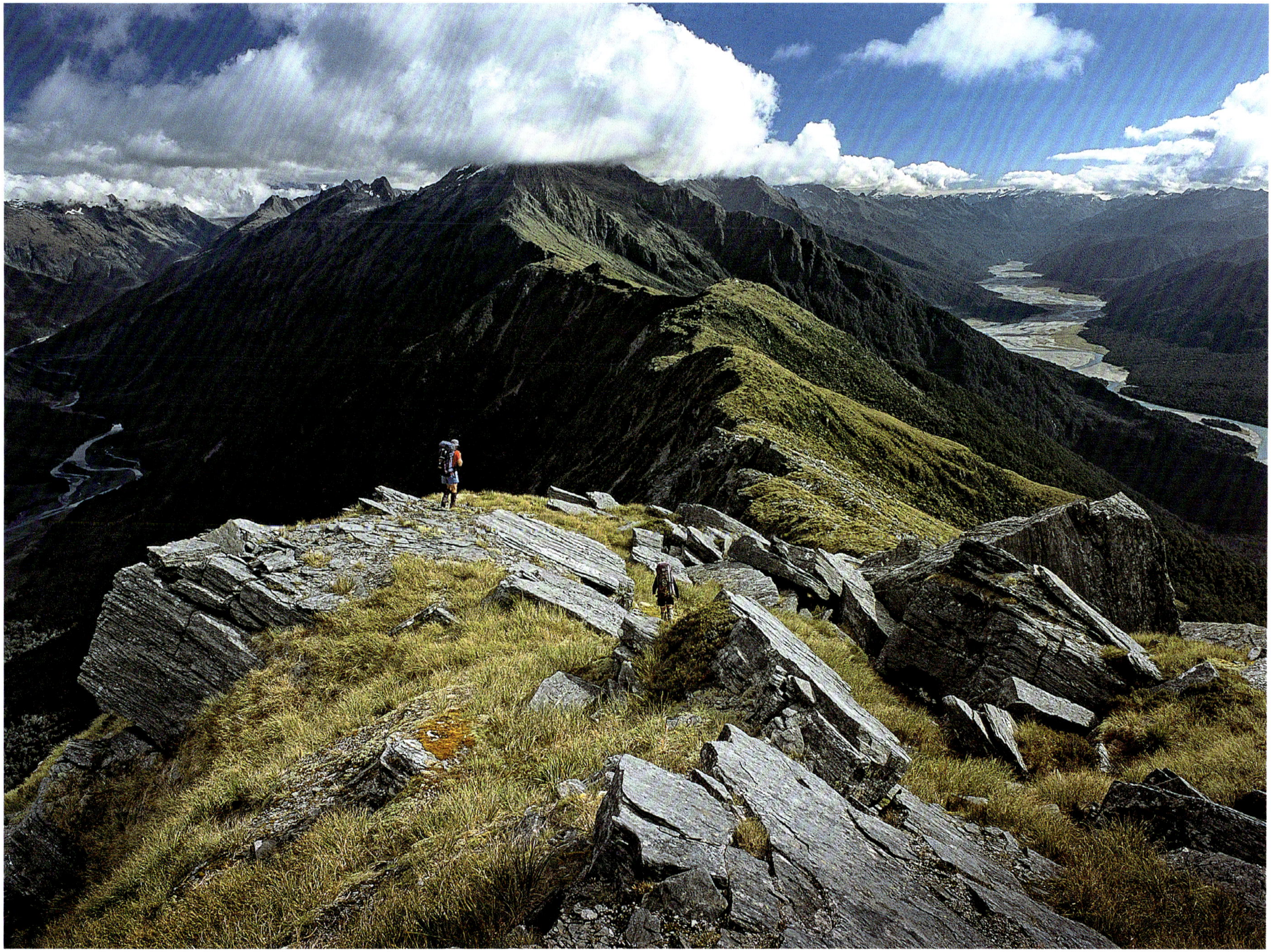

Post, and it worked, but it was still pretty steep. As we climbed, rock wrens kept appearing, flitting about like mountain fairies, so we named it Rock Wren Gully.

Cloud balled up along the Waiatoto faces as we cramponed towards Moonraker, so aptly named after the top sail on old sailing ships. Several kea joined us as we looked down into the greenstone hues of Cloudmaker Lake. Later we swam, Dave cooked, and Barb made pudding beside this idyllic lake nestled in tussock above the Waipara. Investigating a potential rock bivvy, we discovered it was already home to lively, cheeping kea chicks.

The journey from Cloudmaker across the head of Cargo Creek, under the West ridge of Stargazer and over wonderful rock rounds and thin icefields to Colin Todd Hut took about eight hours. The one guy at the hut there asked where we had come from. 'Along the Haast Range.' 'Where's that?' he asked, innocently. I resisted saying he was standing on it. But it seems such a pity that people get so focused on a few 'name' peaks and climbs they stop seeing the peripheral landscape around them or have much interest in it. He was a nice guy, and he put on a brew for us.

We slept out 150 metres up from the hut, and at 3.30 a.m. we were almost stomped on by eager punters keen to climb. We left at six, on a superb day, and on the summit of Aspiring took in 360-degree views, but our eyes were especially focused on where we had come from, along the Haast Range.

Sleeping out that night near Hector Col, we were in good company, with a friend Geoff Wayatt and his client Neil Cram sleeping out nearby. Down in the West Matukituki we visited Scott's Biv, named after Scott Gilkison who was a friend of John's father. Small circles: Scott Gilkison had lectured John at Otago University.

vegetation survey along the northern part of the range had found the place equally as exciting. Earlier, in 1951, a TTC party who had come from the Wilkin and Drake valleys traversed the Haast Range from Fingals Head to Mt Aspiring, climbing most of the peaks along the way. One of them wrote: 'As we approached Corner Post we realised that this was indeed the crucial part of the trip. With packs, our way up the Waiatoto face of Corner Post was not particularly easy.'

When we looked up at the prow leading to Corner Post, it frowned back, severely. We looked over on Waiatoto slopes. Messy slabs discouraged going that way. We poked up a gully on the Waipara side to a saddle beyond Corner

ABOVE Mt Aspiring, the Haast Range and Volta Glacier from Fastness Peak.
OPPOSITE Cloudmaker Lake on the Haast Range.

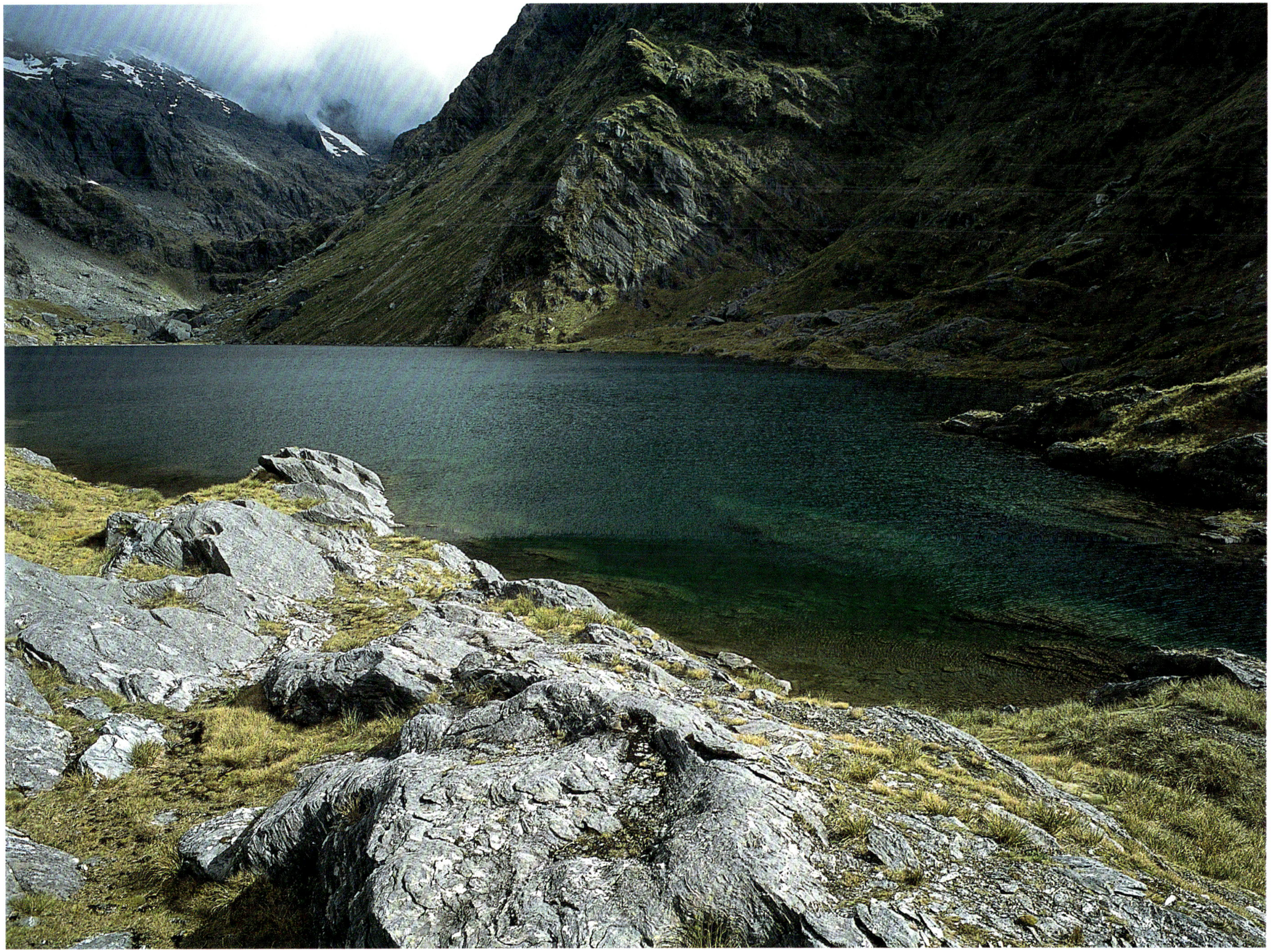

NOT ROCK SOLID: AN EROS ENCOUNTER

WEST MATUKITUKI–ARAWHATA SADDLE–ARAWHATA ROCK–WAIPARA SADDLE–WAIPARA RIVER–MT IONIA–EROS PEAK–HAAST RANGE–MT ASPIRING–BEVAN COL–WEST MATUKITUKI RIVER

18 DAYS: 25 DECEMBER 1970–11 JANUARY 1971
GS WITH NEV LUPTON, LAUCHIE DUFF, DEREK DANIELL, IAN THORNE AND IAN LATHAM

Lots happened on this long, 18-day trip, but it was all eclipsed by one major event on Mt Eros: rockfall. But I'll get to that. We staggered up the West Matukituki with 30-kilogram packs, carrying 20 days' food and climbing gear. Many others have done the same, I know, but it still hurt. I had to prop the pack on logs to get it on my back, and that can't be good for you.

Eventually we reached Liverpool Bivvy. After a brew, the two Aussies there noted the water bucket we used had had a dead rat in it when they arrived. Nice. You can always rely on your neighbours.

Snow and rock on Arawhata Saddle required care with our heavy packs. This saddle was first crossed by Dunedin climbers Eric Miller, J.W. Aitken, H.W. Boddy, F. Hansen and R.G. Stokes, on Boxing Day 1923. It was marked Dart Saddle on their maps, but they soon came to realise they were looking into the Arawhata. Following the Arawhata to Williamson Flat they found an old prospectors' camp, complete with a camp oven and a sluicing nozzle. After investigating the Snow White Glacier they returned over Arawhata Saddle. On the way they visited Arawhata Rock Bivvy, a dry area under a massive boulder over 30 metres high, set among *Hoheria* and prickly shield fern beside the river. We also stopped there, enjoying the bouldering problem it presented and finding a way to the top. Good rock bivvies often have fine dry dust under them, which has ways of ingraining itself into the hands, onto sleeping bags, and into clothes. This one was no different.

Here, we also had the company of over-enthusiastic feathered alarm clocks that went off randomly. They also flogged Nev's real alarm clock and dumped it in the river. Kea have other tricks. I was having a private moment at the base of a small bluff when a small stone landed near me. Then a second one. I looked up to see a kea leaning over, head cocked, getting his eye in. Another stone landed. In the end I was forced to relocate, and only then realised he was tussling and dragging a bigger rock that would probably have cracked my skull. But they totally deserve to get a few human scalps. Government and farmers paid a bounty to kill kea, resulting in at least 150,000 being shot, poisoned and trapped to protect sheep in the 100 years up to 1970. They are now a species in decline.

Next, we crossed Waipara Saddle to reach Bonar Lake and camp by the Waipara River to consider our next moves. Nev and I were keen to climb Mt Ionia, and in the morning we set off up The Wilson, a gully that finished as a headwall composed of very rotten rock. It was pretty dodgy and once up, we weren't going back.

We climbed Mt Ionia up what was predominantly a rock ridge, and summited at four o'clock. Views into the Bascand Glacier revealed wild icefalls and high bluffs, making a return to the Waipara problematic. We continued, arriving on Eros Peak near sunset and we linked into snow tracks heading down, growing more and more uneasy with the route. At dark we tied onto a rock ledge to sit the night out.

Lauchie and Derek had decided to climb Eros on a different approach and with dawn, we found them only 100 metres below in a couloir, as challenged as us. Overhead, strange cracking noises made me look up. Directly above us and only 100 metres away, a rock tower about 10 metres high, and 5 metres by 5 metres, was spurting out puffs of rock dust as it collapsed in front of our eyes.

As it could only thunder down the couloir exactly where we were standing, we ran a few steps to the side, pulled the rope in, pressed ourselves against a small rockwall, with our hearts racing, desperately hoping for no direct hits. No time for anything else.

Then all hell broke loose as the slope we had been on was raked by massive cartwheeling boulders up to 3 metres in diameter, leaping into the air in

OPPOSITE Arawhata Saddle (left), Mt Liverpool (above), Mt Maori (centre) and Mt Maruiwi (right), from Turks Head.

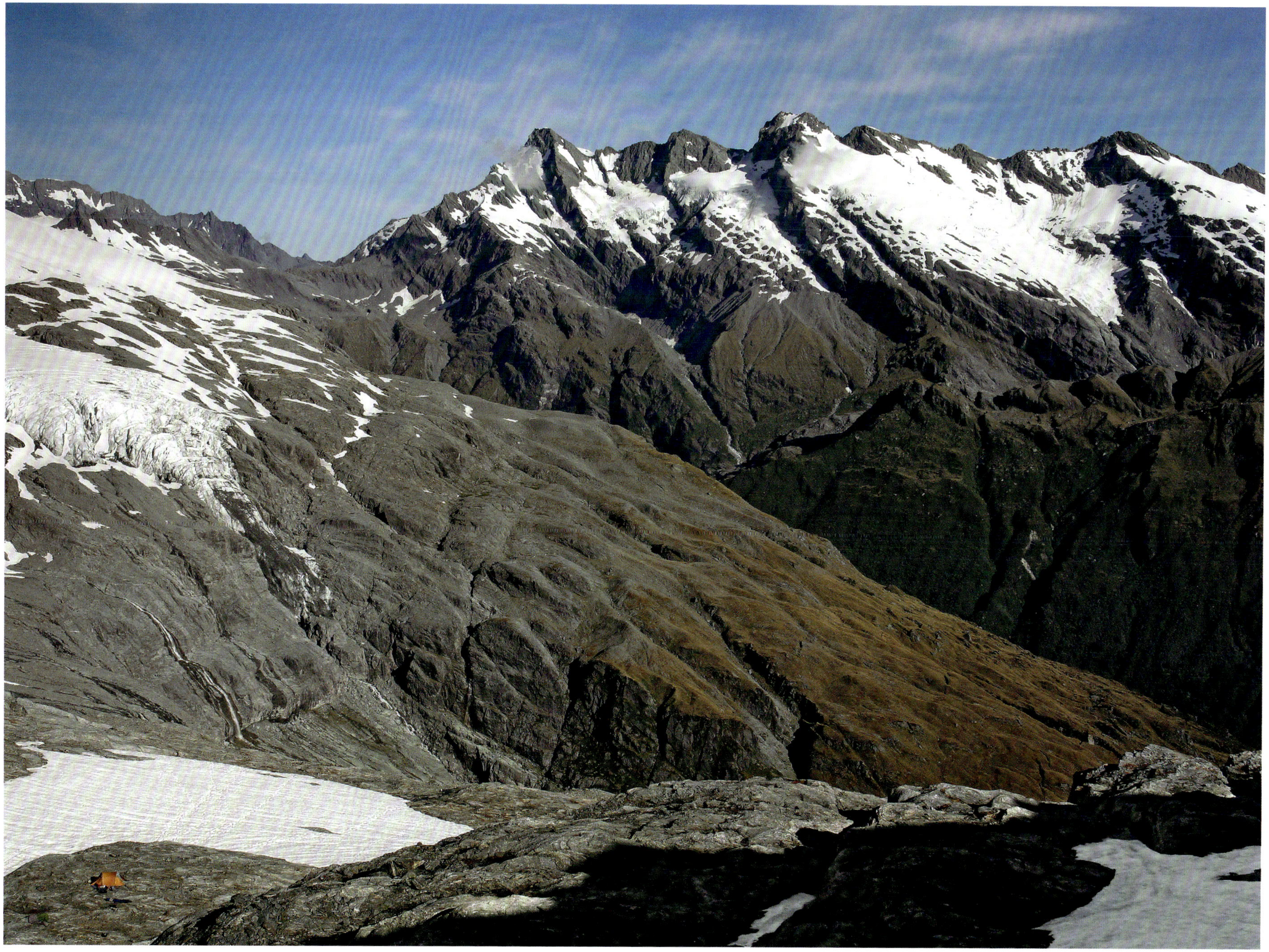

confusion, spinning, crashing and grinding their way down, literally within a metre or two of us. Rock spun over us, but fortunately, I don't know how, there were no direct hits.

Slowly the stones ceased and clattered out of sight down the bluffs below, in ones and twos. The few seconds of silence that followed were complete, the only movement being the thick pall of rock dust we were in, eddying this way and that. A few dry stones dribbled a short way further down and stopped again, caught on the heavy air, which was filled with the powerful smell of crushed rock. The dust flowed slowly down like a funeral procession following the boulders.

'Lauchie, Derek!'

They had been standing on a tiny knob of rock with gutters either side, looking for a route below when the tower collapsed. To reach the side they would've had to climb uphill and they didn't have time for that. We didn't think they had much chance. We called out. No one replied. We called again. Just silence. We discussed how we would tell their families. Minutes later, with the dust pall clearing, they called out. That tiny knob of rock had a little overhang under it where they had managed to shelter. It was beyond lucky. Miraculously, all of us were fine, just drenched in adrenalin and with another life used up.

We sidled out fast, but The Bascand hadn't finished. It poured out from the black ice in its hanging valley over a series of massive waterfalls, in very broken terrain. We picked our way down the bluffs on the true left, using the rope in one place, down-climbing vertical scrub towards the end. With a sense of relief we left it all behind, returned to our camp and focused on the Haast Range across the valley, hoping for a better reception.

Travel in the Waipara River down to The Third Mate Creek was not difficult. Here, we climbed onto the range at Cloudmaker Lake, a place with fantastic surroundings. We swam, we wandered around the lake looking at the flowers and lay in the grass enjoying the scent of tussock.

Later, we traversed across slopes to sleep out between the Iso and Dipso glaciers. On the way we climbed Moonraker, Spike, Stargazer, Main Royal,

LEFT Camp near Waipara Saddle. The trip is not covered in the text, but this was dawn on the first day of 2000.

OPPOSITE Full moon over Mt Eros. Mt Ionia is centre, and Mercer Glacier, right.

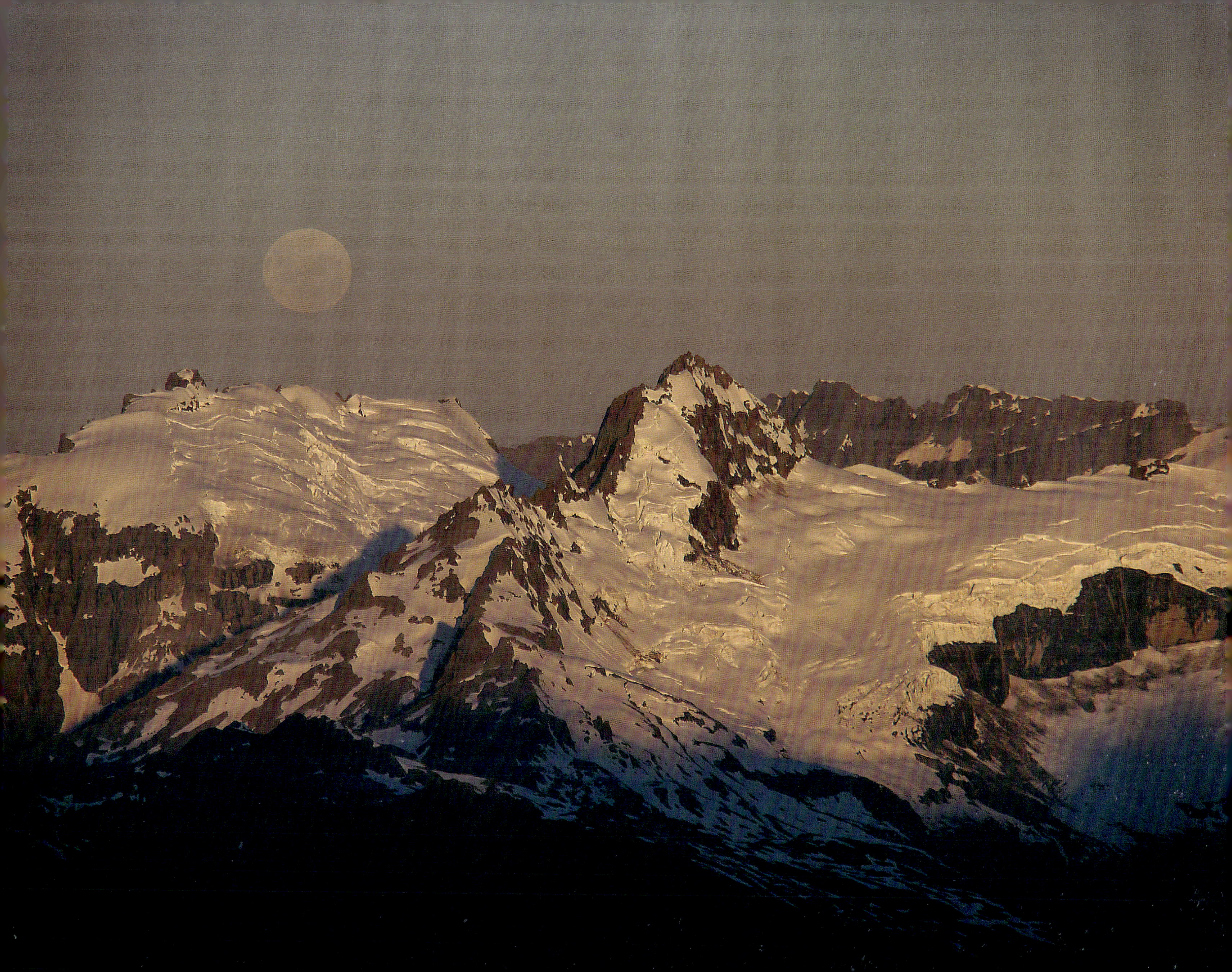

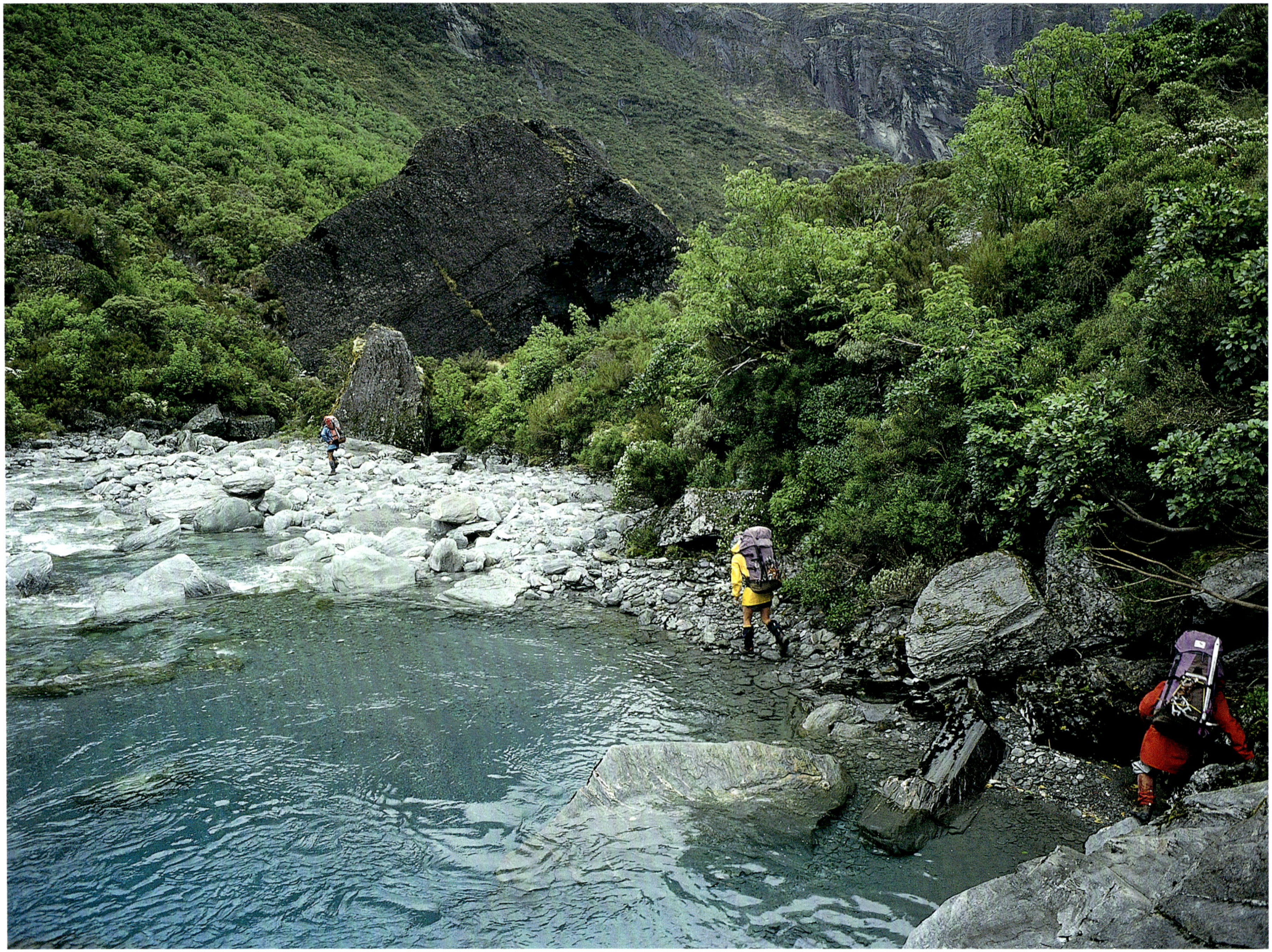

peaks mostly named after ships' sails. Gerhard Mueller named these and other features in the 1880s after the paddle steamer *Waipara*, owned and captained by Mr Bascand, a ship well known on the West Coast in the 1870s. Other names included The Cook (drains the Suet Glacier), The Funnel, The Purser, The Third Mate Creek, Cat O' Nine Tails and Shipowner Ridge.

I learned another early climbing lesson at Colin Todd Hut. The small, old hut was full of people with flash climbing equipment I had only yet seen in catalogues and which left us in awe. Our equipment was spartan and basic and at that stage we naively equated flash gear with mountain competence.

We camped outside and at four the next morning left to climb the north-west ridge of Mt Aspiring. A steely sky, a cold wind and hogsbacks kept us moving. We had a rope but didn't use it, reached the top in a strong bitter wind with cloud now down on us. Racing back, we were below the buttress when we ran into a couple of people: the tech-gear guys. They'd misread the map and had only just sorted where the north-west ridge was.

Considering we were back at Colin Todd Hut by 10.30 a.m., and rain was beginning, we headed for the West Matukituki. Our favoured foods were getting low. We set a compass course for Bevan Col, fumbling down into the gutter below Hector Col in mist. It was now gusty and pouring with rain. No time for delicacies, we took it straight, using the rope in support, swinging the last pack down and someone strong at the back down-climbing. At the last big waterfall, we picked up the ground trail leading past it to the valley floor.

Water flowed everywhere, but the pressure was off us. We could relax, joke, take our time and enjoy the rain itself, watching the drops bounce off leaves, revelling in mossy creeks starting to swell. This is one of the great joys descending from rock and snow – the pleasure of green, the scent of the earth, insects, and the protective security that trees bring.

Joining the Alpine Club was still a year or so away for me, but by evening we were tucked up enjoying the spacious windows in the lounge of the NZAC's Aspiring Hut, watching the rain march ineffectually into them. A perfect way to finish.

OPPOSITE Approaching Arawhata Rock.
RIGHT Rockfall. The pall of rock dust carries a distinctive, acrid smell of flint or cordite. This event happened in the head of the Joe Glacier off the Barrier Range.

VIVA LA VOLTA

EAST MATUKITUKI VALLEY–RAINBOW STREAM–WILMOT SADDLE–VOLTA GLACIER–GLACIER DOME–PURITY GLACIER–BEAUTY RIDGE–PEARSON SADDLE–RABBIT PASS–EAST MATUKITUKI VALLEY

9 DAYS: 1–8 FEBRUARY 2014
GS WITH GARY HUISH, RAYMOND FORD, RUTH BARRATT, CHRIS LEAVER, CALUM MCINTOSH, DOUGLAS WOODS, AARN TATE, DOUG FORSTER AND MERV MEREDITH

ABOVE Approaching Wilmot Saddle from Rainbow Stream. The prominent peak is Moncrieff, with Mt Aspiring higher on the right.
OPPOSITE Ruth (left) and Doug at our camp on Wilmot Saddle, with Mt Aspiring behind.

The Volta Glacier, tucked out of reach behind Mt Aspiring, lies in the Olivine Wilderness, cradled above bluffs that rise like castle walls from the East Matukituki River. Alluring and everywhere difficult to access, the classic packing approach to the Volta up Ruth Ridge is steep. An alternative via Wilmot Saddle passes under the east face of Fastness Peak then climbs on to the Volta at Tartarus Icefall, and we chose this route. It, too, has steep, exposed sections.

We began in the East Matukituki, passing the old Aspinall homestead (now Tititea Lodge, administered by the Mount Aspiring Outdoor Education Trust) and camped in a beech-clearing up the valley. Then, on a fine morning, we swung past the Kitchener Cirque, the Rock of Ages Biv, and headed up the Rainbow Valley. A slow, sweeping climb under bluffs led us to Wilmot Saddle and Sisyphus Peak, one of the best viewpoints in the Southern Alps.

The route we used from Wilmot Saddle across to the Volta had only been pioneered by Erik Bradshaw a few years before. Decades ago I'd looked at it from a camp by Tantalus Rock, and it had looked promising then. Now, by belaying people down using snowstakes buried into the hard earth and crampons on for grip, we carefully negotiated our way lower. Crampons can be very effective in these sort of steep exposed places. We took our time, took care, and there were no problems, but this route down into the upper tussock basin in Ruth Stream, sandwiched between waterfalls and the east face of Fastness Peak, isn't for the faint-hearted.

Heading up to the Volta required the rope again at a small schrund, but by mid afternoon we were on the Main Divide. That night the wind blew hard at our campsite but worse still, the mountain radio predicted gales to follow.

This needed some decisions. Some wanted to return the way we had come. But after the gales the weather was meant to improve, and I had an alternative exit in mind to the north around Beauty Ridge. So, instead, we headed for the east ridge of Glacier Dome and began digging a snowcave with our iceaxes.

There was some skepticism about this, but I've dug dozens of caves with just an iceaxe, and after three or four hours' effort, we had a cosy cave for 10 of us to settle into. Pick your snow and it's not that hard, even in February. We used three entrances to dig in, to keep everyone busy, then closed one up.

Paul Powell wrote eloquently of climbs and storms on the Volta. In 1945 Powell and friends climbed Fastness Peak. In 1965 he returned by plane to

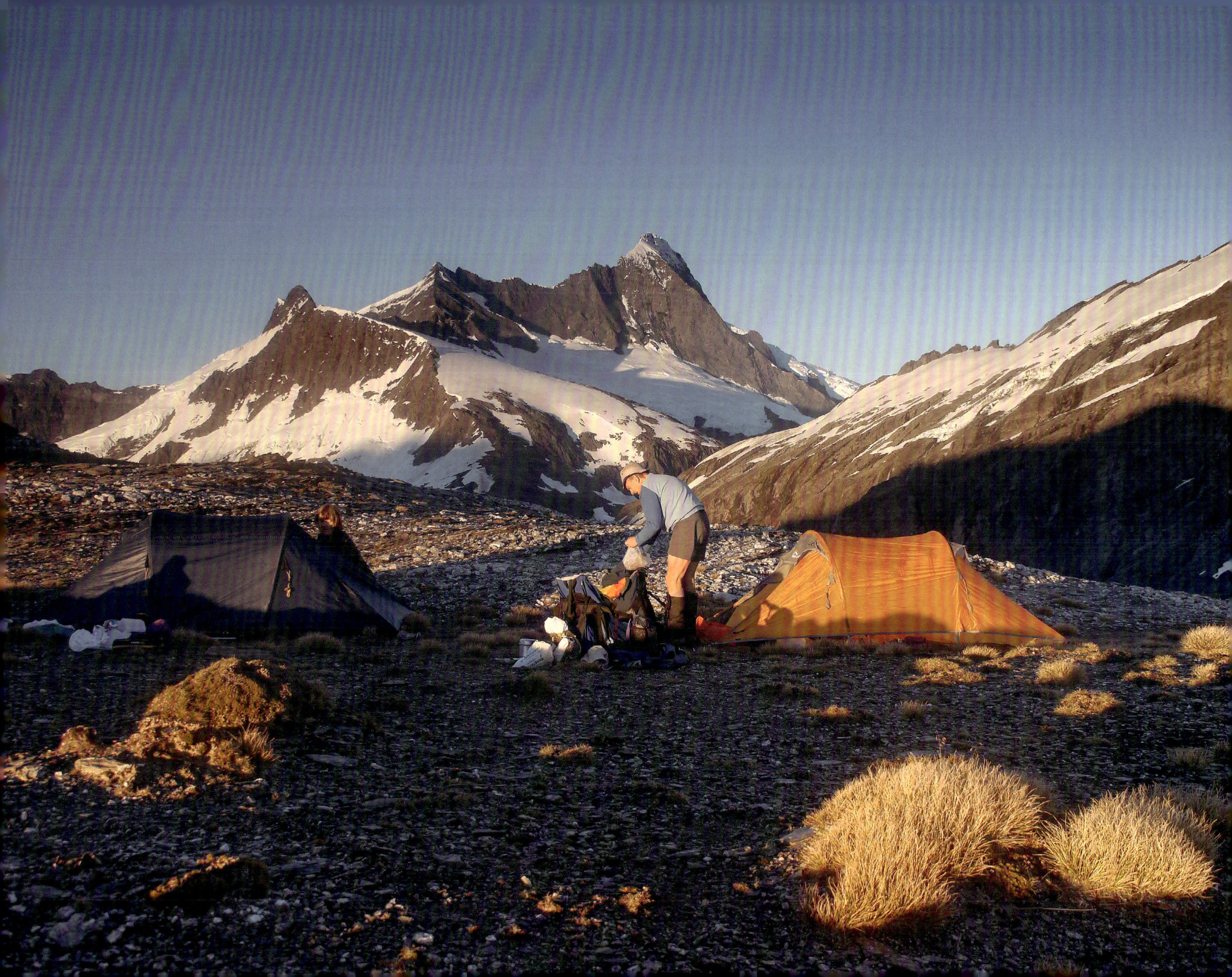

revisit old haunts, including this peak. But the weather trapped the four of them, wrecked their tent, left their clothes and sleeping bags saturated, and drove them into temporary shelter between the rock and snow, and then into a snowcave. They tried to leave via Ruth Ridge, but failed. Feeling trapped, Powell considered using the untried route under the east face of Fastness Peak, but abandoned the idea. Instead, they shivered and waited.

Sometimes weather in the mountains can be like that. You plan, you choose your times, you storm out into it and the weather hits back, bringing you to your knees, unable to stand or even move. Storms in the mountains do what they please, and we cope or not. Powell named the place where they were stuck Tantalus Rock, after the son of Zeus, condemned to eternal frustration in Hades. After nine days – about five of them now overdue – Don Middleton picked them up in a Cessna 185 plane.

For us, it was misty and sometimes drizzling when we looked outside in the morning. That's the great thing about caves. It can be 100-kilometres-per-hour winds outside, or 10 kilometres per hour, and it's all the same. Later, under a dull leaden sky, we took the opportunity to stretch our legs and headed up Glacier Dome.

From Glacier Dome we looked down on the end of Beauty Ridge to the north. It didn't look flash, with big bluffs dropping into the lake in the head of the Purity. I had used this route before in the 1990s, sidling between bluffs on Beauty Ridge and massive walls that curl down to the upper Bettne canyons.

From the snowcave, Merv, Doug and Chris did a water run across the glacier to some rockpools, as melting snow chews through stove fuel, and we tried to avoid it. Meanwhile, Gary cooked dinner. I slept, as befits the leader.

Crunching around on thousands of glinting frost crystals next morning, we crossed over the flat snow plateau between the Volta and the Purity Glacier before descending towards the Bettne bluffs. We approached these as we had approached other difficulties, working together, and once we applied our boots to it we were soon around on the Waiatoto faces, heading over Pearson Saddle, then Rabbit Pass, back to the East Matukituki. By the time we reached the valley floor, legs were sore, backs were sore, throats were dry, and lunch was very attractive. Warm winds and high cloud spoke of a weather change.

Further down, at Junction Flat, we had a break beside Paul Powell's Mountain Tree, a venerable old silver beech. We had gone full circle.

Another link: Powell, who wrote *Men Aspiring* and *Just Where Do You*

ABOVE In a snowcave under Glacier Dome on the Volta Glacier. From left: Chris, Gary, Merv and Calum are cosy and secure.
OPPOSITE On the Purity Glacier. Mt Pickelhaube, right.

Think You've Been?, was also my dentist at one stage many years ago in Dunedin. The mountain tales in Powell's books have inspired me for over 40 years.

His Mountain Tree at Junction Flat was a symbol of homecoming to him, and that's just what it felt like. All that remained was the amble back out through the beech forest, down the flats, a chat to the cows, a river crossing and a swim.

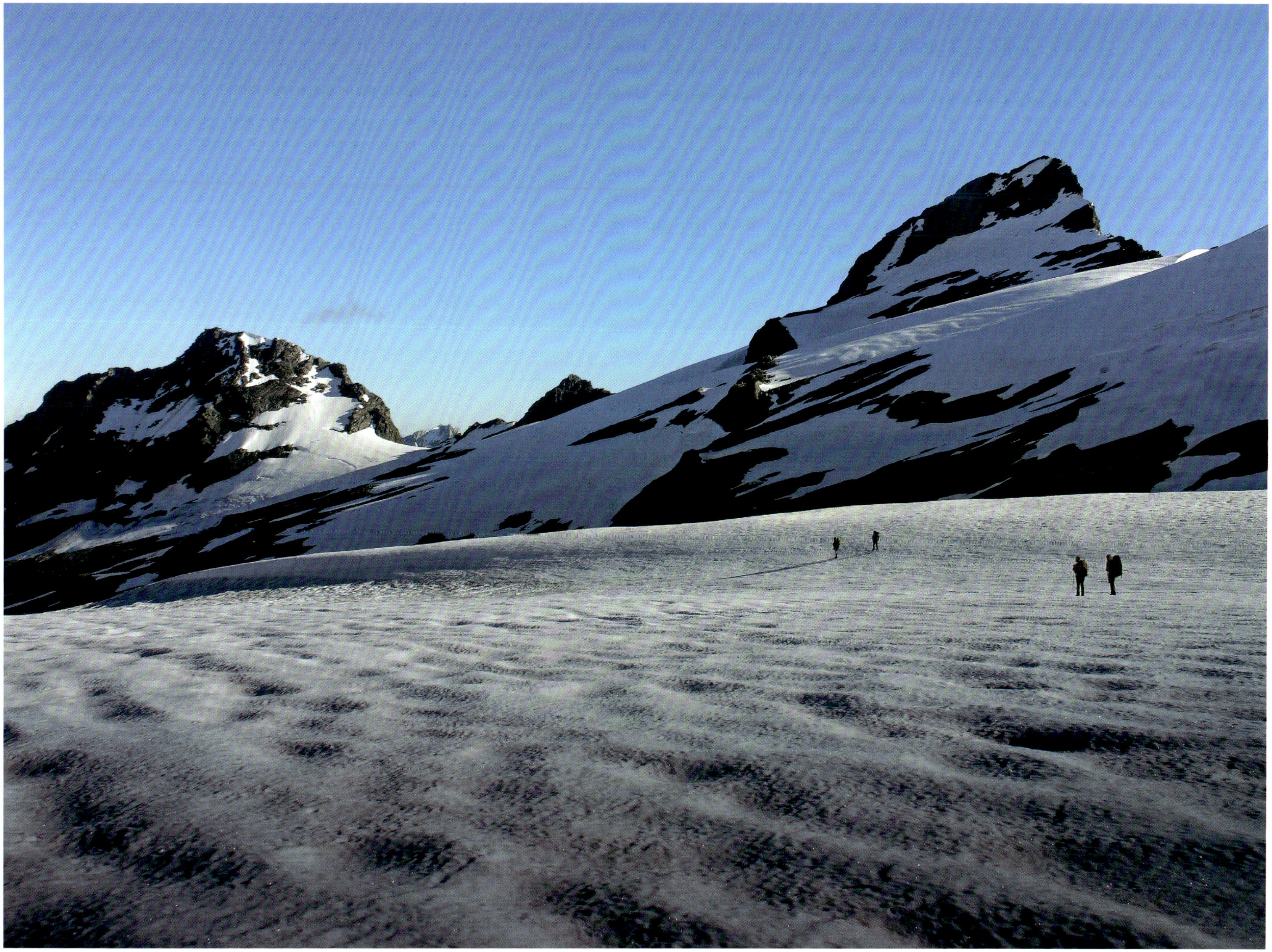

OLIVINE VOLTA TRAVERSE

DESPERATION PASS, THE OLIVINE ICE PLATEAU AND RED MOUNTAIN
2.

A LAND OF BEYOND

IN BARRINGTON COUNTRY

DESPERATION PASS, THE OLIVINE ICE PLATEAU
1.

Ranges: Olivine Range, Thomson Range, Main Divide, Barrier Range, Darran Mountains

Rivers & Creeks: Cascade River, McTavish Ck, Arawhata River, Wilkin River, Waiatoto River, Pyke River, Barrier River, Olivine River, Forgotten River, Joe River, Dart River / Te Awa Whakatipu, Matukituki River, Hollyford River, Hidden Falls Creek, Beans Burn, Rees River

Peaks & Features: Joe Peak, Red Mountain, Telescope Hill, Remote Peaks, Arcade Saddle, Pearson Saddle, Simonin Pass, Stag Pass, Trinity Pass, Invitation Col, McArthur Flat, Pic d'Argent, Ark, The Tower, Forgotten River Col, Futurity Rock, Camp Oven Dome, Williamson Flat, Waipara Saddle, Mystery Col, Arawhata Saddle, Mt Aspiring / Tititea, Volta Gl., Therma Gl., Bonar Glacier, Olivine Ice Plateau, Destiny Peak, Climax Peak, Whitbourn Saddle, Mt Edward, Whitbourn Gl., O'Leary Pass, Derivation Neve, Joe Glacier, Desperation Pass, Seal Col, Fohn Saddle, Daleys Flat, Cattle Flat, Lochnagar, Mt Earnslaw, Scaly Strm

Lakes & Bays: Big Bay, Lake McKerrow, Lake Alabaster

CHAPTER 13

THE OLIVINES & RED MOUNTAIN

The Olivine Range, a land of beyond, has come to represent the epitome of wilderness in New Zealand, a remote place full of mystical mountains requiring commitment and good skills to enter. The jewel in the Olivine crown is the Ice Plateau, draining on one side of the range into tributaries of the Arawhata and on the other into the Pyke. Further north along the range, the country is broken and wild, while to the south the Joe Glacier surrounds are grand in the extreme.

Standing between the Cascade and Pyke rivers, the snows of Red Mountain crown the Red Hills Range, a landscape of barren, burnt-orange ultramafic rock, which is both striking and harsh to walk on. Little grows on it, and the transition from surrounding forest to ultramafic rock at Simonin Pass is as sharp as a knife.

After Māori travellers, mining prospectors explored the area, reaching the Pyke and Hollyford in the 1860s. They left behind some extreme journeys through the ranges, such as those of A.J. Barrington and his mates. The ubiquitous Charlie Douglas and Gerhard Mueller were to follow a decade or so later. Prospector Arawhata Bill crossed O'Leary Pass in 1897 and ranged around the Arawhata, Cascade and Pyke catchments until the 1930s. By this time mountaineers were approaching the Olivine Range and on many fine transalpine trips they explored and climbed its peaks. More of those journeys further on in this chapter.

Most who are heading to the Olivines have one primary objective: to reach the Olivine Ice Plateau and return. For many that becomes a life highlight. The traditional approach follows the Beans Burn over Fohn Saddle to the Olivine–Forgotten River junction, then ascends Forgotten River to Forgotten River Col. This is also a good return route. Basic mountaineering skills and gear are necessary to negotiate small bluffs and crevasses near the col itself.

For mountaineers, a stunning alternate alpine-approach climbs up to Seal Col on the Barrier Range from Dart Valley, traverses the Barrier Range to the Derivation Neve, then sidles the Gates ridge to the Plateau. See *Moir's North*. Allow eight days in fine weather for either option.

OLIVINE–VOLTA TRAVERSE

**JACKSON RIVER–THOMSON RANGE–OLIVINE RANGE–
ANDY GLACIER–CAMP OVEN DOME–WILLIAMSON FLAT–
ARAWHATA RIVER–WAIPARA SADDLE–BONAR GLACIER–
MT ASPIRING–THERMA GLACIER–VOLTA GLACIER–PEARSON
SADDLE–WILKIN RIVER**

20 DAYS: 23 DECEMBER 1975–11 JANUARY 1976
GS WITH MALCOLM GARNHAM AND GRAHAM CLENDON; IAN WILKINS, DAVE SOWRY,
JOE CROFTON, TIM OMUNDSEN AND IAN THORNE ALSO BEGAN THE TRIP ON THE
THOMSON RANGE

I wanted to traverse the Olivine Range. Ian wanted to visit the Volta Glacier. So, we allowed for 20 days and put both places into the same trip. Eight of us met at the Jackson River south of Haast and headed up Carl Creek to camp on the tussock tops of the Thomson Range by Lake Leeb.

The first night, stormy weather wrought havoc among our poorly pitched tents and several sleeping bags were wet. One–nil to the weather. Next night, Christmas Eve, it snowed down into the bush. Two–nil. And on Christmas Day, it snowed and hailed. Three–nil. This was not a good way to start. Mutiny set in, five people abandoned the trip, but then the weather improved. Natural selection can be a brutal process.

The Olivine Range had been traversed once before, over 17 days in February 1973, when Lauchie Duff, Derek Daniell, Paul Clark and Owen Springford from VUWTC came up Martyr Spur from the Jackson River Road and traversed all the way to the Olivine Plateau, exiting via Forgotten River Col, the Olivine Ledge, Fohn Saddle and the Beans Burn. Clark, who was a keen hunter, had carried his rifle the whole way.

In improving weather, Malcolm, Graham and I stayed on or close to the main range all the way from Staircase Mountain to Persephone Col, often finding convenient rocks to bivvy under. At one, below Tararua Peak, bold kea came right under the overhang and flogged Graham's camera case.

The Northern Olivines remained remote and isolated when we were there in the 1970s. As we navigated by map and compass in heavy mist on Bald Mountain we were in a world of our own, imagining how long it might have been since anyone had been here, when fresh bootprints suddenly appeared ahead of us. We weren't as isolated as we thought.

Further along we cramponed up snowy Joe Peak. At Arcade Saddle, we watched the dawn light glow brick-red on the ultramafic rock of Red Mountain and listened to perfect echoes bouncing off nearby rock bluffs. Although not particularly high, the central Olivine peaks through here are quite challenging, rugged and beautiful.

After a quick trip up Toreador Peak from Persephone Col, we descended steep snow slabs onto the Limbo Glacier, crossed Hurricane Col, the Sealy, and then climbed up to Invitation Col. In front of us lay the Trinity Glacier, snaking down to join the Andy Glacier draining the Olivine Ice Plateau. Ice thundered down off cliffs, reverberating.

The terminal of the Andy, though, lay dying: a tongue of ice extending to within 100 metres of the lower end of Lake Williamson. We walked down the old, melting glacier in the middle of the lake, expecting to swim the last section, but ice close to the surface under the murky waters saved most of that. A rock ridge, 150 metres high, blocked the lake in, and the river escaped past it down a slot gorge.

Comparing a sketch by Charlie Douglas from 1884 with today indicates that a thickness of about half a vertical kilometre of solid ice has melted away from the lower Andy Glacier. That is huge. In January 1934, a photo taken by Alex Dickie on a trip with James Speden and George McBride still showed the ice bulging up over the rock ridge.

That trio made the first crossing of the central Olivine Range, from the Pyke Valley up the Barrier Gorge, past Mt Ark and descending the Andy Icefall to the Williamson. James Speden's brother, Gordon, had already crossed Arawhata Saddle in 1928 and they had his detailed notes to follow. High rivers and uncertainty forced Dickie and his party downstream, however, and 26 days after they had set out, Gordon Speden and Captain Mercer flew up the Arawhata and found them, very hungry, at the Waipara Junction.

None of that for us. From the Williamson we climbed over Camp Oven Dome, spending New Year's Eve up there. Down the other side we crossed the Joe and found our food dump at Williamson Flat. This was our eleventh day of the trip and after eight fine days, we were all getting sunburnt. Here, I suffered the ignominy of having my bushshirt and socks flyblown, one of the disadvantages of damp wool. We headed up the Arawhata to Waipara Saddle and sidled through Matukituki Saddle to Bevan Col on the edge of the Bonar Glacier under Mt Aspiring. The second part of our trip was about to begin.

From Colin Todd Hut we climbed Mt Aspiring, then the following day headed for the Therma and Volta, big glaciers feeding out to the west. Under the north-east ridge of Mt Aspiring we had to traverse over fresh ice blocks under active avalanche cliffs. Icefall roulette. Partway across, ice broke away above, and when the first boom sounded, a knot tightened in my stomach. Fortunately, this one didn't reach us.

There were some big crevasses in the Therma, locked together in a jigsaw. In time we navigated through them and dropped onto the Lower Volta Glacier before camping on the Upper Volta near Tantalus Rock on a warm summer evening. Ruth Ridge is the normal exit off the Volta, but I hoped to cross Beauty Ridge near Pickelhaube into the Pearson, and then the Wilkin.

We nearly came unstuck over this plan. In the morning a storm was brewing, and we reached Beauty Ridge at the same time as the cloud. Glimpses down rock bluffs through mist looked horrible, with snow slabs below us actively sliding off at random. We took the best of bad options, cutting a diagonal track down steep snow between bluffs into a rock gut, and finally to easier ground in Jimmy Creek. That was another life used up. In high spirits and thinking the difficulties were over we reached the top of the Waterfall face in the South Wilkin and looked over. Spirits lowered somewhat. This was supposed to be a tramping route. We all took different ways down the bluff (no waratahs back then), all off-route, Graham close to the waterfall, Malcolm and me, further left.

In pouring rain next day we arrived at the six-bunk Top Forks Hut. With 11 people, it was already at double capacity. 'Come on in, we'll find room.' The open fire was going and we were offered a brew.

Inside we met Tom and Pat Barcham, whose 1950s alpine trips I was in awe of; Fred Hollows, originally an Otago climber and well-known international humanitarian and eye surgeon; Ruth Vosseler; and Kurt Suter, an alpine guide who had built De la Beche, Dart and Godley huts. What a bunch! Fred Hollows moved off his bunk into a cat's cradle (made from his climbing rope strung from the rafters), before entertaining us with endless outrageous stories.

Outside, rain drummed on the roof and we were in heaven. This was only our third night in a hut all trip. I'd slept out under the stars for nine, under bivvy rocks for four and in the tent for five nights. Next day we made our way down to Kerin Forks, feeling both trashed and exuberant. Getting here had seemed very improbable after those first wet nights.

ABOVE A classic wilderness mountain. Holloway Peak in the head of Sealy Stream, a tributary of the Pyke River.

OVERLEAF (LEFT) The Joe Valley from Stefansson Peak on the Barrier Range. The Marion Plateau, right, and Mt Aspiring, centre. Williamson Flat is to the left behind Destiny Ridge

OVERLEAF (RIGHT) The Andy Glacier and Olivine Ice Plateau from Mt Gyrae. Climax Peak (right) and Destiny Peak in cloud.

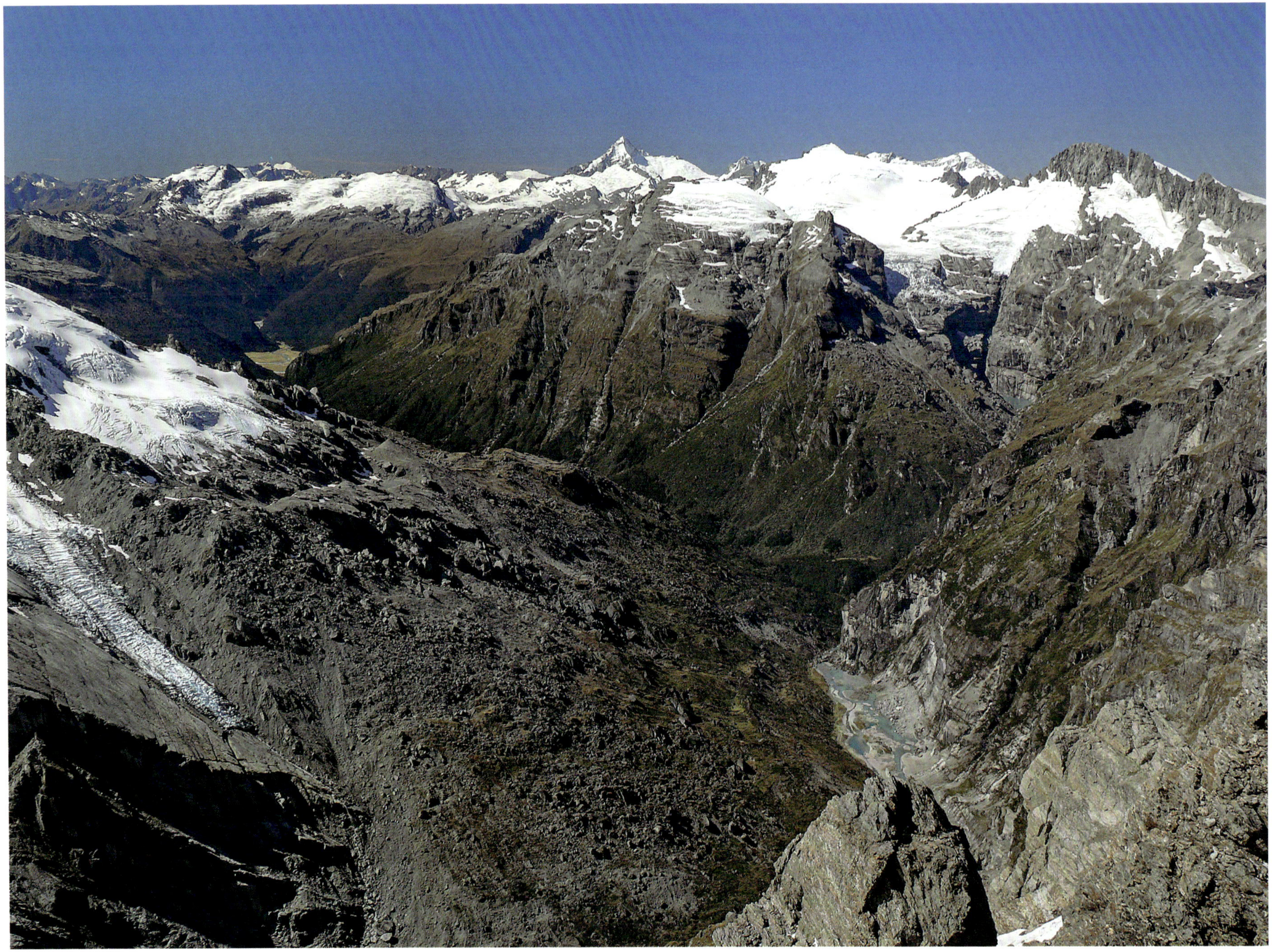

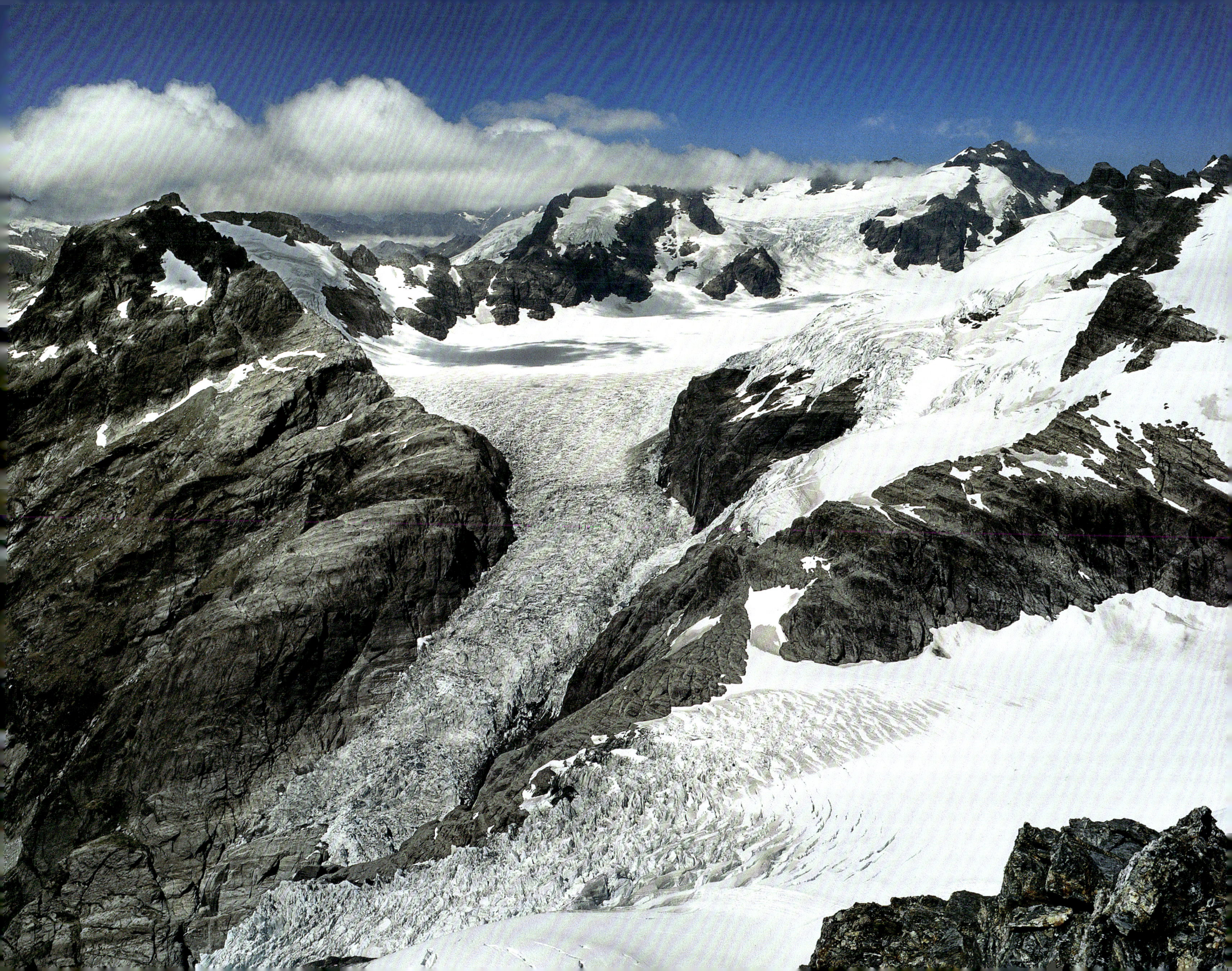

DESPERATION PASS, THE OLIVINE ICE PLATEAU & RED MOUNTAIN

1. DART VALLEY–DESPERATION PASS–JOE GLACIER–DESTINY PEAK–OLIVINE PLATEAU–THUNDERER GLACIER–DERIVATION NEVE–SEAL COL–DART VALLEY

2 DAYS: 9–10 FEBRUARY 1983
GS WITH MIKE ROBERTS

2. DART VALLEY–SEAL COL–DERIVATION NEVE–THUNDERER GLACIER–OLIVINE ICE PLATEAU–TRINITY PASS–TRINITY STREAM–SEALY STREAM–SIMONIN PASS–RED MOUNTAIN–TELESCOPE HILL–BIG BAY–MARTINS BAY

4 DAYS: 19–22 FEBRUARY 1984
GS WITH MIKE ROBERTS

Both these lightweight trips with Mike began in the Dart Valley. I had thought for some years that travel in the Olivines seemed unduly difficult because of the heavy packs people carried. If we were careful and picked our weather, we could go light and fast. The first plan was a two-day return trip to the Olivine Ice Plateau. The second was a four-day trip over the mountains, from the Dart across the Olivine Plateau and Red Mountain to the coast at Big Bay.

First, the Desperation Pass trip.

We left Daleys Flat Hut early, crossed the natural rock bridge of schist boulders spanning the Margaret Burn and reached the bushline at 8.30 a.m. By the time we were on the Barrier Range, however, it was heavily overcast, windy and hailing, so we dropped over Desperation Pass for a look into the Joe. This is big, wild, steep country. A friend, John Rundle, had previously noted that a couloir from the Derivation to the Dilemma Glacier might offer a route down to the Joe Glacier. Just the sort of adventuring I love.

Like John, I had been captured by the stories of Holloway and friends who had some wonderful transalpine expeditions over several summers in the 1930s, in particular 1936. In that year, John T. 'Jack' Holloway, Albert Jackson and E.J. Lilly laid siege to the Barrier Range, determined to cross it to the Joe Glacier then climb peaks on the Olivine Range beyond. They chose Desperation Pass to pack over, and by the time they returned, they had named most of the peaks on the Barrier Range, the head of the Joe, and the Olivine Ice Plateau. They also climbed many of the high peaks.

The names that Holloway and his friends chose were inspired: Climax. Destiny. Derivation. Thunderer (changed to Thunder on current maps). Intervention. Solution and Possibility cols. Futurity Rock. Tower. Darkness. These are titles that have become inseparably linked with the Olivine Mountains. But the name they gave to this pass betrayed their dislike of it: 'We have definitely no further use for Desperation Pass.' In the intervening years we knew of only one other crossing, by Bruce Alexander and party in 1954, and were curious.

From the pass we kicked down a snow gully, swung left over to the Dilemma Glacier and further left to a knob overlooking bluffs. The head of the Joe lay in chaos before us. There was just something about this place, with its rugged and forbidding slabs sandwiched between the Forgotten and the Joe; the roar of raw ice, live ice, dead ice amongst desolate bluffs collapsing on a grand scale. In the midst of it, and looking incongruous, a pair of fragile but fearless rock wren popped up.

A variation of Rundle's couloir worked, using small tussock slopes to bypass a 10-metre fall, then cutting back under bluffs to steep eroding scree. As we reached the glacier, a big rock avalanche boomed and thumped its way down a nearby gully, spilling out across the ice. A billowing plume of rock dust drifted over us. For a raw land in the making, this seemed an appropriate welcome to the Joe.

Tired, we crawled under a bivvy rock and slept. When Holloway and friends were exploring lower down this valley, deer hadn't penetrated it, and they heard kākāpō, kiwi, and saw whio, flocks of parakeets, kea and kaka.

205

PREVIOUS PAGE The Olivine Ice Plateau from the summit of Climax Peak. The high peak across the plateau is Ark.
LEFT Mike on Destiny Ridge, with the Joe Valley under cloud and Mt Gates above the Derivation Neve in the background.
RIGHT Slabs in the head of the Joe Glacier. Climax Peak is to the right.
OVERLEAF (LEFT) Descending Destiny Ridge into the Joe Valley, under Seal Col on the Barrier Range.
OVERLEAF (RIGHT) Red Mountain from Peridot Stream.

Next day we had only been on top of Destiny Peak for five minutes when we started hearing voices. Up popped four climbers from Palmerston North. We were as surprised as they were. But I don't think they believed our plan to be at Daleys Flat Hut that night, the unbelievers.

A long snow slog took us up the plateau, across the Thunderer Glacier to the Derivation Neve and Desperation Pass at 8.30 p.m. It was dark at the bushline below Seal Col, but somehow we chased each other down through trackless beech forest, using torches on a moonless night, to arrive back at Daleys at twelve-thirty. My torch batteries and eyes both needed replacing.

The second trip. Many times I have had to make the choice between my work and my outdoor career. The choice is easy, of course. Do the trip. But the consequences can sometimes be tricky. Mike arrived at my place at the Hillocks ready to go, and I was supposed to work the next two days.

We were dropped off by Gerry Kennedy at the Paradise cattle yards at 10 a.m., complete with packs and four loaves of sandwiches Mike had made. No time wasted preparing lunches on busy days this trip; we could just lie around and eat. Around Chinamans Bluff we ran into Les and Doug Brough and Mal Lapwood. I'd met the Broughs before. These older, cheery twins knew the Otago mountains in detail, and left us with a spring in our step.

Crossing the Dart River at Daleys Flat we ground up through open beech forest again to stop at a tarn high in the tussock, where we could sleep out and watch ice crash off cliffs onto the Margaret Glacier. This was perfect.

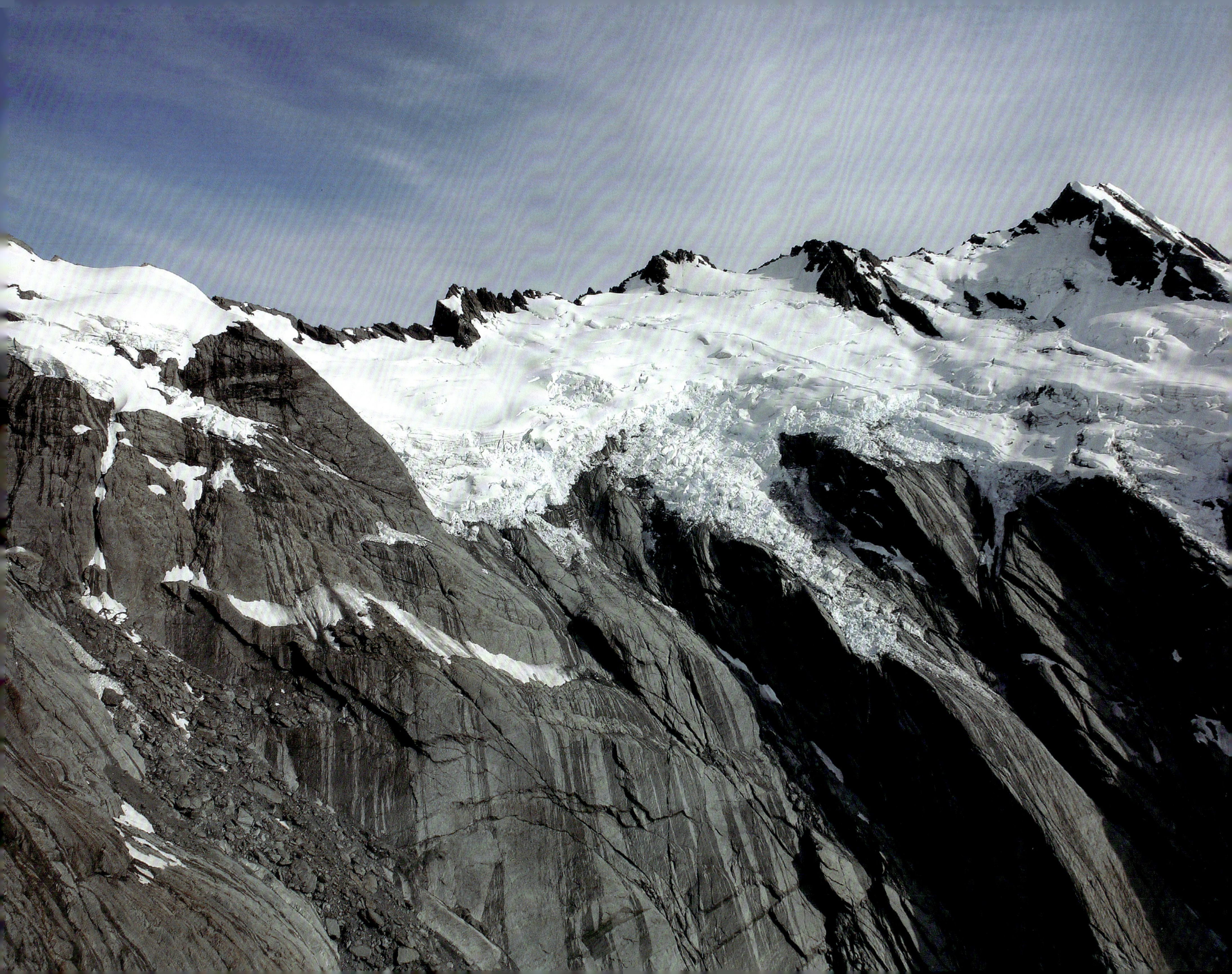

A year on from the Desperation Pass trip, snow conditions were very different. This fickle route from the Derivation Neve across the Thunderer Glacier to the plateau was pioneered by Arnold Heine, Brian Hearfield, John Rundle, and George Thompson on a three-week Christmas trip in 1955. Now, the ice beyond Mt Gates was a mess of schrunds and slots, one of which threatened to derail us. On a belay, Mike carefully balanced over unstable ice blocks, then climbed an icewall on the far side to get back to the snow. There was to be no retreat back over that. We reached Climax Col at 4 p.m.

After plugging steps across the Olivine Ice Plateau we continued over Little Ark. That night we slept out near Trinity Pass on moss and talus in a room the size of the universe, elated. We were making good progress.

In 1976 there had been a lake here at the head of the Trinity Glacier. Eight years later this had become a deep gravel hole with stranded icebergs. Dying glaciers expose older ice that has formed deep down, and the surface crystals can take on a magnified size and clarity, full of subtle watercolours.

Our light packs were paying off, and we both felt good, so we used the morning for a side trip to Trinity Col. Later, we crossed Trinity and Sealy Streams over to Simonin Pass.

Here, we reached the spectacularly abrupt geological boundary between schist and abrasive Red Mountain ultramafic rock, burnt-orange in colour and as barren as Mars. Some of this same rock exists in the Richmond Range south of Blenheim, transported there by the alpine fault. At dusk, kaka called as they flew across the Cascade Valley. As we slept out on the side of Red Mountain, cloud drifted quietly, letting a half moon in and out of the shadow landscape.

Under a leaden sky at 10 the next morning, day four, we were on Red Mountain looking towards Big Bay, still about 20 kilometres away. Our mission was to be there that night. We navigated carefully out along a ridge and down a spur to Chrome Creek and the Pyke River. It was 4.40 p.m.

The sound of surf, then finally the coast, greeted us at 8.30 p.m. where a bright sun was getting ready to dip into the ocean. Leaving the fernbirds, fantails, tomtits, bellbirds and waxeyes behind in the coastal bush, we strode out onto the sand and ditched our clothes. Inevitably a swim; great splashes, body surfing, grins and yelling, the taste of salt, the feel of sore feet. We slept on the beach, with Red Mountain on the horizon, and in the morning we hobbled on down the coast. There were tourist planes at the Hollyford and we were in Glenorchy for tea.

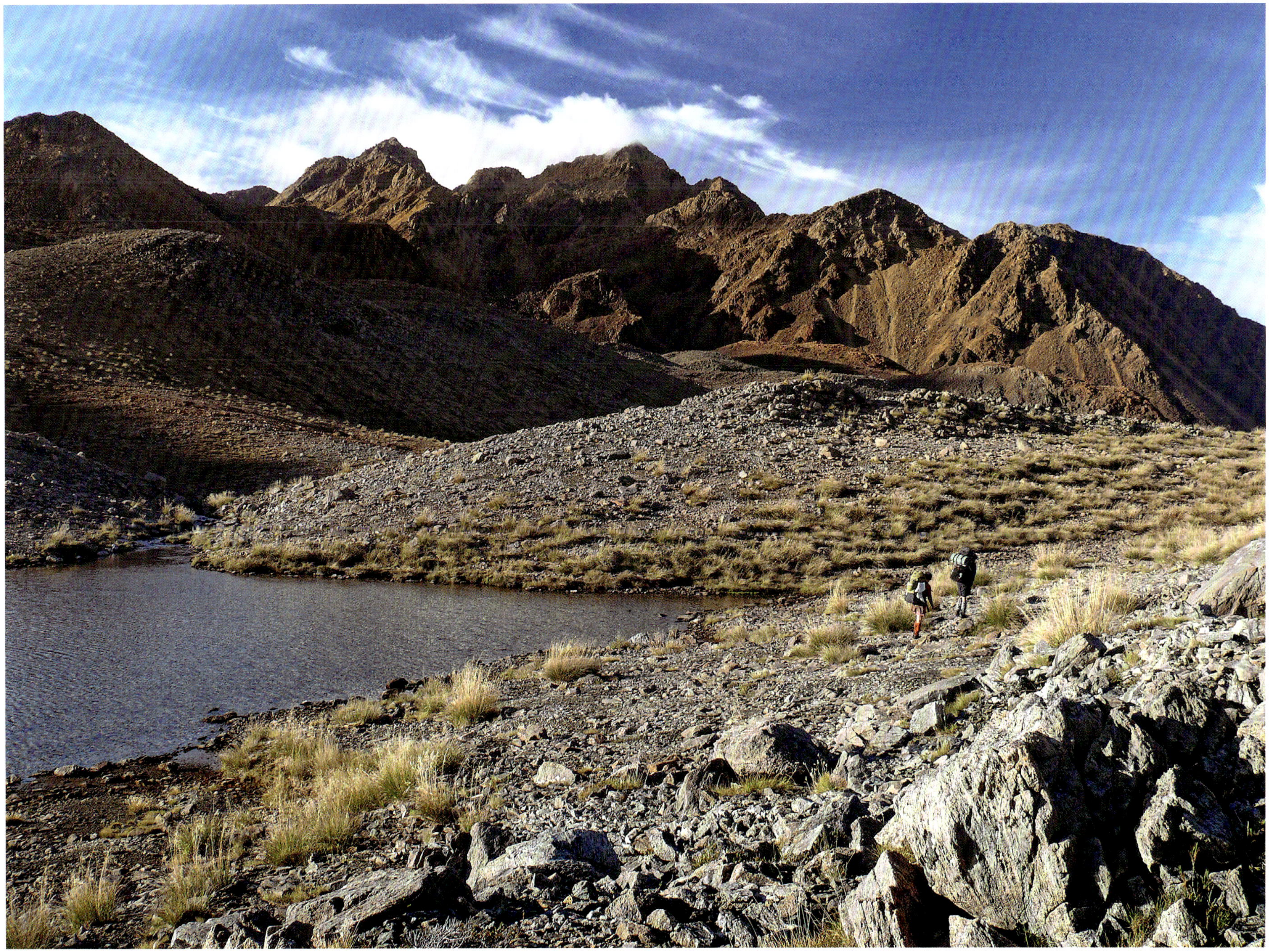

A LAND OF BEYOND

ARAWHATA RIVER–MCTAVISH CREEK–ARCADE SADDLE–REMOTE PEAKS–HALFWAY SADDLE–SIMONIN PASS–LIMBO STREAM–SEALY STREAM–INVITATION COL–TRINITY PASS–LITTLE ARK–OLIVINE ICE PLATEAU–DESTINY RIDGE–JOE RIVER–WILLIAMSON FLAT–MYSTERY COL–WHITBOURN SADDLE–WHITBOURN GLACIER–DART VALLEY

16 DAYS: 28 DECEMBER 1988–12 JANUARY 1989
GS WITH GARY GOLDSWORTHY, CHRIS MANSELL, OWEN SPEARPOINT, NICK BROWN AND FRED LANGFORD

South Westland is big country. We began this trip where McTavish Creek meets the Arawhata River, 35 kilometres beyond the roadend. To get there, local farmer John Nolan took us up-valley in his jetboat. We enjoyed a mild night around the fire, fresh, dry, clean and full of anticipation as dusk drew in.

By morning it was too late to bolt, but as it began to rain we had an inkling of the brutal introduction to follow. With packs of over 30 kilograms and carrying 16 days' food, Gary wrote, 'The whole day was spent grovelling with grossly overloaded packs over, under and around greasy nettle- and bushlawyer-infested boulders and windfalls in pouring rain.' The McTavish Creek experience. Twelve hours of this and hell sounded pretty tame.

I hadn't done myself any favours this trip by experimenting with my footwear. I wore rigid plastic Koflach climbing boots, with socks and wetsuit bootie inners. I had a second pair of dry inners to wear in the snow. It had seemed like a good idea, but wet feet in rigid plastic led to soft, sensitive skin that tended to peel. I also took my medium format (read 'heavy') Mamiya 645 camera, lenses and tripod. The road to hell is paved with good intentions.

At 8 p.m. we stopped for the night on a tussock flat at the bushline studded with tarns, and by good fortune found a spacious, mostly dry bivvy rock to camp under. It did drip in places, and some water needed draining, but we all stayed dry and warmed by the fire. Outside, the rain continued for 48 hours.

Nature happens when you watch, listen and become part of a place. A hind appeared on the flat. Two whio gave a solid territorial display, swimming at me head down and calling. Kaka chortled down in the McTavish. Falling water and mountains rising into the mist brought a spiritual dimension along with the smug satisfaction that wet leatherwood had become impotent now we were above it – it was now just a plant with a wonderful form and colour and smell, with dead wood that burned well in our fire. A day doing nothing, watching the rain, the locals, and maintaining our fire skills.

Beyond Arcade Saddle we climbed up a snow gully onto the Remote Peaks, then glissaded down the Findlay Glacier to camp on Halfway Saddle for New Year's Eve. Two chamois played in the snow, flushes of verdant *Bryum* moss glowed green in wet seeps and we lay around eating chocolates, all the sweeter for the effort involved in getting them here.

Crossing Holland Creek and the Cascade River to Simonin Pass, sidling up into the Limbo and scrambling up scree to Hurricane Col took us into the heart of the central northern Olivine Mountains. This is bold country. The difficulty of travelling between Trinity Glacier and Halfway Saddle has challenged many, inspiring all sorts of journeys over decades to unravel topographical detail and climb a myriad peaks for the first time.

In 1938 Ian and Eric Whitehead, Roland Rodda and J. Findlay crossed Desperation Pass to reach the Olivine Ice Plateau, then pushed on to name the Trinity Glacier, observing that it was fed by three icefalls. They also named Invitation Col, then climbed Mt Temple and the three peaks of Trinity, before also naming Holloway Peak after the man who had explored so much of this area.

Ian Whitehead returned a year later with Murray Benson and J. Findlay to extend that exploration, climbing the highest peak on Jagged Ridge, the Retreat Pinnacles and Toreador Peak, in the head of the Tornado Glacier. On this trip they climbed onto the Olivine Range from the top of Ten Hour Gorge.

Colin Todd made two trips that never reached beyond Trinity Glacier in 1947 and 1948 due to bad weather. In 1951, however, a different approach saw him enter the upper Limbo Valley where they climbed Tempest, Matador and Picador. Enter Stan Conway, John Pascoe, Ray Chapman and Bill Hannah, who, in 1953 climbed the virgin Holloway Peak on a magnificent, mostly

OPPOSITE A mountaineering party on the Olivine Ice Plateau, close to Futurity Rock. Passchendaele Peak is on the left and Climax Peak to the right.

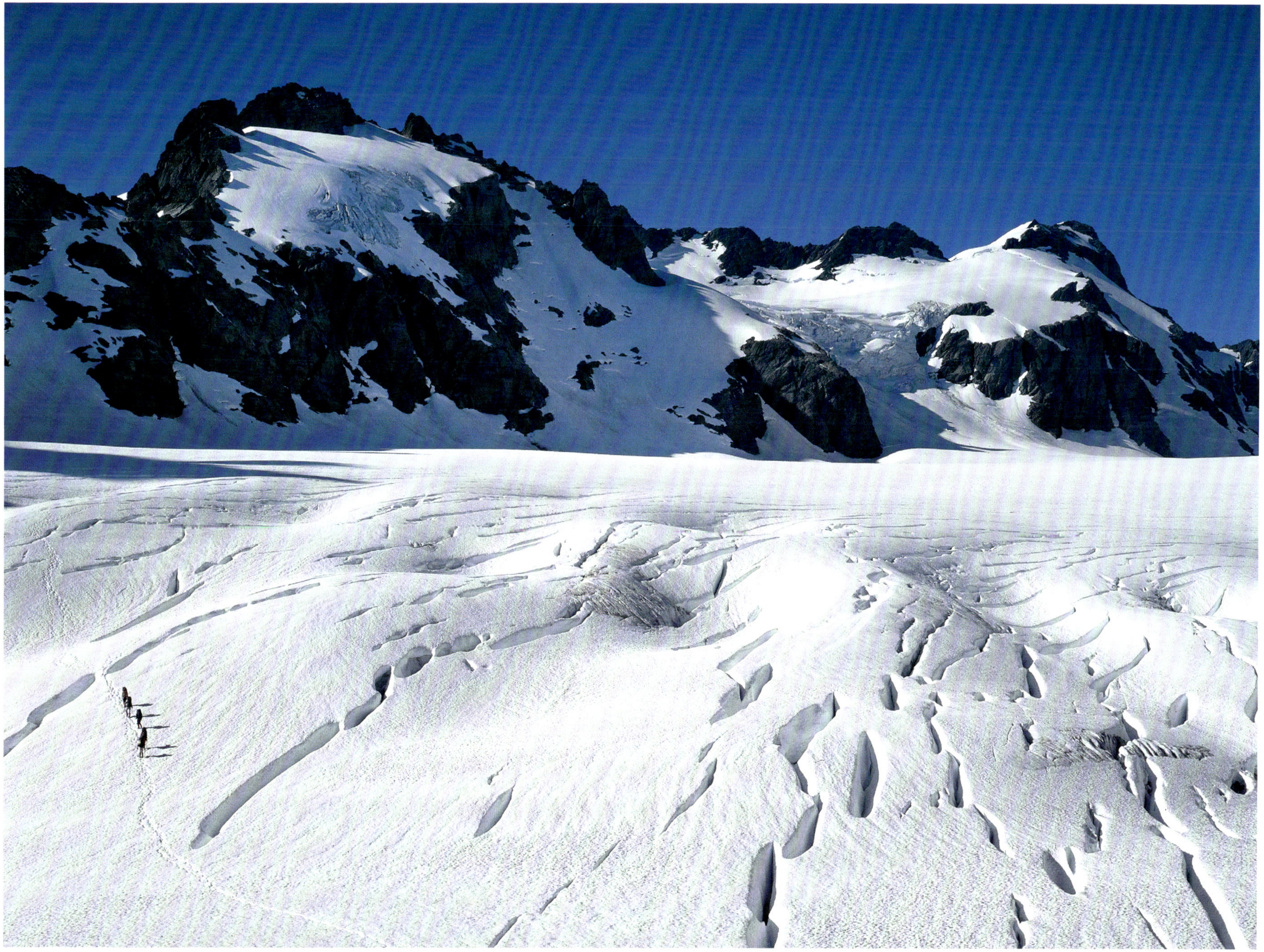

alpine trip from the West Matukituki Valley to Jackson Bay, walking all the way carrying all their provisions, over 21 days.

Many other parties have done their own exploring through here since, including a party from Massey University Alpine Club who climbed the Sealy face of Holloway in 1969. Another, including Les Molloy, summited the unclimbed Typhoon Peak from the Limbo Glacier in 1970.

Since then countless others from all over the country have re-explored this area, especially Otago Tramping and Mountaineering Club and Otago University Tramping Club: staunch, capable people like Dave Craw, Kelvin Lloyd, James Thornton, Nina Dickerhoff and many, many others. Kelvin Lloyd was nicknamed 'E39' after a topo map covering the Olivine area, which he proudly pointed out had no roads on it whatsoever.

Our journey through here took us to the Limbo then up onto Invitation Col. Despite sombre cloud cover and rain, we climbed Mt Temple and descended to camp by the Trinity Glacier.

Over the next few days we climbed Ark, camped on Futurity Rock, climbed Passchendaele, Daedalus, Climax, Destiny and the rock climb of Tower. Then we headed over Destiny into the Joe. From here, the Barrier Range is aptly named. Colossal bluffs rise out of the Joe, big walls of schist, one on top of the other, while wispy streams drift down narrow guts between them, to finally succumb as waterfalls blowing away into the wind before they can reach the valley floor. It is a huge place, full of power, and to journey into it requires big energy.

Downstream we could see O'Leary Pass, where bluffs continued unchecked right around to the Victoria Icefall, draining the Marion Plateau. It is worth a comment. Back in the 1900s, the Victoria Glacier extended into the head of Victor Creek covering those bluffs in one spot, and this became the probable route into the Joe, used by 31-year-old Arawhata Bill in 1897. However, as ice recession made this route more and more difficult, other options were considered. In the early 1950s, a hunter, Dr M.F. Soper of Queenstown, descended through bluffs downstream into Victor Creek. In 1954 a Hutt Valley Tramping Club party of six, led by Arnold Heine, further explored and popularised the current Gulch route by carrying 30-kilogram packs over it. But it remains a transalpine test piece; many will want a rope, and on my trips over it I notice the severity never diminishes.

The Joe is another test piece – at least, it tested us. Big river boulders, scrub, high sides, all beside a dirty, grey, roaring river that bucked and plunged its way down towards the Arawhata at Williamson Flat.

Climbing up from Williamson Flat we reached Mystery Col overlooking the Snow White Glacier and camped on Whitbourn Saddle. Overnight it snowed, and mist came in, but later in the day a clearance saw us beetle up to the summit of Mt Edward.

In March 1914 Major Bernard Head's party made the first ascent. Sadly, Head died soon after at Gallipoli. The second ascent was, appropriately enough, made by Otago climbers R.R. Edwards, G.L. Edwards and C.E. Smith in 1932. Seven years later, in 1939, A.R. 'Bob' Craigie, W.S. Gilkison, E.O. Dawson and J.P. Cook headed up over Whitbourn Saddle from the Dart, exploring and naming the Snow White Glacier and proposing a high-level route that was to become well used between Arawhata Saddle and Williamson Flat. Glacial recession has completely changed that, though, and now a high, smooth wall of schist cuts Mystery Col off from the glacier.

But we had done our dash. We turned to travel out down the Whitbourn and Dart. It had been an exhausting trip, but a great adventure.

OPPOSITE The Joe River is renowned for slow, hard travel.

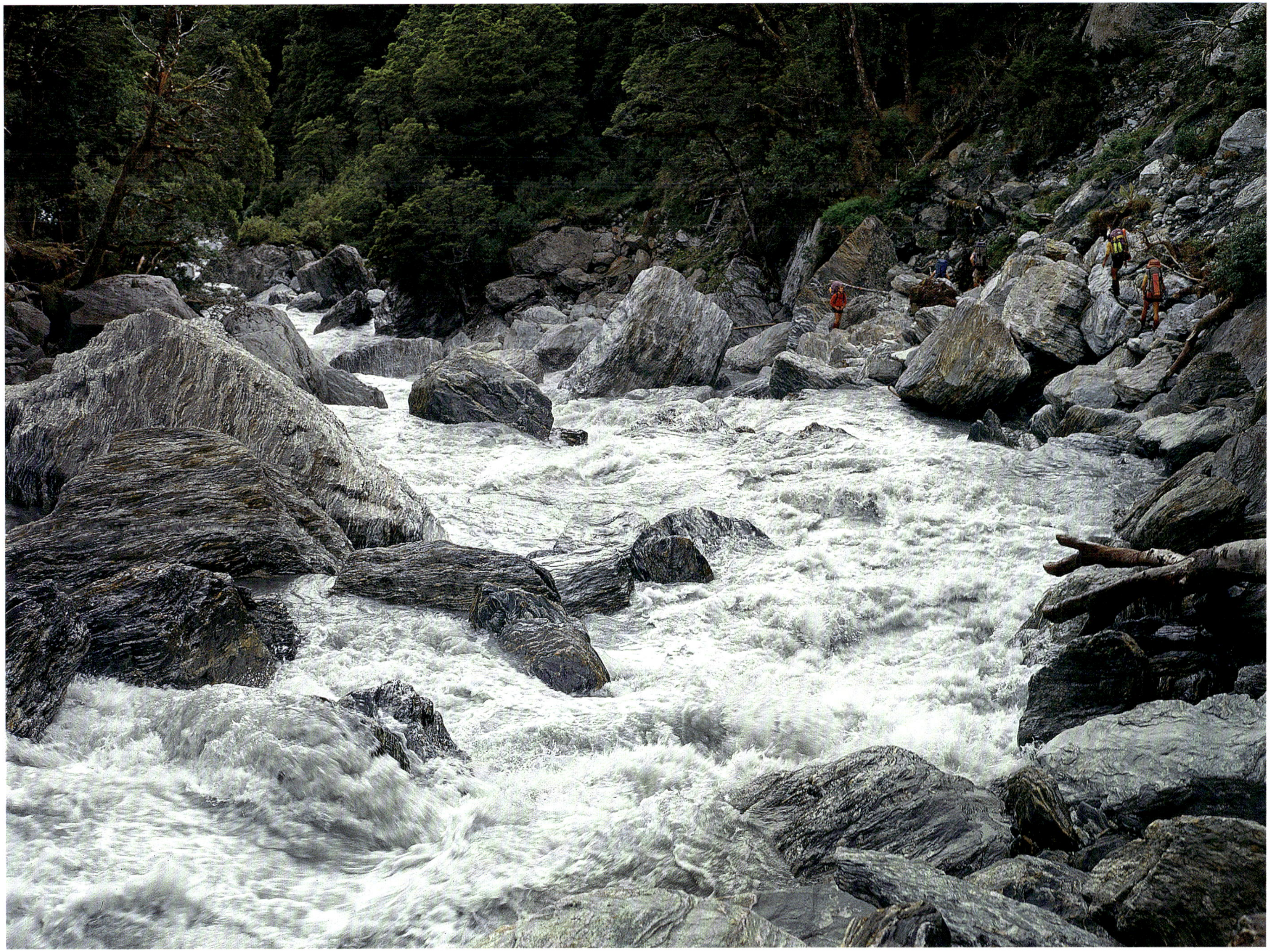

IN BARRINGTON COUNTRY

BIG BAY–PYKE RIVER–STAG PASS–BARRIER RIVER–
PIC D'ARGENT–OLIVINE ICE PLATEAU–FORGOTTEN RIVER
COL–FORGOTTEN RIVER–OLIVINE RIVER–HIDDEN FALLS

7 DAYS: 7–13 FEBRUARY 1999
GS WITH GARY GOLDSWORTHY, BARBARA BROWN AND OWEN SPEARPOINT

We followed in big bootprints: A.J. Barrington's.

From the end of 1863 until June 1864, A.J. Barrington and his mates, including Edward Dunmore, William Bayliss, Joseph McGuirk, Antoine Simonin and James Farrell explored from Lake Wakatipu into the Hollyford, up the Pyke, Gorge and Cascade rivers, and then with winter approaching, tried to cut back home over Red Mountain and the Olivine Range. The result was a gold-prospecting tale of adversity and wilderness survival without equal in New Zealand. Bad weather and snow held them up most of the trip back. Along the way Barrington became separated from his two mates in thick mist on Red Mountain. Weak and alone, trudging in snow, he was forced to abandon much of his load. Days later, completely by chance, he stumbled across his friends again on the Barrier flats under Stag Pass.

Crossing Intervention Saddle, Simonin fell hundreds of metres down a snow couloir and was lucky to survive. While descending the Olivine Gorge their rope broke, plunging Farrell into a cataract and within a whisker of his life. In late May, heavy rain forced Lake Alabaster to rise several metres, flooding their campsite. They abandoned it at ten at night, wading chest-deep for half a kilometre in the dark to solid ground where they walked up and down all night in pouring rain. 'If this night does not kill us we shall never die,' Barrington wrote. All the while they were half starved. When they reached Lake Wakatipu they looked like living skeletons, and were hospitalised. Barrington's diary truly deserves the word 'epic'.

We followed their journey from the Pyke through Stag Pass into the Barrier, the Forgotten, Olivine and Hidden Falls – but only in a broad sense; we followed our own route, which included time on the Olivine Plateau, and it certainly lacked their drama. Near the end they crossed into the Route Burn and Lake Wakatipu. We continued down Hidden Falls to the Hollyford and back to our car again.

Our journey from Big Bay soon had us in the Pyke Gorge, sidling and slipping our way to the Red Pyke River, which we crossed among slippery boulders, camping soon afterwards. The country was in drought, the sandflies were few, and the birdlife prolific. Kaka, riflemen, fantails, bellbirds, riroriro, parakeets and tomtits all came to sing us along as we grovelled through steep ultramafic scrub and boulders.

Pyke Camp on Simonin Flats with its two huts, one a rock-core samples shed and the other a kitchen, was the hub of a controversial prospecting operation in the area during the early 1970s. The afternoon saw us skinny dip in the river and cross Stag Pass into the head of the North Barrier. Ahead lay the Furies, Demon Gap, Darkness and Pic d' Argent.

The Olivine Range is a place many others have also had big adventures in, including club friends of mine, Trev and Thora Jones. There were six of them in their 1951 Christmas trip, and they had reached the Olivine Plateau from the Hollyford via Diorite Stream, Four Brothers Pass and Forgotten River Col. Here they scooped out snow with their dinner plates to build a snowcave, then had several good days' climbing.

Next, Trev, Thora and Brian Hearfield left their cave at 3.30 a.m. on a day trip to climb Darkness Peak. Having achieved this, they decided to explore. They had spied a small moraine lake in the head of the North Barrier River, and it looked inviting. Down there they washed away a week's grime, intending to return on a spur to Mt Ark that they knew had been used in the 1930s by Alex Dickie's party. A storm cut them off at the pass. In blizzard conditions at 1700 metres, they were forced back down to the upper Barrier where 'a frigid New Year's Eve [was] spent with the elements loosing rain, hail, thunder and gale'.

The next day, fatigued and hungry, they backed off Beresford Pass (knowing that also meant crossing Four Brothers Pass and a climb up to Forgotten River Col on empty stomachs) in favour of descending the Barrier Gorge to the Barrier Hut in the Pyke, where there was dry food and hut blankets.

OPPOSITE Morning light across the upper Arawhata, seen from Pic d'Argent at the head of the Williamson Valley in the central Olivines. Mt Aspiring is to the right, with Camp Oven Dome below. Jagged Ridge stands out on the left.

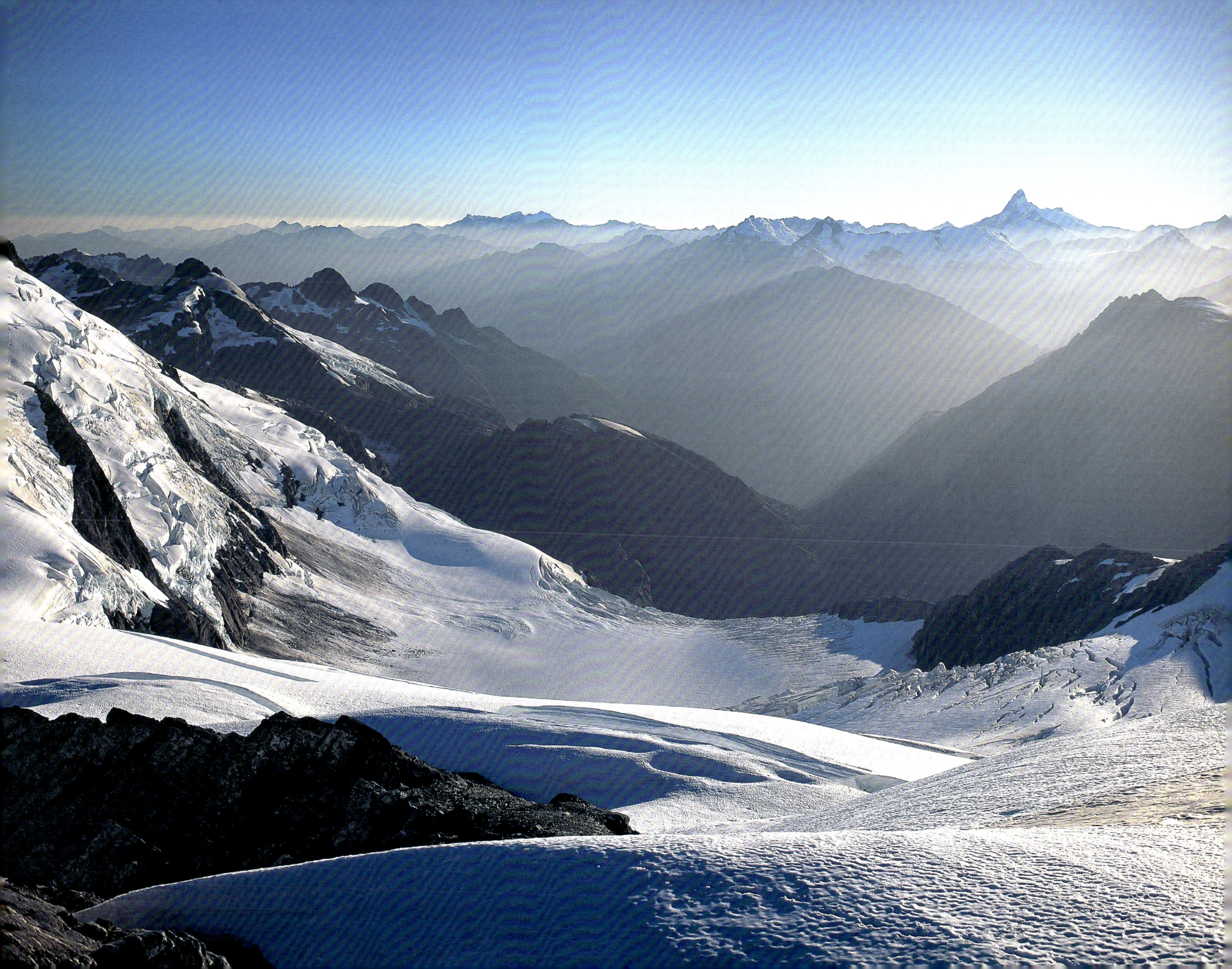

The storm raged on. In deep soft snow on 3 January 1952 they crossed Four Brothers Pass and spent a cold night in old sacks at Forgotten River bivvy rock, before climbing back up to their snowcave on the plateau, where the other three remained storm-bound. It was quite a staunch self-rescue, with no locator beacons back then.

Back to our trip, and from the North Barrier River, we climbed onto Pic d'Argent and camped. The long low rays of sunset burned the slabs of Darkness Peak brick-red, while at dawn, ridges marched across the Arawhata to bold Aspiring as we climbed Gyrae. My medium-format camera loved it all.

Forgotten River Col is the hub of the Olivine universe. Most approach from Forgotten River, using a variety of routes from the Dart and Hollyford. But there are other more recent favourites such as approaches from Daleys Flat to Seal Col, the Derivation Neve and along the Gates Ridge, one side or the other, to the Plateau. Harder routes approach from the Arawhata. It is all in *Moir's*. There are as many routes as there are people's imaginations, and therein lies much of transalpine's fun.

We slept out among rocks above the col, nestled snug and toasty on little earth benches as the afterglow retreated and dew settled for the night. In the morning we descended under bluffs to the Forgotten River bivvy rock. Due to glacial recession, the route from the ice to the benches below often requires a bit of scrambling and route-finding these days, and small pack hauls or lowers. But it's not that hard. It is a climbing route, after all.

How did the Forgotten River get its name? Prior to 1937, maps showed only one river, the Olivine, draining south-west from the Olivine Ice Plateau in a big loop towards Fohn Saddle then north again out to the Pyke. In the summer of 1936/1937, from peaks in the vicinity of Cow Saddle, Holloway realised this was in fact incorrect, and a whole separate catchment just as big as the Olivine drained the Olivine Ice Plateau, entering the Olivine River only 5 kilometres from the Pyke. This was actually a rediscovery, as A.J. Barrington had already descended this 'new' river 70 years earlier. Holloway and friends then corrected the maps and named the river, appropriately, Forgotten.

LEFT In the head of the Barrier River North Branch. The Furies Ridge sits above the bluffs with Demon Gap Icefall to the right.

OPPOSITE The slabs of Darkness Peak with Red Mountain (left), at sunset.

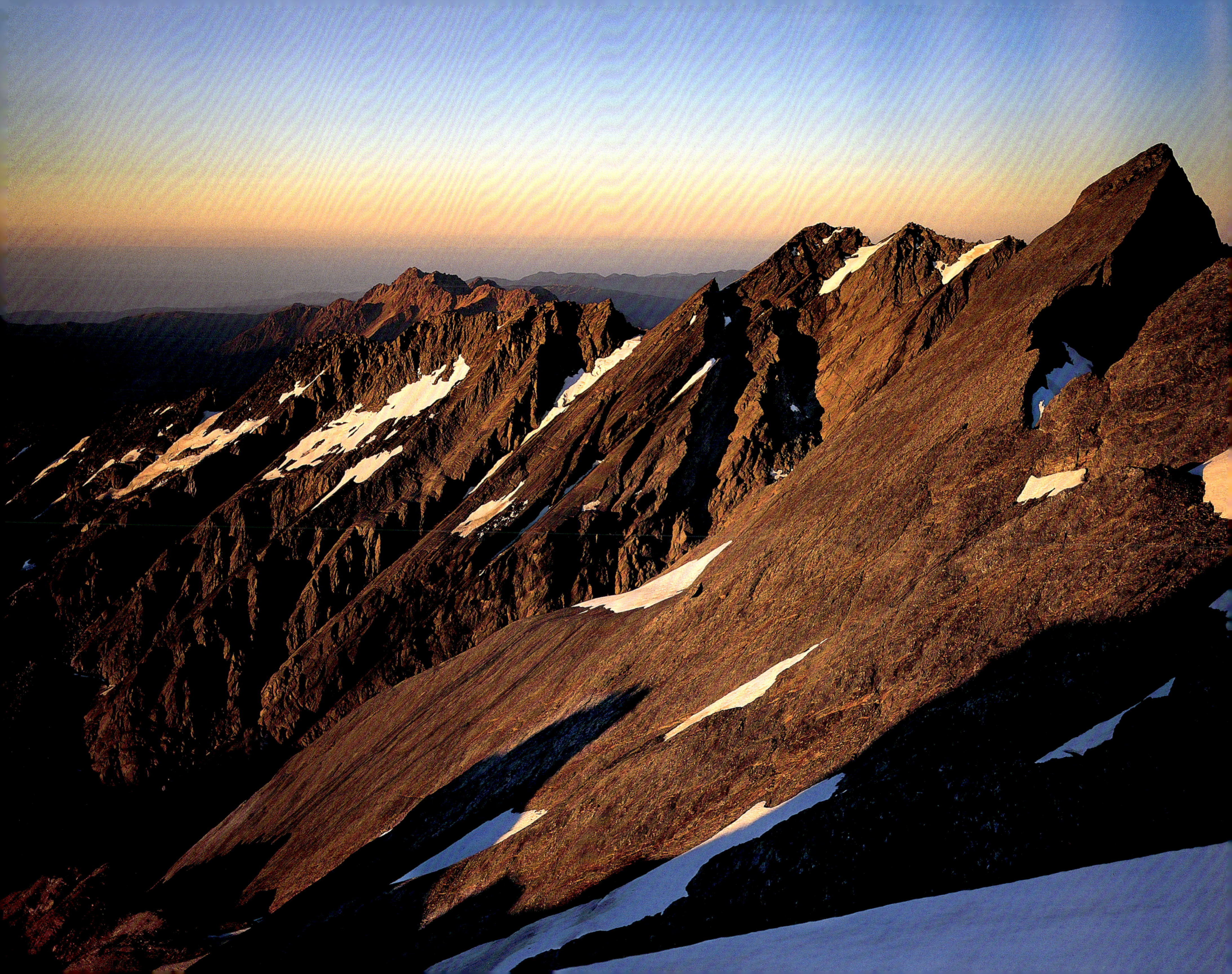

West of the Olivine Range the gorges can be vicious canyons, but flats in the Barrier, Forgotten, Olivine and Hidden Falls are divine. We swum in Forgotten backwaters, contemplated the tranquil blue pool where the shy Forgotten emerges from bedrock under a canopy of cool forest onto the Olivine Flats, and contemplated camping under an old silver beech where the rivers join.

Next day we scrub-scratched up the true left of the Olivine River on ultramafic rock benches before crossing near Fiery Creek and continuing up to Alabaster Flats. Up on Alabaster Pass, rounds of ice-worn bedrock stuck out of the forest like knuckles, offering great views of the Olivine Ledge and river. We continued over the tussock lands of Cow Saddle and down into Hidden Falls Creek.

The Olivine Ledge is part of the Five Pass trip circuit. Central Hidden Falls Creek is a delightful place of flats, kaka, and good travel, but then on the bend it takes a decided turn for the worse. Much worse. We battled our way through vines and boulders, fierce nettle (*Urtica* sp.) and all sorts of other shrubs that lost their shine the more we saw of them. Prickly shield fern and logs. The list seemed to stretch to infinity, but finally we swung south out of the gorge and stumbled dizzily across to the Hollyford track. This was Gary's last trip for a few years, so it was important Hidden Falls Stream gave him something to remember. He not just remembers, he still bears the scars.

LEFT Forgotten River Flats.
OPPOSITE Tucked up for the night under Veints (Cattle Flat) Biv in the Dart Valley, en route to the Marion Ice Plateau.

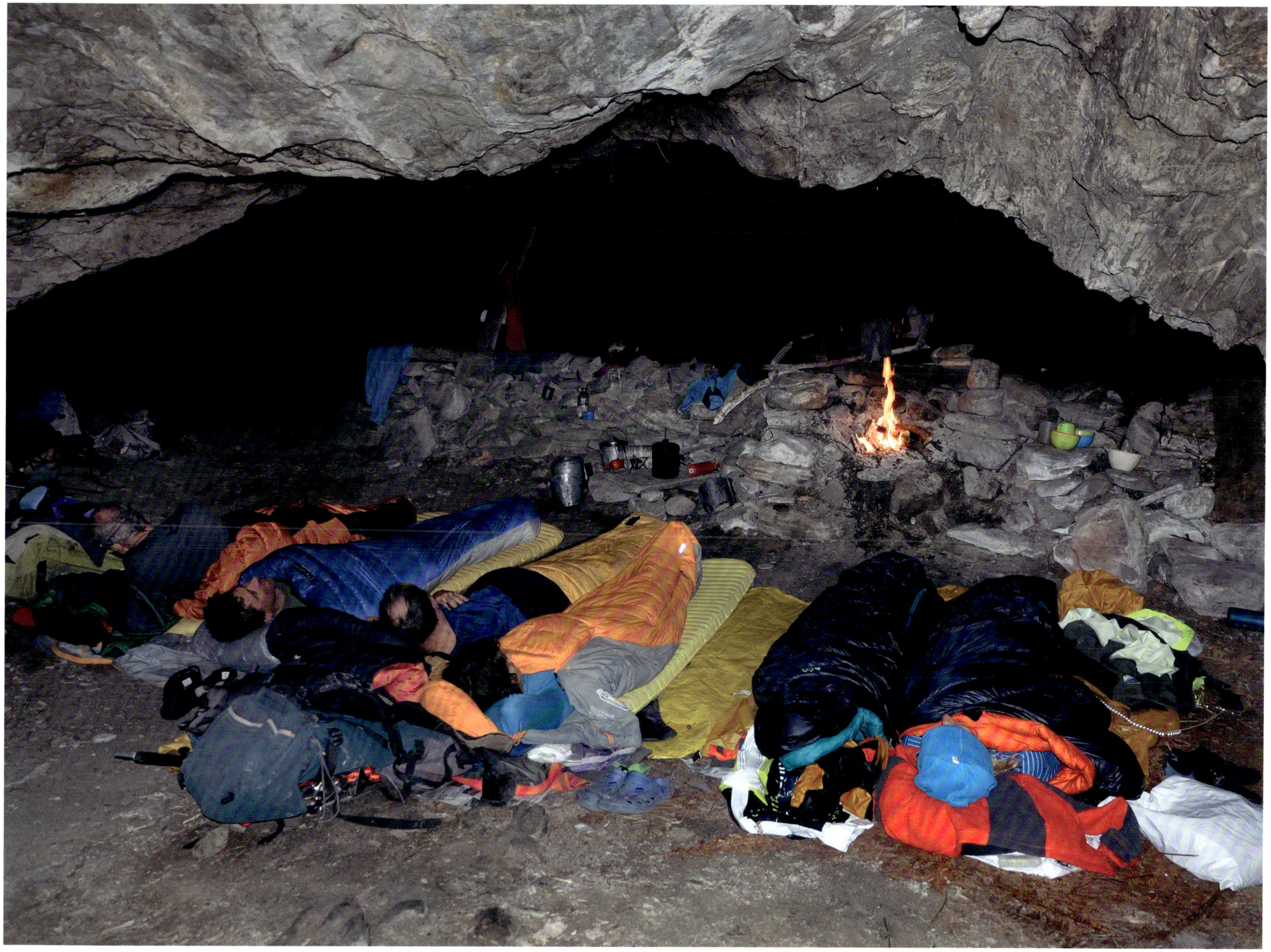

0
5
10 km
N
Milford Sound / Piopiotahi
Anita Bay
Transit River
Kaipo River
Lake Truth
Ngapunatoru Plateau
Lake Never-never
Mt Pembroke
Harrison River
Grave Couloir
Mt Tutoko
Mitre Peak
HARRISON–TUTOKO
Tutoko Valley
DARRAN MOUNTAINS
Sinbad Gully
Llawrenny Pks
TRANSIT–SINBAD
Poison Bay
Lake Moreton
Arthur River
Cleddau River
Mackay Ck
Main Light Valley
Staircase Ck
East Light River
Lake Quill
94
Light Dark Saddle
Dark River
Castle River
Hunter Pass
Prospect Ck
Clinton River
THE LIGHT AND THE DARK
Worsley River
Lake Te Anau

N
Caswell Sound
Charles Sound
Irene River
Nancy Sound
Windward River
Irene Tops
Double Peak
Key Peak
Irene Pass
Rea River
Teardrop Lake
Coronation Peak
WINDWARD RIVER TOPS
CORONATION PEAK
PRECIPICE COVE
Precipice Cove
Bradshaw Sound
Cozette Burn
Camelot River
0
5
10 km

CHAPTER 14
FIORDLAND & THE DARRANS

Fiordland and its northern extension, the Darran Mountains, offer wild remote landscapes on a scale unmatched anywhere else in the country. From the rugged south coast and Puysegur Point, rolling forests and isolated ranges march up between deep fiords, growing higher and steeper the further north they go, until at Milford and the Darran Mountains their spectacular walls reach world-famous proportions. Away from the roads and more developed tracks, this area offers superb alpine and subalpine wilderness journeys.

There are many layers to Fiordland history but the adventures of W.G. Grave and his main companions A.C. Gifford, T.A. Hunter, A. Talbot and A. Grenfell stand out as exceptional. From the first ascent of Grave Couloir in 1898, to the journeys into the Glaisnock in 1903, the Dark River and Sutherland Sound in 1905, the North Clinton, all branches of the Cleddau, the discovery of the Grave Talbot Pass in 1910, the ascent of Mt Pembroke in 1913 with Talbot and J. Lippe, and the ascent of Mt Christina in 1925 with G.M. Moir's party, Grave relished the challenges of bush and alpine journeys in this region.

The classic remote transalpine trip? Choose any mountain range . . . none of the described trips are particularly appropriate classics to recommend. The crossing from the Harrison to the Tutoko has plenty of challenge but Grave Couloir gets cut off in summer. The Light–Dark and Transit–Sinbad areas remain difficult country and can be hard to access. Coronation Peak is tucked deep in Fiordland behind the Murchison Mountains. But there are many other more accessible trips to get going on. This is a region to investigate your own routes, and *Moir's Guide South* is a great place to start, offering untracked routes throughout.

HARRISON–TUTOKO

HARRISON RIVER–NGAPUNATORU PLATEAU–MT TUTOKO–GRAVE COULOIR–TUTOKO VALLEY

7 DAYS: 4–10 FEBRUARY 1972
GS WITH LAUCHIE DUFF

The Harrison Valley is predominantly beech forest with deep piles of moss, more luxuriant to tramp on than the best 80/20 carpet. The valley once had a reputation for bad gorges, but although the river has cut deep slots into the bedrock here and there, those places are generally not difficult to bypass for capable trampers.

Australian Marie Byles and her guide Kurt Suter first came down the Harrison in March 1937. They had come up Stickup Creek from the Hollyford over the Ngapunatoru Plateau (they called it Toru Moana Pass), and then down to Lake Never-never and the Harrison Valley. An attempt on Tutoko was thwarted by weather. They climbed Paranui Peak, and called the Harrison the Brunhilda River. I'm so pleased that didn't stick.

Byles was usually pretty good at naming new features – Lake Never-never and Lake Truth, for instance. She also enjoyed cross-country adventures, and commented: 'I would not give up the crossing of Toru Moana Pass for Tasman, or Sefton, or even Tutoko. After all, those can wait till one is too old for bush-walking.'

In 1972 Lauchie and I needed a friendly fishing-boat skipper to get to Harrison Cove from Milford. We found one in the pub, showed him a letter of support from Chief Ranger Harold Jacobs, and agreed to meet at six-thirty next morning. He dropped us on the beach flats at Harrison Cove and we were on our own.

Later, under overcast skies, we stopped for a late lunch. Our fire produced a billy of tea just as rain began. Upstream, the moss carpet became rather soggy, and as we continued sidling on the true right, the thickening river changed from green to brown. It rained the rest of the day.

It is a feature in Fiordland that rivers split around bush islands, and sometimes these channels may go for some distance. There are some in the Harrison. Going down-valley, all streams lead to Milford, but heading up-valley it can sometimes be roulette whether you're on a shortcut of good travel back to the river or being led up a side creek. We managed a bit of both.

Morning brought perfect stillness, dripping boughs in shafts of sunlight and the strong roller call of mohua and brown creepers in the canopy. We left the Harrison River just below Moulin Creek and climbed a spur that was a reasonably good, if steep, access to the bushline on the true left. We had an incredible lunch spot overlooking Lake Never-never. The name alone inspires, with sparkling lake waters and tussock flats way below in the valley head.

Then later, sidling across snow slopes, we enjoyed the twilight, finally camping on the ridge one col west of Tutoko Saddle (named by Grave's party in 1898 on the first ascent) at the head of Grave Couloir, as it didn't look as though any sly sidles to the saddle would go in torchlight.

We were in good company. Roland Rodda, Paul Powell, Graham Ellis, and Geoff Longbottom had camped near here, on a crossing from the Tutoko Valley to the Harrison via the Ngapunatoru Plateau and Lake Never-never in 1949.

Massey University Alpine Club entered the Harrison from the Kaipo on a north-western approach in 1970, before climbing up to the Ngapunatoru Plateau. As with the Rodda party, weather robbed them of a Tutoko ascent, and they headed out down the Harrison.

Some of the MUAC group came back in 1971 for a Tutoko Valley approach to the peak. This time they were successful at climbing Mt Tutoko, and after an attempt on Grave they returned down Grave Couloir in torchlight and rain. A storm hammered them all the way out to the road.

We were more fortunate. Our ascent of Tutoko began about 9 a.m. Gentlemen's hours. We had only intended a reconnaissance as, first, Paranui Peak had to be climbed. But from there, Tutoko looked stunning. The sky was settled, so why wait? It would mean a night out and we weren't equipped for that but this had never stopped us before. We got cracking.

It was 4.30 p.m. by the time we were on the north-west ridge. For the Darrans, the rock wasn't that good, however, the climbing was relatively straightforward. We pitched twice up a chimney through the final step. Then we were on the summit snows, watching the sun set, and bathed in warm light. Leaving the top at 7.30 p.m., we stopped at dark, 150 metres lower.

Peter Graham and Samuel Turner were first to reach here, in 1924, returning a couple of days later for a better view. The next ascent was a local trio of

RIGHT Mt Tutoko with ice to the right, leading up to Ngapunatoru Pass. This photo is from near Halfway Peak above Stickup Creek, on the route used by Marie Byles and party to cross into the Harrison Valley in 1936.

OVERLEAF (LEFT) A high campsite at sunrise near the Ngapunatoru Plateau in the northern Darran Mountains. The peak is Puketuroto.

OVERLEAF (RIGHT) Lake Truth, in the northern Darrans, typical of many subalpine lakes throughout Fiordland. Rockwalls prevent foot travel around either side of this lake, and packrafts are a great alternative.

Gordon Speden, A. Jackson and G. McBride, seven years later.

It was one of the easier nights I've shivered without bivvy gear. Morning dawned with a yellow horizon sharply cut by mountains – Earnslaw, Aspiring! Tutoko's shadow flung itself out over the sea somewhere down towards Sutherland Sound. Beautiful. Back on the snow we found water in the rocks and slurped. We weren't carrying waterbottles. Returning to the tents I discovered butter supplies had melted and run through my pack, but the jelly we had set was delicious.

Our transalpine trip continued down Grave Couloir into the Tutoko Valley, and that led back to the Milford Road. Grave Couloir gave some trouble. It was February, and one massive schrund near the top ran from side to side. We abseiled down to dodgy loose snowblocks. The rest was plain sailing.

224

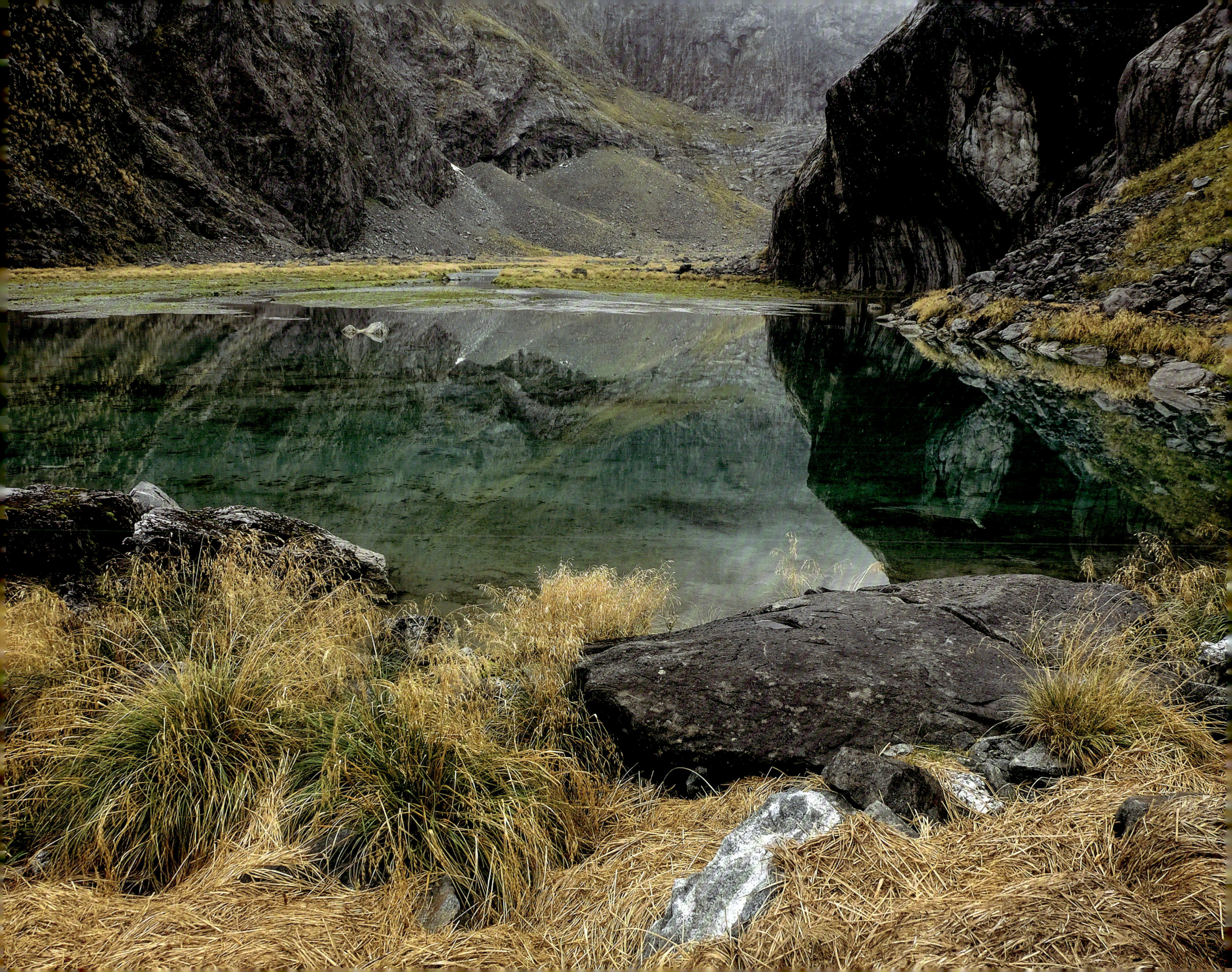

THE LIGHT AND THE DARK

ARTHUR RIVER–STAIRCASE CREEK–MAIN LIGHT VALLEY–EAST LIGHT RIVER–LIGHT-DARK SADDLE–DARK RIVER–HUNTER PASS–PROSPECT CREEK–WORSLEY RIVER

12 DAYS: 13–24 FEBRUARY 1971

GS WITH KEN PEARCE, JOHN GREGORY AND PAUL CLARK

The vertical world of the Light and Dark valleys is the stuff of legend, reinforced by a stunning account of an arduous trip W.G. Grave and friends undertook in 1904 from Lake Te Anau to Sutherland Sound and back via the Dark River, in atrocious weather.

In the late 1930s, others, like the Bowmar brothers of Gore, and Alex Dickie, explored the fringes, climbing peaks overlooking the head of the Dark, and once or twice crossing into it. In 1955, well-known hunter D.B. Banwell and friends also visited the Dark. But it may not have been until 1959 that a party entered the upper Main Light Valley. That's not much more than a decade before our trip in February 1971.

We began at Milford Sound, but needed a boat across to the start of the track. The Tourist Hotel Corporation, who ran regular boats over to pick up their walkers, wouldn't initially take us. Wearing shorts and boots, Ken talked the manager around, and we backloaded to Sandfly Point. At Staircase Creek we headed up towards Sutherland Falls, then continued up a side creek to camp among the green leaves of *Hoheria*. It was drizzling, but we were full of anticipation.

By lunch next day we were on the saddle at the head of Staircase Creek. From here the 1959 party had decided the route directly down was too bluffed, so instead they climbed high in tussock and traversed west, dropping through very steep bush to reach Lake Dale.

We weren't sure of their route, and tried to sidle west from the saddle before descending. That landed us in a heap of bluffs, and after persisting a while with the rope we were glad to retreat. But from our vantage point we had a good look at an unknown and untried possibility straight off the pass

RIGHT Our camp in Staircase Creek, on the way into the Main Light River.
OPPOSITE Light-Dark Saddle (centre) with cloud beyond covering the Light River. The lake in the foreground (right) feeds the Dark River. PHOTO: HENRIETTE BEIKIRCH

itself, and went to reconnoitre it. We had no contoured map, of course. At that stage none existed for isolated areas like this, and we relied on aerial photos.

A very steep, bouldery gut led down between high bluffs, and in less than two hours John and I were on the floor of the Main Light Valley, elated at having found a new route down. Diorite stones, clear emerald pools and *Hoheria* thickets mixed with beech forest and wapiti trails led us along the Main Light towards Lake Dale, where we camped. Paul collected firewood, keeping an eye out for wapiti.

There is something very special about being in places few, if any, have travelled. We enter the unknown, where all is still possible, and look more intently to discover the undiscovered. From Lake Dale we swung across into the true left branch, the East Light.

The East Light Valley has some wonderful travel and flats in the upper reaches, with expansive areas of pale-coloured granite riverstones. We kept looking for chinks through the bluffs under the Light-Dark Saddle up ahead. Unfortunately, the closer we got, the steeper it looked.

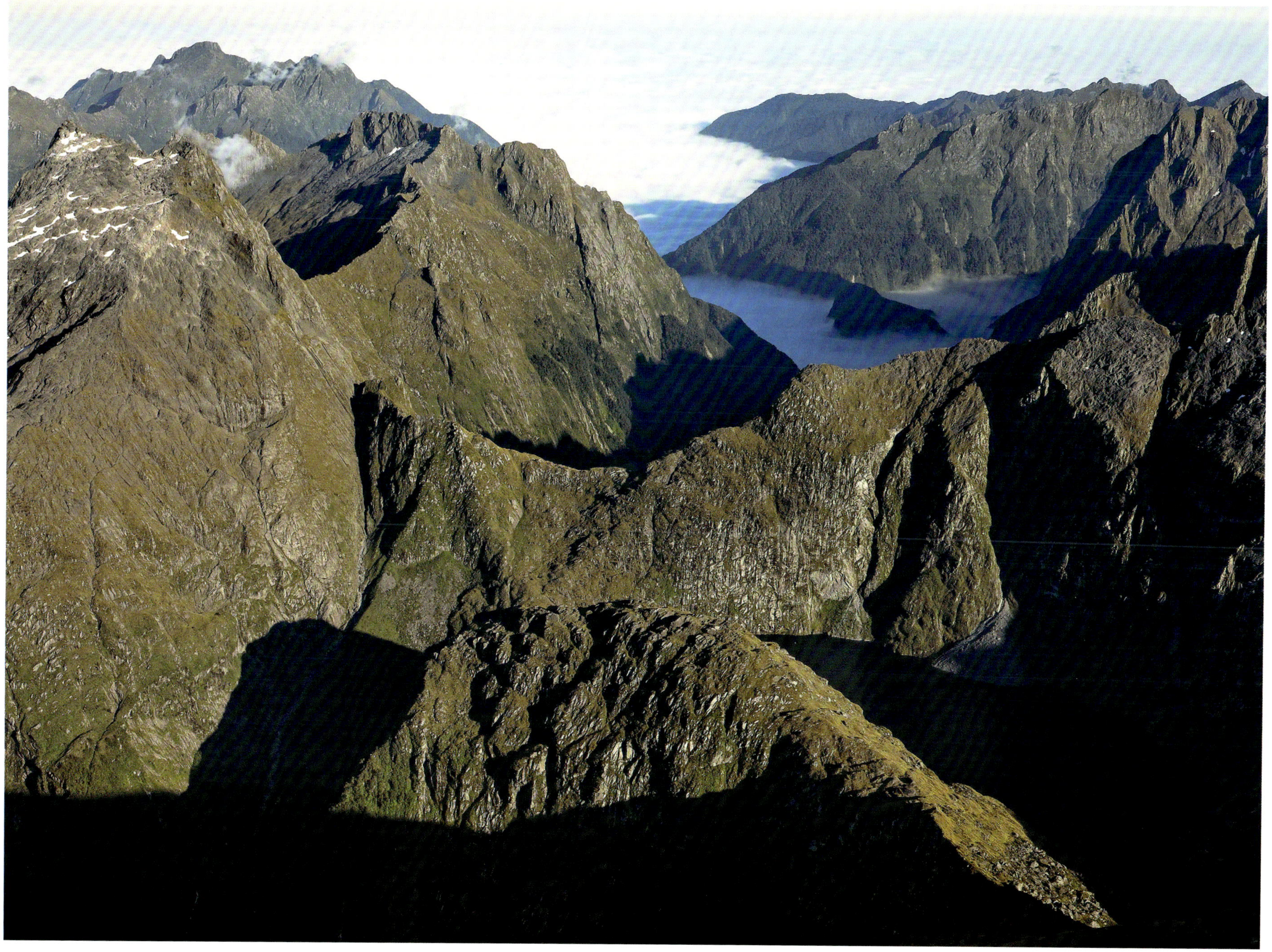

Travelling under forest below the saddle made picking a route up difficult. By the time we reached the bushline we were committed and climbing very steep scrub, sometimes on branches away from the rock face. That inspired strong conversations with the scrub, calling it every name bar its scientific one. With solid packs it was very hard work and there wasn't much left of us when we crawled thankfully over the edge into tussock to rest.

That night we dropped down to a large, nameless alpine lake in the head of the Dark, where I slept out in the tussock. Here we were among mountains less than 3 kilometres from Lake Quill at the top of the Sutherland Falls.

In the morning, with light packs, we went on a day trip along the Light-Dark divide up to the summit of Couloir Peak, and found ourselves 700 metres directly above Lake Quill, which is already 1000 metres above sea level. It was a magic place to be, and spectacular views unfolded everywhere.

A certain person forgot the matches, so our primus brew at lunchtime had to be abandoned, despite hopeful attempts to light fuel with a camera lens. Carrying on to the Castle/Dark divide we dropped down to the head of our nameless alpine lake and had a couple of swims before returning to camp along the opposite side of it. En route, we came across deer remains mixed with old winter snow-avalanche debris below bluffs. That was a rough way to go.

The next part of our mission was to get down to the main Dark River and head up Starvation Creek to Hunter Pass, and so to the Worsley and Lake Te Anau. W.G. Grave and party spent several days in wretched conditions under this pass in bad weather. They didn't name it Starvation Creek for nothing.

> *As bad as ever again next day – to attempt the ascent would have been madness. A spoonful of dried apples was served out to each man that whole day. The following day we were still there. This time our day's allowance was a spoonful of dried milk each. The third day our camp on the mountain was as grim as ever. Still we could not move. A spoonful of cocoa for each man's ration . . . We resolved that no matter what the weather was the next day the grim ascent must be tried. We knew well enough what failure would mean. I think that third day was the most miserable any of us ever spent.*

We followed the same route up Starvation Creek, over Hunter Pass, then down Prospect Creek and the Worsley River to Lake Te Anau. The route up cirque walls to the pass were severely steep with our 25-kilogram packs. It had been an exciting trip into unknown country and we had had a fantastic time.

Three years later, in February 1974, Gilbert van Reenen, Rhys Buckingham and friends crossed Hunter Pass into the Dark, climbed up to the nameless alpine lake under the Light-Dark Saddle, climbed 1682 metres and had a good look around the tops before exiting to Mackinnon Pass as the weather deteriorated. In 1978 a Tararua club party of five led by Pat Begley did the same circuit we had done. In 1980, Dave Craw investigated a route from the Main Light through to Poison Bay.

Others continue to be inspired by the area. A VUWTC party did our trip in reverse in 1981, and others like Danilo Hegg and Henriette Beikirch have enjoyed solo trips on the tops here. I'd like to leave the last comment to Henriette Beikirch: 'Fiordland in particular will remain with me as a place of savage storms, phenomenal scenery, steep bluffs, razor-edged ridgelines, tarns like jewels, and tough travel that really made me earn my place there – it is one of the great wildernesses on Earth.'

OPPOSITE This alpine lake in the head of the Dark River near Light-Dark Saddle backs on to Lake Quill, above the Sutherland Falls. PHOTO: HENRIETTE BEIKIRCH

BELOW South Island edelweiss (*Leucogenes grandiceps*).

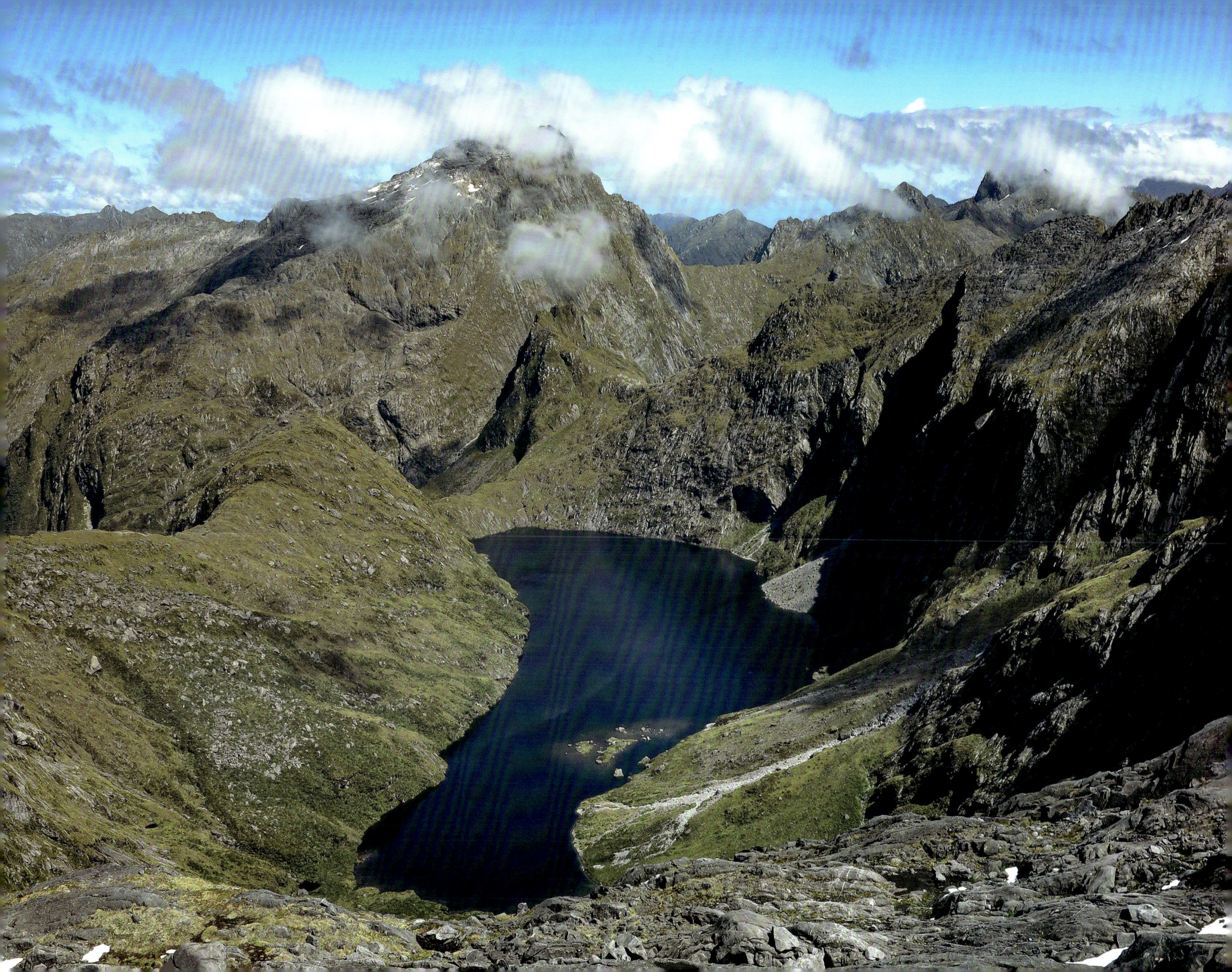

TRANSIT–SINBAD

ANITA BAY–TRANSIT RIVER–SADDLE OVERLOOKING
MACKAY CREEK–TRANSIT RIVER–MITRE/LLAWRENNY PEAK
RANGE CROSSING–SINBAD GULLY–MILFORD SOUND

7 DAYS: 5–11 MARCH 1972
GS WITH DR JIM FINCH AND JOHN GREGORY

Dr Jim Finch, a metallurgical chemist at DSIR, was passionate about Fiordland and the rocks it contained. Jim was also a tramping club friend and enjoyed exploratory adventures where bushbashing and a bit of hardship is often required.

Jim, John Gregory and I jetboated out to Anita Bay in early March 1972, after it became clear heavy swells wouldn't allow us to reach Poison Bay, further down the Fiordland Coast. We were still keen to cross from the Transit into the Poison and Light valleys, then return via Staircase Creek and the Milford Track, but we didn't get that far. This didn't stop us having quite an adventure, though.

Heading inland from Anita Bay, home to tangiwai, a particular form of pounamu, we bashed our way over the steep bush range separating us from the Transit. It was more brutal than we expected, but that may've just been our complacency. Somewhere on the descent we ended up on a knife-edge ridge in the bush, and had to use the rope to lower our packs. Others have found better routes.

The lower Transit Valley has extensive swamps of flax, lawyer, mud, eels, hookgrass, nettle and shrubs. At irregular intervals, deep ditches of murky water blocked our path, and John and I climbed lacebark trees for a view forward. On one of these stops we were entertained by a flock of over 100 bellbirds in one tree, singing their hearts out. Bring on predator-free New Zealand. We retreated back from the swamp to camp on hill slopes among the mosquitoes. Bring on mosquito-free NZ . . . Further up-valley we had a daytime encounter with a kiwi. It headed straight at us, weaving its way dodging left and right, and passing within millimetres. We were as excited as it was.

The spacious lower Transit, with its swamps, flats and deer trails under beech forest, led us south towards Lake Moreton. We never reached the lake. Up under the cirque in the head of the Transit we marvelled at the massive walls that ran around the head of the whole valley, over which the lake emptied as a 400-metre fall. We would have to change our plans.

Rhys Buckingham, with various friends in the early 1970s, took a different approach, looking for routes to Poison Bay and the Transit from Arthur River tributaries. On one trip he reached a saddle overlooking Lake Moreton, and after a couple of attempts reached Poison Bay from there in 1973. Others are still doing new things here. An Otago University Tramping Club party in 2014 climbed a 1714-metre peak between two branches of the Poison River, which they called the Poison Dagger.

With access to Lake Moreton looking impractical from the head of the Transit, we went up the true right fork towards those Arthur tributaries. It led up to the divide overlooking Mackay Creek.

Four hours from camp we were on the saddle in perfect weather, looking down into the creek with its large lake flanked by smooth rockwalls on both sides. You'd need a boat to get past that. Below us we investigated a route into the head of the valley. It wasn't flash, but we decided it would work. The lake wouldn't, though, and alternative routes along the tops in both directions looked decidedly unattractive.

Forty-two years later, in January 2014, an OUTC party of Peter Wilson, Danilo Hegg, James Thornton and Max Olsen headed up Mackay Creek to cross this same saddle we were on. After paddling up the lake they found a route over the range via an unclimbed peak, at 1674 metres. From here they traversed over onto the Transit side, and down to a large tarn at 1000 metres called Lake Liz, where they found the remains of an old wildlife hut put in to search for kākāpō. This A-framed bivvy built of dexion framing and corrugated iron had been in Sinbad Gully in the 1970s, before being relocated here by helicopter. Their trip continued down the Transit Valley then over to Anita Bay for a boat pick-up.

Having had our plans curtailed in the head of the Transit, we now aimed to cross between the Llawrenny Peaks and Mitre Peak from the Transit into

OPPOSITE Midway up the Transit River. PHOTO: DANILO HEGG

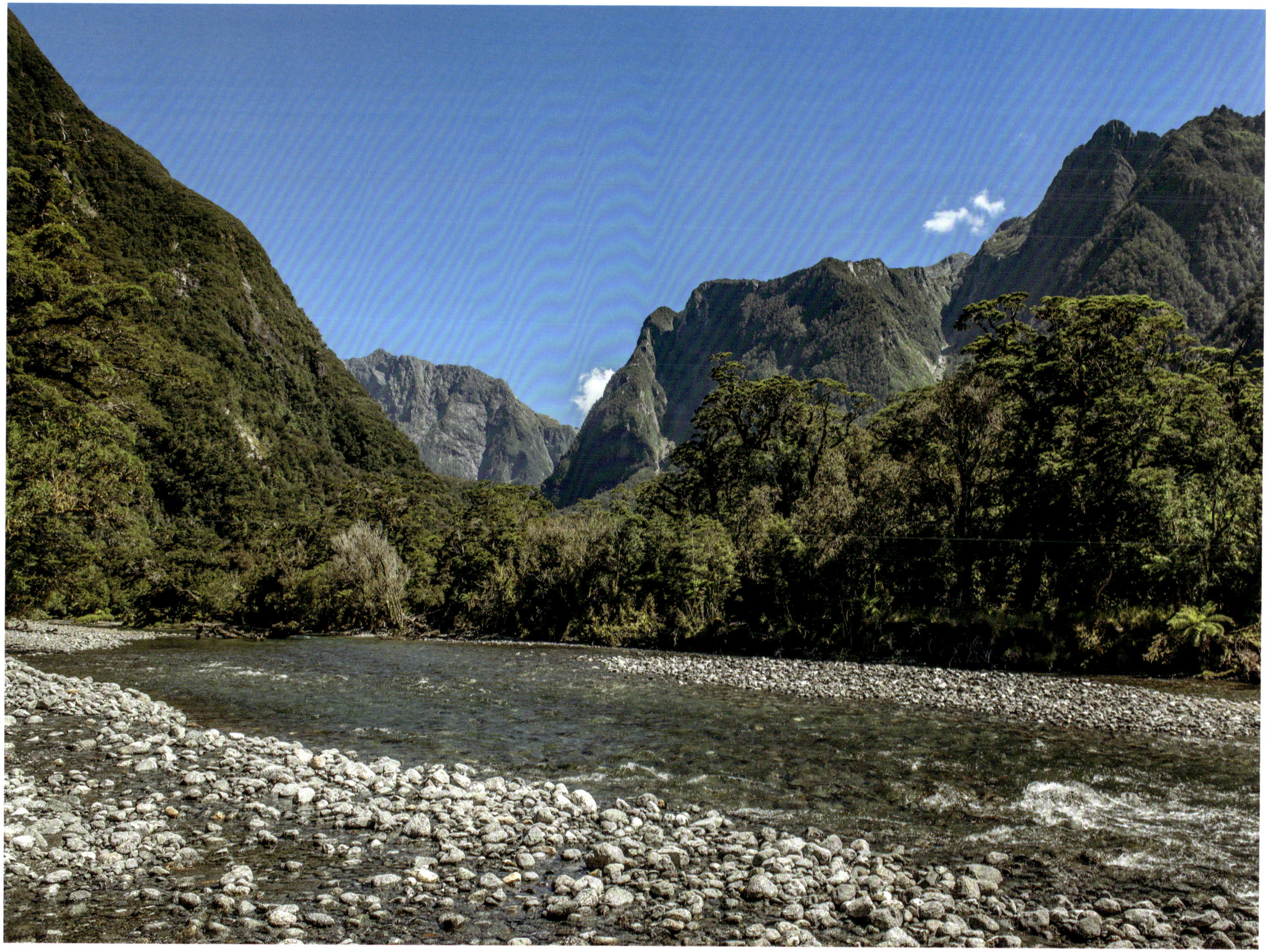

MOW engineer, had been up the Sinbad to the tops and back in 1926.

So it may well be that our trip was the first crossing from the Transit River to the Sinbad Gully. Gilbert van Reenan, Pete Lusk, John Campbell, Martin Heine and Bruce Lusher were to cross in the opposite direction about ten months later.

We may not have had water, but we could now see it coming. Unsettled, thickening high cloud marched steadily in overnight, and we knew our hours were numbered up here. Leaving early, we were on the dividing ridge in an hour, and began to pick our way down, sidling left. At the first trickle on the rocks we had breakfast. Since 2003, big walls in the head of Sinbad Gully have been getting keen attention from rock climbers, but our mission was simply to get to Milford Sound before the weather broke. Lower down, near the scrub band, we sidled right, before zig-zagging down through small waterfalls to the valley floor, arriving about two o'clock.

It was now raining, and we were in a race to beat the floodwaters. Being stuck halfway up Sinbad Gully by flooded streams didn't appeal. We gave it everything, taking every shortcut, using the riverbed as we could, to reach Milford Sound in the dark at eight o'clock.

En route we were brought to a halt by a loud birdcall we didn't know, repeated several times. It was very close by, on the ground, but we couldn't see it. Sinbad Gully was reputed to still have kākāpō in it at that time, and it may well have been one.

Pleased to be at the coast, we had no energy to fiddle around cooking or even boiling water. A few crackers and we were asleep, listening to the rain drum fiercely on the tent. At times like this insomnia is impossible. We slept like the dead, and had all the water we could dream of. By dawn, Sinbad Stream was flooded into the trees on both banks and falls roared everywhere. We were going out by boat. Lucky that.

Sinbad Gully. From the Transit riverbed we picked a reasonable-looking route, and mostly it was, with the odd exception where we used a rope in the bush to cross a rock face with our packs. The day was hot. Intensely hot, and we had no water. At the bushline we had leatherwood and gigantic boulders to force through. When we finally stopped for the day we were still a couple of hundred metres below the saddle.

John and I went looking for water, but all we could find was a bit of sphagnum moss to wring into the billy. It was thick with mud, but we thought we might be able to decant it for dinner. Jim wasn't having any of that. He glugged it down from the billy.

We weren't the first to comment on drought here. In late 1954, J. Ede, R. Cuthill, R.D. Miller and R.W. Blee reached the tops nearby having come up from opposite Dale Point. Thirst and a collapsed party member saw them retreat again. In the same year, Edgar Williams, A. Deans, M. Bassett and R. Copp made the first ascents of Terror and Llawrenny peaks. H.W. Smith, a

ABOVE Mackay Creek, a tributary of the Arthur River. From the Transit Valley we reached a saddle looking into here, but rockwalls on both sides of the lake looked impractical. More recently, the lake has been packrafted by an OUTC party, who then took a high-level route over to the Transit. PHOTO: DANILO HEGG

OPPOSITE Mt Pembroke (right) pokes over the Mitre Peak ridge at sunrise, as seen from the Llawrenny Peaks. Our crossing from the Transit River to Sinbad Gully (foreground) was over the sunlit range to the left. PHOTO: DANILO HEGG

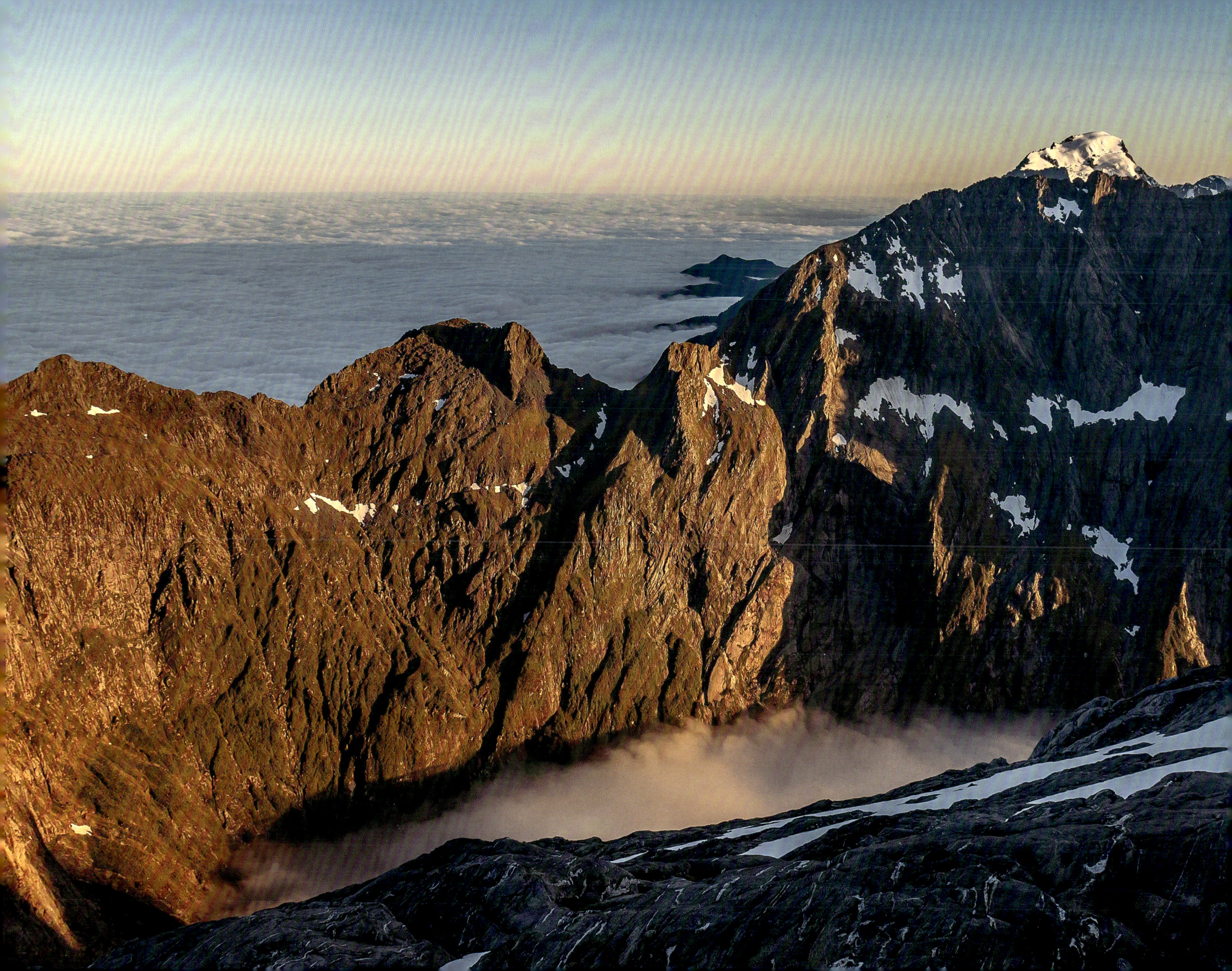

WINDWARD RIVER TOPS –CORONATION PEAK– PRECIPICE COVE

WINDWARD/IRENE TOPS–DOUBLE PEAK–IRENE PASS– CORONATION PEAK–KEY PEAK–REA RIVER–PRECIPICE COVE

7 DAYS: 25–31 JANUARY 2000
GS WITH IAN THORNE

Ian Thorne worked for Fiordland National Park, and was tasked with checking out takahē sign in the head of the Windward River. Ian knew an opportunity, and wanted to use the helicopter as part of his work access to begin an exploratory tops trip in an isolated part of central Fiordland. This sounded great to me.

The Windward River is west of the takahē's normal range in the Murchison Mountains, and we spent a fine first day checking out flats and forest down the valley. In one or two spots, tillers of *Chionochloa flavescens* and *pallens* had been cut and neatly placed in piles, and we found a few poo droppings. Ian concluded it was probably a young roving male.

Back at our campsite under 1231 metres, near a large tarn, we cooked tea on an open fire as the evening settled. Across the Irene Valley, Mt Irene commanded the skyline, looking serene. Tomorrow we would begin our trip, heading south-west along the tops towards Double Peak and Coronation Peak, before continuing west along the tops to Key Peak and beyond, to reach the Rea River about a kilometre from Precipice Cove in Doubtful Sound.

Our first full day was to be a big one. Passing over Double Peak we dropped down to three lakes and, at the outlet to the third, a family of weka strutted around, a brown teal paddled and the ubiquitous seagull flapped and cried. The place was gorgeous.

Over a late lunch, we put the tent up and were away by 3 p.m. with daypacks for an attempt at Coronation Peak on the Museum Range. Sidling through beech forest in the head of Misty River under Irene Pass led us up scrappy bush on to the tops again. Coronation had been climbed before but we had no route knowledge. It all looked a bit more of a commitment than we had time or energy for, but a gravel gully led us onto the southern slopes where there was glacial ice that must be some of the southernmost in the country. Not having crampons, I cut steps across the base and up to the rock.

Scrambling up granite slabs, we came to a steeper chimney and used our light rope to belay. Then it was back to a scramble as we made our way up to the two small summits. On top, we found a cairn and an old May and Baker aluminium container, with wet paper inside. Fiordland does that to paper.

During the mid 1950s, two Canterbury Museum expeditions surveyed the area around Mt Irene. They made the first recorded ascent of Mt Irene in 1953 and named another high mountain Coronation Peak. However, Coronation proved significantly more difficult to climb than Irene. On the second expedition, after a couple of thwarted attempts, A. Carey, T. Couzens and B. Wisely made the first ascent in January 1955. The objectives of the Museum trips were to extend the search for takahē, mapping, look for kākāpō, test for radiation(!), and collect rocks, plants and certain animals, particularly spiders and insects. Each expedition had about 15 members, including Phil Dorizac, a Fiordland natural history legend and R.R. Forster, New Zealand's expert at the time on spiders.

Although the peak is seldom visited, others do reach these places on foot, such as Kelvin Lloyd in 1980, and the OUTC party at Easter 2003 who crossed from Bradshaw Sound to Lake Te Anau.

It was now 7.30 p.m. We could see our campsite kilometres away and 800 metres below us. It was going to be a mission to get back there by nightfall. Dropping off the summit block we managed to avoid the ice and were soon at a notch leading down towards Misty River. Night approaching does fuel the body with adrenalin. We crashed down into the undergrowth and then under silver beech trees in dimming light, before swinging back up a basin towards where we thought our campsite was. Here we started to lose it, and in the dark, just as we realised we weren't sure where in the glades our tent was, we found it at 11 p.m.

With morning, we began a wonderful sojourn along tops towards Key Peak, with small peaks and saddles to cross. In the lower parts, idyllic groves

OPPOSITE Coronation Peak, in the head of the Irene River. Seen here from the north, near Double Peak, on the range above the Windward River.

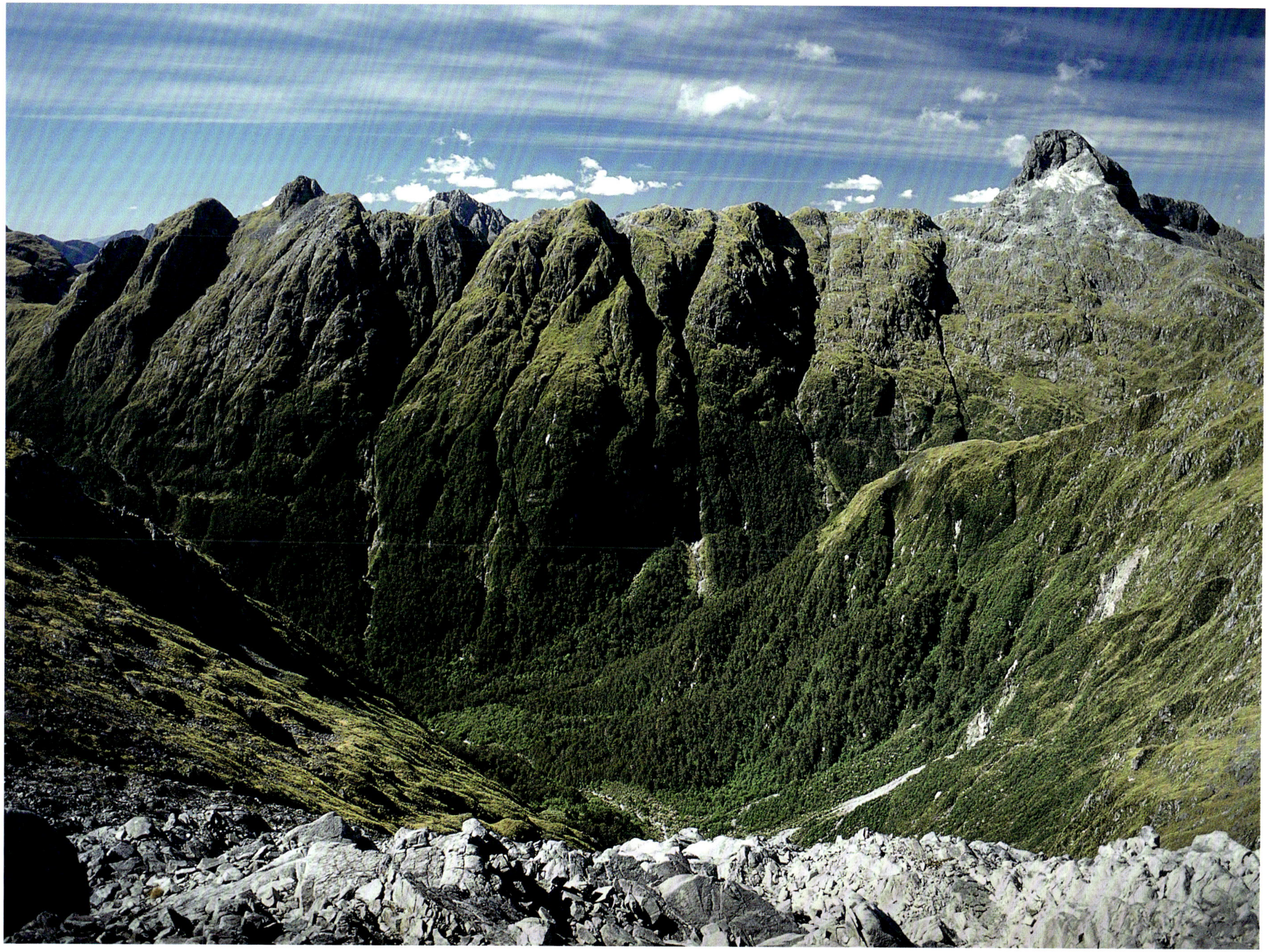

of beech resembled Japanese bonsai gardens, with welcoming campsites and tarns. Travelling on the tops in isolated parts of Fiordland in fine weather must be one of the most glorious things to do on this wonderful planet.

We camped at a saddle before Key Peak, where fine black rock resembled seams of coal. In the morning Key Peak was under cloud, and we resigned to a day in mist, taking care with compass and navigation. Sidling under 1314 metres, we swung south-east down a long straight spur towards the lower Rea River, where travel became very steep at some pinnacles. In the wet it was a bit treacherous, with walls dropping away into nothing. Belays with tenuous anchors and taking care down-climbing with our heavy packs got us through without incident, and we carried on down to the bushline to camp by a tarn. Here, probes in the hollows told us other kiwi liked this spot as well.

In the morning the spur took us down through beech forest to the Rea River. It was raining, and we still had about 2 kilometres of swamps to get through to reach the coast, where we spent our last night, trapped inside a blue Minaret tent completely besieged by sandflies. This wasn't just an attack. They had mustered all the armies in the Kingdom of Fiordland to plague us. I didn't realise it was quite so bad until I got the tent home, and took handfuls of them from between the tent outer and inner. The tent never recovered.

LEFT Fiordland is full of tricky bluffs on the ridges. Ian looking back along the range at our route on the true right of the Misty River above Precipice Cove.
OPPOSITE Shelter from the storm. Robin Saddle Hut, between Mt Irene and Coronation Peak, is an isolated little haven in these conditions.

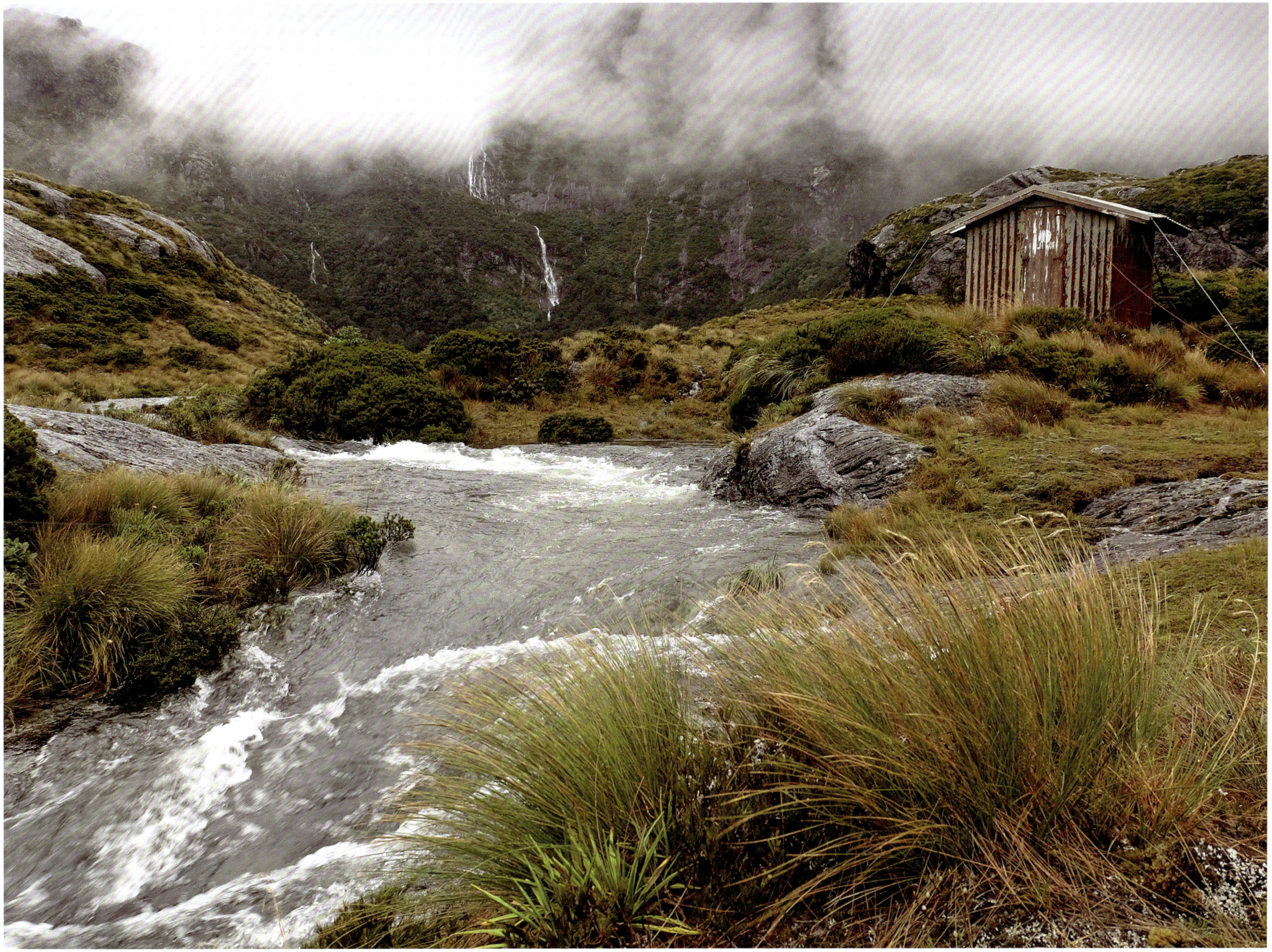

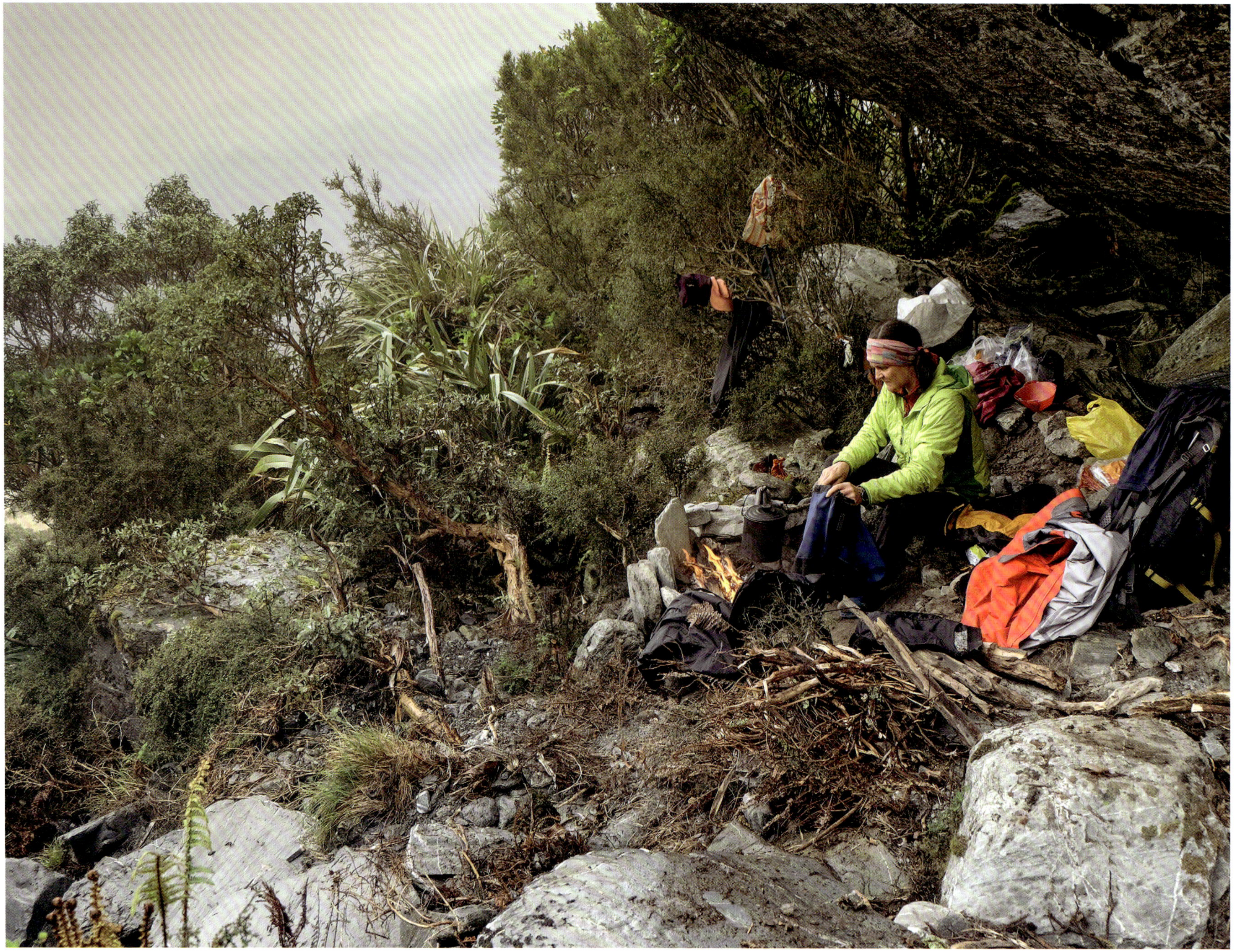

AFTERWORD
BACK OF BEYOND

The fire crackles, moving shadows around in the dusk. Jane and I are warm, dry and snug, but beyond the rock bivvy, water drips incessantly, and the sub-alpine scrub is soaked.

Stillness.

All the upper Callery Valley is cloaked in mist and drizzle, and we watch as fine, floating droplets, small as fairy breath, waft past us.

We have come up the Goatpath, a seldom-used route beside the Franz Josef Glacier, climbing the Minarets on Christmas Day and then descending into the Callery via the Spencer Glacier. Now we are in a waiting game with the weather, and it seems a good time to reflect.

What is the future of the mountains and adventures like this?

There might be more rockfall, and there might be more ice melting, but in human terms, the mountains aren't going anywhere. In transalpine terms, these changes just create new opportunities to investigate and find routes through.

New Zealanders care deeply for their mountains. Nearly 70 years ago, all political parties applauded when the National Parks Act was passed, recognising the intrinsic value of these places, and largely shielding them from commercial activity. Those fundamental values reflected a respect for the mountains, recognising their mana. It's up to us to see this continue.

Humans will always seek to explore. As our technology and affluence changes, the nature of how we explore, and why, will also change. We are no longer exploring to map the land – that can be done by satellites from space – instead, it is for the simple, unpretentious reason of exploring for exploring's sake. I suspect that Eric Shipton in the Karakorams and Marco Polo and any number of explorers were, underneath all the hype, exploring for the same reason.

In transalpine trips, this means finding adventure in the most basic and natural way we can: on foot, with our essentials on our back, seeking challenges in the mountains. The spirit of this is captured in James Elroy Flecker's poem *The Golden Journey to Samarkand*, and regularly quoted in *The Canterbury Mountaineer*:

. . . We are the Pilgrims, master; we shall go
Always a little further: it may be
Beyond the last blue mountain barred with snow . . .

Pilgrims inspired by mountain journeys. It doesn't need to have any deeper meaning than this, but for many it is much more.

Does this style of travelling and climbing in the mountains have a future? We only need to look at enthusiastic university clubs and other keen groups to answer. Increasing numbers of overseas visitors are also discovering the joy of travelling our isolated backcountry on foot.

Fresh eyes and technology are offering new perspectives, too. Packrafts can be used to get past dodgy lake moraine walls, down river sections or across difficult rivers, such as the Landsborough. Recently, friends and I did a trip to the Ngapunatoru Plateau in the Darrans, using a packraft to paddle past rockwalls on Lake Truth. Canyoning in the mountains is also becoming popular. People have been descending gorges for years, but improved gear is taking that to a new level.

Increased support for organised multi-day and multi-sport events from roadend to roadend generates adventures that are often wilderness journeys in their own right. The future of transalpine trips and mountain adventures has never looked so vibrant.

Coupled with that, there is more and more enthusiasm for keeping our remaining wilderness areas untrammelled, free of machines, where people can and do appreciate natural quiet. There is a great egalitarian tradition in New Zealand for doing transalpine trips without guides or aerial access. In part, it is about sharing ownership of the challenges and finding solutions together.

This tradition of 'doing it yourself' is very Kiwi and has been part of the pathway for many capable trampers and climbers. Some have gone on to become guides or instructors of one type or another and some have become involved in clubs and other aspects of outdoor life. They all share a similar love of the mountains and a passion for trips.

The billy has boiled, and it is time for a brew. I'm still having wonderful adventures, and I always look forward to seeing peaks that have become old friends, in different seasons, from different places, bringing new connections.

What the mountains have to offer is endless. The Southern Alps are full of opportunities waiting to be explored and climbed; adventures, ultimately, in the great unknown.

PREVIOUS PAGE Jane out of the rain at the Burton Bivvy Rock, Callery headwaters.
RIGHT Walking poles can be quite useful.

ACKNOWLEDGEMENTS

First, I want to acknowledge the mountains, the rivers and ranges of the Southern Alps, where I have enjoyed so much, learned so much, shared so much and been challenged so much. Also, the departments, whose job it has been to look after these places over the decades, Lands and Survey, Forest Service, and now the Department of Conservation.

My second thanks goes to those with whom I shared these adventures. Without our trips there would be no book. In my early days I benefitted from a vibrant Hutt Valley Tramping Club, then later the New Zealand Alpine Club. Over the last 10 years I have had the support of the Peninsula Tramping Club in leading very enjoyable adventures among the mountains, and some of those stories are in here. Thanks also to Dogtucker, an older group of musterers and climbers including Bill Hood, Peter Bain and others for their deep knowledge and inspiration.

I have drawn on many club publications; they are a goldmine of mountain history and culture, but I want to particularly acknowledge the Tararua Tramping Club's annual, Tararua, the New Zealand Alpine Journals, The Canterbury Mountaineer, produced by the Canterbury Mountaineering Club, and Hutt Valley Tramping, journal of my original club. Wilderness Magazine, too, has many articles off the beaten track.

Friends have helped with various aspects, sometimes directly, sometimes indirectly. I would like to particularly thank Liz Stephenson for her encouragement with the project over many years, and also Rob Frost, Keith (Limbo) Thompson, Gary Huish, Raymond Ford, Ian Gardiner, Rob Brown, Trev Jones, John Simpson, Christine Hardy, Shaun Barnett, John Nankervis, Dennis Page, James Thornton, Nina Dickerhof and Dave Bamford.

Dr Frank Soper in Golden Bay supplied information by letter and phone about the Dragons Teeth history and naming. Jane Forsyth supplied comment on the geology of Garibaldi Ridge. Roger Smith at Geographx drew the wonderful maps that appear with every chapter.

I have used my own photos throughout except for a few in the Fiordland chapter. Here, Danilo Hegg and Henriette Beikirch came to the rescue with quality photos of obscure places, for which I am very grateful.

I want to say a huge thanks to Federated Mountain Clubs and the Mountain and Forest Trust for helping support this project financially. That made a significant difference to the book quality and is deeply appreciated.

Editing can sometimes be a fraught issue for publishers and authors alike, but Jude Watson edited the text sensitively and carefully. Many thanks, Jude. With the encouragement of Robbie Burton, publisher at Potton & Burton, this book has been a joy to do. Robbie believed in the book, and it shows in the careful layout and backing he has provided.

And last but not least, a very special thanks to my fiancé, Jane Morris, for all her wonderful support and patience.

Geoff

BIBLIOGRAPHY, NOTES, REFERENCES & GUIDEBOOKS

There is a wealth of inspiring material on websites, and in books, club journals and other publications relating to transalpine trips. This list is not definitive. It simply stems from my personal connection with our mountain culture and history, and it (sort of) chronologically lists any sources and quotations used within the text. There is a list of current (and older), useful regional guidebooks at the end.

INTRODUCTION

'Some There Are', Lester Masters, from *Unfenced Country and Other Poems*, Hart Printing House, Hastings, c. 1961.

'stormy camp': *Pioneer Work in the Alps of New Zealand: A record of the first exploration of the chief glaciers and ranges of the Southern Alps*, by A.P. Harper, University of California Libraries, 1896, p. 73.

John Pascoe, *The Southern Alps: From the Kaikouras to the Rangitata*, New Zealand Holiday Guides, Pegasus Press, 1951.

'the most joyous days': *Peaks, Packs and Mountain Tracks* by W. Scott Gilkison, Whitcombe and Tombs, Christchurch, 1940, p.105.

Paul Powell, *Men Aspiring*, A.H. and A.W. Reed, 1967.

John Pascoe, *Unclimbed New Zealand: Alpine travel in the Canterbury and Westland Ranges, Southern Alps*, George Allen and Unwin, 1950 (second edition).

Hugh Logan, *Classic Peaks of New Zealand*, Craig Potton Publishing, 2002.

Rodney Hewitt and Mavis Davidson, *The Mountains of New Zealand*, A.H. and A.W. Reed, 1954.

Peter Radcliffe, *Land of Mountains: Tramping and climbing in New Zealand*. Methuen Publications (NZ) Ltd, 1979.

Mark Pickering, *The Hills*, Heinemann Reed, 1988.

John Wilson, *New Zealand Mountaineering, a history in photographs*. Bateman, 2015.

https://www.heddels.com/2015/01/rubber-met-road-history-vibram-soles/

'wilderness threats': Les Molloy and Craig Potton, *New Zealand's Wilderness Heritage*, Craig Potton Publishing, Revised edition 2014, p.206.

'Biv Rocks I have Known', Kelvin Lloyd, *Antics 2003*, OUTC, p.99.

KAHURANGI

'Bitten by the Dragons Teeth', by Rebecca Hayter, *Wilderness*, July 2017, p.36.

https://www.britannica.com/biography/Giuseppe-Garibaldi

Gerald Cover: Don Grady, *Grady's People, Unforgettable people in the top of the South Island*, Nikau Press, 2000, p.157.

'The Matiri', Victoria Froude, *Hutt Valley Tramping*, 1978, p.62.

SPENSER MOUNTAINS

https://en.wikipedia.org/wiki/The_Faerie_Queene.

'Through the Spensers', Tony Nolan, *Tararua*, 1958, p.39.

'Spenserian Variations', John Nankervis, *Tararua*, 1968, p.89.

'Mt Una', R. Husband, *The Canterbury Mountaineer*, 1939, p.78.

E.G. Turbott, *Buller's Birds of New Zealand*, 1967, Whitcombe & Tombs/East-West Center Press, from the 2nd edition, 1888.

R.B. Oliver, *New Zealand Birds*, 1955 (second edition), Reed reprint, 1974, p.435.

KAIKOURA RANGES

'The Nelson Lake District', L.J. Dumbleton, *New Zealand Alpine Journal*, 1948, p.184.

'Pat Begley obituary', Rob Munster, *Tararua*, 1978, p.47.

'Hutton's shearwaters': Geoff Harrow, *The Canterbury Mountaineer*, 1967, p.21.

THE WAIMAKARIRI TO THE HOKITIKA

'*Dracophyllum* species': Alan F. Mark, *Above the Treeline, a nature guide to alpine New Zealand*, Craig Potton Publishing, 2012.

Percy G. Morgan, Bulletin No. 6, *The Geology of the Mikonui Subdivision, North Westland*, New Zealand Geological Survey, 1908.

Samuel Butler, *A First Year in Canterbury Settlement*, A.C. Fifield, London, 1914, p.123.

An account of a one-day, 11-peak traverse in the Mathias by John Pascoe, 'Climbing at the headwaters of the Mathias River, Canterbury', *New Zealand Alpine Journal*, 1931, p.206.

Howard Keene, *Going for Gold, the search for riches in the Wilberforce Valley*, Dept of Conservation, 1995.

Grant Hunter, *Coast to Coast – who was first?* Fifth Camp, 2007, p.18. 'Raureka's Journey', p.91, Three Passes race.

https://teara.govt.nz/en/diagram/7771/record-rainfall

'First Crossing of Clarkes Pass', T.N. Beckett, *The Canterbury Mountaineer*, 1932, p.31.

First crossing of Kea Pass, 'Various expeditions', J.A. Sim, *New Zealand Alpine Journal*, 1936, p.139.

'Frew's Hut proposals', L.W. Boot, *The Canterbury Mountaineer*, 1948, p.229.

'Button Peak', A. Wicks, *The Canterbury Mountaineer*, 1951, p.82.

'Up the Kokatahi', Geoff Spearpoint, *Hutt Valley Tramping*, 1974, p.31.

THE BRACKEN SNOWFIELD

'The first ascent of Mt Whitcombe and crossing of the Strachan Pass', *The Canterbury Mountaineer*, 1932, p.8.

'Across the Seddon Col to the Waitaha', P. Willis, *The Canterbury Mountaineer*, 1939, p.71.

'Park Dome and Mount Evans', S.E. Davis, *The Canterbury Mountaineer*, 1938, p.55.

GNS report, Evans Rockfall, 2014.

'Countdown to Ecstasy: Evans, Bracken County', Ian Wilkins, *Hutt Valley Tramping*, 1975, p.28.

Winter ascent of Malcolm, exiting Blue Lookout: 'Severe Punishment', Guy McKinnon, *The Canterbury Mountaineer*, 2003. p.23.

Visiting Ivory Lake: Tony Gates, *Worn Out Boots, four decades enjoying the New Zealand mountains*, self-published, 2012, p.54.

Ivory Lake Hut: S. Barnett, R. Brown and G. Spearpoint, *Shelter from the Storm*, Craig Potton Publishers, 2012.

THE GARDEN OF EDEN ICE PLATEAU

'First ascent of Newton Pk', L.K. Wilson, *New Zealand Alpine Journal*, 1934, p.347.

First ascent of Dan Pk and Mt Lambert: 'Various Expeditions', J.A. Sim, *New Zealand Alpine Journal*, 1934, p.413.

Naming of the Garden of Eden: 'Exploration of the Perth Glaciers, Westland', J.D. Pascoe, *The Canterbury Mountaineer*, 1935, p.33, p.26.

John Pascoe, *Unclimbed New Zealand: Alpine travel in the Canterbury and Westland Ranges, Southern Alps*, George Allen and Unwin, 1950 (second edition).

The Great Unknown and traverse: 'Tararua Story', B.D.A. Greig, *Tararua Tramping Club*, 1946, p.62.

'Barlow Exploration', D. Parr, *The Canterbury Mountaineer*, 1952, p.147.

'Barlow–Poerua Further Exploration', Gordon Howitt, *The Canterbury Mountaineer*, 1952, p.151.

'The Willberg Range', Arnold Heine, *New Zealand Alpine Journal*, 1952, p.337.

'Willberg Range Exploration', J.T. Cruse, *Tararua*, 1952, p.25.

'Rangitata to the Poerua', Arnold Heine, *New Zealand Alpine Journal*, 1955, p.122.

Paul Powell, *Just Where Do You Think You've Been?* A.H. and A.W. Reed, 1970.

'Garden of Eden Country', Arnold Heine, *Hutt Valley Tramping*, 1972, p.3.

'Gluttony on the Gardens', Geoff Spearpoint, *Hutt Valley Tramping*, 1972, p.6.

'A new Route on Kensington', L. Duff, *The Canterbury Mountaineer*, 1975, Jubilee edition, p.129.

'Kensington', Geoff Spearpoint, *New Zealand Alpine Journal*, 1975, p.42.

The naming of Garden of Eden: Chris Maclean, *John Pascoe*, Craig Potton Publishing, 2003.

Malcolm Peak and Lord River: Bob McKerrow, *Ebenezer Teichelmann*, TARA-India Research Press, 2005, p.203.

Day crossing of the Gardens: 'Over the Gardens and Far Away', Geoff Spearpoint, *New Zealand Alpine Journal*, 2008, p.24.

RANGITATA, THE MOUNTAINS OF EREWHON

'The Second Ascent of Mt D'Archiac', S.H. Barnett, *The Canterbury Mountaineer*, 1933, p.8.

First ascents of Warrior and Amazon: 'A Sojourn in the Lyell', S.A. Wiren, *New Zealand Alpine Journal*, 1933, p.14.

'The Real McCoy – The North Ridge of Warrior', John Nankervis, *Tararua*, 1968, p.29.

'But mountains, for all their benignity, know how to wait': Paul Powell, *Just Where Do You Think You've Been?* A.H. and A.W. Reed, 1970, p.154.

Armoury Range names: T.N. Beckett, *The Mountains of Erewhon*, A.H. and A.W. Reed, 1978, p.89.

Aciphyllastan: 'Footsteps of Drake Expedition', Peter Bain, *The Canterbury Mountaineer*, 1987, p.25.

First ascent of Mt D'Archiac: *The Peaks and Passes of JRD*, J.R. Dennistoun, JRD Publication, 1999, p.126.

ELIE DE BEAUMONT TO AORAKI MT COOK

'Explorations of the Glacier Sources of the Kellery River', George Park, *New Zealand Alpine Journal*, Oct. 1892, p.90.

Grand Traverse of Aoraki Mt Cook: Freda du Faur, *The Conquest of Mt Cook*, George Allen and Unwin Ltd, 1915, p.196.

Callery exploration: 'Three Western Glaciers', D.A. Carty, *New Zealand Alpine Journal*, 1938, p.240.

'Callery Easter', Frank Pearson, *Tararua*, 1964, p.53.

'Scrambles in Patagonia', T. Clarkson, *New Zealand Alpine Journal*, 1973, p.18.

Callery and Elie De Beaumont: 'Games People Play', Geoff Spearpoint, *New Zealand Alpine Journal*, 1977, p.40.

Doole/Englis rescue: 'Middle Peak Hotel', Bob Munro, *New Zealand Alpine Journal*, 1983, p.46.

Rob Hall, 'Aorangi Airmail', *New Zealand Alpine Journal*, 1987, p.10.

Bob McKerrow, *Ebenezer Teichelmann*, TARA-India Research Press, 2005.

THE BALFOUR, NAVIGATOR & SIERRA RANGES

Ascent of Mt Sefton: 'Mr E.A. Fitzgerald's Work in New Zealand', E.A. Fitzgerald, *New Zealand Alpine Journal*, 1895, p.39, 48.

Balfour Glacier: A.P. Harper, *Pioneer Work in the Alps of New Zealand*, T Fisher Unwin, 1896, p.91.

'Tasman from the Balfour', H.E. Riddiford, *New Zealand Alpine Journal*, 1949, p.54.

First ascent Mt Copland from Gulch Glacier: 'The Cook River Valley Revisited', Miss M.L. Roberts, *New Zealand Alpine Journal*, 1932, p.82.

'Various Expeditions', Marjorie Edgar Jones, *New Zealand Alpine Journal*, 1934, p.427.

'Fettes', A.J. Scott, *New Zealand Alpine Journal*, 1935, p.8.

Navigator Range to La Perouse: 'La Perouse from the Strauchon', Tom Barcham, *New Zealand Alpine Journal*, 1953, p.57.

'Cuttance Pass or Saddle', J.R. Jackson, *New Zealand Alpine Journal*, 1958, p.445.

'The Copland Valley', J.M. Wilson, *The Canterbury Mountaineer*, 1964, p.27.

'Virgins behind Sefton', Hugh Wilson, *The Canterbury Mountaineer*, 1967, p.9.

'Copland Virgins', Wayne McIlwraith, *New Zealand Alpine Journal*, 1969, p.113.

'Mary Louise Roberts obituary', *New Zealand Alpine Journal*, 1969, p.287. Foundation member of OSONZAC's, climbed on the Navigator Range peaks.

'In the Halls of the Mountain Kingdom', Geoff Spearpoint, *Hutt Valley Tramping*, 1975, p.30.

'Mt Cook Overview', Pete Sommerville, *New Zealand Alpine Journal*, 1979, p.7.

Freda du Faur, *The Conquest of Mt Cook*. George Allen and Unwin Ltd, 1915, p.224.

Crossing the Douglas neve and an out-of-body experience: Scott Russell, *Mountain Prospect*, Chatto and Windus, 1946, pp.74–76.

Bob McKerrow, *Ebenezer Teichelmann*, TARA-India Research Press, 2005, p.159.

Cook River and Mt La Perouse: 'The Architect', Steve Harris, *New Zealand Alpine Journal*, 2014, p.59.

THE HOOKER WILDERNESS

Karangarua and Landsborough exploration: A.P. Harper, *Pioneer Work in the Alps of New Zealand*, T. Fisher Unwin, 1896, pp.200–215.

John Haynes, *Piercing the Clouds*, Hazard Press, 1994, p.74.

Crossing Fyfe Pass: Norman Hardie, *On My Own Two Feet*, Canterbury University Press, 2006, p.38.

'From East to West via Fyfe's Pass and the Karangarua Pass', S.A. Wiren, *New Zealand Alpine Journal*, 1929, p.14.

Fyfe Pass descent: 'Fettes', A.J. Scott, *New Zealand Alpine Journal*, 1935, p.3.

'Mt Hooker from the Clarke River', M.B. Scott, *New Zealand Alpine Journal*, 1937, p.73.

'The Landsborough – an historical note', Dr B. Wyn Irwin, *New Zealand Alpine Journal*, 1946, p.135.

'A Visit to the Douglas', H.E. Riddiford, *New Zealand Alpine Journal*, 1947, p.49. (includes an upper Landsborough visit)

'The Landsborough. A topographical and historical summary', N. Hardie, *The Canterbury Mountaineer*, 1959, p.98.

Avalanche in head of the Landsborough: Graeme Dingle, *Two Against the Alps*, Whitcombe and Tombs Ltd, 1972, p.66.

http://www.wanganuitrampingclub.net/history/

http://www.nzherald.co.nz/nz/news/article.cfm?c_id=1&objectid=11662933

Naming Mt Fettes: John Pascoe, *Mr Explorer Douglas*, A.H. and A.W. Reed, 1957, p.3 and p.41.

Topographical plan of Clarke and Landsborough Country from Reconnaissance Survey 1887.

https://www.himalayanclub.org/hj/56/18/in-memoriam-11/

Query Peak and Mt Doubtful map positions: James Thornton, *The Climber* 106, summer 2018/19, NZAC, p.20.

FROM THE OKURU TO THE WILKIN

A traverse of the Selborne Range: 'Sun and Sorcery', Geoff Spearpoint, *New Zealand Alpine Journal*, 2012, p.40.

'Five Months on the Coast', Warren Herrick, *New Zealand Alpine Journal*, 1985, p.50.

Rattenbury, Jongens, and Cox. Geology of the Haast Area, GNS Science p.49 (Stargazer rockfall and Waiatoto tsunami in 1991).

Mike Bennett, *The Venison Hunters*, Halcyon Press, 1979.

'Alba to Aspiring', H. Tom Barcham, *Tararua*, 1951, p.5.

Te Naihi, Mt Castor and the Volta Glacier: 'The Dark Side of the Divide – Te Naihi to Volta', Geoff Spearpoint, *New Zealand Alpine Journal*, 1979, p.36.

'Young, Siberia, Ngatau, Okuru, Blue', Geoff Spearpoint, *Hills and Valleys*, December 1974, HVTC.

THE HAAST RANGE, VOLTA GLACIER & MT ASPIRING

W Scott Gilkison, *Aspiring, The Romantic Story of the 'Matterhorn of the South'*, Whitcombe and Tombs, 1951.

Trip to the Volta Glacier: Bob McKerrow, *Ebenezer Teichelmann*, TARA-India Research Press, 2005.

Charlie Douglas Waiatoto exploration: Philip Temple, *New Zealand Explorers*, Whitcoulls Publishers, 1985.

'Stargazer', H.J. Stevenson and W.S. Gilkinson, *New Zealand Alpine Journal*, 1936, p.277.

'Stargazer Again', Peter Weenink, *New Zealand Alpine Journal*, 1936, p.286.

Traverse of Haast Range from the Waipara valley to Jackson Bay: 'Olivine Bound, A three months' record', Gilbert van Reenen, *Massif* 71, MUAC, p.49.

'Alba to Aspiring', H. Tom Barcham, *Tararua*, 1951, p.6.

'West of the Wilkin Part 1', H. Tom Barcham, *New Zealand Alpine Journal*, 1951, p.5.

'The Haast Range Part 2', Graham McCallum, *New Zealand Alpine Journal*, 1951, p.11.

Haast Range traverse, *Wilderness*, Dec 2002, p.20.

First crossing of Arawhata Saddle: 'A Trip Through North West Otago, Christmas 1923', Dr R. Stokes, *New Zealand Alpine Journal*, 1925, p.260.

https://www.keaconservation.co.nz/kea/testing-people-kea-posts/

G.R. Marriner, *The Kea: A New Zealand Problem*, Marriner Bros Printers and Publishers, 1908, p.133.

Haast Range peaks history and naming: W.S. Gilkison and D.J. Galloway, *Handbook to the Mt Aspiring National Park*, Mt Aspiring National Park Board, 1971, p.29.

'The Waipara: A Gem of Nomenclature', F.F. Simmons, *New Zealand Alpine Journal*, 1950, p.283.

'Here Comes the Sun', I. Latham and G. Spearpoint, *Hutt Valley Tramping*, 1971, p.26.

Mt Eros ascent: 'Return to the Waipara', Tom Carter, *Tararua*, 1956, p.67.

Tantalus Rock naming and storm: Paul Powell, *Men Aspiring*, A.H. and A.W. Reed, 1967, p.174.

The Mountain Tree: Paul Powell, *Men Aspiring*, A.H. and A.W. Reed, 1967, p.12.

Therma Glacier comment: Graham Langton, *Mr Explorer Douglas*, Canterbury University Press, 2000, p.121.

'A Ski Traverse of the Southern Alps', Erik Bradshaw, *New Zealand Alpine Journal*, 2011, p.18. & p.22.

THE OLIVINES & RED MOUNTAIN

Graham Langton, *Mr Explorer Douglas*, Canterbury University Press, 2000, p.121. (p.160 colour sketch by Douglas looking across the Williamson Valley to Andy Glacier and Olivines, 1890s.)

Account of Olivine Range crossing: 'From the Hollyford to the Arawhata', Alex Dickie, *New Zealand Alpine Journal*, 1934, p.307.

'The Peaks of the Middle Dart', A Jackson, *New Zealand Alpine Journal*, 1935, p.36.

J.T. Holloway, *New Zealand Alpine Journal*, 1936, p.289. From the Middle Dart to the Back of Beyond (no further use for Desperation Pass).

Naming of Forgotten, p.67, and flyblown eggs eaten by keas: J.T. Holloway, 'Olivine Bound: a three months' record', *New Zealand Alpine Journal*, 1937, p.58.

'Further Olivine Peaks and Passes', J.T. Holloway, *New Zealand Alpine Journal*, 1938, p.204.

'The Northern Olivine Range', Ian Whitehead, *New Zealand Alpine Journal*, 1939, p.31.

Naming of Snow White Glacier: 'Arawhata Roundabout', J.P. Cook, *New Zealand Alpine Journal*, 1939, p.46.

'Northern Olivine Assault', Ian Whitehead, *New Zealand Alpine Journal*, 1940, p.175.

'Journey Through O'Leary Pass', A. Heine, *New Zealand Alpine Journal*, 1955, p.149.

'Over Desperation Pass', B. Alexander, *New Zealand Alpine Journal*, 1955, p.151.

Traverse across the Thunderer Glacier to the Olivine Ice Plateau: 'High Olivine Journey', A.J. Heine, *New Zealand Alpine Journal*, 1956, p.367.

'Typhoon', Les Molloy, *New Zealand Alpine Journal*, 1970, p.411.

'The Exploration of the Northern Olivine Range', D.J. Galloway and Les Molloy, *New Zealand Alpine Journal*, 1971, p.140.

Dart, Olivines, Red Mountain: 'Just a Crazy Dream', Geoff Spearpoint, *New Zealand Alpine Journal*, 1984, p.22.

Twenty-one-day epic from the Matukituki Valley through the Olivines to the Martyr and Arawhata: 'Over the Land to the Sea', John Pascoe, *The Canterbury Mountaineer*, 1953, p.8.

'Olivine Faux Pas – Of Benightment and Whatnot', Trev Jones, *Hills and Valleys*, March 1952, Hutt Valley Tramping Club.

Olivine to Volta traverse: 'Gullible's Travels', Malcolm Garnham, *Hutt Valley Tramping*, 1976, p.22.

'Men at Work', Geoff Spearpoint, *Hutt Valley Tramping*, 1983, p.76.

Arawhata, Olivines, Whitbourn, Dart: 'Big Country, Hard Yakka', Gary Goldsworthy, *Hutt Valley Tramping*, 1989, p.4.

'Last Cruise of the Owl', Gary Goldsworthy, *Hutt Valley Tramping*, 2000, p.59.

Arawhata Bill's first crossing of O'Leary Pass: Ian Dougherty, *Arawhata Bill*, Exisle Publishing, 1996, p.64.

A.J. Barrington's diary: Nancy Taylor, *Early Travellers in New Zealand*, Oxford at the Clarendon Press, 1959, p.387.

Jack Holloway of the Forgotten River: John Pascoe, *Great Days in New Zealand Exploration*, Fontana Silver Fern, 1976, p.166.

Prospecting bulldozer driven along coast to the Pyke Valley: David Young, *Our Islands, Our Selves*, University of Otago Press, 2004, p.177.

FIORDLAND & THE DARRANS

Guide Book to the Tourist Routes of the Great Southern Lakes and Fiords of Western Otago, New Zealand, George M. Moir, Otago Daily Times and Witness Newspapers Co Ltd, 1925, pp.28–29 (Fiordland History), p.49 (Grave–Talbot Pass).

Beyond the Southern Lakes, A.H. and A.W. Reed, 1950, reprinted 1974, p.48, Worsley to Sutherland Sound; p.123, List of explorations and ascents.

'From Lake McKerrow to Milford Sound', Marie B. Byles, *New Zealand Alpine Journal*, 1937, p.50.

'Explorations above the Dark River', Alex Dickie, *New Zealand Alpine Journal*, 1939, p.95.

'First ascent of Mt Grave', Roland Rodda, *New Zealand Alpine Journal*, 1947, p.1.

'Defeat by Drought', R. Cuthill, *New Zealand Alpine Journal*, 1955, p.156.

'Better Luck, (First ascents of Terror and Llawrenny Peaks)', Edgar Williams, *New Zealand Alpine Journal*, 1955.

'First Ascent of Coronation Peak', B. Wisely, *New Zealand Alpine Journal*, 1955, p.160.

'From Lake Te Anau to the Dark River via the Worsley Valley', B. Wisely, *New Zealand Alpine Journal*, 1956, p.392.

'Milford Sound to Lake Te Anau – A new Overland Route. Light and Dark Valleys', A. McDonald, *New Zealand Alpine Journal*, 1959, p.115.

Harrison Valley, Mt Tutoko, Grave Couloir: 'A February of Darranic Delirium', Geoff Spearpoint, *Hutt Valley Tramping*, 1972, p.10.

'The Transit–Sinbad Trip', Jim Finch, *Hutt Valley Tramping*, 1972, p.12.

'Light, Dark, Prospect, Worsley', John Gregory, *Hutt Valley Tramping*, 1972, p.15.

'Coastal Approach to the Northern Darrans', Gilbert van Reenen, *Massif* 1971, p.30.

'Record of the Transit – Struggle Col Expedition of Immeasurable Solidarity', Gilbert van Reenen, *Massif* 1973, p.22 and p.83.

'Overland to Poison Bay', Rhys Buckingham, *New Zealand Alpine Journal*, 1973, p.78.

'Worsley–Prospect Expedition', Gilbert van Reenen, *New Zealand Alpine Journal*, 1974, p.37.

'The Light and the Dark Rivers – Milford to Lake Te Anau', Tony Hay, *Tararua*, 1978, p.35.

'The 1981 VUWTC Fiordland Expedition. Dark–Light traverse', Mike Sheridan, *Heels*, 1982, VUWTC, p.70.

http://nzetc.victoria.ac.nz/tm/scholarly/tei-Heels1982-t1-body-d36.html

Paul Powell, *Just Where Do You Think You've Been?* A.H. & A.W. Reed, 1970, p.130 (Grave); p.151 (Tutoko).

'From Bradshaw Sound to Lake Te Anau', Danilo Hegg, *Antics 2003*, OUTC, p.36 (including a partial ascent of Coronation Peak).

'Mt Irene and Fiordland Exploration', B. Wisely, *New Zealand Alpine Journal*, 1953, p.233.

'Into Darkest Fiordland', Danilo Hegg, *New Zealand Alpine Journal*, 2012, p.30.

'Fiordland Forever', Henriette Beikirch, *New Zealand Alpine Journal*, 2014, p.36.

The Mackay–Transit traverse: 'Turning Transalpine Dreams into Reality', Peter Wilson, *New Zealand Alpine Journal*, 2014, p.54.

'The Virgin of Poison Bay', Max Olsen and James Thornton, *New Zealand Alpine Journal*, 2015, p.22.

'Sinbad', Jarrod Alexander, *New Zealand Alpine Journal*, 2016, p.18.

USEFUL GUIDES FOR TRANSALPINE TRIPS

Ben Winnubst, *Kaikoura–Kahurangi, a guide for climbers*, NZAC, 2006.

Barry Dunnett, *Kaikoura Walks and Climbs*, Nikau Press, 1988.

Sven Brabyn, *Tramping in the South Island, Mount Richmond Forest Park to Arthur's Pass*, Brabyn Publishing, 2003.

Graeme Kates, *Arthur's Pass – a guide for mountaineers*, New Zealand Alpine Club, 2004.

Sven Brabyn, *Arthurs Pass to Mt Cook, a tramping guide*, Brabyn Publishing, 2004.

Yvonne Cook and Geoff Spearpoint, *The Canterbury Westland Alps*, New Zealand Alpine Club and Canterbury Mountaineering Club, 2010.

Remote Huts website for Central Westland: http://remotehuts.co.nz, managed by Andrew Buglass.

Rob Frost, *Aoraki Tai Poutini – a guide for mountaineers*, New Zealand Alpine Club, 2018.

Ross Cullen, *Barron Saddle–Mt Brewster, a guide for climbers*, New Zealand Alpine Club, 2002.

Allan Uren and John Cocks, *The Mt Aspiring Region*, third edition, New Zealand Alpine Club, 2009.

Danilo Hegg and Geoff Spearpoint, *Moirs Guide North*, eight edition, New Zealand Alpine Club, 2013.

Craig Jefferies, *The Darran Mountains*, New Zealand Alpine Club, 2006.

Robin McNeill, *Moirs Guide South*, seventh edition, New Zealand Alpine Club, 2007.

There are many websites offering trip accounts, and the Department of Conservation offers route guides and information, particularly for hut and track facilities.

Various *New Zealand Alpine Journals* have 'spotlight' articles covering specific regions that still have good, useful material in them. They cover a wide range of interests, geology, flora and fauna, tramping and climbing history, and route guide information. Often journals the following year had corrections and additions.

Murchison Valley 1953

Whataroa Valley 1954

Ohau Valleys 1956

Darran Mountains 1957

Kaikoura Mountains 1958

Callery River 1961

Arrowsmith Range 1967

Rees, Dart Valleys 1969